DISABILITY

Edited by

Robert M. Baird, Stuart E. Rosenbaum,
and S. Kay Toombs

DISABILITY

The **SOCIAL**,

POLITICAL,

and

ETHICAL Debate

Prometheus Books

59 John Glenn Drive
Amherst, New York 14228–2119

Published 2009 by Prometheus Books

Inquiries should be addressed to
Prometheus Books
59 John Glenn Drive
Amherst, New York 14228–2119
VOICE: 716–691–0133, ext. 210
FAX: 716–691–0137
WWW.PROMETHEUSBOOKS.COM

13 12 11 10 09   5 4 3 2 1

Library of Congress Cataloging-in-Publication Data

Disability : the social, political, and ethical debate / edited by Robert M. Baird, Stuart E.
    Rosenbaum, and S. Kay Toombs.
        p. cm.
    ISBN 978–1–59102–614–3 (pbk.)
    1. Disabilities—Social aspects. 2. People with disabilities. 3. Sociology of disability.
I. Baird, Robert M., 1937– II. Rosenbaum, Stuart E. III. Toombs, S. Kay, 1943–

HV1568.D5698 2008
362.4—dc22

                                                                        2008007927

Printed in the United States of America on acid-free paper

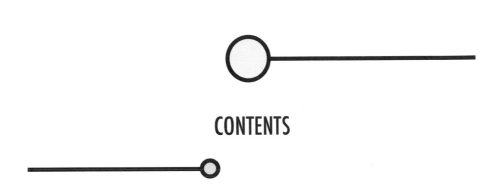

CONTENTS

II. THE CASE OF CHRISTOPHER REEVE

III. THE DISABILITY RIGHTS MOVEMENT: HISTORICAL PERSPECTIVES

IV. DISABILITY, SOCIAL POLICY, AND CITIZENSHIP

V. DISABILITY AND PHYSICIAN-ASSISTED SUICIDE

VI. VALUES AT STAKE IN DISABILITY DEBATES: MORAL AND RELIGIOUS ISSUES

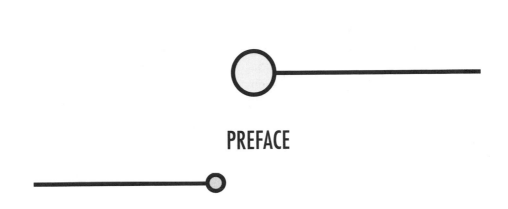

PREFACE

When Prometheus Books began discussing with us the possibility of editing a book on disabilities for the Contemporary Issue series, we immediately thought of including our colleague S. Kay Toombs as a coeditor. No longer teaching in order to spend more time with her husband in retirement, she at first declined. Once she became more aware of the nature of the project, she developed an interest in it and eventually agreed to be a coeditor. The book is significantly better than it would have been without her involvement. Recounting a part of Kay's story will make clear why she is well suited to guide both the organization of the book and the choice of essays, and it will also serve as an introduction to what it means to live with a disability.

Kay was born and educated in England, came to the United States in 1969, and became a US citizen in 1975. Prior to pursuing an academic career, she worked in a variety of administrative and executive secretarial positions in England, North Africa, and the United States. Her association with Baylor University began in 1970 when she was employed as assistant to the executive vice president and chief academic officer; she also began taking courses toward an undergraduate degree.

In March 1973 Kay was diagnosed with multiple sclerosis. Over the next sixteen years she suffered with this progressive, chronic disease in a way that involved periods of acute exacerbation, often requiring hospitalization for intravenous steroid therapy, then periods of remission. During that time she battled a variety of symptoms, including recurring optic neuritis (vision problems), numbness, weakness in her legs (which made walking and keeping her balance difficult), serious bladder problems (requiring hospitalization and eventually self-catheterization), and some problems with bowel control. She also experienced unrelenting fatigue.

During the two years following diagnosis, Kay continued working full-time and taking one or two courses a semester in the University Scholars Program, a program designed for exceptional students that permitted considerable latitude in designing their course of study. In April 1975 she and her husband divorced, having experienced an increasingly strained marriage following her diagnosis and subsequent health problems.

In January 1976 Kay remarried and went to South Africa to live. She continued to work toward her degree, but her plans were delayed by an acute exacerbation of profound weakness in her legs. This required another hospitalization for intravenous steroid therapy and a muscle biopsy on her right leg to rule out other disease possibilities.

The following year Kay and her husband returned to Waco, Texas, and, by the spring of 1977, she had returned to full-time work and was taking two courses a semester toward her degree. As graduation drew near, she took classes full-time, majoring in psychology with many hours also taken in philosophy and journalism. Despite continued health problems, in 1982 she was named Outstanding Student with a Psychology and Philosophy Concentration in the University Scholars Program. She was also elected to Phi Beta Kappa. In the spring of that year she received her BA summa cum laude.

Kay had originally considered entering Baylor's graduate program in psychology, but it required working twelve hours a week under supervision in a clinical setting as well as course work. She knew that this would not be possible with her MS. She decided in the fall of 1982 to enter the graduate program in philosophy.

While working on her philosophy degree she required further hospitalization, at which time it was discovered she had another serious disease (a rare condition involving her carotid arteries and an associated blood disorder) that threatened a major stroke. (Indeed, at that time Kay was already experiencing frequent transient ischemic attacks—ministrokes). This condition culminated in hospitalization in February 1984 for a risky procedure on her carotid artery. In the midst of it all, she completed her master's thesis, graduating in the summer of 1984 with a 4.0 grade point average.

During the 1984–85 academic year, she taught in the Baylor Philosophy Department. By that time using a cane was always necessary for Kay and, in fact, she frequently used a motorized scooter. In 1985 she began the PhD program in philosophy at Rice University in Houston, two hundred miles from Waco, where Baylor University is located. For two years she left Waco at 6:00 a.m. Monday morning, drove to Houston, and attended seminars Monday afternoon, Tuesday morning, and Tuesday afternoon, leaving Houston Wednesday morning at 6:00 a.m. to return to Waco. The third year she drove to Houston once a week during the fall to prepare for comprehensive examinations and once a month in the spring to prepare her doctoral dissertation proposal.

While in the PhD program Kay had two episodes requiring intravenous therapy administered at home, eight hours a day, to counteract exacerbations of the MS. Her ability to walk deteriorated during this time and she began to use increasingly a motorized scooter. In 1989, as she was preparing to write her doctoral dissertation, she was selected as the Lodieska Stockbridge Vaughan Fellow, a competitive fellowship at Rice University awarded to the outstanding graduate student among all departments. Also in 1989 Baylor University presented her with the Baylor University Distinguished Achievement Award.

In 1990 she was awarded the PhD degree from Rice and that fall resumed teaching at Baylor. Kay's ability to walk continued to deteriorate. When she resumed teaching at Baylor, she was using the scooter to go down the hall from her office to the classroom; she then walked (or staggered, as she put it) into the classroom. Over the next few years she lost the ability to walk, but she continued her teaching career, fully dependent on the scooter. In addition to teaching traditional courses in philosophy, she developed a senior-level interdisciplinary medical humanities seminar, Literary and Philosophical Perspectives on Medicine, and a senior-level course, Philosophy and Medicine.

Kay has been active in research, publishing a book and two edited volumes, as well as essays in leading professional journals and chapters in several books. Her writings have been widely recognized, particularly for their ability to communicate the experience of disability and for their insightful analysis of the patient-physician relationship. In 1990 she began traveling frequently throughout the United States, Canada, and Western Europe, lecturing on the experience of disability, the meaning of illness, and the care of patients. On several occasions she traveled alone using a smaller motorized scooter. In recent years she has been accompanied by her husband, whose assistance has become increasingly essential.

As her essay in this volume shows, Kay continues to be concerned that others understand what it means to experience disability. The essay also reflects her interest in the values of society—especially values that contribute to the ability of persons with disabilities to live fruitful lives. Finally, the essay is her reflection on the dignity-enhancing life she and her husband have experienced living in a caring religious community for the past several years.

We dedicate this book to Kay. She has been a model of productive personal and professional life, and she has been a supportive friend.

Robert Baird
Stuart Rosenbaum

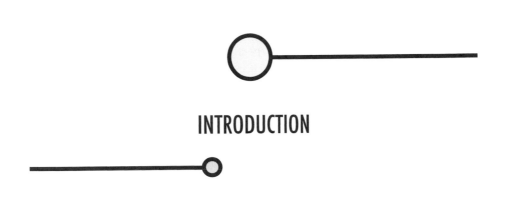

INTRODUCTION

In 2007 Christopher Newport University installed at the entrance to its campus a statue of its namesake, Christopher Newport. Newport was the "swashbuckling sea captain" who commanded the ship that brought English settlers to the Jamestown colony early in the seventeenth century.[1] Newport is also known as a founder of that first successful colony in the New World. The university, established in 1960, was named in his honor. Controversy about the installed statue, crafted by the well-known sculptor Jon Hair, was immediate and intense.

The statue depicted Christopher Newport having two intact arms.

In 1590, while serving as an English mercenary in the Caribbean, Newport lost part of his right arm. In 1607 he commanded the *Susan Constant*, which brought settlers to Jamestown. The settlers saw that his right arm ended in a hook.

Controversy about the statue installed at the entrance to the university focused naturally on sculptor Jon Hair's representation of Newport as normally "armed." Mr. Hair was quoted by the Associated Press as saying, "I wouldn't show an important historical figure like this with his arm cut off." According to the same report, Paul Trible, the university's president, agreed with Mr. Hair's judgment, and a spokeswoman for the university said the university would have no further comment.

How should the statue of Newport have been sculpted? How should Newport have been represented? Is there an issue? Critics of the sculptor argue that Christopher Newport had been without his right arm for seventeen years before he helped to found Jamestown; the disabled Newport, they say, is the one they should honor at the entrance to the university. But Mr. Hair, the sculptor, believes in accord with the administration of the university that this hero should not be portrayed as "maimed."

Mr. Hair's judgment as sculptor is likely an aesthetic judgment of some kind, but if it was an aesthetic judgment, then it is certainly informed by cultural values about what constitutes beauty and physical fitness. Mr. Hair's concern was likely a judgment about how he might represent Christopher Newport in a pleasing and appealing way, a way that might engender or reinforce favorable sentiment toward the university and its namesake. Those who are displeased with Mr. Hair's representation of Newport argue that Newport *was* "maimed" or disabled—a fact that in no way diminishes his personal worth or historical achievements—and that the university's representation of him should acknowledge that fact. Mr. Hair's opponents find his representation of Newport *morally* defective. Mr. Hair's quasi-aesthetic judgment reflects social prejudices about appearance that reveal deep-seated attitudes regarding disability in the minds of the able-bodied. Is Mr. Hair, along with key university administrators, *morally* blind? For some critics of Hair's normally armed sculpture of Newport, the *morally insensitive* rendering of the university's namesake is inexcusable. One might think of them as adding emphasizing qualifiers, like "in this day and age," "in the twenty-first century," and so on. How might any morally sensitive person, especially in an American democratic context, consent to the demeaning of an individual, and perhaps by implication a whole class of individuals who are disabled?

Is the charge of moral blindness credible? How might any university president be unaware of, or blind to, a culturally significant moral issue? Are opponents of the Newport statue straining at a gnat in order to manufacture an issue that, apart from their clamor, would never arise? Is aesthetic sensitivity to the qualities of the work the bottom line in judgments about aesthetic quality? What exactly is the alleged moral offense of Mr. Hair and university president Trible? Is the allegation plausible?

AN ANALOGY WITH RACE

In 1848 Frederick Douglass published his famous memoir about his life as a slave and his struggles to become a free man. Had Douglass been recaptured before finding his way to Massachusetts, he probably would have been returned to his owner, for he was a piece of property. At the time of the publication of his memoir, the institution of slavery was controversial. Many people, many Northerners even, sympathized with Southern slave owners.

Harvard's own distinguished professor of mathematics, Benjamin Peirce, as well as his philosopher son Charles, sympathized with the Southern slave owners and counted them as friends.[2] Were the Peirces morally blind about the institution of slavery? Many people in the twenty-first century would think so: How *could* well-educated, sensitive people consider slavery morally acceptable? In long retrospect, the Harvard professor of mathematics and his philosopher son seem not to have been morally sensitive to the desperate needs of people like Frederick Douglass; they seem not to have been morally sensitive to the depravity of the institution of slavery. And surely they, along with many other Northerners, did not fail to have relevant information about the institution or the plight of individuals who, like Frederick Douglass, suffered under it. Whatever opinion one might form about the moral sensibility or sensitivity of people like the Peirces, one must agree that "in this day and age" slavery is universally morally condemned.

The Civil War and the Emancipation Proclamation changed American culture. Did they change American morals?

Forty years after the Civil War, another black American wrote another definitive work about American morals. W. E. B. Du Bois, the prolific black author, published in 1903 *The Souls of Black Folk*. In his book Du Bois describes and assesses the condition of black people in the American South. There were no slaves in 1903. But neither, according to Du Bois, were there many free black people. The three hundred years of slavery preceding the Civil War had engendered and solidified a large-scale culture—a political, economic, religious, and moral culture—that had swallowed black folks' souls whole. The Emancipation Proclamation might have "freed" the slaves, but it could not recover their souls. Du Bois's accounts of the cultural and moral pathologies of the American South are wrenchingly poignant—forty years *after* the Civil War freed the slaves. How much time is required to recover the souls of a people from a three-hundred-year culture in which they have no souls and are only, like oxen, animals to use for economic gain? And how can those who were, and remain, morally blind recover from their moral pathology?

Is the moral pathology that infected many Americans during those three hundred years of slavery still with us in the twenty-first century? How might it be still with us? Many think the moral pathology of slavery is still swallowing the souls of black folk. Jena, Louisiana, was in 2007 the scene of controversy between black citizens and white citizens, as was Jasper, Texas, in 1998. In September 2007 a large demonstration against racial discrimination occurred in Jena in protest of the county's district attorney's decision to prosecute "the Jena six," six black teenagers who were charged with the attempted murder of Justin Barker, a white teenager. In 1998, in Jasper, Texas, John King and two other white men dragged behind their pickup truck James Byrd, a black man, until he died from the injuries he sustained; a film, *Jasper, Texas*, chronicles the event and its racially charged context.

Well-intentioned people, whether white or black, seem to fall prey to many subtle influences that undermine their moral characters, their moral *sight*. Three hundred years of cultural habit may not be overthrown simply by a four-year war, or by the chaotic efforts in its aftermath to engender new cultural habits.

We know our ideals. We can recite them. They are embodied in the slogan of the French Revolution, in our American Declaration of Independence, and in our Constitution. Living by those ideals is another matter. *Seeing* them in the concrete situations of our everyday lives is difficult.

BACK TO DISABILITY

Just as the Emancipation Proclamation freed slaves, officially giving them the rights of citizens enumerated in the Constitution, the Americans with Disabilities Act of 1990 sought to bring disabled citizens into equity with their normally abled peers. Before 1990 Americans had little legislative guidance focused on the need for equity in social, cultural, and commercial relationships involving disabled Americans. The Americans with Disabilities Act (ADA) provided grounds for equal treatment of disabled Americans.

The Americans with Disabilities Act has four titles. Title 1 prohibits discrimination against persons with disabilities in employment hiring and promotion and in employee benefits. Title 2 prohibits state and local government entities from discriminating on the basis of disability. Title 3 requires all public accommodations to which the general public has access also to be accessible to persons with disabilities. Title 4 requires all telecommunications to be accessible to persons with disabilities.

Just as the Civil War did not solve the problems of equal treatment for black Americans, the ADA also did not solve equal treatment problems for differently abled Americans.

To use an artistic pretense and change the likeness of the university's namesake, charge critics of sculptor Jon Hair and the Christopher Newport University administration, expresses a *morally* inappropriate attitude, not only toward Christopher Newport but also toward the disabled in general. The critics sense *moral* impropriety in the statue, and they sense also a kind of *moral* insensitivity, or *moral* blindness, in the sculptor and the administrators who approved his work.

A similar controversy arose in 1997 around the presentation of the Franklin D. Roosevelt memorial in Washington, DC. Roosevelt was the only American elected to four terms as president, and, as a victim of polio since 1921, he required a wheelchair for mobility during his last years in office. The memorial as originally designed, according to its critics, *denied* Roosevelt's disability. The memorial was revised—by an agreement among critics, the Roosevelt family, the memorial's designer, and the National Park Service—and the first thing visitors see on entering it is FDR sitting in his wheelchair.

THE MORAL ISSUE

How should we think about, or see, those among us who are not "normally abled"? Of course there are problems about what normalcy is, and there are questions about what kinds of inability constitute disability. But the central issue of this volume is evident in the cases of the Christopher Newport statue and the FDR memorial. Is disability a characteristic of individuals that, like race, should be morally irrelevant to understanding their worth or potential for contribution to our common life, and how should we, in moral propriety, think about those among us who are disabled? And if we believe that full inclusion in the American community of those who are disabled is our goal, how may we effectively move toward realizing that goal?

CONTENTS

Part I of this collection, "Experiencing Disability," is a series of short vignettes intended to bring readers a vivid and concrete sense of what it is like to live with a disability in the context of societal values that define "normality" in terms of certain standards of physical fitness, sexuality, youth, appearance, and autonomy. The essays in this section reveal the attitudinal and physical barriers that make difficult the full inclusion of people with disabilities into mainstream culture.

Part II, "The Case of Christopher Reeve," focuses on the controversy about Christopher Reeve, especially about his advocacy of medical solutions, perhaps through stem cell research, for injuries that result in significant disability. Many readers who are not part of the disabled community may be stunned by the attitudinal response of that community to Reeve's determined advocacy of medical solutions for disability. Does Reeve's determined effort to focus financial resources on seeking a cure detract from the need to provide adequate funding to meet the needs of those who live with permanent disability? Does this emphasis also overtly perpetuate the cultural prejudice that it is impossible to live a full and meaningful life in the face of disability?

Part III, "The Disability Rights Movement: Historical Perspectives," provides accounts of the disability rights movement that has emerged during the last part of the twentieth century. Some of the essays in this section also address specifically what it means to be disabled. In describing the political activism of the deaf community at Gallaudet University, for instance, Oliver Sacks moves from a "medical" view of deafness (as a condition to be treated) to a "cultural" view in which the deaf are members of a community that has a complete language and culture of its own.

Part IV, "Disability, Social Policy, and Citizenship," focuses on the course of events that gave birth to the Americans with Disability Act of 1990 and also on the issue of whether that legislation is being adequately implemented. For instance, the essay here by Michael Bérubé raises the question of what our responsibilities are to those who have mental disabilities.

Part V, "Disability and Physician-Assisted Suicide," addresses the question of whether the pursuit of autonomy by those with disabilities should lead to support for physician-assisted suicide. Many within the disability movement believe that social acceptance of physician-assisted suicide puts people with disabilities at unique risk. How does the "right to die" plea for individual autonomy about one's own death specifically affect those with disabilities?

Part VI, "Values at Stake in Disability Debates: Moral and Religious Issues," engages philosophical and religious issues about those who are disabled. A prominent issue here is how we ought morally to treat individuals who are born with disabilities. Peter Singer, a prominent ethicist, argues that we should feel no compunction about putting defective, or disabled, infants to death. Harriet McBryde Johnson, a prominent activist for those who are disabled, engages Singer on behalf of those like herself whom she feels are at great risk from Singer's utilitarian moralist stance. In reflecting on her own experience as a person with multiple sclerosis who lives in a religious community, S. Kay Toombs explores ways in which different value systems both shape our responses to disability and also impact contemporary debates with respect to dignity and end-of-life decisions. Samuel Joeckel's "A Christian Approach to Disability Studies," in addition to providing an overview of disabilities studies, examines the Church's "neglect to do its homework in the area of disability and chronic illness with respect to biblical studies, systematic, historical, and practical theology, especially pastoral care, liturgy, and preaching." The essay is a challenge to the Church to utilize its intellectual and practical resources in responding to disability issues.

RELATED ISSUES

Many of the essays included in this volume address the issue of how disability should be defined and what counts as being disabled. Richard K. Scotch's "Models of Disability and the Americans with Disabilities Act" and Samuel Joeckel's essay detail a variety of definitions of disability, including sociopolitical constructs, medical models, and moral models. Gerald Goggin and Christopher Newell also discuss the social construction of disability in their essay on Christopher Reeve. The essays in the first two parts address social perceptions and constructions of disability, and some of the pieces in part IV address the definition of disability.

The issue of what special rights, if any, should be afforded the disabled is prominent throughout parts IV and V. These issues are also covered in such experiential pieces as Ruthanne L. Curry's essay about her disabled son and the difficulties of getting him into a normal school. "Who Lost the ADA?" by Douglas Lathrop, included in part V, addresses the issue of whether the rights of the disabled should trump those of the able-bodied.

The question of what constitutes discrimination against the disabled is addressed from social, political, and moral perspectives in many of these essays. In some cases that question is the specific focus of a particular essay, as in Carol J. Gill's essay on suicide intervention for people with disabilities and Diane Coleman's testimony on the consequences of legally assisted suicide. Several essays in part VI also address this issue.

The issues addressed in the essays of this collection are of the utmost concern for those prominently involved in debates about disability. We hope this collection provides a significant resource for engaging debates about what is normal and abnormal; about the proper moral, social, and political response to disability in this culture; about relevant suicide, end-of-life, and right to die issues; and about whether aborting a "defective" fetus is morally permissible.

We believe this collection expresses the breadth and depth of concern typical of those who are engaged in thinking about issues of disability. And we hope readers will find the selections provocative of further thought.

Waco, Texas
December 2008

NOTES

1. An Associated Press story reporting this installation appeared in the *Dallas Morning News*, September 9, 2007, 17A.

2. See, for example, Louis Menand, *The Metaphysical Club: A Story of Ideas in America* (New York: Farrar, Straus, and Giroux, 2001); see especially chapter 1, "The Politics of Slavery," and chapter 7, "The Peirces."

EXPERIENCING DISABILITY

1

WALKING WITH THE KURDS

John Hockenberry

There were legs below. Stilts of bone and fur picking around mud and easing up the side of a mountain near the Turkish border with Iraq. Two other legs slapped the sides of the donkey at each step like denim-lined saddlebags. They contained my own leg and hip bones, long the passengers of my body's journeys, and for just as long a theme of my mind's wanderings.

I was on the back of a donkey plodding through the slow, stunned bleed of the Gulf War's grand mal violence. The war was over. It remained only for Desert Storm's aftermath to mop up the historical details wrung out of Iraq. The Kurds were one such detail. It had taken another war, Desert Storm, for the Kurds to unexpectedly emerge from the obscurity they had received as a reward for helping the Allies during the First World War, nearly eight decades before. The Kurds had helped the Allies again this time, but this was just another detail.

In the calculus of victory and defeat echoing through world capitals and

From John Hockenberry, *Moving Violations: War Zones, Wheelchairs, and Declarations of Independence* (New York: Hyperion, 1995), pp. 1–14. Copyright © 1995 John Hockenberry. Reprinted by permission of Hyperion. All rights reserved.

in global headlines, in the first moments of Iraq's surrender there were few details, and fewer human faces. The first pictures of the war were taken by weapons; Baghdad, a city of five million, rendered in fuzzy, gun-camera gray. Snapshots of hangars, bridges, roads, and buildings. No people.

We had won.

They had lost.

The winners were well known: they were the faces on billboards. The smiling, enticing face of the West, its prosperity, and its busy president, George H. W. Bush, were known to the youngest schoolchild in the Middle East. In the West only one Middle Eastern face was as prominent, the face of the demon who became the vanquished, the singular, ever-present Saddam Hussein. The other losers were invisible. As time went on the war began to bleed the faces of its true victims.

Here on the Turkish border it was an open artery of Kurdish faces, streaming out of Iraq and down mountainsides in Turkey and Iran as the world's latest refugee population. Under cover of surrender and Western backslapping, Saddam Hussein had uprooted the mutinous Kurds and sent them packing under helicopter gunship fire north and east and into nations that are neighbors only on the most recent of maps. To the Kurds, the region from northern Iraq to eastern Syria, southeastern Turkey, and western Iran is all one land: Kurdistan. It has been this way for more than one thousand years of warfare and map drawing. So for these Kurdish refugees, border checkpoint traffic jams were just old insults lost in the latest slaughter.

My fists held tight to the saddle and up we went toward the final ridge on the edge of Iraqi Kurdistan. A village called Üzümlü on the Turkish side was the destination. It lay three or more valleys beyond. There, the horizon contained the spilled wreckage of the refugee exodus from inside northern Iraq. Here it was just mountains against the brisk, gray, clouded sky punched through with brilliant patches of blue. Deep below in the valley roared the Zab River, muddy with the melting snowpack's promise of spring.

In March of 1991 the spectacular sky and the brisk air rimmed with intermittent hot alpine sun was a welcome escape from the visa lines and news briefings, SCUD missile attacks, and second-guessing of Saddam, Bush, and Schwarzkopf that so dominated the business of covering Desert Storm. I watched the sky while everyone else stared at their own feet. Ahead and behind, Kurdish men in black slacks walked with enormous sacks of bread on their backs. Like a line of migrating ants, a parade of white bundles snaked up the mountain on black legs.

Neither the heroic foot-borne relief efforts, anticipation of the horrors ahead, nor the brilliance of the scenery around me struck home as much as the rhythm of the donkey's forelegs beneath my hips. It was walking, that feeling of groping and climbing and floating on stilts that I had not felt for fifteen years. It was a feeling no wheelchair could convey. I had long ago grown to love my own wheels and their special physical grace, and so this clumsy leg walk was not something I missed until the sensation came rushing back through my body from the shoulders of a donkey. Mehmet, a local Kurd and the owner of the donkey, walked ahead holding a harness. I had rented the donkey for the day. I insisted that Mehmet give me a receipt. He was glad to oblige. I submitted it in my expense report to National Public Radio. The first steps I had taken since February 28, 1976, cost thirty American dollars.

It was a personal headline lost in the swirl of news and refugees. I had been in such places before. In my wheelchair I have piled onto trucks and jeeps, hauled myself up and down steps and steep hillsides to use good and bad telephones, to observe riots, a volcano, street fighting in Romania, to interview Yasir Arafat, to spend the night in walk-up apartments on every floor from one to five, to wait out curfews with civilian families, to explore New York's subway, to learn about the first temple of the Israelites, to observe the shelling of Kabul, Afghanistan, to witness the dying children of Somalia. For more than a decade I have experienced harrowing moments of physical intensity in pursuit of a deadline, always keeping pace with the rest of the press corps despite being unable to walk. It is the rule of this particular game that it be conducted without a word of acknowledgment on my part. To call attention to the wheelchair now by writing about it violates that rule. My mind and soul fight any effort to comment or complain, even now, years after the events I write about.

This quiet, slow donkey ride was easily the farthest I had gone, out onto a ledge that was never far from my mind during the fifteen years I had used a wheelchair. It was a frightening edge where physical risks loomed like the echoes of loose stones falling into a bottomless canyon, and the place where I discovered how completely I had lost all memory of the sensation, the rhythm, even the possibility of walking. I held onto the saddle or the donkey's neck. The locking of donkey knees and the heavily damped strokes of each donkey leg finding a cushioned foothold in the cold, soft mud of the Iraqi hillside rippled up my hanging limbs and drove into the bones of my arms. My arms were the sentries holding me in place, doing the job of arms and legs once again, as they had for a decade and a half. Though this was the closest to walking that I had felt in all of that time, the job of my arms could not change. FIRST STEPS IN FIFTEEN YEARS. It was a headline composed and discarded, footnote without essay, ridiculous, like the young blond man on the donkey on the mountain. And it was all perfectly true.

In March 1991 I found myself climbing a hillside where civilization was bulldozing a whole people up onto the mud and snow of a place called "no man's land" on maps. It was the end of a very long journey; I had arrived in a place that I could not have imagined. In this soupy outpost, the trucks seemed to have arrived long before the roads. As I watched out taxi windows, I could see that there would come a point where the wheelchair would have to be left behind if I was to make it to the place where early reports said hundreds of thousands of civilians were fleeing Saddam Hussein's terror. Wheels of any kind were out in this terrain. Saddam Hussein had chased the Kurds to the edge of pavement and well beyond. In the pockets of snow, starvation, rock, and mud, only legs could travel.

The story of the Kurds had drawn me from a hotel room in Ankara, onto a plane to Istanbul, then on a charter flight to Van, an old Kurdish city once part of the Armenian empire, on a long, boring drive to the village of Hakkari and then a plunge through the boulder-strewn mountain trails to the border town of Çukurca. I left my wheelchair with the driver from Van beside the road to Çukurca and climbed onto a tawny-colored, medium-size donkey who accepted without a sound what was a more than ample load. Before we began the steep ascent, I had only the time it took to cross a rope-and-plank bridge in a perilous state of disrepair to figure out how to keep my mostly paralyzed body on the animal's back. We crossed over the raging waters of the Zab River in the first weeks of the spring thaw and began the slow, steep climb toward Üzümlü.

The bare facts of what had happened in Iraq and Kuwait in the initial aftermath of Desert Storm read like a random shooting in America: "World outraged as crazed father attacks neighbor then turns guns on family and self." The truth was not as simple. For one thing, Saddam took great pains to make sure that he would not get hurt. Others were neither so lucky, nor did they have much in the way of control over their destiny. The civilians in Baghdad, the Shia of southern Iraq, and the Kurds of the north were all innocent bystanders, caught in the forty-day drive-by shooting that was Desert Storm. Unlike the Kurds, I had some control over my destiny, but in pursuit of this slice of Saddam's long, brutal story I took none of his pains to avoid harm. I would get into northern Iraq any way possible. Whatever difficulties

I might encounter in being separated from my wheelchair in the open mountainous country across the border, I would deal with then. I had made this calculation many times before in covering the Middle East, or in deciding to do anything out in a world not known for its wheelchair-friendly terrain.

I had often thought of riding a donkey in the mountains of western America as recreation but had never found the time to orchestrate such a break in space and time. As a vacation it had seemed like a lot of bother, but here, for the sake of a story, the impulse to toss my own wheelchair to the wind was as natural as carrying a notebook is to other journalists. Still, that I would find myself here, holding on for dear life, with no sense of what lay ahead and certainly no way to control events from the top of a donkey, was unsettling. Was I supposed to be here, or was I in the way? To Mehmet the donkey man, I was just another paying customer.

Feeling out of place was an old sensation, almost as old as the paralysis in my legs. It was a feeling I had among friends, among strangers, and just as often when completely alone. I worried when I held up a check-out line at the supermarket. I smiled sheepishly at restaurant patrons as I made my way through the narrow spaces between the tables to my own place. My anonymity torn from me, I interrupted conversations, intruding on peaceful diners. Was it their eyes or mine that said I was in the way until proven otherwise? I could go away or push ahead. Where wheelchairs could not venture, people working together inevitably could. Still, the choice of pushing ahead through the obstacles or just going away was always a matter of selecting the lesser of two evils. Going away was always a defeat. Pushing ahead was never a victory, and asking for help always reduced the score.

The staring began with the trickle of refugees near the village. They walked slowly, mostly downhill now, toward Turkey. They looked up from their feet at the passenger on the donkey. The incongruity suggested neither disability nor pity. The first refugees we met were the least affected by their week-long trek and a harrowing three days in the mud and snowy cold of the mountainous border region. They carried sacks and misshapen crates of clothing and provisions looted from their own hastily departed neighborhoods in Mosul, Sulaimaniya, Zakho, Kirkuk, and Erbil. Some of the women raised their eyes, wondering why a perfectly good donkey should be wasted on a blond Westerner who seemed to be so well fed. One man suggested to the guide that the donkey would be better suited to carrying a sack of bread, or perhaps a dead or sick person. In Arabic and Kurdish, Mehmet told them that I was a reporter come to see Üzümlü, and that I was unable to walk.

I had been anonymous for a moment; now I was unmasked. The faces of these Kurdish refugees became faces of familiar worry and pity, faces that I had spent so much time thanking. Their concern was appreciated, I told them, but misguided in my case. The men and women gathered around and started to warn me of the dangers ahead. "If you cannot walk, why are you here?" they asked. "There is only death here. People are dying everywhere in Üzümlü. Saddam is killing everyone. Why did America not help us?" they asked. "There is no food. You could die."

I responded just as I did when people wanted to push my chair, or hold a door, or hand me something they thought I was looking at on a supermarket shelf. With a workable, relaxed face of self-assured confidence I could dismiss all of these people politely or rudely, but dismiss them I did. "No need to be concerned." I said. "I've got the door. I am fine. I can make it across the street. No problem. I'm not sick. I don't need a push. I'm not with anyone, no." It was habit, not arrogance that caused me to insist: "I'm just fine here on the donkey in the middle of one hundred and fifty thousand starving, war-terrified refugees."

In Üzümlü, flimsy shelters made of sticks and plastic sheets covered people forced to sleep on crusted mud. A dirty graveyard contained the twenty to fifty people who died each night. The yellow, bloodless, milky- eyed corpse of a child lay next to a partially dug grave. Perhaps two hundred thousand people would pass through here on their way to official Turkish refugee camps. The first had come across minefields, and among the initial group to gather around me and Mehmet and the donkey were a man and the gray-skinned unconscious companion on his back. He had an ugly blackened bandage around his waist, and one of his legs was merely a stump. This man would not make it to the Zab River, let alone the medical facility in Hakkari three hours away by car and already overflowing with casualties. His back and leg had absorbed a mine explosion that had halved his brother. The man carrying him looked at me with authority, pointed at his wounded friend, and said: "There is danger here. He cannot walk . . . we have here many who cannot walk. We have enough," he said with muted anger. "Why are you here?"

I got down off the donkey, sat on the ground, and assembled my tape recorder and microphone. The Kurdish refugees wanted to know why I couldn't walk and if the Iraqis had shot me. Gradually they began to talk.

"The helicopters came and we had to leave. I am a teacher," said one. "I am an engineer," said another.

To an outsider, they were only the sick and the well. Otherwise they were differentiated by the time of day they had decided to flee for the border. Those who fled at night were wearing pajamas under overcoats. Those caught during the day had time to don what looked like their entire wardrobes, especially the children, who stood staring and bundled up like overstuffed cloth dolls. Occasionally someone would walk by in just a thin jacket and torn slacks. Such shivering people explained that they were caught away from home running errands when the gunships came.

Mostly they wanted to talk about "Bush." It was in the bitterest of terms that the leader of Desert Storm was evoked on those cold muddy hills. "Bush is liar. Why he not help us?" "We fight Saddam, but why Bush let Saddam fly helicopters?" They said the word "helicopter" with the accent on the third syllable, and spit it out like an expletive. I sat cross-legged beneath a circle of anger, aiming the microphone to catch the shouting voices.

At that moment, much of the world I knew was reveling in victory. Two days earlier in a conversation with someone from Washington I had learned of the stellar approval ratings for President Bush. Historic peaks in the nineties, enshrining in statistics the apparently unshakable kingship behind the second sacking of Baghdad in a thousand years. As the Kurds might have said, "The warlord Tamerlane did a better job the first time," in 1253. The wind picked up and rattled the plastic sheeting anchored to stubborn mountain shrubs. The plastic made blurry apparitions of the blank young and very old faces inside. A large man stepped up and grabbed my microphone and began to speak in a hoarse, exhausted voice.

"Why is Saddam alive and we are dead? What is for America democracy? Bush is speaking of freedom and here we are free? You see us. They send you to us. You, who cannot stand? You are American, what is America now? Why are you here?" His words echoed out from the hill and mixed with the sobs and squeals of the refugees. To him my presence was an unsightly metaphor of America itself: able to arrive but unable to stand. I could not escape his metaphor any more than I could get off that mountain by myself. These were the questions. And so they remain.

The day was beginning to fade. It was a four-hour ride back down the mountain and at least another hour to file stories to Washington. It was time to go. Mehmet and I hoisted me up onto the donkey and we started our descent. The Turkish army had begun to airlift soldiers by helicopter to the mountaintop to urge the refugees down from Üzümlü and into a camp at a lower elevation. Later the Kurds would discover that this new camp was actually inside Iraq by a couple of hundred yards, a fact Secretary of State

James Baker would learn in a photo op visit to the camp three days later. With its own far less headline-grabbing program of Kurdish oppression in southeastern Turkey, the Turkish government made it clear that it did not want the Iraqi Kurds.

Until the biblical scale of the catastrophe was apparent, the US government was inclined to agree with Turkey. James Baker and George H. W. Bush spoke of territorial integrity in regards to the Kurdish issue. There would be no partitioning of Iraq, they said. The Kurds would have to move . . . again. The Turkish soldiers on the mountain pass fired their automatic weapons into the air, herding people like cattle. The narrow trail down to a spit of Iraqi border territory near the Turkish town of Çukurca was soon clogged with Kurds.

Donkey riding was a slow business. Without any abdominal muscles, my spine twisted and folded with each step. To sit up straight was to get a brief respite from the sharp back pains, but it could only be sustained for a few moments. I held the entire weight of my upper body in my wrists, rubbery and cramped from hours of gripping. They collapsed with each stumble and downward slide of the donkey, pressing my face helplessly into the mane of my tireless friend.

I hadn't figured that the trip down the mountain would be so much harder than the trip up. With the donkey angled upward during the ascent, my weight was pulled back, and holding on had been a simple clinging maneuver. With the donkey descending and angled downward in something of a controlled slide, I had to maintain my weight on my hands, balancing my shifting hips with sheer arm and wrist muscle. The alternative was to tumble down onto the rocks or into one of the many ravines. The crush of refugees narrowed the options for my sure-footed companion and had the effect of periodically spooking him. Mehmet had begun to tire of the earlier novel challenge of escorting the paraplegic on the donkey, and was dragging on the harness. He was also aware that the trail was in considerable danger of jamming into a pedestrian gridlock of desperate refugees.

The sounds of Turkish gunfire caused the donkey to lurch, and me to hold tighter. The rhythm of the donkey's forelegs was intoxicating; it vibrated mechanically up my arms. My whole frame was suspended like a scarecrow on two sticks locked at the elbows. Beneath me walked people clutching their belongings and hurrying to get to shelter before the sun set. Their heads wound along the trail stretching to the horizon.

All around me children stopped to relieve themselves in an agony of diarrhea. In the very same soil, the muddy foot tracks of people and animals filled with snowmelt and rainwater, and children stooped to drink from the puddles. They stood up, and their lips were ringed with brown mud like the remains of a chocolate milk shake. I had drunk nothing all day and had eaten nothing either.

If I was different from other reporters it was in the hydrogen peroxide I carried along with microphones, notebooks, audio tapes, cassette recorders, and cash. Peroxide was the most important item, especially here. In this remote area soaked in mud and surrounded by human waste, there were limits to sanitation. While the closest most reporters came to contaminating their own bodies was by eating a piece of local bread with unwashed hands, for me it was quite different. I use a catheter. Every four hours, every day, for the past fifteen years I have had to insert a tube to empty my bladder. It is a detail which can remain fairly discreetly hidden in most situations. While the processes demanding filling and emptying remained just as urgent here, this environment was hardly optimal for maintaining the near-sterile conditions necessary for using a catheter safely. To expose the catheter to the elements for even a few seconds was to risk infection as definitively as using a contaminated hypodermic syringe risked introducing hepatitis, or worse, into the blood.

After two days my hands had become utterly filthy, and my tattered gloves were soaked through with every local soil. At a certain point one can feel the collective momentum of a human tragedy. With overwhelming power, biological forces penetrate skin, culture, geography, careers, and deadlines. The Kurdish refugees clawed through the mountain foliage, plowing up a rich loam of conquered humanity. I did not want to become fertilizer.

It was not the first time I had encountered potentially lethal mud in the course of covering a story. To prevent infections in such situations, I adopted a simple if crude strategy of self-denial that had served me well in the past. I would go into something of an emergency-induced body shutdown. Nothing in; nothing out. No food meant no waste. No water meant no parasites and therefore no infection.

In an environment without anything resembling a toilet, the inability to stand, squat, or balance above the ground meant that the simplest of bodily functions was impossible to perform without making a mess well outside the specifications of a person's normal notions of human dignity. In this place, human dignity was hard to fathom and beside the point.

But to lose control meant certain contamination. Aside from preventive deprivation, I could ration the peroxide carefully, avoid food and water, and pop vitamin C tablets to keep the acid content and therefore the antibacterial chemistry of my urine high. There was no room for error out here. The weakness that came with intense thirst and having starved for three days, along with being an equal number of travel days from any kind of hospital, would give infection an absolutely lethal head start.

So whatever my face conveyed to the concerned refugees coming down the mountain, I was no more fine than they were, and I was about as confused as to why I was here in this barely inhabitable edge of two warring nations. The accumulated delirium of the war, the Kurdish refugees, and my own deprivation made a dirgelike dream of the donkey ride. From this perch I was again as tall as I used to be. I could see the tops of heads and the shoulders all around me laden with leather straps tied to overstuffed suitcases. In this position my knees seemed farther away from my face. My feet were fully out of view. I had to strain to see them below the flanks of Mehmet's donkey. My abdomen was stretched by my extended and hanging leg bones. It gave me the impression that my lungs had grown larger. None of these details would have mattered to anyone else sitting on a donkey. To me they were a richly hued garment of memory and sensation long lost. In this wondrous garment I was invisible.

The joy of these sensations stood out in surroundings overrun with terror and death. I was unknown and unseen here. There were no presumptions about my body. All that people could tell, unless they were told otherwise, was that I was well fed and blond. Beyond this, nothing was given away. As time went on I ceased even to look like an American journalist. Anonymity intensified the feeling of who I was, where I had come from, and how my own body worked, or didn't. As an American I had no right to be afraid here, I thought. I was safe and distinct from this horror. As a human being I had no way to separate myself from the river of Kurdish flesh making its way toward the valley. In my own invisible way, I was as close to death as they were. As a paraplegic, I was inside a membrane of unspoken physical adversity. There was no reason to expect bodies to function in such conditions, and each additional moment of life required a precise physical calculation. Durability of flesh pitted against the external elements. Each transaction final. The limits fully real. There was no room for mistakes.

I was not alone in contemplating those limits. Each dying person knew who he or she was. Each struggling refugee could see how much he or she had left to wager. The chill of circumstance made the crowd and myself quiet. Energy was conserved. The well-fed Turkish conscripts ahead and behind swaggered and fired their weapons, breaking the collective silence of one hundred thousand people.

Why was I there? It is an imperative of journalists to get the story. It was an imperative of those civilians to make their way off the mountain. There were others. The global imperatives of America to confront Saddam. The imperative of America to go home and beat the drum or lick its wounds. In victory, the United States lifted off from Iraq just as it did from the embassy roof in Saigon in 1975 following defeat in Vietnam. Some Vietnamese clung to the chopper back then. They imagined that despite the circumstances of defeat, the promises of America might be honored elsewhere.

In 1991 those promises seemed hollow and frozen, archived for unborn historians. The Kurds wondered why in victory the Americans would leave them to the wolves more swiftly and surely than the Cambodians and South Vietnamese were abandoned following America's humiliating defeat in Indochina. Aside from the few colorless platitudes thrown their way from Washington, the Kurds had little to do with the business at hand for a triumphant president and his new world. In the anger of the Kurds there was no expectation that America would find their cause worthy, no expectation that their cries would be heard. They had given up on this America without a message and no interest in moving hearts and minds in Iraq. This time when the American chopper lifted off, no one would bother to hold on. Walking in the mud seemed the surer course now.

Fifteen years after lying in an intensive care unit in Pennsylvania I was near the summit of a mountain on the Iraqi border. If this was another event in the struggle for independence and triumph over physical adversity, what about the people who were dying all around me? Was I here to do something for them, or was it for me?

On a donkey among the Kurds at the end of a dreadful back-lot surgical abortion of a war, the paths of truth and physical independence seemed to diverge. I had no good answer for the Kurdish man who insisted that there were already too many people who could not walk in Üzümlü. Why I had gone to Kurdistan was as complicated a question as why Bush's army did not in the first weeks after the war. What seemed an unquestionable virtue had become an excuse for doing something in my case, nothing in the president's.

During the Gulf War, President Bush spoke a lot about how America could regain its sense of mission, its confidence as a world leader, and declare independence from a burden of history. But in a war against historical burdens, the wider battlefield is blocked from view. There is no place for the identity of the people who are simply fighting to save their own miserable lives, the lives that never made it onto the American gun-camera videos, the lives of those we called the enemy, or the Kurdish friends in Iraq we never even knew we had until many thousands of them were dead.

I was fighting my own burdens. Holding on to the flimsy saddle and feeling each donkey step in my back and in my cramped and throbbing fingers, I could see that my entire existence had become a mission of never saying no to the physical challenges the world presented to a wheelchair. It was this that had gotten me through a fiery accident and would provide me with a mission upon which I could hang the rest of my life. I had made the decision to get on that donkey when I had gotten out of a hospital bed years before and vowed never to allow the world to push me. I would pull it instead. In Kurdistan I discovered that the world is a much larger place than can be filled by the mission of one man and his wheelchair.

If the Kurds had truly left me alone and gone about the business of only saving themselves, I would just have died right there, holding my tape recorder. They did not. "I'm fine," I said. There on the mountains between Turkey and Iraq, I had lost my way. It was up to Mehmet, the donkey, and me to find my way back.

In the last valley before the river, the steep trail was teeming with refugees. Just eight hours before it had been deserted and tinged with early spring grass; now each bend had been churned into slippery mud. The donkey was having trouble keeping its footing; Mehmet pulled on the harness as the beast locked knees next to a family pushing a wheel-barrow piled with clothes, utensils, a cassette player, and some toys. The animal would not budge, and Mehmet angrily shoved it and yanked on its tail. The donkey made a spitting noise, moaned, and bolted down a steep slope toward the grass. I held on and twisted as the animal half-tumbled off the trail.

Trail was a generous description for the steep, narrow switchback that folded three times along the gravelly slope. With tens of thousands of refugees clogging the trail, the hillside began to look like a rickety shelf of old books shaking in an earthquake. Every few minutes rocks from the upper trail would be dislodged by someone's feet and tumble down on people one and two tiers below. Shouts and screams would greet the stones. A shower of debris was kicked up by the feet of my fleeing donkey. He landed in a hillock of grass at the river's bank and began to munch and graze with a resolve that suggested that his paraplegic reporter–carrying duties had ended.

I had slipped off the donkey's back farther up the hill. With an exhausted smile, I rolled onto my back, clutched my bag of equipment, and stared up at the sky. The refugees made a moving silhouette against the fiery dusk sky, and the rope bridge over the river was now in darkness. The only sounds were the roar of the river and the shouts of refugees who argued with Turkish soldiers attempting to control access to the bridge.

The crowd was trying to storm a flimsy bridge that could withstand perhaps twenty people at a time without collapsing. The sound of Turkish weapons fired into the air peppered the din. My arms and cramped fingers ached. It felt good to lie down in the cold, wet grass. But I needed to cross that bridge to have any chance at all of filing a story. Without a donkey there seemed to be no way to even approach it from my repose on the river's bank. I turned my head and saw the muddy water raging in frosty darkness. There was no chance of swimming the Zab. The water churned its way around the canyon toward the Tigris, Baghdad, and the Persian Gulf hundreds of miles away. The opposite bank was a traffic jam of relief trucks and makeshift camps, as flimsy shelters from Üzümlü were erected once again along the road to Çukurca. Flickering fires and headlights made shadows on the rocks. Prone and unable to walk on the bank of an unswimmable river with a runaway donkey lost in a crowd of one hundred thousand refugees seemed to be as good an excuse as any for missing a deadline.

Mehmet was taking my predicament much more seriously than I was. He had brought back three men, and insisted on carrying me up to the bridge on a blanket. On the boggy riverbank the blanket quickly became saturated, making it difficult to hold with a body inside. They dropped me half a dozen times and eventually gave up. I laughed. Mehmet's crew went back to attend to their own places in the line to cross the bridge.

I lay there reveling in being invisible. My sore arms were stiff. There was a certain joy in just lying quietly in the grass while the river and the people swirled around me. For two years, more or less, I had been a correspondent in the Middle East. For all that time I had stood out as an American or as a journalist with a microphone; for fifteen years I had been scrutinized continuously because of my wheelchair. But for that moment in Kurdistan surrounded by thousands of refugees covered with mud, without a chair, and lying in the grass I was utterly, completely anonymous.

Mehmet's attempts to move me had brought us closer to the bridge, and the confusion of the mob was almost overhead. Sheep grazed near my head in the growing darkness. Up on the bridge some members of the international press corps had arrived and were shooting pictures. I recognized two faces, though I couldn't remember which newspaper they worked for. But they looked at the man with the backpack and after a moment recognized me. They must have recalled that I used a wheelchair. They looked around with some alarm. No wheelchair to be seen. I shrugged my shoulders at them. I mouthed the words "I'm fine." I chuckled out loud, and said, "I could use a donkey right about now." Like the slow movement of the moon over the sun during an eclipse, my moment of anonymity was passing.

In the end, Mehmet himself, a cigarette in his mouth, carried me on his back up the slope to the bridge. After a screaming argument with the Turkish officer, he carried me across and put me down next to a family with their belongings spread out by the road.

"I am American," I said when asked by a young Kurdish boy.

"Do you know Chicago?" he asked. "I have a brother in Chicago."

I nodded and tried out some broken Arabic on him to pass the time. As darkness fell, the Kurdish taxi driver from Van who had been taking care of my chair for twelve hours found me in the crowd and joyfully hugged me. He had watched the exodus of his Kurdish compatriots with tears in his eyes, and with alarm had watched all day for me to appear in the crowd. He brought my wheelchair over and I hoisted myself into it: it felt so good to move and to feel its support beneath my sore shoulders. There were my feet, just below my knees and my lap, right there below my face. Creased since 1976, my six-foot frame folded itself back into a sitting position once again. After only a day I had forgotten what it felt and looked like.

I took a breath and paused for a moment before I rolled toward where the driver had parked his cab. I looked around. There around me, the noise of the refugees quieted. I saw all eyes watching me. In their staring gazes I was home. I waved good-bye. I made the deadline.

2

I HATE TINY TIM

William G. Stothers

hate Tiny Tim.

TT is on the ropes in Charles Dickens's *Christmas Carol.* Sickly and dependent, TT is getting shakier and shakier on that homemade little crutch. But he is saved from death by old Ebeneezer Scrooge, who sees the light in the nick of time.

Now, before you go apoplectic at my assault on wee Tim, think about how he helps shape some of society's most cherished attitudes—charity and pity (for poor little TT), for example. Tiny Tim, plucky, sweet, and inspirational, tugs at the public heart.

TT has become Disabled Everyone in popular culture. TT is Jerry's Kid.

Society idealizes this sentimental image of disability as a pitiful child in desperate need of help. People feel better when they give a few bucks or a little toy for a kid with a disability.

From *MAINSTREAM Magazine Online*, December 12, 2006. Reprinted with permission.

As an enduring symbol of modern Christmas time, Tiny Tim resonates with a deeper, darker meaning for people with disabilities. The problem is that not all people with disabilities are children, but we all tend to be treated as if we are Tiny Tims.

When I'm in the stores and malls this time of year I get a lot of smiles meant for TT. How do I know? Well, I am a middle-aged bearded and balding adult in a power-driven wheelchair. People, mostly women but some men also, flash smiles at me. Not the kind of smiles most men would hope for from a woman, nor the neutral courtesy smile exchanged by strangers passing on the sidewalk, but that particular precious smile that mixes compassion, condescension, and pity. It's withering to the person on the receiving end.

I hate it. I hate it because this Tiny Tim sentimentality stereotypes people with disabilities and contributes to our oppression. When you think about a person with a disability as someone to feel sorry for, as someone to be taken care of and looked after, it is difficult to think about hiring them as a teacher, an architect, or an accountant. That's part of the reason why the jobless rate among working-age people with disabilities consistently hovers around 70 percent.

And because family, friends, and reborn Scrooges nourish and protect Tiny Tim, the rest of society doesn't have to worry too much about making sure people with disabilities have equal access to education, adequate housing, transportation, and other public facilities.

What about the highly touted Americans with Disabilities Act, you ask? Good question—and good law for the most part. But complaints about violations of the ADA are piling up faster than federal agencies such as the Justice Department and the Equal Employment Opportunity Commission can handle. Inadequate resources are available to enforce the law. And local authorities moan and groan about unfunded federal mandates that they can't afford to implement—such as providing access to *all* citizens.

Every year this country spends more than $200 billion on programs that essentially keep persons with disabilities in a state of dependence, severely restricting us from getting a good education, going to work, or even getting married.

Not all of that money could be saved by removing the penalties on people with disabilities, but billions unquestionably could be saved. Not only would people with disabilities gain independence, but thousands of us would become taxpayers instead of tax users.

These are serious issues affecting people with disabilities and our struggle to be included fully in American life. Remember this the next time those facial muscles begin to activate that Tiny Tim reflex.

TT belongs to Christmas Past. And that's no humbug.

THE EXCEPTIONAL FAMILY
Walking the Edge of Tragedy and Transformation
Ruthanne L. Curry

PROLOGUE

In writing this story as the mother of a physically disabled child, I returned to the handwritten journals which bore witness to our lives of the past sixteen years. From these pages where I had initially tried to make sense of our pain, grief, and occasional triumph emerged recurring themes or threads of meaning. I have attempted in the following story to share these meanings, including excerpts from my own journals which seemed particularly illustrative. Reflecting upon earlier struggles and experiences has been a difficult process, but one which has offered further healing. While this experiential account represents my memory of our family's evolution as an exceptional family, the "story" is a continuing one.

Others, who have kindly shared their thoughts and impressions after reading my story, have suggested that I offer the reader an orientation to our family. We are a family of four: mother, father, older sister, and younger

From *Chronic Illness: From Experience to Policy*, ed. S. Kay Toombs, David Barnard, and Ronald A. Carson (Bloomington: Indiana University Press, 1995), pp. 24–37. Copyright © 1995 by Indiana University Press. Reprinted by permission of the publisher.

brother, Robbie, who is the child with the disability. While our roles as father-physician and mother-nurse practitioner have colored our experiences, it is our voice as an exceptional family which I wish the reader to hear.

WALKING THE EDGE

This is a story about an exceptional family—a family labeled as different because of the son's chronic disability. In many ways, they are ordinary. They go to work, attend school, eat dinner together, get colds, worry about money and their future. Yet always coloring their predictable survival tasks and concerns are the son's needs and society's expectations. People around them may want them to be particularly brave or carefully grateful, as if their "differentness" requires them to be more than just ordinary. To gain entrance or acceptance into the mainstream, they must carry their differentness well or risk being pitied. Few allow them their humanness. Those who do share their journey offer the richest resource.

The journey begins with two major conflicting forces: hope and sorrow. As in most families, the son's beginning was anticipated with much excitement. His unexpected premature birth exposed their vulnerability; they were no longer "normal." Saddened by a lost pregnancy and pummeled by fears of what was to come, the mother adopted a "Mother Bear" stance with the tiny baby. Her son became the first preemie to be breast-fed in the small rural hospital, nurturing both his survival and her hope that he would emerge intact.

> Twelve hours after birth, Robbie is deemed ready for visitors. Delivering prematurely somehow seemed to relegate our status to that of privileged third cousins rather than parents. I would finally be allowed to hold my child. His physician father would wait ten days for Robbie's first touch. Approaching the incubator alone, my hands stroked Robbie's fragile, utterly soft body. Amid wires, beeping equipment, and doubtful glances, I put Robbie to breast as I had my first child. Although smaller and weaker, he responded as she had. We would repeat this scene many times, our shared warmth reassuring us. We belonged together.

Other than prematurity, there were no visible or dramatic markers to identify the insidious damage which had occurred in the baby's brain. Hope continued to gently flourish as the now family of four entered the son's infancy. When the baby was six months of age, however, his inability to sit or roll over allowed the earlier fears surrounding his wholeness to return. Although the parents desperately wanted their child to be "normal," the baby's slow development shouted otherwise. Tentative questions to professionals were often met with comments meant to be helpful and reassuring. Finally, the toll of daily battle with an unknown enemy demanded action and the first of many "experts" entered their lives.

> After months of suppressing doubts about Robbie's development, I seek the opinion of a developmental psychologist. Now, all my rationalizations linking slow development with prematurity crumble before the psychologist's gentle but persistent words. Something, some disease or injury, shrouds Robbie's body as surely as my arms now cradle him. Future visions of children struggling with crutches or clouded intellects kaleidoscope with the reality of the warm baby against me. Worries of what is to come collide with terrible questions about what has happened to our son. Hours later sitting on my couch at home, I feel as though I might drown in the crashing pain. I did not know that our survival would demand repeated encounters with this maelstrom. But this moment would hurt the most.

So the family began to weave their differentness into the everyday tasks of making a life. While other parents went to work or school, this mother took the baby to physical therapy or the ophthalmology clinic or a class for "at risk" babies. No one had spoken a diagnosis, leaving room for continued hope but also ambiguity. Just what were they dealing with anyway? Most of the time, the commitment to doing something minimizes their feelings of helplessness and brings some small progress. At other moments, the continued encounters jar them into realizing just how compromised their son is.

> Each baby class brings more and more healthy babies who roll, crawl, babble, throw things. These incredible creatures are a half, a third Robbie's age. It's like being in the desert and watching someone else drink an incredibly cold drink. I want to shake these other mothers. Do they know how wonderful this all is? But I am too proud to admit my longing.

After several months of many therapy sessions and hearing others comment on their son's problems, the parents choose to begin an all-out assault on whatever process has laid claim to their child. As all successful wars begin with excellent intelligence reports, they turn to specialists in the large medical center in their community. They are ready for the facts.

How strange it feels to be in the role of "patient's mother." The waiting room of the large clinic is tense with families tired from filling out papers, consoling difficult children, and worrying about their impending visit. As I look around at all the children, I am struck by the terrible devastation. So many of them seem helpless and defenseless, as if they are casualties of some awful catastrophe. Is this how others see my child? I want to clutch our son and hide somewhere. Later, the words which have already reverberated in my head are pronounced by the neurologist: cerebral palsy. As he reviews the findings, a door slowly shuts. While there will be no miracle, neither will Robbie die soon. As we leave the clinic carrying our reprieved son, the ghost of Robbie-might-have-been begins to drift away.

While the parents have begun to live with ghosts, others in the family are lagging behind in the journey. The grandparents, seeing their own children's pain and energy depletion, want to help. As they are often separated by time and distance from the day-to-day survival which the parents must face, they are partially insulated from the struggle. They must find their own way to live with this different grandchild.

We have taken the children to visit Whit's parents, hoping for a change in our endless round of clinic appointments and therapy sessions. I sense that they are both excited and nervous about our coming. After all, their questions and understanding have been filtered through our interpretations of what others have told us. Although I want to be sensitive to their possible distress, we are in great need of comfort ourselves. As Whit's mother and I sit on the lakefront shore rocking slowly in the hammock with Robbie, I tentatively expose my hurt.

"It's as if someone has died," I tell her. I can feel her recoil. My words have been too honest.

"You just have to be strong," she replies. I wonder if I must be strong for her as well as my son.

Like many other families, this one is linked by the usual holiday dinners and birthday parties. These expected encounters promote repeated inoculation to Robbie's assets as well as his liabilities and allows the other, more distant family members to become comfortable with his slumping body posture or raking grasp. Some move more easily into his style, and offer the friendly acceptance the parents crave for him.

> My mom and dad have come to Florida to enjoy their grandchildren and escape the cold. Mary K. is jumping with "Grandma" projects to do, and I am again glad to have some adult conversation. As I merge breakfast routine into getting Mary K. ready for preschool, Mom and Dad take Robbie. I glance over at the happy, ordinary sounds coming from our couch. My parents are tickling Robbie and blowing bubbles with total glee. The young baby, who is more likely to cry or fuss, is responding with giggling abandon. They have taught Robbie to laugh. How simple, but how needed.

Family members learn to savor these moments of happiness, tucking them into their collective memory to sustain them on other less sunny days. The roller coaster of hope and sorrow, physical exhaustion and encouragement continues to require balance reactions which they are learning to cultivate. Guilt, rage, fear, and frustration repeatedly threaten to suck them down into perpetual grief, but the son always seems to pull them back with his sheer commitment to be.

> June 22nd—almost the longest day—how I feel that our lives seem to be composed of "long" days. How absurd that I should want to give up at times. My son is the one with the disability. I could walk away if I really wanted to, yet can he? Sometimes I just want to be with him without all the "should's" of doing therapy at home, clinic appointments, reinforcing appropriate behavior, nurturing, and dressing, while fighting off the guilt monster. I wonder what he really wants. He tries to tell me with cries or by tightening his body. I am so used to reading his nonverbal ways that I almost missed his first "real" talking. Today he called me "Ma" for the first time. After two and a half years, he can finally call me, acknowledge me as a person. While other children have been able to crawl after their parents, he has had to cry or fuss to seek us out. Now he has another way to engage us besides crying.

Language validates many of the ways in which the family see Robbie, an individual who seems to grasp quickly much of what occurs around and with him. While family members have bridged their relationship with him through touch, holding, smiling, carrying, and generally bringing the world to him, his verbal reciprocity now further reinforces their efforts to work with him. In contrast, daily encounters with less observant or informed individuals force the family to somewhat reluctantly share their impressions with strangers. Advocacy is not in their everyday vocabulary but soon becomes mandatory.

> Lunch at McDonald's, a most American custom, is even more than just lunch with the kids. Robbie has finally taken to eating meat—McDonald's hamburgers. Even this is ironical after all the homemade baby food and other "healthy" concoctions I have created. He attacks the food in his usual less-than-precise style. At the adjoining table the children have obviously raised some questions to their now uncomfortable mother who starts muttering and casting us furtive glances. I can feel the anger starting to seep into my awareness. Although I am a nurse, I would seriously like to clobber this woman for telling her children "he is a victim" and "not to look." Do I owe her an explanation? Somehow, if I am to help my son see himself differently than this woman does, I must do something. I smile at the children and begin my awkward public relations attempts.
>
> "It's o.k. to wonder what happened that he moves differently than you do. His brain was hurt around the time he was born, but he's not sick (I have learned some kids think they might "catch" it) and in many ways is just like you."
>
> The kids now sense the floor is open to questions. When will he walk? Why does his eye look away? Will he die? I gulp. Am I ready for this? Scared or not, I have waded into this and best bumble some sort of finish. I hear myself explaining haltingly that we hope he will walk, that he will not die soon, and his eye seems different because those muscles are not working together. The kids, satisfied with those answers, return to their hamburgers. I look down at the crushed french fry in my hand.

Over the subsequent months and years, it is often the children who help the family find their way. Friends' children, occasional visiting cousins, and most of all the daughter, Mary K., often figure out how to live with Robbie. Five-year-old Mary K. and her friends pile their supplies around Robbie in the red wooden wagon and venture off in the make-believe "frontier" behind their house. Other toddlers play alongside him briefly and take his toys; Robbie learns to verbally try to stop them. The children of new acquaintances sometimes also provide a bridge to other parents.

> My new neighbor Linda bikes by our backyard where Rob and I are "experiencing" the sandbox Whit has created. On the back of Linda's bike is her

son, Tim, who is a few months younger than Rob. Linda is bubbly and friendly, calling out to us and introducing herself. We chat and at some point I feel I must explain Robbie's obvious differences from her son. Somehow, this part always feels like a test. Will my "orientation" to Robbie's difficulty honestly present his compromises without scaring people away? Linda responds with a mixture of interest and friendly concern. When she mentions that she plays tennis every week, I offer to have Tim stay with us while she plays. We are always looking for playmates. She agrees, but on the condition that I leave Rob with her for an equal amount of time. I am startled. Linda is the first friend to offer to brave Robbie alone.

Other mother-child pairs become part of the family's efforts to rescue their lives. Bike rides to the park, picnic lunches, and walks through neighborhoods relieve the isolation of nurturing a young child eighteen hours a day. Sharing everyday events and the boundless energy of other mothers' children allows the parents to see their son as more like other children than so singularly dissimilar. The family needs these friends and strangers-become-friends like they need food. Despite their need, the parents sense there are rules for this game of social integration. Most of the time they feel they should initiate contact, explaining the disability to newcomers and readily appreciating inclusion. Part of their consciousness is always censoring what they share lest they lose their "admission" to the ordinary. They find an emotional closet in which to store their feelings. The closet is opened only with a few tested friends or in moments of reckless bravery.

When their son is three years old, the parents have the opportunity to experience a divergent world where disability is now the entering ticket. They leave familiar home territory and travel to Washington, DC, living for five weeks in a college dormitory with thirty other parents and children growing up with disabilities. All these people have come together to offer their children as "practice subjects" for therapists learning new techniques to help their children.

Initially, I realize we are checking each other out, wondering about the children's problems, curious about adaptations others have found, and amazed that there could be so many of us. We are all like wounded geese, still flying on an altered course to assist our children. While our lives have never been the same since our children arrived, we have all survived. That in itself is a miracle. I am humbled by the commitment of these other parents and immensely relieved that I am not alone. I am also aware that my troubles sometimes pale in comparison to what other parents are managing. Somehow known problems seem less overwhelming than scenarios I never imagined. It is our commonality of experience, however, which leads to new understanding.

One night, Celia, home economist by training and mother of blond, chipper Kristen, and I share a moment over chicken noodle soup prepared in the dorm kitchen. Celia has ventured into that gray land called "the future," wondering whether Kristen will be a "domestic ambulatory"— someone who can walk around the house but not to the store. This has already proceeded beyond the bounds of the usual chats I have had back home but I hear a familiar thread of my own thoughts. Suddenly, Celia looks up at me.

"What if she can't cook for herself?" she asks.

I am not sure how to respond. Is she asking whether Kristen will be dependent on her or others? I know this song except mine involves my son getting a job. I realize we may define our children by what matters to us rather than who they are. I hear myself offering Celia the idea that her tenacious, bright but stubborn daughter might become a lawyer and hire a housekeeper. Celia laughs with relief, partly because I have suggested a hopeful solution but more because we have been afraid together.

Five weeks of intensive therapy and spontaneous, close relationships with other "different" parents lead the family down new paths. Fifty therapists, thirty children and parents, and ten therapy faculty all blend into a stimulating "soup" of alternatives and energy. Until now, the parents have repeatedly struggled with a bipolar concept of their child; he would walk, talk, learn, socialize, and grow up or he would be disabled. They actively resisted seeing his disability as part of who their son was because to do so seemed to be giving up. To be disabled also seemed to mean passivity, helplessness, victimization. Out of their experiences with these other parents and therapists emerges a fresh recognition of who their son might be, a person who happens to have severe movement problems. He also "happens" to have a wonderful smile, an intense will, and a bright mind. They are beginning to learn how to live with the enemy, but are still vigilant that the cerebral palsy be allowed few concessions.

Blond, hazel-eyed Robbie leans against the gigantic beach ball while the therapist attempts to reduce his marked stiffness. Near the end of the hour-long session, which he has tolerated with little crying today, the therapists rock him slowly onto his feet. He stands with their help, an almost casual awareness that he is both relaxed and upright at the same time. Another mother quickly snaps a polaroid picture, as I am so engrossed by the independent movement, but it is his expression of belonging in this body which I will remember.

The family's growth during the summer of therapy away from home facilitates new skills and social courage. After participating in a parent session focusing on education, the parents decide to merge their hope for a preschool experience for their son with their commitment to push local school board members toward offering an early education program. The school administration has deferred the family's inquiries to the elected members of the board, who must decide whether money will be spent to start an early education program. The parents contact the individual board members one by one and arrange to meet with them. Several are supportive of the concept of early education, while others apparently need help understanding the problems and possible solutions.

> Robbie and I are again on our way to meet Whit and school board member number three at the restaurant of his choice to discuss the lack of preschool opportunities. As we enter the restaurant, Mr. H. politely shakes our hands. Although he attempts to mask his surprise that we have included Robbie, I recognize the now familiar averted gaze and general uncomfortableness. I sense this will not be easy. After presenting our now well-rehearsed "talk" and reminding the board member of the intent of Public Law 94–142, we pause, waiting for him to respond. By now our food has arrived and Robbie has begun to awkwardly feed himself. I have ordered him a pancake, a food with which I knew he would have some success but produce limited mess.
>
> Mr. H. nodding his head toward Robbie asks, "Why does your son need a program? I mean, he can feed himself." Because, I want to say, life should be more than eating pancakes.

While the parents continue to juggle their developing advocacy with their son's needs, their impatience grows. Their efforts at increasing their own awareness and knowledge about their son's disability repeatedly point toward early intervention. They are racing a developmental clock which is already several years late. An educational experience will also offer another way for their son to begin to learn how to live with his peers. The parents decide to explore other regular community preschools.

Tomorrow Robbie and I are to attend a private preschool. Through phone calls and luck, I have found the director of a community college program which trains special education aides and a preschool director willing to consider Robbie's attendance with one of these trainees. Tomorrow will be another "coming out"—of facing new people and new situations where the possibility exists for misunderstanding, comparison and rejection. Yet, tomorrow is, more importantly, another opportunity for everyone to grow a little—Robbie, the teachers, the "normal" kids. Please let my determination help us see the possibilities.

The preschool experiment works. Again the children lead the way with their pragmatic curiosity and problem solving. Once they grasp the new child's limitations and abilities, they learn to move with him in a dance of give and take. Sometimes they run away and he cannot follow. Other times, they are more likely to play alongside him or laugh at his spontaneous participation. The parents are encouraged by their child's language explosion, his willingness to reach out toward other children, his evolving trust in others outside his own family. From the lack of a special education setting has emerged an early model for integration. The family will continue to seek other integrated school settings as Robbie grows older. If he is to have a life beyond therapy, clinic visits, and family protectiveness, he must learn to deal with the fears and questions of others now. They have figured out that school is a microcosm of society; learning is more than knowing one's letters and numbers.

As family members continue to move reluctantly into arenas they never envisioned, the problem of helping their son form an identity which both includes and goes beyond his disability impacts everything they do. Through their small advocacy efforts and contacts with professionals who deal with disabilities, they are now visible outside their circle of friends and neighbors. The system appears to see them as a compromised but marketable example.

Before running out the door to therapy, I grab the phone. One of the public school therapists whom I barely know wants to know if smiling, five-year-old Robbie might be the March of Dimes poster child. Immediate conflict starts to churn in my gut. I am torn between wanting to be a team player through doing a good deed for the community and a nagging sense that this somehow just does not feel right. I have learned to ask questions before "buying" anything.

"What does the March of Dimes use their money for?" I ask her. "Does any of it go for the treatment or programs the children need?"

She explains that the money is used for research to prevent prematurity, birth defects, and other health problems with which the children are born. I hear myself fumbling with an answer tinged with irritation and sadness.

"I'm sorry," I explain, "but I don't feel comfortable telling my son that he is doing this to prevent other children like him. We're trying to help him understand where he fits into a world that is often more confused than he is about his problems. I can't put him out there as something to "prevent." This poster thing also seems to use these kids to collect money, yet you tell me none of it goes toward addressing their problems now. That feels sort of dishonest."

I realize I have given away potential "celebrity" status for Robbie by declining their invitation. I have also risked being labeled an ungrateful parent. But I think I have been true to what I really want for him. Free lunches and pictures in the newspaper are not going to help him push his wheelchair into a community that sees him as something that should not have happened.

Ten years later, Robbie will choose to "walk" his wheelchair thirteen miles in the March of Dimes Walk-a-thon as part of his Boy Scout service project. There will still be no newspaper pictures, just quiet accomplishment in doing something for others. The journey between possible poster child and teenage contributor, however, will require the family to rework earlier struggles. "Anniversaries" often force open the closeted feelings and offer bittersweet opportunities for growth.

Just-turned six-year-old Robbie sits in a small child-sized chair, secured by a velcro strap and a homemade knee abductor. Many of his schoolmates surround him as he opens their carefully chosen presents. There are all sorts of books and bookmarks, for the children have observed Robbie's new mastery of reading. There is also a slate upon which Robbie can easily draw and a car which he can activate by just pushing down. I am appreciative of the children's and their parents' sensitivity to what might be an appropriate gift for Robbie with his limited mobility. We have had a fun day, playing with the children and helping Robbie participate in the games he has planned. As we clean away the cake crumbs and shredded paper, I am thankful for the friends who have helped make this a "typical" happy birthday. Although I smile as I remember Robbie directing me in the party peanut hunt, I feel another year of hoped-for progress needing readjustment. In many ways I keep losing him over and over—relinquishing the child that never was, letting the dreams, however unrealistic, slip away, reshaping my vision of what he might be. We have come so far, always trying compassionately and persistently to push and guide him toward his own life. Yet, I am forever wondering if we have held him too close, found the right therapy or education, given the most genuine parts of ourselves 29 hours a day. Sometimes it seems as if we want him too much. Sometimes I want for just one moment for the disability to let him be.

In their recurrent encounters with sadness, the family attempts to find some explanation or meaning. Having been figuratively struck by lightning, they realize the unfairness of life's events. Neither do they believe in a "grand plan" theory; no higher force has selected them or the child for martyrdom or punishment. Just as they will never know what biological process or medical oversight led to the son's problems, neither will they be able to foresee the future. What has happened is put aside; what will come is dealt with as a present-day here-and-now dilemma. They learn to slowly, repeatedly forgive themselves for possible past mistakes and current omissions.

I am alone in the library, writing in the journal which has long been my honest friend. As I write, I am aware that the guilt I sometimes feel is now only a vague reminder of a way of living that helped me cope for so many years with fear. When something terrible happens in your life, you either feel that "it finally got you" or you see the total absurdity of that fearful superstition. For so long I believed that if I followed the rules, gave my best, or did the "right" thing, I might accomplish something or at least escape some painful fate. Now I know that if there ever were any rules, they have been broken. What an incredible sense of freedom Robbie has given me.

As the family continues to grow alongside the child with the disability, they learn to rely upon a core of discovered beliefs. These sometimes painfully forged "truths" about themselves, the child, and the world in which he will someday live without them are woven into their daily lives. Often when they are exhausted from the physical and emotional demands of caring for the child, their frustration makes them ask the "why" and "where are we going" questions. There are, of course, the immediate, concrete goals for the child, such as learning to drink from a straw or to drive a new electric wheelchair. The once ultimate goal of walking, so symbolic of independence, is now fading, however. The family must again choose between despair and redefinition.

We have nervously assembled in the large community college auditorium for the Montessori end-of-the-year school play. Our daughter Mary K., several grandparents, friends, and therapists have all come to watch "Peter Pan," who will be played by a blond boy in a red wheelchair. Robbie's incredible memory and unselfconscious singing have landed him the lead. During the play, several lines are muffed, a mermaid trips on her tail, and Robbie's voice projects less than optimally. For the exhilarating "I'm Flying" scene, a creative costume designer has rigged a way for Robbie to fly across the stage. As I anxiously hope the harness will hold Robbie, a stage hand gives Robbie/Peter a big push. Robbie looks more like a suspended fish than a trapeze artist, but the imagery is there. Robbie, who may never walk, is flying. In many ways, he has also learned to fly with his spirit.

What the parents may want for their son and what they think he may want for himself frequently distill into intangibles. While they have become credible troubleshooters at integrating their son into his surroundings, they often return to their sense of underlying purpose to direct their actions and renew their efforts. Self-esteem, love, and the ability to be touched by the moments of life serve as the family's anchors.

We have just come back from another three weeks of intense therapy with our friend and therapy "expert" Chris. Going to work with Chris is like taking your child in for a major overhaul of ideas, approaches, and creative equipment. She, like many of the therapists who have listened, cared, and given their best, infuses us with energy and a "can do" attitude. Somehow she knows how to help us translate our dreams into what we need to do today without overwhelming us. Watching her touch Robbie involves seeing more than the obvious movements. She asks him with her hands to continually let go of his spasticity, to trust her to lead his body into subtle new sensations. In offering him a guided way to try something different, she validates who he is now and who he might become. I am aware that therapy is considerably more than creating possibility for movement. The intense relationship between the therapist and Robbie reflects many of the less visible experiences I want for him—to try and not quite master it but still count for who he is now. As I observe Chris and Robbie work together, I remember a line in "The Little Prince."

"It is only with the heart one can see rightly," the fox says to the Little Prince. "What is essential is invisible to the eye."

As other individuals care for and about the child, the parents' perceptions of their son are reinforced. Acceptance of his evident disability is more than a scientific diagnosis and evaluation of what he can or cannot do. To be able to hope for love for their child in the larger world outside their family, the family members need help in molding a loveable and loving individual. While the parents expend incredible energy, time, and interest in addressing the disability, they also learn to treat him more as a child than as a health problem. This requires vigilant awareness. While their son has many needs and limited abilities, their expectations are often directed by the behavior of their daughter. Her development serves as a compass for the uncharted course they travel with their son.

> Vibrant, talkative Mary K. runs through the house collecting materials for her next drama production. Her more quiet friend Laura follows, pushing Robbie in his child-size wheelchair. Robbie is not too sure he wants to participate, but the girls coax him into giving it a chance. Lesson 241: If one wants to be included, one needs to be flexible. After the children's magic show in which Robbie produces a puppet rabbit from an old hat with Mary K.'s sly assistance, they decide to go swimming. Lesson 242: Disability or not, life moves quickly. As we later play in the pool, I remember that Mary K. will be leaving soon for four weeks of overnight camp. We will all miss her dearly. That feeling leads to another "lesson." Every child needs the opportunity to get away from her or his parents. In our family, I must fight to protect Mary K.'s right to move away from us. I must also find a way for Robbie to leave us.

Leaving the family's immediate circle of care and understanding does occur through school, through driving the wheelchair down the street, and eventually by going away to camp. Each separation arouses manageable fears which are amplified versions of what the parents experienced with their daughter. Will their son be physically safe? Will others acknowledge his abilities and allow him to try? Will he have fun? Can they trust him to find his way, however hard that may be? Some separations are more difficult than others.

> As we kiss Robbie good night, my words of encouragement attempt to mask my concern. Tomorrow Robbie will face the first of many surgeries. For ten years he and the hours of therapy have kept the surgeons as mere observers. Although tempted to seek surgical "fixes" for Robbie's problems, I have chosen to trust the therapists more. Now we are forced to decide between possibly limiting future mobility and surgically transferring muscles, which may compromise what little function he has. I have always

wanted options in his care and demanded participation. I am acutely aware though that our responsibility exacts a price. Robbie will have to live with the consequences of our decision. Will he blame us if things do not go well?

Hours later, as we wait for the surgery to be over, the crisis of an unknown outcome allows prior battles to resurface. I remember how it felt each time I explained my way into the newborn nursery years ago, wondering what had happened to my child in my absence. What if Robbie were to die now? For so long we have fought to find a way around, through, over, or in spite of the disability, so that the child in Robbie might have a chance. What if this is a gamble we should never have taken?

Other surgeries will provoke similar fears. While the disability requires the family to dance with it rather than attempt to control it, hospital settings often overlook much of what the family has mastered. Even in a healthcare environment, where physical compromises are everyday occurrences, patronization and underestimation appear. While the parents know there are few ways in which medicine may help their son, they hoped that their fellow healthcare professionals might see the individual in their child.

I arrive in the pediatric intensive care unit where Robbie has stayed after his third surgery. He will be moved today to the pediatric floor after a quiet night. The nurse who has cared for him has attempted to give him choices in his care and he seems relatively pain-free. As I remove the Walkman headset from his ears, the nurse comments on how he listened all night to his Bill Cosby tapes. Robbie has learned that humor is definitely one way to deal with this experience. Chuckling herself, the nurse remarks on how strange it was to hear Robbie laugh through the night. Her comments reveal how absent this place is of laughter. I wonder also if she thinks disabled people are incapable of having fun in other settings.

Several days later on the pediatric floor, Robbie and his older, but mentally younger roommate, Tom, are watching a television program together. A young, abrupt woman resident whips into the room, yanks the curtain closed and proceeds to do an invasive procedure on the roommate. Frightened, Tom begs her to stop.

Suddenly, immobile Robbie yells to the physician, "He doesn't understand what you are doing. You need to tell him or leave him alone."

The resident peers around the curtain, unsure as to who initiated this directive. Embarrassed by two teenagers, she is not sure how to proceed. She eventually examines the roommate but Robbie has managed to assert himself from a prone position.

As the teenager grows up, issues which have always been there assume new importance. While their son was young, the parents dealt with the uncertainty of his future through believing that they must somehow outlive him. Gradually they realize the impracticality and unhealthiness of this idea. Again they will have to trust him to deal with the outside world, just as he has negotiated other difficult situations. Their son will still need some "road maps" and occasional directions, but hopefully they have given him the essentials.

The almost empty college gym echoes with the voices of the basketball players Robbie has come to watch. One of the university sports information directors has invited him to observe practice, having learned of Robbie's obsession with sports and his budding interest in a sports information career.

Years ago, I once asked Robbie if there were things he wished he could do. He answered simply, "I'd like to be able to run—not walk, but RUN."

Today as I watch him intently follow the players' moves, I know he is attempting to run with them through his head. There will be the predictable real and psychological obstacles. Will he be able to attend college, live with other young adults, find a job? Will someone appreciate his strengths and see who he may continue to become?

He and the sports information director are now going over player statistic sheets and talking about the press coverage for tomorrow's game. I am just another observer of the practice session. And that is what it has all been about. . . .

YOUNG AND DISABLED

Nancy Mairs

Lunchtime. Your favorite café. Blinking away the dust and glare of the street, your gaze falls on a woman at the corner table. Her dark hair swings softly against cheeks as flawless as porcelain, and her chin rests on the slender fingers of one hand. In her beige silk blouse and ivory linen suit, she has the crisp appearance of someone who holds a powerful job and does it well. She leans forward to say something to the man across from her, and when he throws his head back with a deep laugh, her eyes sparkle.

Yourself, you're having a bad-hair day, and a zing up your calf tells you you're going to have to dash into the drugstore for a new pair of pantyhose before returning to your office, where the world's most boring report lies on your desk, still only half read. You stayed awake half the night worrying whether your boyfriend will take the job he's been offered in Denver, and now your brain feels as soggy as a fallen log under a thick layer of moss. But your stomach is rumbling, so you head for a table in the back.

As you pass the woman, you see with a start that she's sitting in a wheelchair. "Oh, the poor thing!" you think. "How courageous she is to fix herself up and get out of the house on a day as hot as this. And what a thoughtful man—her brother, it must be—treating her to lunch to cheer her up." In an instant, your mossy brain has dredged up an entirely new creature. The person you first noticed—the glamorous career woman enjoying a flirtation over lunch—is no more real, of course, than this pitiful invalid putting a brave face on her misery. Both are projections of your own imagination—your desires, your dreads. But because you admire the first, you're more likely to want to know her; the second, because she makes you uneasy, will remain a stranger.

The "you" I refer to is as much my young self as she is anyone else. In those days, I knew almost no one with a disability. When I was a child, one of my uncles had become partially paralyzed by polio, but he moved to Florida and I seldom saw him after that. Although two of my college classmates had been disabled, one quite severely, and I remember watching in wonder as she maneuvered her crutches over paths made treacherous by the New England winter, I didn't happen to know—or did I avoid knowing?—either of them well. Those were the days before buildings were ramped, elevators installed, and bathrooms modified for accessibility, and I can't imagine how complicated and exhausting and downright dangerous their lives must have been. No wonder relatively few disabled people ventured out into the world.

Then I became one of them. When my neurologist diagnosed my multiple sclerosis, he told me that I had a "normal" life expectancy. But, he didn't have to tell me, I wouldn't have a "normal" life, not the one I had prepared myself to live. I was going to be "disabled," more severely as time went on, and I had no idea how to live such a life. Could I go on teaching, and if so, would anybody want to hire me? Would my husband still find me sexually attractive, and could he accept my increasing need for help? Would my children resent having a mother who couldn't do everything that other mothers could? How would I survive if they all abandoned me? Did I even want to live to find out the answers to these questions?

As such questions suggest, I subscribed to the major social myths about the "disabled woman": that she lacks the health or competence to hold a job; that no man could want her or care for her, either physically or emotionally; that disability can only damage, never enhance, friendships and family relationships; that suicide is an understandable, even a rational, response to physical impairment, rather than the symptom of depression it is known to be in nondisabled people. Above all, I felt permanently exiled from "normality." Whether imposed by self or society, this outsider status—and not the disability itself—constitutes the most daunting barrier for most people with physical impairments, because it, even more than flights of steps or elevators without braille, prevents them from participating fully in the ordinary world, where most of life's satisfactions dwell.

Gradually, I stopped thinking of myself as an outcast, and over the years I have watched the social barriers crumbling as well. As technological advances permit disabled people to travel, study, and work, and as the media incorporate their pictures and stories into articles, advertising, television programs, and films, their presence becomes more familiar and less frightening. Many of them are eager to promote this process, as *Glamour* magazine discovered by asking readers with disabilities to write about their histories and the effects that their physical circumstances have had on their work, their friendships, and their love lives. Letters and faxes flooded in from several hundred women (and a handful of men), ranging in age from sixteen to eighty-five but most in their twenties and thirties, who were "intrigued," "excited," and "thrilled" at being asked to emerge from the shadows. Having the chance to collate these for an article I wrote for the magazine, I became charmed by the frankness, grit, and good humor these women displayed.

The challenge in compressing their replies—many of them covering several closely typed or handwritten pages—lay in fairly representing their diversity. Their disabilities varied so widely that it was difficult—even deceptive—to generalize about such women, who may have less in common with each other than they do with some nondisabled women and who may even be made uneasy by women with disabilities different from their own. As Peggy Merriman, who was diagnosed with multiple sclerosis when she was nineteen, protested, "The general public seems to have an easier time (or simply unconsciously prefers) dealing with people with disabilities by lumping us all together and assuming that we all have the same problems and, what is worse, that *all* we deal with or have in our life is our disability." But defining someone solely in terms of what she cannot do tends to distort her life: "I feel I have been neatly tucked into a category with no room to move," wrote twenty-one-year-old Naomi Passman, whose legs were paralyzed in infancy by a spinal tumor, but "the last thing I need are limits!" I hope that, as these women speak, "disability" will emerge as one element of their complicated personalities and not as a confining category.

Nevertheless, as every woman who wrote to *Glamour* has long since found out, breaking free of a category doesn't abolish the realities of the disability itself, which may include weakness, fatigue, deformity, physical pain, bouts of illness, and reliance on technical assistance like crutches, wheelchairs, or hearing aids. In a society that equates "vitality" and "beauty" with physical soundness, a disabled woman must come to terms with serious shortcomings often earlier and even more urgently than others. In this process, these women have learned from experience what many their age understand only intellectually, that life itself is imperfect: the best-qualified person doesn't always get the job; the most loving heart doesn't always find a mate. Although a few responded to such knowledge with bitterness or apathy, most seemed to take it as a challenge. Their lives might not be "perfect" by conventional social standards, but they were determined to live productively and passionately anyway.

Those who were disabled from birth, by conditions like spina bifida and cerebral palsy, had to cope with being "different" during the time when social conformity seems most compelling. For many of them, childhood was anything but carefree, since they often faced both painful medical treatments and the taunts of "normal" schoolmates. Their reactions to their situations often diverged, however, as revealed by the responses of two women with osteogenesis imperfecta, a genetic disorder that causes bones to fracture very easily. "My parents were somewhat over-protective, which is highly understandable," wrote Felicia Wells Williams, a young African American woman who was born with several ribs and both arms already broken. "However, some of their apprehensiveness about my 'fragile' condition rubbed off on me. As a young child, I was told to be careful and think of the consequences of my actions. So I became fearful of certain things—heights, falling down stairs, etc. I spent a lot of my childhood being a spectator—watching others have fun." Konie Gardner, with the same diagnosis, recalled that her parents assigned her Saturday chores just like her five brothers and sisters and gave her every opportunity to try whatever she wanted. "I was always an accepted kid in the neighborhood, too, and even though I could not physically participate in many of the games, etc., I was an enthusiastic spectator and never felt left out by anyone." Whereas one felt she was missing the fun, the other had fun just watching.

Many received the kind of encouragement Kim Silvey reported: born with dislocated hips that required ten operations while she was growing up, Kim "wasn't one to hide and not be seen by anybody," thanks to her parents, who "instilled in me confidence and the belief that I could do anything I wanted, and that's the attitude I grew up with and the one I still hold today." She added, "It would have been so easy for them to coddle me and try to keep me out of the 'evil eye' of the world and to try to shelter me from the pain others could inflict upon me. I credit my being who I am today to my parents' unwillingness to hide me because I didn't fit the 'normal' mold."

Even those with supportive parents often found other children cruel. "With a toe first walking style, slurred speech and nearly no fine motor coordination, I was not what anyone considered popular," recalled Barbara McGuire, thirty-four, born with cerebral palsy and educated in regular classes. "I was the first to get 'cooties' (call me if you don't remember this social disease of elementary school kids); the last to get rid of them; the first to get teased; the last to get picked in gym." From early on, "boys were terribly mean," and by junior high school girls were, too, "to impress the boys." Only after entering an all-girls' high school did she begin to make lifelong friends.

The struggle for approval from nondisabled peers can have humorous consequences, as Juli Delzer, born with a 60 percent hearing loss in both ears, revealed. As a child, "I was so painfully shy about my deafness that it was embarrassing to let people know that I couldn't hear. I came up with what I call 'deaf answers.' If someone asked me a question that I didn't hear, I would answer with 'yes,' 'no,' or 'I don't know,' hoping that I had covered the bases and given an appropriate answer. This didn't work so well when I moved to a new school. In gym class one day, someone turned around to ask, 'What's your name?' To which I answered, 'I don't know.'" Now, planning to do small animal husbandry in the Peace Corps before she begins veterinary school, Juli has grown self-assured enough to give up these "deaf answers," but still, she wrote, "I am very aware of my handicap in relationships with men. They can't whisper sweet nothings in my ear because I would be forced to look at them and whisper back, 'What?'"

In addition to a sense of humor, pride did much to carry these women through their awkward childhood years. "On the day I received my first hearing aid, when I was nine years old, my doctor assured me my long hair would easily hide it," wrote Madeline Cohen, a student at Stanford Law School who was also born deaf. "In response, I pulled my hair into a pony tail and walked out of his office with my nose in the air."

The dependencies of childhood—for nurture, instruction, and approval from adults—were often especially hard for these women to outgrow, though virtually all of them appear to have succeeded. The transition was not always a happy one. "As a child I was very much treated like a cosseted princess: dressed in beautiful clothes and sheltered from the outside world," wrote thirty-two-year-old Karyna Laroche, whose muscular dystrophy requires her to rely on caregivers for virtually all her needs. An outstanding student, she attended a special school for disabled students until, at thirteen, she transferred to a regular high school, where "I finally realized just how different I was from other kids, how being disabled was only considered cute and socially acceptable when one is young, otherwise it is a social embarrassment." The shock was so great that, despite outward success, "inwardly I only wanted to die. My first suicide attempt occurred at the age of 16 and suicide plans and attempts continued until I turned 30." Only then did she discover "just how lucky I was to be living on my own (which I love), to have great friends, and to have the chance to build a life based on my needs rather than on others' expectations of me."

More often, simply entering adulthood brought a new rush of self-confidence. When Michele Anne Hope Micheline, a student at Emory University whose spina bifida, though relatively mild, has necessitated a number of operations on her left foot, developed a severe ulcer on her normal right foot during her freshman year, the doctors wanted to amputate the infected bone. "I realized," she reported, "almost like a slap on my face, that I was old enough to tell them that [surgery] was NOT how I wanted it. I had a right to say no, to get a second opinion. To grasp my life." Finding a doctor in whom she had complete confidence, who was able to save all but half of her big toe, and having her left foot reconstructed, she assumed responsibility for her own well-being. She has come to terms with the fact that she will always have to deal with a disability and that doctors, though useful, "can't give you a perfect foot. They can't give you what God didn't. You have to find a substitute within yourself for what you are lacking."

Some respondents had already reached adulthood when, like me, they developed a disabling disease or else were injured in skiing, motorcycle, automobile, or on-the-job accidents—even, in one case, a tornado. After I learned that I had multiple sclerosis, the transitions I had to make, involving the development of a new sense of who I was and what I was good for, required mourning the loss of the "old me" as I confronted a new one who seemed like a stranger. The active young wife and mother faded: no longer could I run after my young children or dance with their father. When my waist-length hair grew too heavy for my weakening hands to wash and brush, I had to cut it off, and suddenly I felt no longer carefree and sexy but practical and matronly.

With degenerate conditions like mine, self-definition may have to be revised in this way again and again as new limitations develop.

For those struck by sudden catastrophe, the need to adjust may have come instantly, but the process itself took time. Muffy Davis was fifteen, training to be an Olympic ski racer, when an accident on the slopes left her paralyzed from mid-chest down. "It always amazed me when people would say, 'I don't know how you do it. I could never do it!' You don't have a choice, you just do it! What most people don't realize is that they would do this also. They see a disabled person and immediately put themselves in that person's shoes. What they don't realize is that disabled person didn't just get to wherever she was right away. It took time and grieving, but slowly day by day she got better, and eventually she was right back to attacking life, like she had been before her disability." After graduating from Stanford and before beginning medical school, Muffy plans to "give myself a shot at ski racing again, this time as a disabled athlete. I don't want to have any regrets when I get older." Thanks to adaptive sports equipment, such a goal is within her reach.

Whether gradually or suddenly, disabilities that occur in adulthood require revisions of identity that can yield fresh insight, as Madeline Cohen, who has a degenerative retinal disease in addition to her 85 to 90 percent hearing loss, discovered during a three-week Outward Bound experience after college graduation. "Had I stumbled over your disability survey announcement a few years ago, I might have continued flipping through the magazine with little more than a passing glance," she wrote, because she did not grow up defining herself as disabled. On Outward Bound, she encountered "a virtual assault of obstacles. Not the least of these was learning to recognize my limitations, voice them to my group members, and accept assistance from those around me. The latter was (and remains) the most difficult." As the days went by, she came to perceive that "everyone in my group carried special needs [one, for instance, was terrified of heights, and Madeline was able to talk him through a scary climb] and that by accepting assistance, I was acknowledging my participation in the cooperative human endeavor. Since that time, I have been learning to define myself as a 'person with a disability.'"

Regardless of when their disabled lives began or what pattern they have followed, all the respondents confronted the same issues in the "cooperative human endeavor" known as life as did their nondisabled peers. "People seem surprised and often patronizing when they find out I have a job and a social life," wrote Peggy Merriman, who works for a nonprofit agency assisting released prisoners, as though disability drained away all the interest taken by normal young women (and some of us who are not so young!) in finding meaningful work and developing personal relationships. On the contrary! Despite the enormous variety of their experiences, virtually all the respondents devoted much of their energy to the issues surrounding career and love.

A number were still undergraduate or graduate students, majoring in a variety of fields from art history to animal physiology. Those who had finished school worked in similarly diverse areas, among them education, management, law, healthcare, and fashion design. Disability often required them to be both flexible and resourceful. "At first I wanted to become a vet," wrote Naomi Passman, "but saw how much lifting was involved and decided against it." Determined to work with animals, she applied to become an apprentice trainer of assistance dogs, but the director of the school turned her down. "I couldn't believe that a person who provided a service for the disabled would not hire me because I *was* disabled!" Undaunted, she found another program. "I am an Apprentice Assistance Dog Trainer and an Independent Living Specialist. I LOVE my work," she reported.

Even though the Americans with Disabilities Act is supposed to prevent the kind of rejection Naomi experienced, a few of the respondents had encountered outright bias, including retaliation by employers if they applied for workers' compensation after being injured on the job. Felicia Wells Williams, with a bachelor's degree in social work, started her career as an entry-level receptionist. "Once after observing blatant discrimination, I filed an equal employment opportunity suit with the Defense Contract Administration/Department of Defense," she recounted. "With the help of some knowledgeable friends, I not only won my case, but I was given the higher grade plus back pay." Defending one's rights can be tricky, however, since the nondisabled tend to expect people with disabilities to be unfailingly cheerful and passive, as Felicia has learned: "Some people say I am arrogant but I believe if I were of normal height/not disabled, I would be called 'confident' rather than 'bossy' or 'pushy.'"

More subtle forms of intolerance can make the workplace a chilly one for disabled women. "Because my symptoms tend to be invisible, I haven't experienced any real bias or discrimination" as a policy advisor to an elected official, reported Cece Hughley Noel, who has had multiple sclerosis since 1987. "However, on the days that I need a cane it is very difficult for me emotionally. People who I work with every day fail to recognize me on the street. They tend to avert their eyes from 'cripples' and don't meet my eyes or hear my 'hello.' It can be devastating to win their praise for taking charge

of a meeting one day, only to be ignored as a 'gimp' on the street, the next."
Dealing with pain and fatigue every day, Cece has found herself being
resented as well as ignored: "My co-workers get 'snitty' sometimes when I
take a break and lie down in my office or leave early."

In addition, Cece wrote, "I've used up all my vacation and sick leave this
year and feel as though my back is up against the wall." Some of the respondents, finding themselves in similar situations, have had to give up their jobs,
and their comments revealed that in our work-driven society, where what
you "do" determines who you "are," lack of employment can erode one's
sense of self-worth (not to mention one's bank account). As Stephanie
McCarty, who managed a bookstore for ten years until her MS symptoms
forced her to go on Social Security Disability, put it, "I often feel flustered
when I am asked what I 'do' for a living (they wouldn't believe what I do
just to live) and don't quite know what to say. I take classes in pottery, spend
a great deal of time in the library (and doctor's office), keep myself busy on
my home computer, and concentrate on staying healthy. But these things all
seem pretty benign when I am talking to someone with a 'career.'"

Whether they held paid jobs or not, these women craved social contact,
even at the risk of awkward encounters. Many recognized that what seems
to be rudeness on the part of nondisabled people often arises from ignorance
and fear, which can be more crippling in their own way than a physical disability, and that the best way to relieve these is through education. Their
advice was pragmatic: Treat a disabled person as an intelligent and responsible adult. (If she's not, that's her problem, not yours.) Remember that not
all disabilities are apparent before you accuse her of malingering or shout at
her for taking a handicapped parking space. NEVER take one of these yourself, even if you'll "only be a minute." If she does have an obvious disability,
before rushing to her aid, ask "How may I help?" and then follow her
instructions carefully, or you may both wind up in a heap on the floor. If she's
in a wheelchair, sit down whenever possible so that you can converse eye-
to-eye, not eye-to-navel. Don't ask her any questions more personal than
you'd feel comfortable answering yourself. ("What's wrong with you?" is
probably not one of them.) Above all, don't offer her pity. She probably
doesn't need it. (And when she does, she can take care of the job herself.)

Many spoke warmly of friends who offer, as one anonymous respondent
who was left partially paralyzed by a brain tumor put it, "kindness without
condescension." Most of these friends were not disabled, although some of
the women still in college reported involvement in disabled students' groups,

and most accommodated a disability without much fuss. With both her hearing and her vision impaired, Madeline Cohen has found that "the people who know me best are great about things like repeating themselves, steering me through dark bars and parking lots, and understanding when I miss the thread of a large, noisy conversation and say something ridiculously unconnected. My friends are used to seeing me bump into any object lower than hip level, collide with small children, and look around blankly for someone standing directly in front of me; they do as much as possible to help me avoid such mishaps without making me feel inadequate or foolish."

Sometimes thoughtless friends cause pain without meaning to. Maree Larson, an assistant producer for a video production company who has spina bifida, recalled attending a political rally with some friends, all but one of whom "walked up the steps and took their seats in the third row," while her wheelchair required her to stay in the first. "Soon, my friend was persuaded to join the others ('but only for a minute,' she said), and I was left by myself for the remaining 20 minutes before the rally began." Even friends who are sympathetic in one area can be insensitive in another, as Konie Gardner discovered when it came to dating: "I can't begin to count the number of times that well-meaning friends would say to me, 'I'll set you up with . . .' and every time, and I do mean every time, they never once did. I don't think people realize how much a person like me clings to every promise, suggestion, or hint that is made in this regard."

In general, these women found romantic and sexual relationships much more difficult to establish and sustain than simple friendships. A number were troubled by the prevailing social perception of disabled women as incapable of and uninterested in sex: "In this culture people with disabilities are expected to be perpetual children which means that sexual expression would not be appropriate and may be considered perverted," observed Pat Danielson, whose juvenile rheumatoid arthritis was diagnosed when she was four; and twenty-three-year-old Kimberly Mangiafico, who has spinal muscular atrophy, protested that her wheelchair gives most men "the impression that I cannot have sex, which is totally not true. I have a great sexual self-image and I am really comfortable in my own skin." Others recognized internal barriers, like Naomi Passman, who reflected, "I have had boyfriends and even a first love. That part has never been a problem for me; however, when it comes to being sexually involved that's when walls go up. Quite honestly, for me it has not been other people's perceptions that have affected the relationships, it has been my own."

Knowing that they, like nondisabled women, will be judged initially on their appearance, many reported taking great care with their clothes, makeup, and hair. Some were aware of the obvious ironies of this emphasis, like Peggy Merriman, who asked a male friend, "in my most unconcerned and disinterested voice, if he thought any guy would *ever* want to meet or go out with me or even be seen with me, if I was using a wheelchair" and was told, "I don't think it really matters that you're in a wheelchair, because you're so pretty." "Here I was," she went on, "ashamed and embarrassed, because of my physical body. Here he was, praising me and telling me I had nothing to worry about, because of my physical body. He didn't say, 'It doesn't matter, because you are so interesting and intelligent,' or even, 'It doesn't matter, because you have such a cute dog, and anyone who wants to play with him knows you and he are a package deal, unfortunately.' *That* is me; that's who I am."

No matter how pretty or smart a woman may be, or how cute her dog is, "dating and initiating a relationship is difficult though because all of the typical rules never seem to apply when you are in a wheelchair," noted Muffy Davis. "Guys feel that they can really flirt with a girl in a chair but they don't see it as anything serious," since she presumably doesn't expect to be asked out. "Also girls with disabilities can put all the moves on guys and yet the guys will never interpret things the right way." Although she has found that she often has to take the lead, "I really like it when, every once in a while, a guy makes the first move."

Too often, however, he doesn't make any move at all. "I am 27 years old and still a virgin, not that that is bad, but only that it is really not by my choice," wrote Kim Silvey. "I had a date to my prom when I was a junior in high school and went out on a couple of 'just friends' dates in college, but that is it." But disability didn't take away her dreams: "I want nothing more in life than to get married and have a soul-mate, best friend, and lover for life. As each birthday comes and goes, I feel the reality of such happening getting smaller and smaller, and I feel cheated and angry."

Those who had succeeded in establishing relationships often found them complicated, physically and emotionally, by disability. "I worry about what weird noises my body is making that he can hear and I don't," Juli Delzer confided. And a woman who asked to remain anonymous wrote, "Unfortunately, spina bifida did affect my sexual functioning, and I'm not able to achieve orgasm. While we've been able to have a reasonably satisfying sex life without intercourse, I know it bothers my partner that I'm non-orgasmic. I think he sometimes sees it as his failure. I'm very responsive to foreplay with my breasts and around my neck, but am truthfully disappointed myself not to be able to climax." "Due to numbness, weakness, fatigue, and bladder problems we sometimes have to be creative with our lovemaking," noted Stephanie McCarty. A sense of humor also helps: "Often, in the heat of passion, one of my hearing aids will be pressed against a chest, an arm, or a pillow," creating an electronic squeal, wrote Madeline Cohen. "My line, dating back to junior high school: 'Whoops! That's my parents checking up on me.'"

Sometimes the urgency to find a partner contributed to an unwise choice, leading to grief. At twenty-nine, Frances Wallen was paralyzed from the waist down when an eighteen-wheeler ran a stop sign and struck her red Mazda RX-7. "Before the accident I'd been dating someone fairly seriously," she recalled. "He was wild and unreliable, but I was crazy about him and our affair was very hot. After the accident he was there for me every day and we talked about marriage. I wanted as much of my life back as possible, and figured that this was my last shot at love with someone who could see me without pity. My new husband didn't pity me—he resented me, and took great pleasure in draining me dry financially. I figured he would settle down eventually, but he didn't. We divorced after a year and a half, and I added a broken heart to my list of all my other broken body parts."

But there were happy stories as well. One respondent's husband had abandoned her and their three small children when she was still only mildly disabled by a childhood bout with polio; later, post-polio syndrome caused increasing pain and fatigue, a limp, and breathing problems. At this point, she became friends with a man at the agency where she worked. "He talked to me and we found common ground in our children and love of music," she recollected. "While out in the field I came back to agency headquarters occasionally, and he'd be there, interested in my latest news. When I was moved back on my medical transfer, last year, our friendship grew. I told him, up front, about the polio and the part it played in my life. We married in April 1994. He is there for me, supportive and encouraging and loving. In his eyes I am beautiful; the fact that I have polio doesn't interfere. Through him, I am learning to do my best without exhausting all my energy to 'measure up.' Through him, I've found self-acceptance, self-pride, and love. I look in the mirror and see *normal*."

Fortunately, this experience was far from unique. As Muffy Davis pointed out, "The phone does ring less often, but the guys who do call and are interested are of a higher quality." She's been with one of them for two and a half years now, and many other respondents reported similar good fortune, finding partners who were perceptive, patient, affectionate, and above all reassuring. One respondent, whose brain tumor left her with partial paralysis, as well as hair loss and weight gain, wrote, "Naturally, I don't feel very sexy anymore. Yet my husband has continued to treat me with kindness and tenderness. Because of his accepting attitude, my self-esteem has not plummeted entirely." Barbara Maguire, married with two small sons, reflected on her fear that her cerebral palsy might be a burden to her family: "Perhaps my biggest fear is for my husband to someday find out that I am not worth the struggles we've had. He assures me that he is the lucky one and that I am the one 'putting up' with him." "I presently have someone in my life and he is a sweetheart," wrote twenty-five-year-old Stacey Fujii, whose lupus was diagnosed on her twenty-third birthday. "Although he is a surfer, he will do things with me that do not involve the sun, like going out to dinner, to a movie or for a walk on the beach at night. It was very hard for me at first because I felt as if I were holding him back. I was also very insecure about the person I am now, but he always tells me I am beautiful and incredible for what I had to go through. He takes the best care of me and never says I am different, just special."

Not perfect, perhaps, but both normal and special: just the way every women needs to feel. And aided by parents, teachers, friends, lovers, and/or sheer self-determination, the majority of the women who responded had achieved some sense of their own ordinary yet unique qualities. Like Madeline Cohen, they had gained an insight into the human condition which enabled them to see their disabilities as "simply a part of who I am, just as other people have lost parents, gone through divorces, overcome learning disabilities or major illnesses, pulled themselves out of socioeconomic deprivation, or emigrated from war zones." Surely not all would go as far as Kimberly Mangiafico when she wrote that "if I was suddenly given the chance to be able to walk, I would not take it. My being in a wheelchair is part of who I am." But most would understand the self-acceptance her statement implies.

Over all, the women who chose to reveal themselves to *Glamour* were bright, tough, competent, sometimes angry, often funny, and very self-assured—hardly a whiner in the bunch! Theirs were not, as cancer survivor Pat Wallace put it, "triumph-over-tragedy stories" (though there were plenty of tragedies and some triumphs, too) but adventure stories. Stephanie McCarty echoed the sense I often have of exploring uncharted territory: "I feel I have been sent on a journey. I wasn't given a guidebook, so I'll have to draw my own map." In undertaking to live as full human beings in a world intent on reducing them to a set of dysfunctional limbs and organs, they had grown much more vigorous than their sometimes fragile bodies would suggest. As I read and digested their words, I felt honored to count myself among their number.

5

TOUCHING THE ROCK

An Experience of Blindness

John M. Hull

DOES HE TAKE SUGAR?

16 JULY 1984

At church, one of the vergers approached Marilyn as she was standing with me, and said to her, "Marilyn, is it John's wish to go forward to the Communion Rail?" Marilyn made no reply, I turned towards him and said with a smile, "Yes, thank you very much, I will be going forward." There was a slight sound of surprise, and I gathered that the kindly man was somewhat flustered because I had overheard what he had said. I assured him that I would be quite all right, and would go up accompanied by Marilyn as I normally did. I thanked him for his concern. I think that he was assuming I was deaf. Why not tap me on the elbow, and ask me whether I intended to go forward, and whether I would need any assistance? I would appreciate this thoughtful gesture. To speak *about* me, in the third person, to someone else, is another matter.

This situation often seems to arise when I am getting in a car with a group of other people. "Will you put John in the back with you?" "No, I'll put him in the front with you." "All right, you put him in then." At this point I interjected, crying out with an exceedingly loud voice, "John is not *put* anywhere, thank you very much. John is asked if he has any preferences about where he sits." At this, all my friends laughed uproariously and were covered with apologies and confusions. On a similar occasion recently I shouted out, "Hey, you guys, don't you talk about me as if I am not here." This, again, brought shouts of laughter and a mixture of apologies, agreements and congratulations.

It is, of course, very embarrassing for intelligent and sensitive people when they are caught out like this, in using the "Does he take sugar?" approach to a disabled person. These people are all sensitive, and well aware of the humiliation which this approach implies. So the question arises, why do they do it? . . .

ACOUSTIC SPACE   27 APRIL 1984

. . . I have been spending some time out of doors trying to respond to the special nature of the acoustic world. I am impressed by the many different aspects of reality, the range and depth of the contact points between myself and something created by sound.

The tangible world sets up only as many points of reality as can be touched by my body, and this seems to be restricted to one problem at a time. I can explore the splinters on the park bench with the tip of my finger, but I cannot, at the same time, concentrate upon exploring the pebbles with my big toe. I can use all ten fingers when I am exploring the shape of something, but it is quite difficult to explore two objects simultaneously, one with each hand. It is true that, if many people were poking me, I would feel all the prods with various parts of my body, but this would not tell me very much about the world, only about my body.

The world revealed by sound is so different. It is true that I cannot listen to two different tape-recorded books at the same time, but that has to do with speech. I am thinking of the way in which sound places one within a world.

On Holy Saturday I sat in Cannon Hill Park while the children were playing. I heard the footsteps of passersby, many different kinds of footsteps. There was the flip-flop of sandals and the sharper, more delicate sound of high-heeled shoes. There were groups of people walking together with different strides, creating a sort of patter, being overtaken now by one, firm, long stride, or by the rapid pad of a jogger. There were children, running along in little bursts, and stopping to get on and off squeaky tricycles or scooters. The footsteps came from both sides. They met, mingled, separated again. From the next bench, there was the rustle of a newspaper and the murmur of conversation. Further out, to the right and behind me, there was the car park. Cars were stopping and starting, arriving and departing, doors were being slammed. Far over to the left, there was the main road. I heard the steady, deep roar of the through traffic, the buses and the trucks. In front of me was the lake. It was full of wild fowl. The ducks were quacking, the geese honking, and other birds which I could not identify were calling and cranking. There was continual flapping of wings, splashing and squabbling, as birds took off and landed on the surface or fought over scraps of bread. There was the splash of paddleboats, the cries of the children, and the bumps as two boats collided. Parents on shore called out encouragement or warning. Further away, from the larger expanse of the lake, there was the different sound of the rowing boats as they swished past, and beyond that was the park. People were playing football. I heard the shouting, running feet, the impact of leather upon leather as the ball was kicked. There seemed to be several groups playing different games. Here there were boys; further over in that direction there seemed to be a group of young children playing. Over this whole scene there was the wind. The trees behind me were murmuring; the shrubs and bushes along the side of the paths rustled; leaves and scraps of paper were blown along the path. I leant back and drank it all in. It was an astonishingly varied and rich panorama of movement, music and infor-mation. It was absorbing and fascinating.

The strange thing about it, however, is that it was a world of nothing but action. Every sound was a point of activity. Where nothing was happening, there was silence. That little part of the world then died, disappeared. The ducks were silent. Had they gone, or was something holding their rapt atten-tion? The boat came to rest. Were people leaning on the oars, or had they tied it to the edge and gone away? Nobody was walking past me just now. This meant that the footpath itself had disappeared. I could only remind myself of its direction by considering that it ran parallel to the bench upon which I sat. Even the traffic on the main road had paused. Were the lights red? When there is rest, everything else passes out of existence. To rest is not to be. Mine is not a world of being; it is a world of becoming. The world of being, the silent, still world where things simply are, that does not exist. The rockery, the pavilion, the skyline of high-rise flats, the flagpoles over the cricket ground, none of this is really there. The world of happenings, of movement and conflict, that is there.

The acoustic world is one in which things pass in and out of existence. This happens with such surprising rapidity. There seems to be no intermediate zone of approach. There is a sudden cry from the lake, "Hello Daddy!"; my children are there in their paddleboat. Previously, a moment ago, they were not there. Not until they greeted me with a cry could I distinguish them from the rest of the background sounds. There was no gradual approach. While the world which greets me in this way is active, I am passive. I cannot stop these stimulations flooding me. I just sit here. The creatures emitting the noise have to engage in some activity. They have to scrape, bang, hit, club, strike surface upon surface, impact, make their vocal cords vibrate. They must take the initiative in announcing their presence to me. For my part, I have no power to explore them. I cannot penetrate them or discover them without their active cooperation. They must utter their voice, their sound. It is thus a world which comes to me, which springs into life for me, which has no existence apart from its life towards me.

The intermittent nature of the acoustic world is one of its most striking features. In contrast, the perceived world is stable and continuous. The seen world cannot escape from your eyes. Even in the darkness, you can use a torch and force things into visibility, but I have only very limited power over the acoustic world.

Here is another feature of the acoustic world: it stays the same whichever way I turn my head. This is not true of the perceptible world. It changes as I turn my head. New things come into view. The view looking that way is quite different from the view looking this way. It is not like that with sound. New noises do not come to my attention as I turn my head around. I may allow my head to hang limply down upon my chest; I may lean right back and face the sky. It makes little difference. Perhaps there is some slight shading of quality, but the acoustic world is mainly independent of my movement. This heightens the sense of passivity. Instead of me having to search things out and uncover fresh portions of my world by my own effort as I fix my gaze first here then there, in the acoustic world there is something which is rather indifferent to my attempts to penetrate it. This is a world which I cannot shut out, which goes on all around me, and which gets on with its own life. I can, of course, train myself to pay attention to it; I can learn to distinguish this from that sound, become more practiced in judging distance and so on. Nevertheless, my ears remain fixed in a stationary head; while my eyes, if I could see, would be darting here and there with innumerable movements in a head which is itself moving.

Acoustic space is a world of revelation.

6

I'M LISTENING AS HARD AS I CAN

Terry Galloway

At the age of twelve I won the swimming award at the Lions Camp for Crippled Children. When my name echoed over the PA system the girl in the wheelchair next to me grabbed the box speaker of my hearing aid and shouted, "You won!" My ear quaking, I took the cue. I stood up straight—the only physically unencumbered child in a sea of braces and canes—affixed a pained but brave grin to my face, then limped all the way to the stage.

Later, after the spotlight had dimmed, I was overcome with remorse, but not because I'd played the crippled heroine. The truth was that I was ashamed of my handicap. I wanted to have something more visibly wrong with me. I wanted to be in the same league as the girl who'd lost her right leg in a car accident; her artificial leg attracted a bevy of awestruck campers. I, on the other hand, wore an unwieldy box hearing aid buckled to my body like a dog halter. It attracted no one. Deafness wasn't, in my eyes, a blue-

From *With Wings: An Anthology of Literature By and About Women with Disabilities*, ed. Marsha Saxton and Florence Howe (New York: Feminist Press at the City University of New York, 1987), pp. 5–9. Reprinted by permission from the April 1981 issue of *Texas Monthly*.

ribbon handicap. Mixed in with my envy, though, was an overwhelming sense of guilt; at camp I was free to splash in the swimming pool, while most of the other children were stranded at the shallow end, where lifeguards floated them in lazy circles. But seventeen years of living in the "normal" world has diminished my guilt considerably, and I've learned that every handicap has its own particular hell.

I'm something of an anomaly in the deaf world. Unlike most deaf people, who were either born deaf or went deaf in infancy, I lost my hearing in chunks over a period of twelve years. Fortunately I learned to speak before my loss grew too profound, and that ability freed me from the most severe problem facing the deaf—the terrible difficulty of making themselves understood. My opinion of deafness was just as biased as that of a person who can hear. I had never met a deaf child in my life, and I didn't know how to sign. I imagined deaf people to be like creatures from beyond: animal-like because their language was so physical, threatening because they were unable to express themselves with sophistication—that is, through speech. I *could* make myself understood, and because I had a talent for lip-reading it was easy for me to pass in the wider world. And for most of my life that is exactly what I did—like a black woman playing white, I passed for something other than what I was. But in doing so I was avoiding some very painful facts. And for many years I was inhibited not only by my deafness but my own idea of what it meant to be deaf.

My problems all started when my mother, seven months pregnant with me, developed a serious kidney infection. Her doctors pumped her full of antibiotics. Two months later I was born, with nothing to suggest that I was anything more or less than a normal child. For years nobody knew that the antibiotics had played havoc with my fetal nervous system. I grew up bright, happy, and energetic.

But by the time I was ten I knew, if nobody else did, that something somewhere had gone wrong. The people around me had gradually developed fuzzy profiles, and their speech had taken on a blurred and foreign character. But I was such a secure and happy child that it didn't enter my mind to question my new perspective or mention the changes to anyone else. Finally, my behavior became noticeably erratic—I would make nonsensical replies to ordinary questions or simply fail to reply at all. My teachers, deciding that I was neither a particularly creative child nor an especially troublesome one, looked for a physical cause. They found two: I wasn't quite as blind as a bat, but I was almost as deaf as a doornail.

My parents took me to Wilford Hall Air Force Hospital in San Antonio, where I was examined from ear to ear. My tonsils were removed and studied, ice water was injected into my inner ear, and I underwent a series of inexplicable and at times painful exploratory tests. I would forever after associate deafness with kind attention and unusual punishment. Finally a verdict was delivered: "Congenital interference has resulted in a neural disorder for which there is no known medical or surgical treatment." My hearing loss was severe and would grow progressively worse.

I was fitted with my first hearing aid and sent back home to resume my childhood. I never did. I had just turned twelve, and my body was undergoing enormous changes. I had baby fat, baby breasts, hairy legs, and thick pink cat-eye glasses. My hearing aid was about the size of a small transistor radio and rode in a white linen pouch that hit exactly at breast level. It was not a welcome addition to my pubescent woe.

As a vain child trapped in a monster's body, I was frantic for a way to survive the next few years. Glimpsing my reflection in mirrors became such agony that I acquired a habit of brushing my teeth and hair with my eyes closed. Everything I did was geared to making my body more inhabitable, but I only succeeded in making it less so. I kept my glasses in my pocket and developed an unbecoming squint; I devised a smile that hid two broken front teeth, but it looked disturbingly like the grin of a piranha; I kept my arms folded over my would-be breasts. But the hearing aid was a different story. There was no way to disguise it. I could tuck it under my blouse, but then all I could hear was the static of cotton. Besides, whenever I took a step the box bounced around like a third breast. So I resigned myself: a monster I was, a monster I would be.

I became more withdrawn, more suspicious of other people's intentions. I imagined that I was being deliberately excluded from schoolyard talk because the other children didn't make much of an effort to involve me—they simply didn't have the time or patience to repeat snatches of gossip ten times and slowly. Conversation always reached the point of ridiculousness before I could understand something as simple as "The movie starts at five." (The groovy shark's alive? The moving stars that thrive?) I didn't make it to many movies. I cultivated a lofty sense of superiority, and I was often brutal with people who offered the "wrong" kind of help at the "wrong" time. Right after my thirteenth birthday some well-meaning neighbors took me to a revivalist faith healing. I already had doubts about exuberant religions, and the knee-deep hysteria of the preacher simply confirmed them. He bounded to my side and put his hands on my head. "O Lord," he cried, "heal this poor little lamb!"

I leaped up as if transported and shouted, "I can walk!"

For the first few years my parents were as bewildered as I was. Nothing had prepared them for a handicapped child on the brink of adolescence. They sensed a whole other world of problems, but in those early stages I still seemed so normal that they just couldn't see me in a school for the deaf. They felt that although such schools were there to help, they also served to isolate. I have always been grateful for their decision. Because of it, I had to contend with public schools, and in doing so I developed two methods of survival: I learned to read not just lips but the whole person, and I learned the habit of clear speech by taking every speech and drama course I could.

That is not to say my adolescent years were easy going—they were misery. The lack of sound cast a pall on everything. Life seemed less fun than it had been before. I didn't associate that lack of fun with the lack of sound. I didn't begin to make the connection between the failings of my body and the failings of the world until I was well out of college. I simply did not admit to myself that deafness caused certain problems—or even that I was deaf.

From the time I was twelve until I was twenty-four, the loss of my hearing was erratic. I would lose a decibel or two of sound and then my hearing would stabilize. A week or a year later there would be another slip and then I'd have to adjust all over again. I never knew when I would hit bottom. I remember going to bed one night still being able to make out the reassuring purr of the refrigerator and the late-night conversation of my parents, then waking the next morning to nothing—even my own voice was gone. These fits and starts continued until my hearing finally dropped to the last rung of amplifiable sound. I was a college student at the time, and whenever anyone asked about my hearing aid, I admitted to being only slightly hard of hearing.

My professors were frequently alarmed by my almost maniacal intensity in class. I was petrified that I'd have to ask for special privileges just to achieve marginal understanding. My pride was in flames. I became increasingly bitter and isolated. I was terrified of being marked a deaf woman, a label that made me sound dumb and cowlike, enveloped in a protective silence that denied me my complexity. I did everything I could to hide my handicap. I wore my hair long and never wore earrings, thus keeping attention away from my ears and their riders. I monopolized conversations so that I wouldn't slip up and reveal what I was or wasn't hearing; I took on a disdainful air at large parties, hoping that no one would ask me something I couldn't instantly reply to. I lied about the extent of my deafness so I could avoid the stigma of being thought "different" in a pathetic way.

It was not surprising that in my senior year I suffered a nervous collapse and spent three days in the hospital crying like a baby. When I stopped crying I knew it was time to face a few things—I had to start asking for help when I needed it because I couldn't handle my deafness alone, and I had to quit being ashamed of my handicap so I could begin to live with its consequences and discover what (if any) were its rewards.

When I began telling people that I was *really* deaf I did so with grim determination. Some were afraid to talk to me at any length, fearing perhaps that they were talking into a void; others assumed that I was somehow an unsullied innocent and always inquired in carefully enunciated sentences; "Dooooooooo youuuuuuuu driiinnk liquor?" But most people were surprisingly sympathetic—they wanted to know the best way to be understood, they took great pains to talk directly to my face, and they didn't insult me by using only words of one syllable.

It was, in part, that gentle acceptance that made me more curious about my own deafness. Always before it had been an affliction to wrestle with as one would with angels, but when I finally accepted it as an inevitable part of my life, I relaxed enough to do some exploring. I would take my hearing aid off and go through a day, a night, an hour or two—as long as I could take it—in absolute silence. I felt as if I were indulging in a secret vice because I was perceiving the world in a new way—stripped of sound.

Of course I had always known that sound is vibration, but I didn't know, until I stopped straining to hear, how truly sound is a refinement of feeling. Conversations at parties might elude me, but I seldom fail to pick up on moods. I enjoy watching people talk. When I am too far away to read lips I try reading postures and imagining conversations. Sometimes to everyone's horror, I respond to things better left unsaid when I'm trying to find out what's going on around me. I want to see, touch, taste, and smell everything within reach; I especially have to curb a tendency to judge things by their smell—not just potato salad but people as well—a habit that seems to some people entirely too barbaric for comfort. I am not claiming that my other senses stepped up their work to compensate for the loss, but the absence of one does allow me to concentrate on the others. Deafness has left me acutely aware of both the duplicity that language is capable of and the many expressions the body cannot hide.

Nine years ago I spent the summer at the University of Texas's experimental Shakespeare workshop at Winedale, and I went back each year for eight years, first as a student and then as a staff associate. Off and on for the last four years I have written and performed for Esther's Follies, a cabaret theater group in Austin. Some people think it's odd that, as deaf as I am, I've spent so much of my life working in the theater, but I find it to be a natural consequence of my particular circumstance. The loss of sound has enhanced my fascination with language and the way meaning is conveyed. I love to perform. Exactly the same processes occur onstage as off—except that onstage, once I've memorized the script, I know what everybody is saying as they say it. I am delighted to be so immediately in the know. It has provided a direct way to keep in touch with the rest of the world despite the imposed isolation.

Silence is not empty; it is simply more sobering than sound. At times I prefer the sobriety. I can still "hear" with a hearing aid—that is, I can discern noise, but I can't tell you where it's coming from or if it is laughter or a faulty drain. When there are many people talking together I hear a strange music, a distant rumbling in my consciousness. But when I take off my hearing aid at night and lie in bed surrounded by my fate, I wonder, "What is this—a foul subtraction or a blessing in disguise?" For despite my fears there is a kind of peace in the silence—albeit an uneasy one. There is, after all, less to distract me from my thoughts.

But I know what I've lost. The process of becoming deaf has at times been frightening, akin perhaps to dying, and early in life it took away my happy confidence in the image of a world where things always work right. When I first came back from the Lions Camp that summer I cursed heaven and earth for doing such terrible wrong to me and to my friends. My grandmother tried to comfort me by promising, "Honey, God's got something special planned for you."

But I thought, "Yes. He plans to make me deaf."

EXPECTING ADAM

Martha Beck

Four days after hearing the diagnosis, I still wasn't able to eat or sleep. My body seemed to have decided not to go forward with any normal functioning until it heard better news. Better news was not to be had. I looked. I looked everywhere. Information about Down syndrome was surprisingly hard to find at Harvard, but I read what I could find with desperate intensity. Later, when the people around me had time to marshal better resources, I would learn a few not-so-awful things about my son's condition. But those first few days, I swallowed thousands of appalling bits of information from insensitive and outdated sources. I swallowed them without even chewing.

I have seen the same sort of craving for information in people who have lost loved ones to illness or injury. They rivet all their attention on the postmortem analysis or the police report or the black box, clinging to the facts of the case as though understanding the cause of death will soften its horrible

Excerpt from Martha Beck, *Expecting Adam* (New York: Times Books, 1999), pp. 211–23. Copyright © 1999 by Martha Beck. Used by permission of Times Books, a division of Random House, Inc.

finality. As far as I can tell, this never really works. When all the data are in, when the case is closed and sealed, the dead are still dead.

My situation in the months before Adam's birth was in some ways better than this, and in other ways worse. On the one hand, I was still having a baby. He still bounced around on my bladder and invited me down for the occasional game of Prod. On the other hand, the more I learned about all the possible problems connected with Down syndrome, the more I became afraid of him. I went into a state of alternating protectiveness and terror toward the baby. Half the time the exploratory thumps from my insides seemed to come from a monster, like that disgusting creature in the movie *Alien* that rips its way out of a crew member's abdomen and sets out to eat every human it encounters. Then, just when I was ready to lose my mind, I would accidentally glance at the ultrasound picture of Adam floating around in the amniotic fluid like a perfect, sweet-faced doll, and feel a love so strong it shattered the fear like a pure, high tone shatters crystal. Then I would set out to read more about Down syndrome, by way of becoming a better mother, and the fear would begin to harden all over again.

The little mustard-yellow book I'd bought at the Coop was the worst. It had last been updated in about 1950, when people with Down syndrome were rarely seen outside of institutions. I understand now, and I want to state for the record, that putting a person with Down's into an institution is like forcing an otter to live in a Pringle's can. There is nothing wrong with the social adaptability of people like Adam. They are as gregarious as any "normal" person, more so than many, and thrive on loving interaction. They also learn social skills as quickly as any child given normal treatment. It makes me sick to think of the thousands of children who were raised in institutions before the last couple of decades. Isolated, bored, and aching with loneliness, many literally turned their faces to the wall and died by the time they were in their teens or early twenties. The mustard book described this as the normal life course for the human beings it called "mongoloid idiots."

Oh, that book was full of tasty treats for the parent of a child with Down's. I've met hundreds of parents whose decisions about their children's lives were made on the basis of such incredible misinformation. My book declared grandly that the birth of a Down syndrome child generally destroyed the mother's mental health, as well as the life of any older sisters that might be in the family (brothers, it said, were exempt, since they were not expected to fill a caretaking role). It gave absolutely false information about the inability of such children to control their bodily functions, and their antisocial inclinations. It listed the typical IQ for "mongoloids" as about 35, and by way of comparison, mentioned that the IQ of a chimpanzee is about 50 and that of the average *oak tree* is 3. (I don't know how you'd test the IQ of an oak tree, but apparently the authors of this particular book got one to answer at least a few questions.) It was impossible for me to keep myself from calculating that this meant my son's IQ would be about 130 points below the average of my oft-tested siblings, and only 32 points higher than the plants in Harvard Yard.

A year later, when we had moved to Utah and I was doing research for my dissertation, I ran across that mustard-yellow book in a box of reference materials. By that time, Adam was an adventurous, affectionate little boy who loved to draw, tickle his sister, and explore all our floor-level kitchen cabinets. I had learned a great deal about the fear and misjudgment that had been leveled at people with Down syndrome for so many years. Just a glance at that book yanked me abruptly back to the days after Adam's diagnosis, when I hadn't learned any of these things, when I'd forced myself to read and accept claims that were both untrue and brutally unkind. Before I was aware of having moved, I slammed that book across the room so hard that pages flew like feathers when it hit the wall. I chased it down, grabbed it, and tore it straight across and then down the middle, with the same kind of fevered strength that enables a mother to lift a life-crushing weight, like a tractor or a stereotype, off her pinned and struggling child.

In the days following Adam's diagnosis, however, I seemed to have no strength at all. I made a halfhearted effort at sleeping but barely even tried to eat. It had been difficult enough before, with the nausea killing my appetite. Once I heard about the Down syndrome, it simply became impossible. After four days of numbness and physical decline, I finally admitted to myself that I probably needed another IV. It wasn't as if this was a new idea—I'd been getting them regularly for months—but the thought of going back to University Health Services was almost unbearable. The place had become so aversive to me that I would go blocks out of my way to avoid walking past it. It took a lot of misery to get me to the point of going inside and mentioning that I was, once again, dehydrated. I felt like a plant that had to be watered every few days. An oak tree, perhaps.

Nevertheless, it was with considerable relief that I finally lay down on one of the clinic's two beds and allowed yet another fledgling Florence Nightingale to try to lace the IV needle into my legendary veins. They were so limp from dehydration that this particular nurse punctured all the available forearm locations and ended up inserting the drip in my ankle. I didn't mind at all, though, because before she even got started with the needle, she read my chart and turned to me with a look of such compassion that it almost unhinged me. Then she set her cool, soft hand on mine and whispered, "He's going to be a beautiful baby. I have a brother." This is the way families who have an Adam talk to each other, a gentle, indirect language that requires very little explanation. I cried the whole time that nurse was there, and it had nothing to do with needles.

By the time the glucose solution had begun to plump up my veins and my head cleared a little, it was 8:00 p.m. and dark as death outside. The admitting physician had recommended that I spend the night at the infirmary, to see if I would be able to hold down food once my stores of electrolytes were replenished, so I settled in and prepared to try to sleep.

The infirmary was a small room with four beds, steel ones, bolted to warped linoleum under harsh fluorescent lights. I had been there twice before, once when a friend of mine sicked out of a test by eating a bar of soap, and again when one of John's roommates had developed some sort of psychogenic paralysis, also because of exam anxiety. That infirmary filled right up around exam time. The night I stayed there, however, was near the beginning of the spring semester, and the room was nearly empty. There was only one patient besides me, a woman named Maude who worked in the dormitory kitchens. Maude had an extraordinarily thick Boston accent and a face like a lump of bread dough, from which her eyes peered like inset raisins. She told me that she was in the infirmary because she was unable to pee without a catheter. The doctors were trying to figure out why.

Maude voiced my own feeling that the fluorescent lighting was extremely unpleasant. After pressing our "call nurse" buttons for a while with no result, we decided that I should get out of bed and hop over to switch it off, holding my plugged-in ankle carefully so as not to rip out the IV. My mission accomplished, Maude switched on a little reading light she had brought from home, casting a small yellow glow. "Is this going to keep you awake, Mather deah?" she asked kindly.

I shook my head and closed my eyes. My body was feeling better as it absorbed liquid, but my soul hurt so much I could hardly talk. I didn't think I would be able to sleep.

"I'm just going to stay awake," said Maude, "because I have a visitor coming. I'm helping my friend study for the bar exam."

I opened one eye and said, "Oh. That's good."

I was a little surprised that Maude should be helping someone become an attorney, then immediately berated myself for being so classist. Still, I was surprised again when Maude's friend showed up. I had expected another woman, maybe someone Maude's age who had decided to go back to school. The friend turned out to be a huge, twenty-something African American man named Emory, who wore so much jewelry that it jingled faintly whenever he moved. Maude didn't introduce us; she thought I was asleep, which was fine with me. I watched through my eyelashes as Emory pulled the visitor's chair close to Maude's bed and handed her a book.

"Okay," he said. "Quiz me."

At the sound of his voice, I opened my eyes all the way and looked at him in wonder. It was one of those almost inhumanly beautiful voices, like the deep, echoing hum of a cello played softly. Emory kept his voice down, to avoid waking me, and I found that just by concentrating on his lovely voice, I could go to that soothing, half-conscious state between waking and sleeping. To this day, whenever I get a little anxious, I go back to the sound of Emory's voice.

"Wheah should I staht, deah?" said Maude.

"Anywhere." Emory told her.

"All right, then," she said. "Margarita."

There was a pause before Emory said, "Three parts tequila, one part triple sec, juice from half a lime. Salt the glass rim. Frozen or on the rocks."

They weren't looking at me, over in my darkened corner of the room. This was good, because I'm not sure exactly what expression showed up on my face as I realized that when Maude had said "bar exam," she'd meant *bar* exam.

"Whiskey sour," she said, and Emory responded, "Four parts rye whiskey, one part lemon juice, a teaspoon of sugar. Garnish with a maraschino cherry and a slice of orange."

That was the first time since Adam's diagnosis that I had yanked out of my introverted despair and into a kind of lightheartedness. I remembered my older sister, in the midst of a hellish divorce, mentioning that life would be completely unbearable if it weren't so hilarious. I began to laugh under my breath, and then the tears came again, and I began to relax. The sound of Emory's voice, listing the mellifluous recipes for various alcoholic drinks, soothed me to sleep like a lullaby.

The next morning I was awakened by four doctors, who marched into the room in a vaguely military procession. Three of them looked young and were unfamiliar to me; the fourth was one of the many doctors connected to the clinic's obstetrical unit. This doctor, whom I will call Grendel, was a popular topic of conversation among the women who came to University Health Services for their prenatal care. Everyone wanted Grendel to be on call when they actually delivered their babies. He was supposed to be a wonder in the delivery room: gracious and concerned and incredibly skillful. However, no one wanted to have Grendel conduct her prenatal exams. He apparently didn't think much of these routine appointments, and his bedside manner tended to be aloof, if not downright disdainful.

I myself had been examined by Grendel only once, about three months into my pregnancy. I was used to chatting a little with the doctors before the actual exam, on the old-fashioned grounds that it's nice to be on speaking terms with a person before you allow him or her unlimited access to your genital region. When I'd spoken to Grendel, he'd look at me with an expression of disgust and answered not a word. During the entire exam, he remained silent except to ask me medical questions. He never looked at my face or smiled. He left me with the impression that I was distinctly unworthy of his time and attention. Judging from what other patients said about their appointments with Grendel, this seemed to have been his usual demeanor.

I was therefore very surprised to see Grendel approach my bed in the infirmary that morning, trailing his three disciples. The younger physicians lined up against the wall beside my bed, while Grendel walked right up and peered earnestly into my eyes. He was short, with very thick glasses, through which his eyes peered with peculiar intensity, and the skin on his face was very tight, as though it had been stretched across his bones. He had no visible lips.

I blinked, pulling myself awake, wondering what Dr. Grendel was doing at my bedside. At some level, I jumped to the conclusion that since mine was now officially a "high-risk" pregnancy, Dr. Grendel had decided it was worth his time. I felt a surge of relief, knowing his reputation as a superb obstetrician and believing that, somehow, his presence would give my baby a better chance.

"Good morning, Martha," said Grendel. I was amazed. He virtually never addressed his patients at all, much less by their first names. His voice was friendly and kind, with a little sadness around the edges.

"Morning," I said.

"Do you mind if I sit down?" The only visitor's chair was still over by Maude. Grendel patted the foot of my bed, and I nodded. He sat down sidesaddle.

"How are you feeling?" he asked.

I thought about it. "Better," I said. "I'm not sure I'll be able to keep down any food, but I feel like I could try."

Grendel nodded, the skin on his neck relaxing and then stretching tight again. "Your chart says that you haven't eaten for four days."

I felt myself blush, embarrassed. "I know. I tried."

Grendel gave a long sigh, looking away from me and down at the toes of his shoes. "We all know what you're trying to do," he said gently.

I glanced at the three young doctors, who were looking on with apparent interest. "You do?" I said. I myself didn't know what I was trying to do. I was hoping they could tell me.

"There are more efficient ways to take care of this problem than starving yourself until the fetus dies," said Grendel.

I stared at him. "Excuse me?"

"Martha, it's obvious," he said. He looked at me again, his face suddenly stern. "Why else would you stop eating?"

For a minute I just opened and closed my mouth without making any noise, like a fish. Then I said, "But I've been sick all along. And upset, and—"

"Exactly," Grendel cut in. "You're upset. I think it's time to let us take care of it for you."

I was getting the picture. I felt myself go cold inside, as though I had swallowed liquid nitrogen.

"Martha, listen to me," said Grendel urgently. His piercing little eyes were full of concern. "I have been in this business for a very long time. I've had several cases like yours, and in every case, the woman has made . . . uh . . . the other decision."

I was beginning to tremble. I wished that I had my clothes on, instead of the hospital napkin. I didn't know what to say.

"You are also the youngest woman I have ever dealt with on this particular problem," said Grendel. He paused meaningfully, glancing up at the three student doctors arrayed along the wall.

It took me a second to catch on. Then I said, "You think I'm making this decision because I'm too young to know better?"

Grendel didn't even look at me. He and the three disciples nodded at each other.

I felt dizzy, overwhelmed. It was true that I was young and inexperienced, but the chief effect that I could see was that I didn't know how to assert myself with world-renowned obstetricians.

"You realize," Grendel went on, "that you are placing a very heavy burden on yourself and your entire family. Did you know that eighty percent of couples who have a child with this condition end up divorcing?"

I swallowed, though my mouth was very dry. "No," I said. "I didn't know that."

"I would not make the choice that you have made," he went on steadily. "I have never known anyone who would."

The other doctors were watching me intently, as if I were a tree that Grendel was chopping down and they were waiting to see me topple.

"I don't know," I mumbled. "I guess I just . . . I just can't reject him."

It was a miserably inadequate statement. My real feeling, the one I couldn't articulate yet, was that my entire life hinged on knowing that there were people who would continue to love me unconditionally, even if I were damaged, even if I were sick. Such love was the only thing that had sustained me during the turmoil of the past months. If I eliminated my child because of his disability, if I put him out of my life, I would be violating the only thing that was keeping me alive. I'd be ripping the rug out from under my own feet.

Grendel was looking at me with obvious frustration. The skin across his cheekbones tightened even more as he pursed his lips.

"Well, I can't do the operation against your will," he said. "Of course, if a patient came in here with a malignant tumor and refused to let me remove it, I couldn't do that operation either. Even if we all knew what was best."

The other doctors nodded.

It is difficult to convey the fear and despair I felt as the weight of their collective disapproval bore down on me. It was like a wall of ice backing me slowly into a corner. I could hardly breathe. I remember wishing desperately that Dr. Grendel would move away from me, get off the bed, give me some space.

Since that time, beginning a few months after Adam's birth, I have addressed a number of medical conferences on the topic of ethics related to the new obstetrical technologies. My firm opinion is that women should be given all relevant medical information and then allowed to make up their own minds about whether or not to abort their fetuses. Invariably, I am approached after these conferences by doctors—never nurses, always doctors—who disagree with me. They argue quite explicitly that they are highly trained professionals, that their opinions are far more informed than the average pregnant woman's, and that they are therefore in a much better position to make the right decision about any particular woman's abortion than the woman herself. Some of these physicians are pro-lifers who would never abort a fetus with Down syndrome; others would do so without exception. I would like to take this opportunity to invite all such doctors (and I recognize that they represent a minority of their profession) to fold it five ways and put it where the sun don't shine.

Oh, I'm sorry—do I sound a little bitter? Hm. Perhaps that's because, in the years since that encounter with Dr. Grendel, I have had so many physicians wedge their personal prejudices into my life, into Adam's life, and call it medical advice. Dr. Grendel, who had never seen a woman elect to keep a Down syndrome baby, was as ignorant as the most severely retarded child when it came to the actual consequences of my choice. I doubt very much that he had ever really known anyone with Down syndrome. I'd bet my life he'd never loved such a person.

I once spoke to an entering class of Harvard Medical School students about my pregnancy and my decision. Adam was asleep on my lap at the time, wearing a bow tie and a dreamy expression. After the speech, I was approached by an elderly professor whose name I forget. He had just become the grandfather of a little girl with Down's. As he talked to me, he stroked Adam's soft blond hair and wept. He loved his granddaughter with inexplicable openness, and the experience had changed his whole life. Now there's a doctor with some real information to offer the parents of a retarded baby. Whoever said that love is blind was dead wrong. Love is the only thing on this earth that lets us see each other with the remotest accuracy.

I suppose that I am grateful to Dr. Grendel for showing me so explicitly the prejudice of the Harvard medical community. I called the nurse-practitioner after he left, to ask if any of the other obstetricians connected with Harvard were in favor of my decision to continue the pregnancy. She didn't think so. So after that morning visit, I knew where I stood. Most, if not all, of the doctors I would interact with for the remainder of my pregnancy disagreed with my decision; would have considered it wiser to do away with the baby they were helping me protect. An awkward situation, to be sure.

At the time that Dr. Grendel sat on my bed and tried to talk some sense into me, it was almost more than I could bear. After all, I was a good girl, a conscientious student, a high achiever. I always did what the grown-ups said to do, especially when they were prestigious and successful grown-ups. I knew that I was still certain I didn't want an abortion, but I was completely unskilled in the practice of disagreeing with an authority figure—let alone a whole team of authority figures like Grendel and the Go-Gos. . . .

Grendel was launching into a recitation of various horrible things about children with Down syndrome when that voice—the calm, inaudible voice I had heard a few times before—drowned out the doctor's voice with a simple question.

Why is he doing this?

I looked at Grendel closely, suddenly feeling like an observer rather than a patient. Why, indeed. This man always made a great show of being too busy even to look at his patients. Why was he spending this inordinate amount of time trying to convince me to abort a child he would probably never even see?

As I considered this question, a strange thing began to happen. . . . I looked at Grendel's face, and there, just behind the tight-stretched skin, I seemed to see another face appear. It was Grendel, but not the wise and solemn physician who was displaying his technique to the three students. This face was terrified. The fear in its eyes . . . [was] heavily laced with pain, old pain, pain so deep it had become a way of life.

Grendel was scared to death.

This kind of seeing has happened to me many times since. I believe it happens to everyone. It happens when you meet some smiling person and walk away with the distinct impression that the person means you no good. It happens when a teenager lashes out at you, and instead of anger you suddenly see the bewildered battle he is fighting inside himself. It happens when you strike up an acquaintance and, within fifteen minutes, know you have made a friend. I believe our intuition is far more delicate, and accurate, than we allow ourselves to admit. I had to be pushed to the brink of complete breakdown before I let myself trust mine, or even notice what it was telling me. But that day in the infirmary, it was so incredibly vivid, so visual, that it stunned me. My fear of Grendel was completely gone. The doctor was like a bee, a snake, a dog; he was attacking me only because he felt that I threatened his survival.

Why should this be? I relaxed and looked frankly at the second face that drifted, panicky and bewildered, behind Grendel's strange, taut skin. I examined this new face with some care. The fear in it spoke to me of a lifetime spent desperately avoiding the stigma of stupidity, of failure, of not measuring up. I knew plenty of premeds at Harvard, and as a group I think they were even more obsessed than the rest of us with climbing to the very top of the prestige heap. They were famous for things like razoring out the pages in the reserved readings for their courses, so that none of their classmates could study the material. It was said that it took two Harvard premeds to change a lightbulb, one to change the bulb and the other to push the ladder out from under him. Dr. Grendel had fought his way through the increasingly rarefied ranks of such people to achieve the apex of his profession. Something had driven him all that way, and it wasn't just affection for his patients. I was convinced, looking at his fear-face, that Grendel's entire philosophy of life centered on obliterating the stupid little boy inside him. It was that person he feared, desperately feared, and this was why he was begging so earnestly for a chance to obliterate the stupid little boy inside me.

I looked at Grendel, and I looked at his acolytes. They, too, had their fears and their agendas. It was obvious to me as I looked through the new set of eyes Adam had given me. As Grendel finished his closing arguments, I stretched out to my full length on the bed, pushing the doctor slightly aside with my feet.

"Thank you," I said. "You can go now."

Grendel and the gang stared at me in frustration and disbelief. The doctor chewed his lip with obvious anxiety, the fear-face trembling under his physical visage like that of a man facing execution. Eventually, he heaved a huge sigh and rubbed his hands together emphatically, making a clear point to the other doctors that he was washing his hands of this matter, once and for all. As they filed out of the room, Adam gave me a cheerful wallop just below the navel. Grendel was last in line, and before he left, his fear face, though not his flesh-and-blood head, turned to look behind him with those terrified eyes. I could see the fear, as clear as day, but I didn't feel it. Briefly, for the first time since I had bought the mustard-yellow book and started soaking in the prejudices against the developmentally disabled world, I was not afraid at all.

JAMIE

Michael Bérubé

My little Jamie loves lists: foods, colors, animals, numbers, letters, states, classmates, parts of the body, days of the week, modes of transportation, characters who live on Sesame Street, and the names of the people who love him. Early last summer, I hoped his love of lists—and his ability to catalogue things *into* lists—would stand him in good stead during what would undoubtedly be a difficult "vacation" for anyone, let alone a three-year-old child with Down syndrome: a three-hour drive to Chicago, a rush-hour flight to LaGuardia, a cab to Grand Central, a train to Connecticut—and then smaller trips to New York, Boston, and Old Orchard Beach, Maine. Even accomplishing the first of these mission objectives—arriving safely at O'Hare—required a precision and teamwork I do not always associate with my family. I dropped off Janet and nine-year-old Nick at the terminal with the baggage, then took Jamie to long-term parking with me while they checked in, and then entertained Jamie all the way back to the terminal, via bus and shuttle train. We sang about the driver on the bus, and we counted all the escalator steps and train stops, and when we finally got to our plane, I told Jamie, *Look, there's Mommy and Nick at the gate! They're yelling that we're going to lose our seats! They want to know why it took us forty-five minutes to park the car!*

All went well from that point on, though, and in the end, I suppose you could say Jamie got as much out of his vacation as might any toddler being whisked up and down New England. He's a seasoned traveler, and he thrives on shorelines, family gatherings, and New Haven pizza. And he's good with faces and names.

Then again, as we learned toward the end of our brief stay in Maine, he doesn't care much for amusement parks. Not that Nick did either, at three. But apparently one of the attractions of Old Orchard Beach, for my wife and her siblings, was the small beachfront arcade and amusement park in town, which they associated with their own childhoods. It was an endearing strip, with a roller coaster just the right size for Nick—exciting, mildly scary, but with no loop-the-loops, rings of fire, or oppressive G forces. We strolled among bumper cars, cotton candy, games of chance and skill, and a striking number of French-Canadian tourists: perhaps the first time our two little boys had ever seen more than one Bérubé family in one place. James, however, wanted nothing to do with any of the rides, and though he loves to pretend-drive and has been on bumper cars before, he squalled so industriously before the ride began as to induce the bumper cars operator to let him out of the car and refund his two tickets.

Jamie finally settled in next to a train ride designed for children five and under or thereabouts, which, for two tickets, took its passengers around an oval layout and over a bridge four times. I found out quickly enough that Jamie didn't want to *ride* the ride; he merely wanted to stand at its perimeter, grasping the partition with both hands and counting the cars—one, two, three, four, five, six—as they went by. Sometimes, when the train traversed the bridge, James would punctuate it with tiny jumps, saying, "Up! up! up!" But for the most part, he was content to hang onto the metal bars of the partition, grinning and counting—and, when the train came to a stop, pulling my sleeve and saying, "More, again."

This went on for about half an hour, well past the point at which I could convincingly share Jamie's enthusiasm for tracking the train's progress. As it went on my spirits began to sink in a way I do not recall having felt before.

Occasionally it will occur to Janet or to me that Jamie will always be "disabled," that his adult and adolescent years will undoubtedly be more difficult emotionally—for him and for us—than his early childhood, that we will never *not* worry about his future, his quality of life, whether we're doing enough for him. But usually these moments occur in the relative comfort of abstraction, when Janet and I are lying in bed at night and wondering what will become of us all. When I'm *with* Jamie, by contrast, I'm almost always fully occupied by taking care of his present needs rather than by worrying about his future. When he asks to hear the Beatles because he loves their cover of Little Richard's "Long Tall Sally," I just play the song, sing along, and watch him dance with delight; I do not concern myself with extraneous questions such as whether he'll ever distinguish early Beatles from late Beatles, Paul's songs from John's, originals from covers. These questions are now central to Nick's enjoyment of the Beatles, but that's Nick for you. Jamie is entirely sui generis, and as long as I'm with him I can't think of him as anything but Jamie.

I have tried. Almost as a form of emotional exercise, I have tried, on occasion, to step back and see him as others might see him, as an instance of a category, one item on the long list of human subgroups. *This is a child with Down syndrome,* I say to myself. *This is a child with a developmental disability.* It never works: Jamie remains Jamie to me. I have even tried to imagine him as he would have been seen in other eras, other places: *This is a retarded child.* And even: *This is a Mongoloid child.* This makes for unbearable cognitive dissonance. I can imagine that people might think such things, but I cannot imagine how they might think them in a way that prevents them from seeing Jamie *as* Jamie. I try to recall how I saw such children when I was a child, but here I guiltily draw a blank: I don't remember seeing them at all, which very likely means that I never quite saw them *as* children. Instead I remember a famous passage from Ludwig Wittgenstein's *Philosophical Investigations:* "'Seeing-as' is not part of perception. And for this reason it is *like* seeing, and then again *not* like." Reading Wittgenstein, I often think, is something like listening to a brilliant and cantankerous uncle with an annoying fondness for koans. But on this one, I know exactly what he means.

As Jamie counted the train cars and urged them up, up, up for maybe the sixteenth time, I actually began to see him differently—and then to catch myself doing it. Seeing, then seeing-as, then seeing. He was not like the other children his size who were riding the train with the usual varieties of distress and delight, and he was *noticeably* different. I began to see other parents looking at him with solicitude, curiosity, pity . . . and I thought, well, it's better than fear or disgust, but I still don't like it. Once last year, on our way back from visiting a local apple orchard, Janet told me that she'd seen other parents looking at James with an expression she read as *So that's what they're like when they're little*, and she said she'd sent those parents telepathic messages saying, *Don't be looking at my child, who's perfectly well behaved; keep an eye on your own child, the one who's pushing everybody else out of the wagon.* But this was different. Here, at a ride for small children, Jamie seemed clearly . . . limited. Not just unwilling, but somehow *unable* to enjoy the ride as "normal" children were supposed to enjoy it.

Finally, one mother approached us and asked Jamie (I was glad she asked us by asking Jamie directly, instead of asking me) if he would like to ride the train with her daughter. "Would you like to go on the train with this little girl?" I said, hoisting him up. "Noooooooo," said James, arching his back and repelling as best he could. "Down, down," he added, pointing to the ground. "Thanks very much," I said to the girl's mother. "He just loves watching the train, but he really doesn't want to go on. It was very nice of you to ask." She stayed by us for the duration of her daughter's ride, during which I engaged Jamie in a discussion of whether his classmates might ride the train:

"Does Madison ride a train?"

Jamie nodded "hm" (a shorthand "yes" he learned from his mother), then cocked his head and went into his "list" mode: "How 'bout . . . um . . . Keegan." Sometimes when Jamie gets pensive and says, "How 'bout, um," he's really thinking hard; sometimes, I think, he's just going through a routine he's learned from watching what pensive people do.

"Oh yes, Keegan rides a train," I assured him.

"How 'bout . . . um . . . Thaniel."

"Yes, Nathaniel also rides a train." (Good *th,* I thought.)

"How 'bout . . . um . . . Timmy."

"Timmy can ride a train."

"Are those his friends?" the girl's mother asked me.

"Yeah," I replied. "I'm hoping he'll get the idea that he can go on the train, too. Failing that, I'll settle for reminding him that he goes back to day care next week." But by this time I couldn't care less whether he went on the damn train; I just wanted him to vary his routine, to stop clutching the bars and saying "up, up, up." Not only for his benefit, or for the benefit of anyone who might be looking at him, but for my benefit: I was getting thoroughly bored with Jamie's take on the amusement park.

Suddenly I realized why Jamie's demeanor had been bothering me, why he had begun to seem like a "limited" child, a mere member of a *genus*: He was reminding me of a passage in William Faulkner's *The Sound and the Fury*, an image of Benjy Compson clutching the front gate and watching the "normal" children fearfully pass him by:

> *Aint nothing going to quiet him, T.P. said. He think if he down to the gate, Miss Caddy come back.*
>
> *Nonsense, Mother said.*
>
> I could hear them talking. I went out the door and I couldn't hear them, and I went down to the gate, where the girls passed with their booksatchels. They looked at me, walking fast, with their heads turned. I tried to say, but they went on, and I went along the fence, trying to say, and they went faster. Then they were running and I came to the corner of the fence and I couldn't go any further, and I held to the fence, looking after them and trying to say.

And then I remembered the very young Benjy, held tenderly by his sister Caddy after their mother has called him a "poor baby":

> we stopped in the hall and Caddy knelt and put her arms around me and her cold bright face against mine. She smelled like trees.
>
> "You're not a poor baby. Are you. Are you. You've got your Caddy. Haven't you got your Caddy."

It's one of the novel's earliest portraits of Caddy Compson: unlike her obsessively self-dramatizing mother, she loves Benjy too much to allow herself the distance of pity. The scene could not be more important to the emotional drama of Faulkner's novel. Caddy is so compelling and sympathetic a character precisely because she alone, of all the Compsons, consistently treats Benjy with a tenderness and compassion that never descends to condescension. Benjy is in this sense the key to the novel's moral index: *Whatsoever you do to the least of my brothers* . . . and when Caddy is banished from the household Benjy loses the only blood relative who has empathy enough to understand his desires. Not for nothing are Caddy and Benjy among the most unforgettable characters in the literature of our century. For all its famous narrative pyrotechnics, *The Sound and the Fury* is at bottom a novel of characters: doomed Caddy, brooding Quentin, demonic Jason, stoic Dilsey, and retarded Benjy, whose primary senses and emotions are painfully acute but who has no sense of the passage of time, no sense of good or evil. Most of Faulkner's readers know that the title of the novel alludes to the final soliloquy of Shakespeare's *Macbeth:*

> *Life's but a walking shadow, a poor player*
> *That struts and frets his hour upon the stage,*
> *And then is heard no more. It is a tale*
> *Told by an idiot, full of sound and fury,*
> *Signifying nothing.*

And, I suppose plenty of people (though all too few of my students) know that Benjy is part of a noble lineage in Western Lit, from *King Lear* to Dostoyevsky to *Forrest Gump*. But not too many readers know that Faulkner based his portrait of Benjy Compson on a local Mississippi man with Down syndrome.

Later that night we went out for—what else?—seafood. Jamie loves fish, particularly salmon, and he is both entertained and perplexed by picturebook portraits of grizzly bears plucking and devouring live salmon from the river. "Are you like a hungry bear?" I ask James. "Do you gobble the salmon all up?" "Hm," Jamie nods, and he's not kidding: we've seen him pack away half a pound of salmon at a sitting, all the while putting one index finger to pursed lips and saying, "More."

So James had a great time at dinner, as we expected. Then, after dinner, he felt like tooling around the restaurant a little. It was a large place and touted itself as a "family" restaurant, which meant it allowed for a lot of high chairs, booster seats, small portions, spills, dropped utensils, and noise. I figured a wandering toddler, supervised by Dad, wouldn't constitute a breach of decorum. Luckily, a whole section of the restaurant lay empty—about ten tables against the wall, on a platform raised two steps above the rest of the floor, punctuated by a bar and a TV. For now, the area was serving as a station for waitresses on break and hockey fans watching game four of the Stanley Cup finals between Detroit and New Jersey. "Well, I know you want to see the game," Janet said to me. "Why don't you just shepherd him over there?"

So I kept one eye on the Stanley Cup finals and one eye on Jamie, as he methodically walked to each table, babbled spiritedly to himself, and shuttled back and forth to a small slate fireplace—dormant, of course, in late June. But it wasn't until he got to a table near me that I overheard some of his babbling: "Taco," he was saying. "Hm. Chicken. Okay." He nodded, and then off he went to the fireplace.

I frowned. *No, it can't be.* But then, he *is* awfully mimetic, isn't he? Doesn't he pretend to make coffee in the morning? Doesn't he try to toss the salad, set the table, and sweep up all the debris under his chair after dinner?

But he wouldn't come up with something so elaborate. Not at three years of age. Well, wait. Here he comes. He stops at one table, then proceeds to another where he seems, by his account, to be depositing pizza and burgers. I know the menu: all of these are items from his list of favorite foods. I abandon the hockey game, take a seat at a nearby table, and call him over. "Jamie?" He walks over. "Are you the waiter?"

"Hm," he hms brightly, eyes wide, clearly delighted that I've picked up on this.

"Can you get me . . . let's see . . . a tuna sandwich?"

"Tuna!" he half-shouts in a hoarse little voice, and heads back to the fireplace. Did I imagine him pretending to write that down? I must have imagined it. He's extraordinarily mimetic, all right, as so many children are, but he doesn't usually get the tiny details; he's more comfortable with the general idea. I mean, he moves the dustbuster around, but he doesn't get *all* the rice, not by a long shot. He knows the route Janet traverses to make coffee, but he doesn't understand that the water has to go *into* the coffee pot. He's three years old, and like the Cat in the Hat, he makes a mess. But I know I *wanted* to think he wrote down my order.

He eventually got back to my table, but I don't remember whether he remembered that I'd asked for a tuna sandwich. By this point I was lost in the same kind of reverie that had possessed me at the amusement park, only this time I knew Jamie had no literary antecedents. He had decided that this wing of the restaurant was his, that these tables were peopled by customers wanting tacos, chicken, pizza, burgers, fries, and tuna (no green beans, no peach melba, no broccoli, no strawberries), that the fireplace was the kitchen, and that he was the waiter. This was the child who'd seemed so "limited" at the amusement park? The adults who'd seen him that afternoon may have seen him as a retarded child, as a disabled child, as a child to be pitied; and the children, if they were children like the child I was, may not have "seen" him at all. They certainly wouldn't have seen the distinct little person with whom I went to the restaurant that evening—a three year old whose ability to imitate is intimately tied to his remarkable ability to imagine, and whose ability to imagine, in turn, rests almost entirely on his capacity to imagine *other people.* Sure, his imagination has its limits; they're evident in the menu. He imagines people who order *his* list of foods, and yes, that list is (by any nutritionist's standards) limited. But the ability to imagine what other people might like, what other people might need—that seems to me a more crucial, more *essential* ability for human beings to cultivate than the ability to ride trains round and round. After we got back to our motel, after New Jersey had won the Cup, after the kids were finally asleep, I looked out over the beach and wondered whether Janet and I would always be able to understand what Jamie wants and needs, and whether our ability to imagine his desires will be commensurate with his ability to imagine ours.

Meanwhile, as Jamie was fussing about bumper cars, serving entrees to imaginary diners, and splashing in the waves, the 104th US Congress was debating how to balance the federal budget by slashing programs for the disabled and the mentally handicapped; electricians and construction workers in New Haven were putting the final touches on preparations for the 1995 Special Olympics World Games; researchers with the Human Genome Project were trying to locate the biochemical basis for all our variances; and millions of ordinary human beings, all of them women, were undergoing prenatal testing for "severe" genetic defects like Down syndrome.

Jamie has no idea what a busy intersection he's landed in: statutes, allocations, genetics, reproduction, representation—all meeting at the crossroads of individual idiosyncrasy and sociopolitical construction. "Value" may be something that can only be determined socially, by collective and chaotic human deliberation; but individual humans like James are compelling us daily to determine what *kind* of "individuality" we will value, on what terms, and why. Perhaps those of us who can understand this intersection have an obligation to "represent" the children who can't; perhaps we have an obligation to inform our children about the traffic, and to inform the traffic about our children. As those children grow, perhaps we need to foster their abilities to represent themselves—and to listen to them as they do. I strongly suspect that we do have those obligations. I am not entirely sure what they might entail. But it is part of my purpose . . . in representing Jamie, to ask about our obligations to each other, individually and socially, and about our capacity to imagine other people. I cannot say why it is that we possess the capacity to imagine others, let alone the capacity to imagine that we might have *obligations* to others; nor do I know why, if we possess such things, we so habitually act as if we do not. But I do know that Jamie has compelled me to ask these questions anew, just as I know how crucial it is that we collectively cultivate our capacities to imagine our obligations to each other.

THE CASE OF CHRISTOPHER REEVE

FAME AND DISABILITY

Christopher Reeve, Super Crips, and Infamous Celebrity

—⊙ *Gerard Goggin and Christopher Newell*

W hen we think of disability today in the Western world, Christopher Reeve most likely comes to mind. A film star who captured people's imagination as Superman, Reeve was already a celebrity before he took the fall that would lead to his new position in the fame game: the role of super-crip. As a person with acquired quadriplegia, Christopher Reeve has become both the epitome of disability in Western culture—the powerful cultural myth of disability as tragedy and catastrophe—and, in an intimately related way, the icon for the high-technology quest for cure.

The case of Reeve is fascinating, yet critical discussion of Christopher Reeve in terms of fame, celebrity, and his performance of disability is conspicuously lacking (for a rare exception see McRuer). To some extent this reflects the comparative lack of engagement of media and cultural studies with disability (Goggin). To redress this lacuna, we draw upon theories of

This article was first published in *M/C Journal: A Journal of Media and Culture* 7, no. 5 (November 2004). Reprinted by permission.

celebrity (Dyer; Marshall; Turner, Bonner, & Marshall; Turner) to explore the production of Reeve as celebrity, as well as bringing accounts of celebrity into dialogue with critical disability studies.

Reeve is a cultural icon, not just because of the economy, industrial processes, semiotics, and contemporary consumption of celebrity, outlined in Turner's 2004 framework. Fame and celebrity are crucial systems in the construction of disability; and the circulation of Reeve-as-celebrity only makes sense if we understand the centrality of disability to culture and media. Reeve plays an enormously important (if ambiguous) function in the social relations of disability, at the heart of the discursive underpinning of the otherness of disability and the construction of normal sexed and gendered bodies (the normate) in everyday life. What is distinctive and especially powerful about this instance of fame and disability is how authenticity plays through the body of the celebrity Reeve; how his saintly numinosity is received by fans and admirers with passion, pathos, pleasure; and how this process places people with disabilities in an oppressive social system, so making them subject(s).

AN ACCIDENTAL STAR

Born September 25, 1952, Christopher Reeve became famous for his roles in the 1978 movie *Superman*, and the subsequent three sequels (*Superman II, III, IV*), as well as his role in other films such as *Monsignor*. As well as becoming a well-known actor, Reeve gained a profile for his activism on human rights, solidarity, environmental, and other issues.

In May 1995 Reeve acquired a disability in a riding accident. In the ensuing months, Reeve's situation attracted a great deal of international attention. He spent six months in the Kessler Rehabilitation Institute in New Jersey, and there gave a high-rating interview on US television personality Barbara Walters's *20/20* program. In 1996, Reeve appeared at the Academy Awards, was a host at the 1996 Paralympic Games, and was invited to speak at the Democratic National Convention. In the same year Reeve narrated a film about the lives of people living with disabilities (Mierendorf). In 1998 his memoir *Still Me* was published, followed in 2002 by another book, *Nothing Is Impossible*.

Reeve's active fashioning of an image and "new life" (to use his phrase) stands in stark contrast with most people with disabilities, who find it difficult to enter into the industry and system of celebrity, because they are most often taken to be the opposite of glamorous or important. They are objects of pity, or freaks to be stared at (Mitchell & Synder; Thomson), rather than assuming other attributes of stars. Reeve became famous *for* his disability, indeed very early on he was acclaimed as *the* preeminent American with disability—as in the phrase "President of Disability," an appellation he attracted.

Reeve was quickly positioned in the celebrity industry, not least because his example, image, and texts were avidly consumed by viewers and readers. For millions of people—as evident in the letters compiled in the 1999 book *Care Packages* by his wife, Dana Reeve—Christopher Reeve is a hero, renowned for his courage in doing battle with his disability and his quest for a cure.

Part of the creation of Reeve as celebrity has been a conscious fashioning of his life as an instructive fable. A number of biographies have now been published (Havill; Hughes; Oleksy; Wren). Variations on a theme, these tend to the hagiographic: *Christopher Reeve: Triumph over Tragedy* (Alter). Those interested in Reeve's life and work can turn also to fan Web sites. Most tellingly perhaps is the number of books, fables really, aimed at children, again, on a characteristic theme: *Learning about Courage from the Life of Christopher Reeve* (Kosek; see also Abraham; Howard).

The construction, but especially the consumption, of Reeve as disabled celebrity, is consonant with powerful cultural myths and tropes of disability. In many Western cultures, disability is predominantly understood as a tragedy, something that comes from the defects and lack of our bodies, whether through accidents of birth or life. Those "suffering" with disability, according to this cultural myth, need to come to terms with this bitter tragedy, and show courage in heroically overcoming their lot while they bide their time for the cure that will come. The protagonist for this script is typically the "brave" person with disability; or, as this figure is colloquially known in critical disability studies and the disability movement—the super-crip.

This discourse of disability exerts a strong force today, and is known as the "medical" model. It interacts with a prior, but still active charity discourse of disability (Fulcher). There is a deep cultural history of disability being seen as something that needs to be dealt with by charity. In late modernity, charity is very big business indeed, and celebrities play an important role in representing the good works bestowed on people with disabilities by rich donors. Those managing celebrities often suggest that the star finds a charity to gain favorable publicity, a routine for which people with disabilities are generally the pathetic but handy extras. Charity dinners and events do not just reinforce the tragedy of disability, but they also leave unexamined the structural nature of disability, and its associated disadvantage.

Those critiquing the medical and charitable discourses of disability, and the oppressive power relations of disability that it represents, point to the social and cultural shaping of disability, most famously in the British "social" model of disability—but also from a range of other perspectives (Corker and Thomas). Those formulating these critiques point to the crucial function that the trope of the super-crip plays in the policing of people with disabilities in contemporary culture and society. Indeed, how the figure of the super-crip is also very much bound up with the construction of the "normal" body, a general economy of representation that affects everyone.

SUPERMAN FLIES AGAIN

The celebrity of Christopher Reeve and what it reveals for an understanding of fame and disability can be seen with great clarity in his 2002 visit to Australia.

In 2002 there had been a heated national debate on the ethics of use of embryonic stem cells for research. In an analysis of three months of the print media coverage of these debates, we have suggested that disability was repeatedly, almost obsessively, invoked in these debates ("Uniting the Nation"). Yet the dominant representation of disability here was the cultural myth of disability as tragedy, requiring cure at all cost, and that this trope was central to the way that biotechnology was constructed as requiring an urgent, united national response. Significantly, in these debates, people with disabilities were often talked about but very rarely licensed to speak. Only one person with disability was, and remains, a central figure in these Australian stem cell and biotechnology policy conversations: Christopher Reeve.

As an outspoken advocate of research on embryonic stem cells in the quest for a cure for spinal injuries, as well as other diseases, Reeve's support was enlisted by various protagonists. The current affairs show *60 Minutes* (modeled after its American counterpart) presented Reeve in debate with Australian critics:

PRESENTER: Stem cell research is leading to perhaps the greatest medical breakthroughs of all time. . . . Imagine a world where paraplegics could walk or the blind could see. . . . But it's a breakthrough some passionately oppose. A breakthrough that's caused a fierce personal debate between those like actor Christopher Reeve, who sees this technology as a miracle, and those who regard it as murder. ("Miracle or Murder?")

Sixty Minutes starkly portrays the debate in Manichean terms: lunatics standing in the way of technological progress versus Christopher Reeve flying again tomorrow. Christopher presents the debate in utilitarian terms:

> CHRISTOPHER REEVE: The purpose of government, really in a free society, is to do the greatest good for the greatest number of people. And that question should always be in the forefront of legislators' minds. ("Miracle or Murder?")

No criticism of Reeve's position was offered, despite the fierce debate over the implications of such utilitarian rhetoric for minorities such as people with disabilities (including himself!). Yet this utilitarian stance on disability has been elaborated by philosopher Peter Singer, and trenchantly critiqued by the international disability rights movement.

Later in 2002, the premier of New South Wales, Bob Carr, invited Reeve to visit Australia to participate in the New South Wales Spinal Cord Forum. A journalist by training, and skilled media practitioner, Carr had been the most outspoken Australian state premier urging the federal government to permit the use of embryonic stem cells for research. Carr's reasons were as much industrial as benevolent, boosting the stocks of biotechnology as a clean, green, boom industry. Carr cleverly and repeated enlisted stereotypes of disability in the service of his cause. Christopher Reeve was flown into Australia on a specially modified Boeing 747, free of charge courtesy of an Australian airline, and was paid a hefty appearance fee. Not only did Reeve's fee hugely contrast with meager disability support pensions many Australians with disabilities live on, he was literally the only voice and image of disability given any publicity.

CONSUMING CELEBRITY, CONTESTING CRIPS

As our analysis of Reeve's antipodean career suggests, if disability were a republic, and Reeve its leader, its polity would look more like plutocracy than democracy; as befits modern celebrity with its constitutive tensions between the demotic and democratic (Turner).

For his part, Reeve has criticized the treatment of people with disabilities, and how they are stereotyped, not least the narrow concept of the "normal" in mainstream films. This is something that has directly affected his career, which has become limited to narration or certain types of television and film work. Reeve's reprise on his culture's notion of disability comes with his starring role in an ironic, high-tech 1998 remake of Alfred Hitchcock's *Rear Window* (Bleckner), a movie that in the original featured a photojournalist injured and temporarily using a wheelchair. Reeve has also been a strong advocate, lobbyist, and force in the politics of disability. His activism, however, has been far more strongly focused on finding a cure for people with spinal injuries—rather than seeking to redress inequality and discrimination of all people with disabilities.

Yet Reeve's success in the notoriously fickle star system that allows disability to be understood and mapped in popular culture is mostly an unexplored paradox. As we note above, the construction of Reeve as celebrity, celebrating his individual resilience and resourcefulness, and his authenticity, functions precisely to sustain the "truth" and the power relations of disability. Reeve's celebrity plays an ideological role, knitting together a set of discourses: individualism; consumerism; democratic capitalism; and the primacy of the able body (Marshall; Turner).

The nature of this cultural function of Reeve's celebrity is revealed in the largely unpublicized contests over his fame. At the same time Reeve was gaining fame with his traditional approach to disability and reinforcement of the continuing catastrophe of his life, he was attracting an infamy within certain sections of the international disability rights movement. In a 1996 US debate disability scholar David T. Mitchell put it this way: "He's [Reeve] the good guy—the supercrip, the Superman, and those of us who can live with who we are with our disabilities, but who cannot live with, and in fact, protest and retaliate against the oppression we confront every second of our lives are the bad guys" (Mitchell, quoted in Brown). Many feel, like Mitchell, that Reeve's focus on a cure ignores the unmet needs of people with disabilities for daily access to support services and for the ending of their brutal, dehumanizing, daily experience as other (Goggin & Newell, *Disability in Australia*).

In her book *Make Them Go Away* Mary Johnson points to the conservative forces that Christopher Reeve is associated with and the way in which these forces have been working to oppose the acceptance of disability rights. Johnson documents the way in which fame can work in a variety of ways to claw back the rights of Americans with disabilities granted in the *Americans with Disabilities Act*, documenting the association of Reeve and, in a different fashion, Clint Eastwood as stars who have actively worked to limit the applicability of civil rights legislation to people with disabilities. Like other successful celebrities, Reeve has been assiduous in managing his image, through the use of celebrity professionals including public relations professionals. In his Australian encounters, for example, Reeve gave a variety of media interviews to Australian journalists and yet the editor of the Australian disability rights magazine *Link* was unable to obtain an interview. Despite this, critiques of the super-crip celebrity function of Reeve by people with disabilities did circulate at the margins of mainstream media during his Australian visit, not least in disability media and the Internet (Leipoldt, Newell, and Corcoran, 2003).

INFAMOUS DISABILITY

Like the lives of saints, it is deeply offensive to many to criticize Christopher Reeve. So deeply engrained are the cultural myths of the catastrophe of disability and the creation of Reeve as icon that any critique runs the risk of being received as sacrilege, as one rare iconoclastic Web site provocatively prefigures (Maddox). In this highly charged context, we wish to acknowledge his contribution in highlighting some aspects of contemporary disability, and emphasize our desire not to play Reeve the person—rather to explore the cultural and media dimensions of fame and disability.

In Christopher Reeve we find a remarkable exception as someone with disability who is celebrated in our culture. We welcome a wider debate over what is at stake in this celebrity and how Reeve's renown differs from other disabled stars, as, for example, in Robert McRuer's reflection that:

> . . . at the beginning of the last century the most famous person with disabilities in the world, despite her participation in an 'overcoming' narrative, was a socialist who understood that disability disproportionately impacted workers and the power[less]; Helen Keller knew that blindness and deafness, for instance, often resulted from industrial accidents. At the beginning of this century, the most famous person with disabilities in the world is allowing his image to be used in commercials . . . (McRuer 230)

For our part, we think Reeve's celebrity plays an important contemporary role because it binds together a constellation of economic, political, and social institutions and discourses—namely science, biotechnology, and national competitiveness. In the second half of 2004, the stem cell debate is once again prominent in American debates as a presidential election issue. Reeve . . . [represents] disability in national culture in his own country and internationally, as the case of the currency of his celebrity in Australia demonstrates. In this light, we have only just begun to register, let alone explore and debate, what is entailed for us all in the production of this disabled fame and infamy.

EPILOGUE TO "FAME AND DISABILITY"

Christopher Reeve died on Sunday 10 October 2004, shortly after this article was accepted for publication. His death occasioned an outpouring of condolences, mourning, and reflection. We share that sense of loss.

How Reeve will be remembered is still unfolding. The early weeks of public mourning have emphasized his celebrity as the very embodiment and exemplar of disabled identity: "The death of Christopher Reeve leaves embryonic-stem-cell activism without one of its star generals" (*Newsweek*); "He Never Gave Up: What actor and activist Christopher Reeve taught scientists about the treatment of spinal-cord injury" (*Time*); "Incredible Journey: Facing tragedy, Christopher Reeve inspired the world with hope and a lesson in courage" (*People*); "Superman's Legacy" (*The Express*); "Reeve, the Real Superman" (*Hindustani Times*). In his tribute New South Wales Premier Bob Carr called Reeve the "most impressive person I have ever met," and lamented "Humankind has lost an advocate and friend" (Carr). The figure of Reeve remains central to how disability is represented. In our culture, death is often closely entwined with disability (as in the saying "better dead than disabled"), something Reeve reflected upon himself often. How Reeve's "global mourning" partakes and shapes in this dense knot of associations, and how it transforms his celebrity, is something that requires further work (Ang et al.).

The political and analytical engagement with Reeve's celebrity and mourning at this time serves to underscore our exploration of fame and disability in this article. Already there is his posthumous enlistment in the United States presidential elections, where disability is both central and yet marginal, people with disability talked about rather than listened to. The ethics of stem cell research was an election issue before Reeve's untimely passing, with Democratic presidential contender John Kerry sharply marking his difference on this issue with President Bush. After Reeve's death his widow Dana joined the podium on the Kerry campaign in Columbus, Ohio, to put the case herself; for his part, Kerry compared Bush's opposition to stem cell research as akin to favoring the candle lobby over electricity. As we write, the US polls are a week away, but the cultural representation of disability—and the intensely political role celebrity plays in it—appears even more palpably implicated in the government of society itself.

REFERENCES

Abraham, Philip. *Christopher Reeve*. New York: Children's Press, 2002.

Alter, Judy. *Christopher Reeve: Triumph over Tragedy*. Danbury, Conn.: Franklin Watts, 2000.

Ang, Ien, Ruth Barcan, Helen Grace, Elaine Lally, Justine Lloyd, and Zoe Sofoulis (eds.). *Planet Diana: Cultural Studies and Global Mourning*. Sydney: Research Centre in Intercommunal Studies, University of Western Sydney, Nepean, 1997.

Bleckner, Jeff, dir. *Rear Window*. 1998.

Brown, Steven E. "Super Duper? The (Unfortunate) Ascendancy of Christopher Reeve." *Mainstream: Magazine of the Able-Disabled*, October 1996. Repr. 10 Aug. 2004 <http://www.independentliving.org/docs3/brown96c.html>.

Carr, Bob. "A Class Act of Grace and Courage." *Sydney Morning Herald*. 12 Oct. 2004: 14.

Corker, Mairian, and Carol Thomas. "A Journey around the Social Model." *Disability/Postmodernity: Embodying Disability Theory*. Ed. Mairian Corker and Tom Shakespeare. London and New York: Continuum, 2000.

Donner, Richard, dir. *Superman*. 1978.

Dyer, Richard. *Heavenly Bodies: Film Stars and Society*. London: BFI Macmillan, 1986.

Finn, Margaret L. *Christopher Reeve*. Philadelphia: Chelsea House Publishers, 1997.

Fulcher, Gillian. *Disabling Policies?* London: Falmer Press, 1989.

Furie, Sidney J., dir. *Superman IV: The Quest for Peace*. 1987.

Gilmer, Tim. "The Missionary Reeve." *New Mobility*. November 2002. 13 Aug. 2004 <http://www.newmobility.com/>.

Goggin, Gerard. "Media Studies' Disability." *Media International Australia* 108 (Aug. 2003): 157–68.

Goggin, Gerard, and Christopher Newell. *Disability in Australia: Exposing a Social Apartheid.* Sydney: UNSW Press, 2005.

———. "Uniting the Nation? Disability, Stem Cells, and the Australian Media." *Disability & Society* 19 (2004): 47–60.

Havill, Adrian. *Man of Steel: The Career and Courage of Christopher Reeve.* New York: Signet, 1996.

Howard, Megan. *Christopher Reeve.* Minneapolis: Lerner Publications, 1999.

Hughes, Libby. *Christopher Reeve.* Parsippany, NJ: Dillon Press, 1998.

Johnson, Mary. *Make Them Go Away: Clint Eastwood, Christopher Reeve and the Case against Disability Rights.* Louisville: Advocado Press, 2003.

Kosek, Jane Kelly. *Learning about Courage from the Life of Christopher Reeve.* 1st ed. New York: PowerKids Press, 1999.

Leipoldt, Erik, Christopher Newell, and Maurice Corcoran. "Christopher Reeve and Bob Carr Dehumanise Disability—Stem Cell Research Not the Best Solution." *Online Opinion,* 27 Jan. 2003. <http://www.onlineopinion.com.au/view.asp ?article=510>.

Lester, Richard, dir. *Superman II.* 1980.

———. *Superman III.* 1983.

Maddox. "Christopher Reeve Is an Asshole." 12 Aug. 2004 <http://maddox .xmission.com/c.cgi?u=creeve>.

Marshall, P. David. *Celebrity and Power: Fame in Contemporary Culture.* Minneapolis and London: University of Minnesota Press, 1997.

McRuer, Robert. "Critical Investments: AIDS, Christopher Reeve, and Queer/ Disability Studies." *Journal of Medical Humanities* 23 (2002): 221–37.

Mierendorf, Michael, dir. *Without Pity: A Film about Abilities.* Narr. Christopher Reeve. 1996.

"Miracle or Murder?" *60 Minutes.* Channel 9, Australia. March 17, 2002. 15 June 2002 <http://news.ninemsn.com.au/sixtyminutes/stories/2002_03_17/story _532.asp>.

Mitchell, David, and Synder, Sharon, eds. *The Body and Physical Difference.* Ann Arbor: University of Michigan Press, 1997.

Oleksy, Walter G. *Christopher Reeve.* San Diego, CA: Lucent, 2000.

Reeve, Christopher. *Nothing Is Impossible: Reflections on a New Life.* 1st ed. New York: Random House, 2002.

———. *Still Me.* 1st ed. New York: Random House, 1998.

Reeve, Dana, comp. *Care Packages: Letters to Christopher Reeve from Strangers and Other Friends.* 1st ed. New York: Random House, 1999.

Reeve, Matthew, dir. *Christopher Reeve: Courageous Steps.* Television documentary, 2002.

Thomson, Rosemary Garland, ed. *Freakery: Cultural Spectacles of the Extraordinary Body*. New York: New York University Press, 1996.

Turner, Graeme. *Understanding Celebrity*. Thousands Oak, CA: Sage, 2004.

Turner, Graeme, Frances Bonner, and David P. Marshall. *Fame Games: The Production of Celebrity in Australia*. Melbourne: Cambridge University Press, 2000.

Wren, Laura Lee. *Christopher Reeve: Hollywood's Man of Courage*. Berkeley Heights, NJ: Enslow, 1999.

Younis, Steve. "Christopher Reeve Homepage." 12 Aug. 2004 <http://www.fortune city.com/lavender/greatsleep/1023/main.html>.

10

MORE THAN AN INSPIRATION

Robert F. Molsberry[*]

C hristopher Reeve is something of an enigma for the disability community. He is probably the most well known and visible example of a person with a disability in the world. He's a celebrity and a quadriplegic. Like E. F. Hutton, when he speaks, people listen. The disability community has been looking for a powerful spokesperson who might make an impact on how society regards people with disabilities. Unfortunately, many people with disabilities believe Reeve is using his influence in ways that perpetuate stereotypical perceptions. Here, in his book *Still Me,* he takes the simple, everyday challenge of living with a disability and casts it as a heroic undertaking:

When the first Superman movie came out, I gave dozens of interviews to promote it. The most frequently asked question was: "What is a hero?" I

*Editor's note: Robert F. Molsberry is senior pastor of the United Church of Christ-Congregational in Grinnell, Iowa. A pastor, father, and triathlete, Molsberry became paraplegic following a near-fatal hit-and-run accident in 1997.

From Robert F. Molsberry, *Blinded by Grace: Entering the World of Disability* (Minneapolis: Augsburg Books, 2004), pp. 57–61. Copyright © 2004 Augsburg Fortress. Reprinted by permission of the publisher.

remember how easily I'd talk about it, the glib response I repeated so many times. My answer was that a hero is someone who commits a courageous action without considering the consequences. A soldier who crawls out of a foxhole to drag an injured buddy back to safety, the prisoners of war who never stop trying to escape even though they know they may be executed if they're caught. . . .

Now my definition is completely different. I think a hero is an ordinary individual who finds the strength to persevere and endure in spite of overwhelming obstacles. The fifteen-year-old boy down the hall at Kessler who had landed on his head while wrestling with his brother, leaving him paralyzed and barely able to swallow or speak. Travis Roy, paralyzed in the first eleven seconds of a hockey game in his freshman year at college. Henry Steifel, paralyzed from the chest down in a car accident at seventeen, completing his education and working on Wall Street at age thirty-two, but having missed so much of what life has to offer. These are real heroes, and so are the families and friends who have stood by them. (Reeve, 1998, p. 273)

Pardon me for raining on the parade of the media love fest that has surrounded Reeve since his accident, but I disagree. People who face difficult circumstances in everyday life, I maintain, are not heroes at all. They are simply ordinary individuals doing what they have to do in order to survive. Besides not being an accurate description of how most people with disabilities feel about their experiences, Reeve's interpretation both diminishes the word *hero* and also diminishes the person who is struggling simply to live out her or his life with the hand dealt. Don't narrow our experience—even if in the process you place it on a pedestal. It may be flattering, but it's wrong. Some people with disabilities may be heroic. But some aren't. Some people with disabilities would crawl (or roll or stumble or shuffle) out of their foxhole, if they could, to rescue an injured buddy. Some wouldn't. So don't be too quick to pass judgment on an experience that looks challenging to you. Do your homework first. Get involved in that life before you make a judgment about it.

That's what is wrong with the major telethons. Have you ever watched one of those things with a critical eye toward the experience of disability that they portray? They never examine the preconceived notion that people with disabilities are universally suffering as a result of their ailments, that their condition is a tragedy to be pitied, that those with disabling conditions who manage to live useful lives are heroic figures for overcoming a terrible situation, and finally, that your tax-deductible dollars can prevent this from happening. Telethons open the purse strings by tugging on the heartstrings. They're good at what they do, and, to their credit, they have raised astonishing amounts of money for their causes. The "Jerry Lewis Muscular Dystrophy Association Telethon," for example, has raised over 1 billion dollars for the Muscular Dystrophy Association. But at what cost? Is there ever the slightest effort made to get behind the stereotype to try to understand the experience of a person with a disability, in all its complexity and ambiguity? The fundraising formula doesn't come close to describing my experience of disability, for example. Is it possible that "Jerry's Kids" might be more than objects of pity or admiration? Jerry's not going to let on, if that's the case, because that knowledge would cut into his fundraising margin. Who wants to give money to a person with a disability who seems to have accepted her or his condition, who's managing quite well with a disability, thank you very much? Many people with disabilities would much rather have the public *understand* their condition than to contribute money to *reverse* it. . . .

Inspiration is an easy, knee-jerk reaction to people with disabilities. Hide behind that perception and you don't have to get your hands dirty trying to discover the rich and intricate complexity hidden there. I have been the subject of no fewer than six local television news features. I was featured prominently in an hour-long program covering the 2000 San Diego Marathon, which played all over the country on the Outdoor cable channel. Articles about me have appeared in a half-dozen papers. Each feature had the same exact spin. Each reporter presented my story as an inspiration. Why? Is it a conspiracy? Do they get together and compare notes? Or is it sloppy journalism, slapping an easy interpretation—that will sell newspapers and television features—of a complex reality? "Disabled Pastor Overcomes Obstacles: He's such an inspiration!" "It's the amazing story of one man's faith getting him through a devastating accident." "This man of the cloth is now a man of the roads." "Riding in RAGBRAI is nothing short of a miracle for this true road warrior." Who do they think I am, Mel Gibson? They never wrote about me when I was nondisabled, even when I did things that I thought were much more heroic. Why not? I worked just as hard then. And I'm sure there are people who, in their daily living, face a more daunting task more doggedly than I tackle marathons. Why aren't they featured?

One woman with a disability, June Price, editor of *Living Smart* magazine, wrote an account of how the media attention on "inspirational" achievements of more-active people with disabilities affects her.

Part of me is in awe of these athletes as they pour forth their last ounce of energy in quest of gold. But another part of me resents that these brawny specimens waste their precious resources on "games" when I need every scrap of my strength just to survive another day! . . . I kept thinking of my many friends for whom reaching to scratch their nose is a monumental task. They don't get high fives or their photos on a bulletin board. . . . What really makes a winner, after all, is not what we can achieve compared to others, but what we can achieve given what we have to work with. (Price, 2000, p. 10)

Price recalls seeing a program about a mountain climber scaling some craggy summit in the dead of winter. It demanded all his effort. His fingers were frozen, arms exhausted as he struggled upward. She writes, "So? I thought. What's the big deal? Isn't this exactly what I go through every winter when I'm outside in the numbing cold trying to push my joystick?" (Ibid.)

I have to admit I'm shamefully flattered by media attention of my post-disability achievements. I don't apologize for it. I think most people would be proud. I'm just surprised by it, and, deep down, more than a little embarrassed. At my first marathon I was invited for television interviews in the motel suite reserved for elite athletes. They even had a sign at the door announcing it. "Elite Athletes." I had known that such watering holes for the privileged gazelles existed, but I had never seen one. And I had surely never been invited to one. There was free food and drink laid out on long tables. International athletes sat around talking and watching television. I had Ann take my picture in front of the sign. I've had that photo enlarged and it serves as an ego boost. But, however much I enjoy impressing people, I realize at a deeper level that this is a narrow definition of who I am. It's not very accurate, either, if you come right down to it. I'm still no better than a middle-of-the-pack weekend athlete. I'm just more competitive now because the field is so limited. There is only one other wheelchair racer I'm aware of in Iowa, and only one handcyclist who can challenge me on the roads. There's no one I'm aware of closer than either coast who does triathlons from a wheelchair. Permit me a little gloating, at least.

It seems as though some people judge my efforts on the basis of degree of difficulty, like figure skating or competitive diving. In these events, the competitors get points for how difficult their attempts are. Two divers are competing. One does a simple dive well. The second diver doesn't perform as well, but he does a more difficult dive. The second diver might just win the competition because of the greater degree of difficulty. At the Salt Lake City Olympic Games, Russian officials lodged a complaint over the scoring in figure skating. It was clear to all who watched that the young US skater Sara Hughes skated better than the Russian, but there was some legitimacy to their claim because the Russian skater performed a more difficult program.

What if life were judged that way? It seems like that is how the media and others choose to look at my adjustment to disability. A lackluster sermon last Sunday? That's okay, because you were dealing with a bladder infection at the time and your degree of difficulty was way up there. Your minister never visits you? He's still a great minister, because it's so difficult for him to get around now. Sometimes, I confess, I wish that's how life were judged. Sometimes, in fact, that is the way I find myself rationalizing my efforts. "Bob is getting out of bed now. A hush has fallen over the crowd. He's sitting up. Oh, it's a painful day today. Just look at that grimace on his face. He's toughing it out today. Look at that concentration. It wouldn't surprise me if he were to lie back down today. Another five minutes marshalling his strength and then try again. But no! He's moving. He's moving! He has a hand on his wheelchair. Leaning, leaning, leaning, and—yes!—Bob is up. He has transferred into his chair. And a magnificent transfer it was, too. Considering what Bob must be going through this morning, I'd give him at least a 9.8 for that maneuver. Let's see what the judges have to say."

But life isn't judged by degree of difficulty. Life is judged, if at all, by what you do with what you've been given. Are you a competent steward of the resources at your disposal? Do you give back? Do you dive headfirst into this adventure called life, and surface after with gratitude in your heart? Do you love?

If life were judged by the challenges each of us had overcome, then everyone would be getting extra points for something or other. One person needs glasses to read. Another is short. Others are balding or overweight or suffer from arthritis or are old or young or ugly or too beautiful. One woman struggles in the aftermath of divorce. A man has lost his parents. Every newspaper would be stuffed with features about people doing things that seem heroic to someone else. There wouldn't be any room for real news. We'd all have handicap-parking tags. We'd all be inspirations.

Then where would we be?

BIBLIOGRAPHY

Price, June. "My Spin: The Olympics of Life." *New Mobility*, October 2000.

Reeve, Christopher. *Still Me*. New York: Random House, 1998.

Robert F. Molsberry. *Blindsided by Grace: Entering the World of Disability*. Minneapolis: Augsburg Books, 2004.

11

CHRISTOPHER REEVE'S SUPER BOWL AD SCORED A TOUCHDOWN

But It Has Provoked a Surprisingly Negative Reaction among Disabled Groups. Why?

John Williams

I have never understood the animosity that many of my friends with disabilities show toward Christopher Reeve. A talented actor, writer, director, and producer, Reeve suffered a severely damaged spinal cord in a horse riding accident several years ago. Today, most of the world knows he's a quadriplegic. He never asked to be severely limited in what he can do physically. He never asked for the attention his disability automatically guaranteed him. And I'm sure he never asked to become a universal role model, symbol, and leader in the struggle to find a cure for spinal cord injuries and other disabling diseases.

By virtue of his fame and personality, Reeve's role as a spokesman for the disabled community was thrust upon him. He could easily have become a recluse and said, "No, I do not want that role." He did not.

Having met him several times, I know Reeve is a fighter. He wants to

From *Business Week Online*, February 11, 2000. Reprinted by permission of the publisher.

walk again. He wants to ride again. He wants to hold his wife and children in his arms. He wants to work. He wants to be independent. These are his dreams, the same as those of many other disabled people, and we should respect them and encourage him to use every resource at his command—his fame, his personality, his friends—to achieve his dream and give hope to others with spinal cord injuries.

SECOND THOUGHTS

But a great deal of controversy and anger has surrounded the actor, much of it coming from people with disabilities. The latest example: Reeve's appearance in a Super Bowl ad for Nuveen, an investment-management company, in which the paralyzed actor seems to stand up and walk across a stage to present an award.

I must admit, at first I, too, was upset. How phony, I thought. (The ad was a computer simulation of Reeve's head on the body of a man in a tuxedo.) Why would Reeve do this, I thought?

Later, when I saw the ad again, I had second thoughts. This was really a Big Idea, an emotional moment packaged with a thought-provoking message—the importance of hope, the importance of investing in the future and in technology that could open the floodgates of opportunity for disabled people worldwide.

"MOTIVATING VISION"

I asked Reeve why he agreed to do the ad. "It is a motivating vision of something that can actually happen," he said via a spokesman. "Leading scientists around the world all agree that it is only a question of money and time before people who have suffered from spinal cord injuries will be able to recover. And so in order to help people visualize what the future will bring, I thought this ad would be very helpful.

"Rather than just imagining a spinal cord victim walking in the future, I thought it would be even more powerful to see it actually happening. The response I got from people all over the world, both the general public and people who suffer like me from spinal cord injuries, has been overwhelmingly positive," he said, through the spokesman.

But a backlash is building. Columnist Dr. Charles Krauthammer—whose own spinal cord was damaged in a diving accident when he was young—denounced the ad in his syndicated column on February 1 as "disgracefully misleading." Krauthammer, who uses a wheelchair, said Reeve was trying to foist his false hopes upon others. "His propaganda undermines those—particularly the young and newly injured—who are struggling to face reality, master it, and make a life for themselves from their wheelchairs."

I have heard many other disparaging comments about the ad and read many angry letters from other people with disabilities. Part of the reaction seems to derive from the fact that Reeve was paid for his appearance. (The advertising agency, Fallon Elligott of Minneapolis, declines to disclose how much Reeve was paid to appear in the $2 million Super Bowl air-time buy.) It's true that often a huge gap exists between the incomes of people either born with disabilities or who become disabled before they have a chance to achieve their earning potential and those who become disabled in midlife. Because Reeve is financially successful, class resentment seems to have developed.

The other factor that seems to be at work is a tinge of jealousy. Reeve has captured the spotlight, even though he has been disabled for "only" four years—that at least is the way many of my friends and colleagues appear to view it. This is insulting to Reeve. I don't share the sentiment. I like his message of hope, and I like the message of investment. We have a stingy US Congress that would rather slash R&D funding for spinal cord injuries and other disabling conditions than increase it. Cutting funding will delay finding a cure.

The greatest investment we can make is in people who develop technology and in people who can benefit from it—this is a message that must get out. People with disabilities need more access to technology, and if Congress won't invest in development, then we should encourage the private sector to provide money.

NEAR-MIRACLES

Of course commercial reasons were behind the ad. In fact, says Fallon Elligott, it was designed to spur a dialogue between the medical and financial communities on the monetary value of investing in research that could lead to breakthroughs in treatment.

According to Fallon Elligott, "Reeve was approached because he is a courageous individual with a powerful message. He's very focused on his legacy. Seeking a cure for paralysis from spinal cord injury is not just about him. We're proud to help provide an opportunity for him to share his message with millions."

I don't know how long it will take to find a cure for paralysis. Some doctors believe a major breakthrough will occur within the next two decades. Others, such as Krauthammer, aren't so optimistic. But with the advances researchers are making in biotechnology, medical near-miracles will happen, and we will need to redefine "disability" and "disabling conditions." That will be a wonderful thing.

Despite the unwillingness of Congress to assume a leadership role in finding cures for disabilities, technology can advance the human condition and improve lives. I believe the message from Christopher Reeve is that investing in technology is really investing in human development. This is a legacy that will help future generations. Is Reeve a rich, deluded glory-seeker? No. I say he's a courageous risk-taker.

12

WISHING FOR KRYPTONITE

A Response to Christopher Reeve's Pursuit of Cure

● *William J. Peace*

hortly after Christopher Reeve was paralyzed in a horseback riding acci-dent in 1995, he vowed he would walk again before he was fifty years old. Such vows are hardly unusual after a traumatic injury. To make the same claim—and to devote all one's time, effort, and money to such a vow—seven years later is decidedly so.

Already paralyzed for over a decade when Reeve was injured, I thought many of Reeve's proclamations about walking again were misguided. I blamed the press for printing such empty rhetoric and hoped, given time, he would learn that such statements were counterproductive. At worst, I thought his interest in walking again would become a side interest and that he would return to his acting career. Hopelessly naive and surrounded by all the wrong people, though, Reeve has not deviated from his desire to walk again. Indeed, as the years have passed, he has become increasingly obnoxious about his expectations.

Since his paralysis, Reeve has spent huge sums of money on "exer-

From *Ragged Edge Online*, September 24, 2002.

cising" his body and has used his celebrity to lobby for stem cell research. He has also created a foundation whose goal is the cure of paralysis. While his ultimate goal, a cure for spinal cord injury, is laudable, the manner in which he is going about it is deeply offensive. Disability rights activists cringe when he is quoted and I am convinced his activities have not only hindered but harmed disability rights.

In the past I have refrained from criticizing Reeve in part because I refused to believe an intelligent person with a disability could be so narrow-minded and oblivious to the stigma associated with disability. However, Reeve's latest ABC television documentary, *Christopher Reeve: Courageous Steps*, was the last straw for me. I sat stunned when Reeve informed the viewer that he "willed" his body to move his finger. When I heard this pronouncement, replete with the appropriate drama and gasps from loved ones, for the first time I too wished I could will my body to move. Had I been able to, I would have kicked my TV.

Already wealthy and well connected in Hollywood, Reeve is not your average paralyzed person. Since his injury he has antagonized those active in the fight for disability rights and insulted innumerable disabled people who are more concerned with social injustices than a cure for paralysis.

It is not just Reeve's proclamations that are misguided. The breathless comments of those beholden to him are just as bad. "If there is anybody that's going to get out of this [paralysis], it's him," said Chris Fantini. "Nobody in his condition ever worked as hard for this long."

Fantini is absolutely correct: no one has spent such an inordinate amount of time and money—nor surrounded himself with a staff of people—for a goal that is so unrealistic. No single individual has spent so much and done so little for others in a similar situation. And no one has ever been as oblivious to the fact that all the ramps, elevators, and lifts he uses were fought for by the people he is actively alienating—a fact I find a cruel irony, for the people who fought so hard for disability rights have enabled a monster to be unleashed.

The gross disparity between Reeve and his paralyzed brethren is readily transparent in one scene from the documentary. The viewer sees Reeve lowered into a pool, surrounded by at least a dozen people, including one of his doctors. Once in the pool, Reeve is assisted by at least four people—and the viewer is supposed to be awed by the fact he is supposedly able to move his legs with five-pound ankle weights on them! This tremendous expenditure of energy is part of an ongoing rehabilitation process directed by John W.

McDonald of the Washington University in St. Louis Activity Based Recovery Program. Of one thing I am sure: there is only one respirator-dependent quad in the continental United States who can pay to mobilize so many people.

Here's what I kept thinking about during this scene (and the others like it designed to pull at viewers' heartstrings): what about the other people with injuries similar to Reeve's? What are they doing? Are they, too, living in a palatial home in Westchester County? Are they surrounded by a dozen people looking for the slightest movement? Are they being cared for by a staff of people and flying to St. Louis to participate in the program Reeve is active in? Do they have a multimillion-dollar foundation in their name? Does a major medical school like Washington U. send out press releases and devote part of its Web site to their progress? I think not.

With neither access to such high-level medical care nor the financial resources to hire full-time employees, how many C2 ventilator-dependent quads are dead or rotting away in nursing homes?

I am convinced Reeve simply does not care about others with similar spinal cord injuries and that he uses his privileged position to distance himself from other disabled people. I have never read nor heard Reeve bemoan the fact the unemployment rate among disabled people in the United States is about 66 percent. Or that the vast majority of people with spinal cord injuries lack access to basic healthcare and are routinely hospitalized for problems such as skin breakdowns that could easily be avoided.

I do not begrudge Reeve's wealth or position. I do take exception to his belief that he is somehow different. Despite the fact he has limited movement and has recovered some sensation, he remains a ventilator-dependent quad. I also do not believe that the recovery of sensation and limited movement is all that unusual in quads long after the original injury.

In separating himself from other disabled people, Reeve has lost a golden opportunity to raise awareness of the myriad problems disabled people encounter daily. As I too live in Westchester County, I never cease to be amazed by his complete lack of interest in wheelchair access. The New York Rangers raise funds for the Christopher Reeve Foundation as part of an event called Super Skate. In spite of this fundraiser, wheelchair seating at Madison Square Garden is appallingly inadequate. Disabled people sit in the aisles and are routinely bumped and jostled. I sincerely doubt Reeve faces the same obstacles when he wishes to see a Ranger game with his family— nor does he consider what it is like for others who would like to attend such a game—or try to do anything about those obstacles for others.

Reeve would like to blame government restrictions on stem cell research for his failure to walk. "If there had been full government funding of embryonic stem cell research," he said, "I believe we would be in human trials by now. And there might have been a possibility of realizing the goal [of walking again] that I stated in 1995." Such speculation may let Reeve sleep better at night, but it does absolutely nothing to enhance the quality of his life or others. Unfortunately, disabled people will continue to endure further observations and declarations of this nature by Reeve.

In the documentary's only scene that accurately depicted the reality of life for a ventilator-dependent quad, we see Reeve obviously and profoundly disappointed with the failure of his effort to breathe independently of the ventilator. Here he quietly reveals that his most ardent wish is to be free of the respirator—a modest wish in light of his desire to walk again. In this attempt to wean off his ventilator, I wish him well.

As to his desire for a cure, though—when he engages the media in this disability-disowning folly, I wish someone would quietly place some kryptonite nearby.

CHRISTOPHER REEVE

1952–2004

John Schatzlein

Many sports and entertainment industry stars have been affected by spinal cord injury (SCI). Undoubtedly the most visible of these, Christopher Reeve had the most severe level of injury resulting in the need for a ventilator for breathing since his 1995 injury. Reeve has perhaps the most documented efforts for recovery of any individual with SCI in the last twenty years. He went through many of the same difficulties we all faced when we acquired our spinal cord injuries.

In a split second, "faster than a speeding bullet," a spinal cord injury can change our lives. The sudden onset of the changes in the body's ability to control its functions, the fear of dependency on others, or the presumption that we will never be as valued or as capable as we were before the injury cause us to immediately look for a way to make it go away. It also makes us look at who we are, where we have been, or where we might have gone. Having explored those answers, we ask the scary question . . . : Where are we going from here?

First printed in John Schatzlein, "Christopher Reeve: 1952–2004," *Access Press* 15, no. 11, November 10, 2004. Reprinted by permission.

Like most people right after a spinal cord injury, for me the search for a cure started immediately. My family and I (at age fourteen), were told in May of 1963 that the cure was right around the corner. Forty-one years later in my case, and nine years later in Reeve's case, it is still "right around the corner." More enlightened professionals, however, are saying a cure MAY be around the corner with the number of efforts being pursued.

Individuals with SCI, scientists, and research teams all around the world are making tremendous efforts to crack the complexities of a cure. Hope must be maintained while being balanced with the need for forward life continuance and positive movement. Hopefully the time to a cure is a bit shorter now, although it's important to keep one's body in its best condition through activity, exercise, and nutrition as the research continues.

While Christopher Reeve waged his battles with health issues, he maintained hope for a cure, optimizing what he could do to stay as healthy as possible while continuing to move forward productively and capably—leading a life of fulfillment and spiritual contentment. For me personally, this type of contentment means that I am taking control of my life and its direction, I have acknowledged the impact of the spinal cord injury and have chosen to move onward to the best of my ability at this time.

The passing of Christopher Reeve points out the complexity of the body system interactions after a severe spinal cord injury, especially for a quadriplegic but for paraplegics also. On Saturday, October 9, 2004, he fell into a coma after going into cardiac arrest while at home. Reeve was being treated for a pressure wound that he developed, a common complication for people living with paralysis. In his last week, the wound became severely infected, resulting in a serious systemic infection.

Reeve had the economic ability to have the best care and assistance available. He could afford the latest therapeutic activities, from electrical stimulation cycling three times weekly or more, cardiovascular strengthening, to the latest surgical procedure facilitating finger or hand closure/grip. He had the ability to travel to research sites and participate in trials with support staff and family. Even with independent financial resources, however, a small skin breakdown that might seem insignificant at the time can lead to a rapidly progressing systemic shutdown.

With the thirty-five years I have worked and associated with persons with SCI, I know that these secondary complications, such as skin breakdowns, bladder/kidney infections, and excessive swelling of the lower extremities, can all suddenly get worse. We all have to take the responsibility to prevent these occurrences where we can and have all secondary issues checked. Christopher Reeve's untimely passing reminds us that we must get off these sores and not push them to infections. We have perhaps been lucky that ours did not progress as rapidly, or cause system-wide shutdown and death.

Reeve was a man who grasped what it meant to acknowledge what his SCI was in his life and move it forward to its maximum. With his family's efforts, he raised the issue of SCI cure research to a high visibility level in recent years. We also cannot overlook the efforts of the Paralyzed Veterans of America (PVA), or United Spinal Association (formerly Eastern PVA-New York) or the National Spinal Cord Injury Association's research-funding efforts dating back to the '50s. Kent Waldrep's National Paralysis Foundation and Rick Hanson's Canadian Man in Motion Foundation started in the early '70s with the Miami Project starting in 1985.

Here in Minnesota, the Spinal Cord Society started in 1978 with a sole focus on a cure, to this day utilizing no government funding. In the mid '90s the Morton Cure Paralysis Fund was established. The majority of their funding in recent years has gone to the Spinal Cord Injury Project at Rutgers University, home of Dr. Wise Young, named America's top spinal cord injury research scientist by *Time* magazine. In the last three years, they have accepted grant proposals from other laboratories for specific projects and have approved three of them. Two of these projects are in Minnesota, at laboratories at the University of Minnesota Twin Cities and the Mayo Clinic in Rochester, Minnesota. The third is at the research department of Boston Children's Hospital.

Reeve's great acting presence and visibility certainly increased awareness of the sudden onset of SCI. His will to overcome a significant injury, far more severe than many, provides a role model that can be pointed to for many years to come.

Many individuals have reported that after their spinal cord injury, their lives were enhanced, full of love and warmth and exciting adventures. They also say they felt for a long time the societal pressures to not be different or functionally limited. What many say now is that they are fine with who they are and what they have accomplished during their lives. Maybe when the breakthrough comes, they will make sure it works consistently before they have to get "fixed."

My way of thinking, as with many of my friends, is that I don't need to walk at first, but maybe some of the other functions I would like to have will be available in my lifetime. In the meantime we are going to keep moving forward, take on the challenges of living whole and productive lives, and in our own ways we'll thank Reeve for the fight he waged to make life more complete for others. Our thoughts are with his family and all families that go through catastrophic changes and move forward the best ways they can.

THE DISABILITY RIGHTS MOVEMENT

Historical Perspectives

14

THE DISABILITY RIGHTS MOVEMENT

A Brief History

As our parents, children, friends, and neighbors, people with disabilities are—and always have been—everywhere. The history of the disability rights movement, however, is relatively new. While people with disabilities have always been members of most communities, it is only within recent memory that they have begun to recognize themselves as a cohesive social group.

There are nearly 54 million people with disabilities in the United States. As the largest single minority in this country, they represent a potentially formidable voting bloc. Yet many people with disabilities claim that they are still an unrecognized minority. The disability rights movement intends to change all that, and to bring the needs, concerns, and rights of people with disabilities to national attention.

Historically, the condition of having a disability—in any society—has been viewed as tragic. In pre-industrial times, when people with disabilities often were unable to support themselves or their families, they were seen as

From *U.S. Society & Values, USIA Electronic Journal* 4, no. 1, January 1999.

social dependents, objects of pity or recipients of charity. In the early years of the United States, society assumed a paternalistic approach towards people with disabilities—often institutionalizing them in special homes or hospitals. People with disabilities were looked upon as patients or clients who needed curing. In those institutions, medical professionals and social workers were considered the primary decision makers, rather than the people with disabilities themselves.

As a result, these people found themselves excluded from the larger society. While the assumption was that people with disabilities needed to be rehabilitated from their "problems," great numbers had conditions for which there was no known cure at the time. And so society provided no room for integration, thereby perpetuating myths of inequality.

In the first half of the twentieth century, however, the United States' involvement in two world wars had a profound effect on the way people with disabilities were viewed and treated by the culture at large. As thousands of disabled soldiers returned home, society made provisions for them to re-enter the work force. The first vocational rehabilitation acts were passed by the US Congress in the 1920s to provide services to World War I veterans with disabilities.

The biggest changes, though, came in the throes of the civil rights movements of the 1960s. As African Americans, women, and other social minorities gained political influence, so, too, did people with disabilities.

A pivotal moment in the history of the disability rights movement may have been the admission of Ed Roberts to the University of California at Berkeley in 1962. Paralyzed from the neck down due to a childhood bout with polio, Roberts overcame opposition to gain admission, and he was housed in the campus hospital. A headline in a local newspaper proclaimed, "Helpless Cripple Attends UC Classes."

Within a short period of time, several other men and women with disabilities joined him on campus. Dubbing themselves the "rolling quads," they banded together to fight for better services and for permission to live independently, rather than at the hospital. With a grant from the US Office of Education, they created the Physically Disabled Students Program, the first of its kind on a college campus. It was, in effect, the beginning of the independent living movement.

This movement rests on the concepts of consumer control, self-reliance, and economic rights. It rejects the supremacy of medical professionals in decision making and advocates the right to self-determination by people with disabilities. The first center for independent living opened in Berkeley in 1971, with an eye towards providing peer support, referral services, advocacy training, and general information. Today, there are more than two hundred such centers across the nation.

With the success of the independent living movement, people with disabilities began to band together on behalf of their civil rights. In the early 1970s, they lobbied Congress to add civil rights language for people with disabilities to pending legislation. In 1973, the legislature passed the revised Rehabilitation Act. Its most important aspect was Section 504, a one-sentence paragraph prohibiting any program or activity receiving US government financial assistance from discriminating against qualified individuals with disabilities.

On a parallel track to the disability rights movement was a campaign to provide access to educational services for children and youth with disabilities. The Education for All Handicapped Children Act, passed in 1975, ensured equal access to public education for such students. Renamed the Individuals with Disabilities Education Act (IDEA) in 1990, it called for a free and appropriate public education for every child with a disability, to be delivered in the least restrictive environment. IDEA promotes the concept of inclusion, requiring that students with disabilities be educated in general education settings, alongside students without disabilities, to the greatest extent appropriate.

Despite these pieces of legislation, people with disabilities did not gain broad civil rights until the enactment of the Americans with Disabilities Act (ADA) in 1990. Modeled after the Civil Rights Act of 1964, this landmark US Government anti-discrimination law ensures equal access to employment opportunities and public accommodations for people with disabilities. The ADA guarantees that no person with a disability can be excluded, segregated, or otherwise treated differently than individuals without disabilities. With this act, Congress identified the full participation, inclusion, and integration of people with disabilities into society as a national goal.

With increased access to employment opportunities and public services, though, discrimination does persist—with obstacles to full participation in housing, transportation, education, and access to public accommodations. Many of these obstacles are the result of ongoing ignorance and lack of public awareness. This has led to the disability culture movement.

The legislative changes represented the first phase in the quest for disability rights. The second is what disability expert Dr. Paul Longmore calls "a quest for collective identity," an exploration of what it means to have a disability in today's society.

Disability culture is aimed at fostering pride in one's disabilities, creating positive self-images, and building a society which not only accepts, but also celebrates, diversity. It calls for the collection of disability history, the establishment of disability studies in academia, and the support of artistic expressions of the disability experience through poetry, art, music, and dance.

"Gradually, people with disabilities are finding their history and cultural legacy," says Carol Gill, a psychologist who has studied disability culture at length. "They are seeking support and validation in the community—the family—of other disabled people."

15

THE SECOND PHASE

From Disability Rights to Disability Culture

Paul K. Longmore

The movement of disabled Americans has entered its second phase. The first phase has been a quest for disability rights, for equal access and equal opportunity, for inclusion. The second phase is a quest for collective identity. Even as the unfinished work of the first phase continues, the task in the second phase is to explore or to create a disability culture.

This historic juncture offers a moment for reflection and assessment. It is an opportunity to consider the aims and achievements of the disability movement over the past generation and in the last few years.

In August 1985, the *Disability Rag* reported an incident that captured the essence of the disability movement's first phase:

'It comes to a point where you can't take it any more,' said Nadine Jacobson, sounding for all the world like Rosa Parks. She and her husband Steven were arrested July 7th for refusing to move from seats in the emergency exit row of a United Airlines flight on which they were to leave

First printed in *Ragged Edge Online*. Copyright © 1995 by Paul K. Longmore. Reprinted by permission.

Louisville after the National Federation of the Blind convention here. 'You lose some of your self-respect every time you move,' she told Louisville Times reporter Beth Wilson. United has a policy of not letting blind people sit in emergency exit rows, because it believes they might slow an evacuation in an emergency, though there seems to be no airline policy against serving sighted passengers in emergency exit rows as many drinks as they want for fear they might become too intoxicated to open an emergency door properly in the event of a disaster. NFB members say it's discriminatory treatment, plain and simple. The airline says it is not. The Jacobsons pleaded 'not guilty' to the charge of disorderly conduct.

Six months later, *The Rag* related that the Jacobsons had been acquitted of the charge. A half year after that, in the fall of 1986, it announced that Congress had passed the Air Carrier Assistance Act, which amended the Federal Aviation Act to prohibit discrimination against persons with disabilities in airline travel. Yet over the next three years, *The Rag* reported instances of discrimination against blind and wheelchair-riding travelers, FAA regulations that restricted the rights of disabled airline passengers, including a rule prohibiting them from sitting in exit rows, and the opposition of the NFB, the Eastern Paralyzed Veterans Association, and American Disabled for Accessible Public Transportation (ADAPT) to these practices and policies.

Despite the problem with its implementation, the Air Carrier Assistance Act was one of some fifty federal statutes in a quarter century of legislation that reflected a major shift in public policymaking regarding Americans with disabilities. That process began in 1968 with the Architectural Barriers Act and culminated in 1990 with the ADA. In between came such legislative high points as Section 504 and P.L. 94–142. This body of laws departed significantly from previous policies because it sought not just to provide more "help" to persons regarded as disadvantaged by disability, but rather expressed and implemented a fundamental redefinition of "disability" as a social more than a medical problem.

The new-model policies coincided with, and to a degree reflected, the emergence of disability rights activism. Airline accessibility was only one of the issues spurring that activism. Deaf and disabled activists moved on everything from the presidency of Gallaudet University to the pervasive impact of telethons. But whatever the particular issue at hand, activists were redefining "disability" from the inside.

This activism was the political expression of an emerging consciousness among a younger generation of Americans with disabilities. A 1986 Louis Harris survey of adults with disabilities documented that generational shift in perspective. While only a minority of disabled adults over the age of 45 regarded people with disabilities as a minority group like blacks or Hispanics, 54 percent of those aged 18 to 44 agreed with the perspective. In addition, substantial majorities in every age bracket believed people with disabilities needed legal protection from discrimination, but the largest percentage of respondents holding that view was in the youngest age group, 18 to 30. Yet only one-third were aware of Section 504. It appeared that the great mass of disabled people had not yet become politically active. Their views reflected a proto-political consciousness, the emerging minority group consciousness of a new generation.

That younger generation has spurned institutionalized definitions of disability and of people with disabilities. At its core, the new consciousness has repudiated the reigning medical model, which defines "disability" as physiological pathologies located within individuals. That definition necessarily prescribes particular solutions: treatments or therapies to cure those individuals or to correct their vocational or social functioning. Cure or correction has been viewed as the only possible means by which people with disabilities could achieve social acceptance and social assimilation.

Those who are not cured or corrected have been defined as marginalized by disability. They have been relegated to invalidism. This has meant not just physical dependency or institutionalization, but, most fundamentally, social invalidation.

While the medical model claims to be scientific, objective, and humane, within its practice has lurked considerable ambivalence toward the people it professes to aid. In one respect, the medical model has been the institutionalized expression of societal anxieties about people who look different or function differently. It regards them as incompetent to manage their own lives, as needing professional, perhaps lifelong, supervision, perhaps even as dangerous to society.

The new disability perspective has presented a searching critique of the medical model. It has argued that by locating the problem in the bodies of individuals with disabilities, the medical model cannot account for, let alone combat, the bias and discrimination evident in such actions as the mistreatment and arrest of Nadine and Steven Jacobson. Indeed, disability rights advocates have argued that the implementation of the medical model in healthcare, social services, education, private charity, and public policies has institutionalized prejudice and discrimination. Far from being beneficial, or even neutral, the medical model has been at the core of the problem.

In the place of the medical model, activists have substituted a sociopolitical or minority group model of disability. "Disability," they have asserted, is primarily a socially constructed role. For the vast majority of people with disabilities, prejudice is a far greater problem than any impairment: discrimination is a bigger obstacle for them to "overcome" than any disability. The core of the problem, in the activists' view, has been historically deep-seated, socially pervasive, and powerfully institutionalized oppression of disabled people.

To combat this oppression, the disability movement not only called for legal protection against discrimination, it fashioned a new idea in American civil rights theory: the concept of equal access. Traditional rehabilitation policy defined accommodations such as architectural modifications, adaptive devices (wheelchairs, optical readers), and services (sign language interpreters) as special benefits to those who are fundamentally dependent. Disability rights ideology redefined them as merely different modes of functioning, and not inherently inferior.

Traditional civil rights theory permitted differential treatment of minorities only as a temporary expedient to enable them to achieve parity: Disability rights ideology claimed reasonable accommodations as legitimately permanent differential treatment because they are necessary to enable disabled persons to achieve and maintain equal access.

"Access" could have been limited to physical modifications in the personal living and work environments of disabled individuals. Instead, disability activists have pressed forward a broad concept of equal access that has sought to guarantee full participation in society. To ensure equal opportunity, they have declared, equal access and reasonable accommodations must be guaranteed in law as civil rights.

To nondisabled opponents, disabled activists have not sought equal opportunities, they have demanded special treatment. Disabled people could not, the critics have complained, on the one hand, claim equal opportunity and equal social standing, and, on the other, demand "special" privileges, such as accommodations and public financial aid (e.g., health insurance). Disabled people could not have it both ways. According to majority notions, equality has meant identical arrangements and treatment. It is not possible in American society to be equal and different, to be equal and disabled.

On this basic issue of the nature of equality and the means of accomplishing it, disabled activists and their nondisabled opponents have had radically different perceptions. And that difference was not new in the 1970s and '80s. It had a long history.

To take just one example, in 1949 a spokesman for the National Federation of the Blind testifying before a Congressional committee argued simultaneously for Aid to the Blind (ATB), a social welfare program of financial assistance, and for what today would be called civil rights. The disability of blindness was a physical condition that incurred significant expense and limitations, he argued, and therefore required societal aid. But it was also a social condition that involved discriminatory exclusion. He quoted the famous legal scholar and blind activist Jacobus ten Broek's "Bill of Rights for the Blind" to the effect that the real handicap [of] blindness, far surpassing its physical limitations, was "exclusion from the main channels of social and economic activity."

Throughout the history [of] disabled activism, advocates like this NFB spokesman simultaneously called for "social aid" and civil rights. Like their nondisabled opponents, they saw no contradiction in this position. It was possible in America, they implicitly proclaimed, to be equal and to require aid and accommodations, to be equal and different. Indeed, for Americans with disabilities, any other approach to equality seemed impossible.

The disability movement critique of the medical model has also argued that the complete medicalization of people with disabilities has advanced the agenda of professional interest groups. People with disabilities have served as a source of profit, power, and status.

An estimated 1.7 million mentally, emotionally, or physically disabled Americans have been defined as "incurable" and socially incompetent and have been relegated to medical warehouses. Another 10 to 11 million disabled adults, 70 percent of working-age adults with disabilities in the United States, are unemployed and welfare dependent, while uncounted others languish below the poverty line.

According to the disability movement analysis, the immediate causes of this marginalization have been public policies. Healthcare financing policies force disabled people into institutions and nursing homes rather than funding independent living. Income maintenance and public health insurance policies include "disincentives" that penalize disabled individuals for trying to work productively. Disabled adults have also been relegated to dependency because of continuing widespread inaccessibility and pervasive job market discrimination.

But according to this analysis, the ultimate cause of their marginalization is that people with disabilities are highly profitable. For that reason, they have been kept segregated in what is virtually a separate economy of disability. That economy is dominated by nondisabled interests: vendors of over-priced products and services; practitioners who drill disabled people in imitating the "able-bodied" and deaf people in mimicking the hearing; a nursing home industry that reaps enormous revenues from incarcerating people with disabilities.

Thus, concludes this analysis, millions of deaf and disabled people are held as permanent clients and patients. They are confined within a segregated economic and social system and to a socioeconomic condition of childlike dependency. Denied self-determination, they are schooled in social incompetency, and then their confinement to a socially invalidated role is justified by that incompetency. According to this critique, disabled issues are fundamentally issues of money and power.

The disability rights movement marked a revolt against this paternalistic domination and a demand for disabled and deaf self-determination. That revolt and that demand have been at the center of the controversy over telethons. Who should have the power to define the identities of people with disabilities and to determine what it is they really need? Or parallel to this dispute, how could the hearing majority on the Gallaudet University board of trustees reject two qualified deaf educators to select yet another hearing president? "Who has decided what the qualifications [for president] should be?" asked Gallaudet student government president Greg Hlibok. "Do white people speak for black people?" Hence the students' demand for a deaf majority on the board of trustees.

But the attack on the medical model has gone beyond merely questioning the motives of nondisabled interest groups. At a still deeper level, that critique has explained the relentless medicalization of people with disabilities as an attempt to resolve broader American cultural dilemmas. In a moment of intense social anxiety, it has helped reassure nondisabled people of their own wholeness as human beings, their own authenticity as Americans. It has done so by making "disability," and thus people with disabilities, the negation of full and valid American humanity.

In order for people with disabilities to be respected as worthy Americans, to be considered as whole persons or even approximations of persons, they have been instructed that they must perpetually labor to "overcome" their disabilities. They must display continuous cheerful striving toward some semblance of normality. The evidence of their moral and emotional health, of their quasi-validity as persons and citizens, has been their exhibition of the desire to become like nondisabled people. This is, of course, by definition, the very thing people with disabilities cannot become.

Thus, they have been required to pursue a "normality" that must forever elude them. They have been enticed into a futile quest by having dangled before them the ever-elusive carrot of social acceptance.

Recognition that "overcoming" is rooted in nondisabled interests and values marked the culmination of the ideological development of the disability movement's first phase. And that analytical achievement prepared the way for a transition into the second phase.

The first phase sought to move disabled people from the margins of society to the mainstream by demanding that discrimination be outlawed and that access and accommodations be mandated. The first phase argued for social inclusion. The second phase has asserted the necessity for self-definition. While the first phase rejected the medical model of disability, the second has repudiated the nondisabled majority norms that partly gave rise to the medical model.

That repudiation of dominant values has been most obvious in the rejections of the medically proclaimed need to be cured in order to be validated. At the time of the Gallaudet student revolt, Eileen Paul, cofounder of an organization called Deaf Pride, proclaimed, "This is a revolt against a system based on the assumption that deaf people have to become like hearing people and have to fit into the dominant hearing society."

As they spurned devaluing nondisabled definitions, deaf people and disabled people began to celebrate themselves. Coining self-affirming slogans such as "Disabled and Proud," "Deaf Pride," and "Disability Cool," they seized control of the definition of their identities. This has been not so much a series of personal choices as a collective process of reinterpreting themselves and their issues. It is a political and cultural task.

Beyond proclamations of pride, deaf and disabled people have been uncovering or formulating sets of alternative values derived from within the deaf and disabled experiences. Again, these have been collective rather than personal efforts. They involve not so much the statement of personal philosophies of life, as the assertion of group perspectives and values. This is a process of deaf cultural elaboration and of disabled culture building.

For example, some people with disabilities have been affirming the validity of values drawn from their own experience. Those values are markedly different from, and even opposed to, nondisabled majority values.

They declare that they prize not self-sufficiency but self-determination, not independence but interdependence, not functional separateness but personal connection, not physical autonomy but human community. This values formation takes disability as the starting point. It uses the disability experience as the source of values and norms.

The affirmation of disabled values also leads to a broad-ranging critique of nondisabled values. American culture is in the throes of an alarming and dangerous moral and social crisis, a crisis of values. The disability movement can advance a much-needed perspective on this situation, it can offer a critique of the hyperindividualistic majority norms institutionalized in the medical model and at the heart of the contemporary American crisis. That analysis needs to be made not just because majority values are impossible for people with disabilities to match up to, but more important, because they have proved destructive for everyone, disabled and nondisabled alike. They prevent real human connection and corrode authentic human community.

Another manifestation of the disability movement's analysis and critique has been the attempts over the past dozen years to develop "disability studies" within research universities. Every social movement needs sustained critical analysis of the social problems it is addressing. Such movements develop their own cadres of intellectuals and scholars who arise from the community and often connect it with academic institutions. Disability studies has been conceived as a bridge between the academy and the disability community.

But what should disability studies look like? Professor Simi Linton, a disabled scholar/activist, and her colleagues at Hunter College in New York have proposed a useful working definition of disability studies:

"Disability Studies reframes the study of disability by focusing on it as a social phenomenon, social construct, metaphor and culture, utilizing a minority group model. It examines ideas related to disability in all forms of cultural representation throughout history, and examines the policies and practices of all societies to understand the social, rather than physical and psychological, determinants of the experience of disability. Disability Studies both emanated from and supports the Disability Rights Movement, which advocated for civil rights and self-determination. The focus shifts the emphasis away from a prevention/treatment remediation paradigm, to a social/cultural/political paradigm. This shift does not signify a denial of the presence of impairments, nor a rejection of the utility of intervention and treatment. Instead, Disability Studies has been developed to disentangle impairments from the myth, ideology and stigma that influence social interaction and social policy. The scholarship challenges the idea that the economic and social status and the assigned roles of people with disabilities are inevitable outcomes of their condition."

This definition captures the fundamental features of disability studies as it has grown out of the disability rights movement.

If disability studies is to serve the disability community and movement effectively it needs to define an agenda. That project should include the following goals:

Disability studies should serve as an access ramp between the disability community and research universities. It must forge a fruitful connection between the disability community movement and such institutions.

The traffic of ideas and persons on that ramp should flow in both directions. It must be a two-way street. The disability perspective, the insights, experience, and expertise of people with disabilities, must inform research, producing new questions, generating new understandings.

At the same time, academic researchers can help bring new rigor to the disability rights movement's analysis and activism. Collaboration between scholars and advocates can produce a deeper critique of disability policy and the social arrangements that affect people with disabilities and can generate a more fully elaborated ideology of "disability" and disability rights.

Complementing these endeavors, disability studies should also forge a link with disabled artists and writers. This collaboration can support the current flowering of disability arts. It will also promote disability-based cultural studies that can uncover disabled values, explain the social/cultural construction of "disability" by the majority culture, and critique dominant nondisabled values.

To implement this agenda, disability studies must obtain support for faculty and graduate students. That support must come in two forms: funding to pay for research and teaching, and affirmative action to recruit faculty and students with disabilities to develop disability studies. We need to build a phalanx of disabled disability studies scholars and intellectuals.

To succeed and to remain true to its purpose, disability studies needs the active support and involvement of the disability community. Disability studies can then help advance both phases of the disability movement.

Those two phases are not separate and successive chronological periods. They are complementary aspects of the disability movement. The concept of equal access represents a politics of issues. It is the effort of Americans with disabilities to build an infrastructure of freedom and self-determination. The proclamation of disability and deaf pride and the elaboration of disability and deaf cultures express a politics of identity. It is an affirmation, a celebration of who we are, not despite disability or deafness, but precisely because of the disability and deaf experiences.

These two phases of the disability movement are reciprocal. Each is essential to the other. Together they declare who we are and where we intend to go.

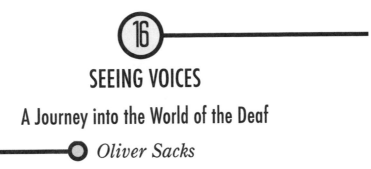

SEEING VOICES

A Journey into the World of the Deaf

Oliver Sacks

Wednesday morning, March 9, 1988: "Strike at Gallaudet," "Deaf Strike for the Deaf," "Students Demand Deaf President"—the media are full of these happenings today; they started three days ago, have been steadily building, and are now on the front page of the *New York Times*. It looks like an amazing story. I have been to Gallaudet University a couple of times in the past year, and have been steadily getting to know the place. Gallaudet is the only liberal arts college for the deaf in the world and is, moreover, the core of the world's deaf community but, in all its 124 years, it has never had a deaf president.

I flatten out the paper and read the whole story: the students have been actively campaigning for a deaf president ever since the resignation last year of Jerry Lee, a hearing person who had been president since 1984. Unrest, uncertainty, and hope have been brewing. By mid-February, the presidential

From Oliver Sacks, *Seeing Voices: A Journey into the World of the Deaf* (New York: Vintage Books, 1989). Used by permission of Vintage Books, a division of Random House, Inc.

search committee narrowed the search to six candidates—three hearing, three deaf. On March 1, three thousand people attended a rally at Gallaudet to make it clear to the board of trustees that the Gallaudet community was strongly insisting on the selection of a deaf president. On March 5, the night before the election, a candlelight vigil was held outside the board's quarters. On Sunday, March 6, choosing between three finalists, one hearing, two deaf, the board chose Elisabeth Ann Zinser, vice chancellor for Academic Affairs at the University of North Carolina at Greensboro—the hearing candidate.

The tone, as well as the content, of the board's announcement caused outrage: it was here that the chair of the board, Jane Bassett Spilman, made her comment that "the deaf are not yet ready to function in the hearing world." The next day, a thousand students marched to the hotel where the board was cloistered, then the six blocks to the White House, and on to the Capitol. The following day, March 8, the students closed the university and barricaded the campus.

Wednesday afternoon: The faculty and staff have come out in support of the students and their four demands: (1) that a new, *deaf* president be named immediately; (2) that the chair of the board, Jane Bassett Spilman, resign immediately; (3) that the board have a 51 percent majority of deaf members (at present it has seventeen hearing members and only four deaf); and (4) that there be no reprisals. At this point, I phone my friend Bob Johnson. Bob is head of the linguistics department at Gallaudet, where he has taught and done research for seven years. He has a deep knowledge of the deaf and their culture, is an excellent signer, and is married to a deaf woman. He is as close to the deaf community as a hearing person can be.[1] I want to know how he feels about the events at Gallaudet. "It's the most remarkable thing I've ever seen," he says. "If you'd asked me a month ago, I'd have bet a million dollars this couldn't happen in my lifetime. You've got to come down and see this for yourself."

*   *   *

When I had visited Gallaudet in 1986 and 1987, I found it an astonishing and moving experience. I had never before seen an entire community of the deaf, nor had I quite realized (even though I knew this theoretically) that Sign might indeed be a complete language—a language equally suitable for making love or speeches, for flirtation or mathematics. I had to see philosophy and chemistry classes in Sign; I had to see the absolutely silent mathematics department at work; to see deaf bards, Sign poetry, on the campus, and the range and depth of the Gallaudet theater; I had to see the wonderful social scene in the student bar, with hands flying in all directions as a hundred separate conversations proceeded. I had to see all this for myself before I could be moved from my previous "medical" view of deafness (as a "condition," a deficit that had to be treated) to a "cultural" view of the deaf as forming a community with a complete language and culture of its own. I had felt there was something very joyful, even Arcadian about Gallaudet and I was not surprised to hear that some of the students were occasionally reluctant to leave its warmth and seclusion and protectiveness, the coziness of a small but complete and self-sufficient world, for the unkind and uncomprehending big world outside.[2]

But there were also tensions and resentments under the surface, which seemed to be simmering, with no possibility of resolution. There was an unspoken tension between faculty and administration—a faculty in which many of the teachers sign and some are deaf.[3] The faculty could, to some extent, communicate with the students, enter their worlds, their minds; but the administration (so I was told) formed a remote governing body, running the school like a corporation, with a certain "benevolent" caretaker attitude to the "handicapped" deaf, but little real feeling for them as a community, as a culture. It was feared by the students and teachers I talked to that the administration, if it could, would reduce still further the percentage of deaf teachers at Gallaudet and further restrict the teachers' use of Sign there.

The students I met seemed animated, a lively group when together, but often fearful and diffident of the outside world. I had the feeling of some cruel undermining of self-image, even in those who professed "Deaf Pride." I had the feeling that some of them thought of themselves as children, an echo of the parental attitude of the board (and perhaps of some of the faculty). I had the feeling of a certain passivity among them, a sense that though life might be improved in small ways here and there, it was their lot to be overlooked, to be second-class citizens.

Thursday morning, March 10: A taxi deposits me on Fifth Street opposite the college. The gates have been blocked off for forty-eight hours; my first sight is of a huge, excited, but cheerful and friendly crowd of hundreds barring the entrance to the campus, carrying banners and placards, and signing to one another with great animation. One or two police cars sit parked outside, watching, their engines purring, but they seem a benign presence. There is a good deal of honking from the traffic passing by. I am puzzled by this, but then spot a sign reading "HONK FOR A DEAF PRESI-

DENT." The crowd itself is both strangely silent and noisy: the signing, the Sign speeches, are utterly silent; but they are punctuated by curious applause, an excited shaking of the hands above the head, accompanied by high-pitched vocalizations and screams.[4] As I watch, one of the students leaps up on a pillar and starts signing with much expression and beauty. I can understand nothing of what he says, but I feel the signing is pure and impassioned—his whole body, all his feelings, seem to flow into the signing. I hear a murmured name, Tim Rarus, and realize that this is one of the student leaders, one of the Four. His audience visibly hangs on every sign, rapt, bursting at intervals into tumultuous applause.

As I watch Rarus and his audience, and then let my gaze wander past the barricades to the great campus filled with passionate Sign, with passionate soundless conversation, I get an overwhelming feeling not only of another mode of communication but of another mode of sensibility, another mode of being. One has only to see the students, even casually, from the outside (and I felt quite as much an outsider as those who walked or drove casually by) to feel that in their language, their mode of being, they *deserve* one of their own, that no one not deaf, not signing, could possibly understand them. One feels, intuitively, that interpretation can never be sufficient, that the students would be cut off from any president who was not one of them.

Innumerable banners and signs catch the brilliant March sun: "DEAF PREZ NOW" is clearly the basic one. There is a certain amount of anger—it could hardly be otherwise—but the anger, on the whole, is clothed in wit: thus a common sign is "DR. ZINSER IS NOT READY TO FUNCTION IN THE DEAF WORLD," a retort to Spilman's malapropos statement about the deaf. Dr. Zinser's own comment on *Nightline* the night before ("A deaf individual, one day, will . . . be president of Gallaudet") has provoked many signs saying: "WHY NOT MARCH 10, 1988, DR. ZINSER?" The papers have spoken of "battle" or "confrontation," which gives a sense of a negotiation, an inching to and fro. But the students say: "Negotiation? We have forgotten the word. 'Negotiation' no longer appears in our dictionaries." Dr. Zinser keeps asking for a "meaningful dialogue," but this in itself seems a meaningless request, for there is no longer, there never has been, any intermediate ground on which "dialogue" could take place. The students are concerned with their identity, their survival, an all-or-none: they have four demands, and there is no place for "sometime" or "maybe."

Indeed Dr. Zinser is anything but popular. It is felt by many not only that she is peculiarly insensitive to the mood of the students—the glaring fact that they do not want her, that the university has been literally barricaded against her—but that she actively stands for and prosecutes an official "hard line." At first there was a certain sympathy for her: she had been duly chosen and she had no idea what she had been thrown into. But with the passing of each day this view grew less and less tenable, and the whole business began to resemble a contest of wills. Dr. Zinser's tough, "no-nonsense" stance reached a peak yesterday, when she loudly asserted that she was going to "take charge" of the unruly campus. "If it gets any further out of control," she said, "I'm going to have to take action to bring it under control." This incensed the students, who promptly burned her in effigy.

Some of the placards are nakedly furious: one says "ZINSER—PUPPET OF SPILMAN," another "WE DON'T NEED A WET NURSE, MOMMY SPILMAN." I begin to realize that this is the deaf's coming of age, saying at last, in a very loud voice: "We're no longer your children. We no longer want your 'care.'"[5]

I edge past the barricades, the speeches, the signs, and stroll onto the large and beautifully green campus, with its great Victorian buildings setting off a most un-Victorian scene. The campus is buzzing, visibly, with conversation. Everywhere there are pairs or small groups signing. There is conversing everywhere, and I can understand none of it; *I* feel like the deaf, the voiceless one today—the handicapped one, the minority, in this great signing community. I see lots of faculty as well as students on the campus: one professor is making and selling lapel buttons ("Frau Zinser, Go Home!"), which are bought and pinned on as quickly as he makes them. "Isn't this great?" he says, catching sight of me. "I haven't had such a good time since Selma. It feels a little like Selma and the Sixties."

A great many dogs are on the campus. There must be fifty or sixty on the great greensward out front. Regulations on owning and keeping dogs here are loose; some are "hearing ear" dogs, but some are just dogs. I see one girl signing to her dog; the dog, obediently, turns over, begs, gives a paw. This dog itself bears a white cloth sign on each side: "I UNDERSTAND SIGN BETTER THAN SPILMAN." (The chair of Gallaudet's board of trustees has occupied her position for seven years while learning hardly any Sign.)

Where there was a hint of something angry, tense, at the barricades, there is an atmosphere of calm and peacefulness inside; more, a sense of joy, and something like festivity. There are dogs everywhere, and babies and children too, friends and families everywhere, conversing volubly in Sign. . . . It is rather like Woodstock, much more like Woodstock than a grim revolution.

Earlier in the week, the initial reactions to Elisabeth Ann Zinser's appointment were furious and uncoordinated; there were a thousand individuals on the campus, milling around, tearing up toilet paper, destructive in mood. But all at once, as Bob Johnson said, "the whole consciousness changed." Within hours there seemed to emerge a new, calm, clear consciousness and resolution; a political body, two thousand strong, with a single, focused will of its own. It was the astonishing swiftness with which this organization emerged, the sudden precipitation, from chaos, of a unanimous, communal mind, that astonished everyone who saw it. And yet, of course, this was partly an illusion, for there were all sorts of preparations and people behind it.

Central to this sudden "transformation" and central, thereafter, in organizing and articulating the entire "uprising" (which was far too dignified, too beautifully modulated, to be called an "uproar") were the four remarkable young student leaders: Greg Hlibok, the leader of the student body, and his cohorts Tim Rarus, Bridgetta Bourne, and Jerry Covell. Greg Hlibok is a young engineering student, described (by Bob Johnson) as "very engaging, laconic, direct, but in his words a great deal of thought and judgment." Hlibok's father, who is also deaf, runs an engineering firm; his deaf mother, Peggy O'Gorman, is active in lobbying for the educational use of ASL; and he has two deaf brothers, one an actor, one a financial consultant. Tim Rarus, also born deaf, and from a deaf family, is a perfect foil for Greg: he has an eager spontaneity, a passion, an intensity, that nicely complements Greg's quietness. The four had already been elected before the uprising—indeed while Jerry Lee was still president—but have taken on a very special, unprecedented role since President Lee's resignation.

Hlibok and his fellow student leaders have not incited or inflamed students. On the contrary, they are calming, restraining, and moderating in their influence, but have been highly sensitive to the "feel" of the campus and, beyond this, of the deaf community at large, and have felt with them that a crucial time has arrived. They have organized the students to press for a deaf president, but they have not done this alone: behind them there has been the active support of alumni, and of deaf organizations and leaders all around the country. Thus, much calculation, much preparation, preceded the "transformation," the emergence of a communal mind. It is not an order appearing from total chaos (even though it might seem so). Rather, it is the sudden manifestation of a latent order, like the sudden crystallization of a supersaturated solution—a crystallization precipitated by the naming of Zinser as president on Sunday night. This is a qualitative transformation, from passivity to activity, and in the moral no less than in the political sense, it is a revolution. Suddenly the deaf are no longer passive, scattered, and powerless; suddenly they have discovered the calm strength of union.

In the afternoon I recruit an interpreter and with her help interview a couple of deaf students. One of them tells me:

> I'm from a hearing family . . . my whole life I've felt pressures, hearing pressures on me—"You can't *do* it in the hearing world, you can't *make* it in the hearing world"—and right now all that pressure is lifted from me. I feel free, all of a sudden, full of energy now. You keep hearing "you can't, you can't," but I *can* now. The words "deaf and dumb" will be destroyed forever; instead there'll be "deaf and able."

These were very much the terms Bob Johnson had used when we first talked, when he spoke of the deaf as laboring under "an illusion of powerlessness," and of how, all of a sudden, this illusion had been shattered.

*   *   *

. . . Far from being childlike or incompetent, as they were "supposed" to be (and as so often they supposed themselves to be), the students at Gallaudet showed high competence in managing the March revolt. This impressed me especially when I wandered into the communications room, the nerve center of Gallaudet during the strike, with its central office filled with TTY-equipped telephones.[6] Here the deaf students contacted the press and television, invited them in, gave interviews, compiled news, issued press releases, round the clock, masterfully; here they raised funds for a "Deaf Prez Now" campaign; here they solicited, successfully, support from Congress, presidential candidates, union leaders. They gained the world's ear, at this extraordinary time, when they needed it.

Even the administration listened—so that after four days of seeing the students as foolish and rebellious children who needed to be brought into line, Dr. Zinser was forced to pause, to listen, to reexamine her own long-held assumptions, to see things in a new light and, finally, to resign. She did so in terms that were moving and seemed genuine, saying that neither she nor the board had anticipated the fervor and commitment of the protestors, or that their protest was the leading edge of a burgeoning national movement for deaf rights. "I have responded to this extraordinary social movement of deaf people," she said as she tendered her resignation on the night of March 10 and spoke of coming to see this as "a very special moment in time," one that was "unique, a civil rights moment in history for deaf people."

*   *   *

Friday, March 11: The mood on campus is completely transformed. A battle has been won. There is elation. More battles have to be fought. Placards with the students' four demands have been replaced with placards saying "3½," because the resignation of Dr. Zinser only goes halfway toward meeting the first demand, that there be a deaf president immediately. But there is also a gentleness that is new, the tension and anger of Thursday have gone, along with the possibility of a drawn-out, humiliating defeat. A largeness of spirit is everywhere apparent—released now, I partly feel, by the grace and the words with which Zinser resigned, words in which she aligned herself with, and wished the best for, what she called an "extraordinary social movement."

Support is coming in from every quarter: three hundred deaf students from the National Technical Institute for the Deaf arrive, elated and exhausted, after a fifteen-hour bus ride from Rochester, New York. Deaf schools throughout the country are closed in total support. Deaf people flood in from every state. I see signs from Iowa and Alabama, from Canada, from South America, as well as from Europe, even from New Zealand. Events at Gallaudet have dominated the national press for forty-eight hours. Virtually every car going past Gallaudet honks now, and the streets are filled with supporters as the time for the march on the Capitol comes near. And yet, for all the honking, the speeches, the banners, the pickets, an extraordinary atmosphere of quietness and dignity prevails.

Noon: There are now about twenty-five hundred people, a thousand students from Gallaudet and the rest supporters, as we start on a slow march to the Capitol. As we walk a wonderful sense of quietness grows, which puzzles me. It is not wholly physical (indeed, there is rather a lot of noise in a way—the ear-splitting yells of the deaf, as a start), and I decide it is, rather, the quietness of a moral drama. The sense of history in the air gives it this strange quietness.

Slowly, for there are children, babes-in-arms, and some physically disabled among us (some deaf-blind, some ataxic, and some on crutches) slowly, and with a mixed sense of resolve and festivity, we walk to the

Capitol, and there, in the clear March sun that has shone the entire week, we unfurl banners and raise pickets. One great banner says, "WE STILL HAVE A DREAM," and another, with the individual letters carried by fourteen people, simply says: "HELP US CONGRESS."

. . . There are many speeches—from Greg Hlibok, from some of the faculty, from congressmen and senators. I listen for a while:

> It is an irony [says one, a professor at Gallaudet] that Gallaudet has never had a deaf chief executive officer. Virtually every black college has a black president, testimony that black people are leading themselves. Virtually every women's college has a woman as president, as testimony that women are capable of leading themselves. It's long past time that Gallaudet had a deaf president as testimony that deaf people are leading themselves.

I let my attention wander, taking in the scene as a whole: thousands of people, each intensely individual, but bound and united with a single sentiment. After the speeches, there is a break of an hour, during which a number of people go in to see congressmen. But most of the group, who have brought packed lunches in on their backs, now sit and eat and talk, or rather sign, in the great plaza before the Capitol and this, for me, as for all those who have come or chanced to see it, is one of the most wonderful scenes of all. For here are a thousand or more people signing freely, in a public place, not privately, at home, or in the enclosure of Gallaudet, but openly and unself-consciously, and beautifully, before the Capitol.

The press has reported all the speeches, but missed what is surely equally significant. They failed to give the watching world an actual vision of the fullness and vividness, the unmedical life, of the deaf. And once more, as I wander among the huge throng of signers, as they chat over sandwiches and sodas before the Capitol, I find myself remembering the words of a deaf student at the California School for the Deaf, who had signed on television:

> We are a unique people, with our own culture, our own language—American Sign Language, which has just recently been recognized as a language in itself—and that sets us apart from hearing people.

. . . *Sunday evening, March 13*: The board met today, for nine hours. There were nine hours of tension, waiting . . . no one knowing what was to come. Then the door opened, and Philip Bravin, one of the four deaf board members and known to all the deaf students, appeared. His appearance, and not Spilman's, already told the story, before he made his revelations in Sign. He was speaking now, he signed, as chair of the board, for Spilman had resigned. And his first task now, with the board behind him, was the happy one of announcing that King Jordan had been elected the new president.

King Jordan, deafened at the age of twenty-one, has been at Gallaudet for fifteen years; he is dean of the School of Arts and Sciences, a popular, modest, and unusually sane man, who at first supported Zinser when she was selected.[7] Greatly moved, Jordan, in simultaneous Sign and speech, says:

> I am *thrilled* to accept the invitation of the board of trustees to become the president of Gallaudet University. This is a historic moment for deaf people around the world. This week we can truly say that we together, united, have overcome our reluctance to stand for our rights. The world has watched the deaf community come of age. We will no longer accept limits on what we can achieve. The highest praise goes to the students of Gallaudet for showing us exactly even now how one can seize an idea with such force that it becomes a reality.

With this, the dam bursts, and jubilation bursts out everywhere. As everyone returns to Gallaudet for a final, triumphal meeting, Jordan says, "They know now that the cap on what they can achieve has been lifted. We know that deaf people can do anything hearing people can except hear." And Hlibok, hugging Jordan, adds, "We have climbed to the top of the mountain, and we have climbed together."

Monday, March 14: Gallaudet looks normal on the surface. The barricades have been taken down, the campus is open. The "uprising" has lasted exactly one week. . . . "It took seven days to create the world; it took us seven days to change it." This was the joke of the students, flashed in Sign from one end of the campus to another. And with this feeling they took their spring break, going back to their families throughout the country, carrying the euphoric news and mood with them.

But objective change, historical change, does not happen in a week, even though its first prerequisite, "the transformation of consciousness," may happen, as it did, in a day. "Many of the students," Bob Johnson told me, "don't realize the extent and the time that are going to be involved in changing, though they do have a sense now of their strength and power. . . . The structure of oppression is so deeply engrained."

And yet there are beginnings. There is a new "image" and a new movement, not merely at Gallaudet but throughout the deaf world. News reports, especially on television, have made the deaf articulate and visible across the entire nation. But the profoundest effect, of course, has been on the deaf themselves. It has welded them into a community, a worldwide community, as never before.

NOTES

1. One can be very close to (if not actually a member of) the deaf community without being deaf. The most important prerequisite besides a knowledge of and sympathy for deaf people is being a fluent user of Sign: perhaps the only hearing people who are ever considered full members of the deaf community are the hearing children of deaf parents for whom Sign is a native language. This is the case with Dr. Henry Klopping, the much-loved superintendent of the California School for the Deaf in Fremont. One of his former students, talking to me at Gallaudet, signed, "He is Deaf, even though he is hearing."

2. The deaf world, like all subcultures, is formed partly by exclusion (from the hearing world), and partly by the formation of a community and a world around a different center, its own center. To the extent that the deaf feel excluded, they may feel isolated, set apart, discriminated against. To the extent that they form a deaf world, voluntarily, for themselves, they are at home in it, enjoy it, see it as a haven and a buffer. In this aspect the deaf world feels self-sufficient, not isolated. It has no wish to assimilate or be assimilated; on the contrary, it cherishes its own language and images, and wishes to protect them.

One aspect of this is the so-called diglossia of the deaf. Thus a group of deaf people, at Gallaudet or elsewhere, converse in Sign among themselves; but if a hearing person should enter, they at once switch to signed English (or whatever) for a time, returning to Sign as soon as he is gone. ASL is often treated as an intimate and highly personal possession, to be shielded from intrusive or foreign eyes. Barbara Kannapell has gone so far as to suggest that if we all learned Sign, this would destroy the deaf world. See Barbara Kannapell, "Personal Awareness and Advocacy in the Deaf Community," in *Sign Language and the Deaf Community*, ed. C. Baker and R. Battison (Silver Spring, MD: National Association of the Deaf, 1980), p. 112.

3. Even those teachers who sign tend, however, to use a form of signed English rather than ASL. Except in the mathematical faculty, where a majority of the teachers are deaf, only a minority of the faculty now at Gallaudet is deaf—whereas in Edward Gallaudet's day a majority were deaf. This, alas, is still the case generally

with regard to the education of the deaf. There are very few deaf teachers of the deaf; and ASL, for the most part, is either not known to, or not used by, hearing teachers.

4. Although the deaf are sometimes supposed to *be* silent, as well as to inhabit a world of silence, this may not be the case. They can, if they wish to, yell very loudly, and may do this to arouse the attention of others. If they speak, they may speak very loudly, and with very poor modulation, since they cannot monitor their own voices by ear. Finally, they may have unconscious and often very energetic vocalizations of various sorts, accidental or inadvertent movements of the vocal apparatus, neither intended nor monitored, tending to accompany emotion, exercise, and excited communication.

5. This resentment of "paternalism" (or "mommyism") is very evident in the special edition of the students' newspaper (the *Buff and Blue*) published on March 9, in which there is a poem entitled "Dear Mom." This starts:

> *Poor mommy Bassett-Spilman*
> *How her children do rebel,*
> *If only they would listen*
> *To the story she would tell*

and continues in this vein for thirteen verses. (Spilman had appeared on television, pleading for Zinser, saying, "Trust us—she will not disappoint you.") Copies of this poem had been reproduced by the thousand. One could see them fluttering all over campus.

6. It should not be thought that even the most avid signer is against other modes of communication when necessary. Life for deaf people has been altered immensely by various technical devices in the past twenty years, such as close-captioned TV, and teletypewriters (TTY; now TDD, or telecommunication devices for the deaf)—devices that would have delighted Alexander Graham Bell (who had originally invented the telephone, partly, as an aid for the deaf). The 1988 strike at Gallaudet could hardly have got going without such devices, which the students exploited brilliantly.

7. Although the choice of King Jordan delighted almost everyone, one faction saw his election as a compromise (since he was postlingually deaf), and supported instead Harvey Corson, superintendent of the Louisiana School for the Deaf, and the third finalist, who is both prelingually deaf and a native signer.

17

A PSYCHOLOGICAL VIEW OF DISABILITY CULTURE

Carol J. Gill

A s I am not an anthropologist, sociologist, or historian, I make no claim to understanding culture from any of those perspectives. As a psychologist, however, I have become interested in the impact of culture on the emotional well-being of individuals. Moreover, my interest is deepened by my own minority group membership (Disabled people).

My former work as a clinical psychologist spanned sixteen years and hundreds of clients ranging in age from adolescence through end-of-life, both with disabilities and without. Having conducted my doctoral research on identity development, I was often concerned with the pressures and rewards of minority group identity in my clients. Particularly, I was impressed by the way cultural affiliation mediated the effects of social devaluation in persons from the African American, Latino, Asian, non-Christian, and gay communities.

In the mid-1980s, I accepted an invitation to attend Shabbat at a Jewish temple recognized for its efforts to integrate people with disabilities into its

From Carol J. Gill, "A Psychological View of Disability Culture," *Disability Studies Quarterly* 15 (Fall 1995): 16–19. Copyright © 1995 by *Disability Studies Quarterly*. Reprinted with permission of the publisher.

activities. It turned out to be a great opportunity for an "outsider" like me to learn more about Jewish cultural expression. The evening left an indelible mark. I saw how re-telling history and folklore, explaining symbols, sharing rituals, teaching customs to children, and how eating, laughing, weeping, embracing, and singing together united and fortified a diverse minority community in the space of three hours!

That year, I also attended an incredible disability community event in Southern California: the mournful yet triumphant commemoration of the annihilation of more than two hundred thousand Disabled people in Hitler's Germany. A Deaf survivor of the holocaust recounted the horror and destruction of her people. We (Deaf, physically and cognitively Disabled participants) lit candles, told the story, viewed the photos, cried together, and proclaimed to each other "Never again!" It was the first official Disabled people's cultural event I had ever attended.

Also that year, I began to present publicly my thoughts about disability culture. I addressed a chapter meeting of the California Association of the Physically Handicapped (CAPH).

Using a family model to describe our orphanlike dependence on an arrogant, rejecting able-centric parent culture, I suggested to the twenty-some assembled members that we could oppose our social devaluation through developing a strong disability community-family and elaborating a proud disability culture. To my amazement, the majority of my audience broke into tears. They spontaneously took turns describing their ideal of a disability culture and how it would heal them.

A few months later, I did the cover-featured interview with *Disability Rag* on the benefits of focusing on disability culture. It failed to generate much direct reader response, but Disabled people across the country still pull that issue out of their briefcases and wheelchair bags to show me that they've kept it.

THE FUNCTIONS OF A DISABILITY CULTURE

From the time of the CAPH speech, I have focused on four major functions served by the development of a disability culture.

1) Fortification—The definition and expression of our value as a community charges us up and enriches our lives, giving us energy and endurance against oppression.

2) Unification—As we hear ad nauseam, people with disabilities are a heterogeneous community encompassing different ages, races, genders, socioeconomic statuses, etc. The expression of our beliefs and heritage in cultural activities, however, brings us together, encourages mutual support, and underscores our common values.

3) Communication—Our developing art, language, symbols, and rituals help us articulate to the world and signal to each other who we are as a distinct people.

4) Recruitment—The expression of our culture is a positive and defiant conversion of our social marginalization into a celebration of our distinctness. It encourages people with disabilities (particularly new and young Disabled persons) to "come out" as part of the community, allowing them finally to integrate their disabilities into their individual identities and offering them a sense of group "belonging."

CORE VALUES

I have been constructing a list of the core values of the disability culture—the values that undergird our political struggles that are reflected in our art, conversations, goals, and behaviors. They include:

1) An acceptance of human differences (e.g., physical, functional, racial, intellectual, economic/class).

2) A matter-of-fact orientation toward helping; an acceptance of human vulnerability and interdependence as part of life.

3) A tolerance for lack of resolution, for dealing with the unpredictable and living with unknowns or less-than-desired outcomes.

4) Disability humor—the ability to laugh at the oppressor and our own situations, to find something absurdly hilarious in almost anything, however dire.

5) Skill in managing multiple problems, systems, technology, and assistants.

6) A sophisticated future orientation; an ability to construct complex plans taking into account multiple contingencies and realistically anticipated obstacles.

7) A carefully honed capacity for closure in interpersonal communication; the ability to read others' attitudes and conflicts in order to sort

out, fill in the gaps, and grasp the latent meaning in contradictory social messages.

8) A flexible, adaptive approach to tasks; a creativity stimulated by both limited resources and experience with untraditional modes of operating.

DISABILITY CULTURE—WHAT IS IT?

It is not simply the shared experience of oppression. If that were all our culture was, I would agree with those who doubt the probability of a disability culture. The elements of our culture include, certainly, our longstanding social oppression, but also our emerging art and humor, our piecing together of our history, our evolving language and symbols, our remarkably unified worldview, beliefs, and values, and our strategies for surviving and thriving. I use the word "remarkably" because I find that the most compelling evidence of a disability culture is the vitality and universality of these elements despite generations of crushing poverty, social isolation, lack of education, silencing, imposed immobility, and relentless instruction in hating ourselves and each other.

Our culture has been submerged by the profundity of our oppression and the forces that have divided us from each other. But any time disabled people have been able to come together, culture has flourished—in hospital wards, in special schools, at charity camps, during sit-ins, during creative workshops, in peer-support groups, in the hotel corridors of disability conferences, in jail. Furthermore, these scattered spurts of cultural development bear a significant resemblance to each other. For example, a Disabled woman in the Southern states described the themes of her childhood play with other Disabled girls in an orthopedic hospital. She recalled the creativity, cooperation, and multilevel humor satirizing the nondisabled culture that she and her playmates employed to cope with their marginalization and to promote group spirit. Her story was remarkably similar to that of a Disabled friend from Scandinavia.

At the Society for Disability Studies in 1994, Larry Voss and I quoted interview responses from Disabled adult participants in our education study. Afterward, we were swamped by members of the audience from across the United States and from Japan and Canada who said their experiences and interpretations of those experiences had been virtually identical to our interviewees.

The disability rights and independent living movements have accelerated the transmission of our culture. As I travel around the country or speak by phone to Disabled persons overseas, I am struck by the common usage and understanding of such terms as "AB," "supercrip," "overcoming," "medical model," and such concepts as crip time [a flexible standard for punctuality], normalization, and passing. Our emotional reactions and beliefs regarding issues such as eugenic abortion, nursing homes, community access, entitlement to accommodation, media images, and "special" anything are becoming universal. This is due, I believe, not only to our exchange of more information, but also to our transmission of values about life with a disability.

Maybe "culture" is not the proper term for a set of elements deriving from a mixture of: 1) inherent differences; 2) societal treatment; and 3) transmitted facts, interpretations, and preferences. But what better term is there for that collection of common views and expressions that increasingly characterize Disabled people everywhere? What else do you call that familiar, comfortable rhythm of shared meanings that Disabled people, even strangers, fall into when they meet? That wide-ranging compatibility is difficult to convey to those outside of our community, however sensitive they may be to disability rights issues. (Maybe that is one reason that some of our most aware non-disabled allies and Disabled persons who are fighting hard to "make it" in the majority culture oppose the notion of disability culture.) Several Disabled individuals I know have independently referred to that in-sync feeling (when in the company of other Disabled persons) as "coming home."

I have also noticed that once we began to attach to these common elements the label "culture," Disabled people of all kinds began to rally behind it with a fervor I have rarely seen. In less than a decade, "disability culture" has become a popular term among our people whether activist or not, young or old, scholarly or undereducated. I detect an underlying assertion in this embrace of the term that goes something like, "Yes, we have learned something important about life from being Disabled that makes us unique yet affirms our common humanity. We refuse any longer to hide our differences. Rather, we will explore, develop, and celebrate our distinctness and offer its lessons to the world."

IV

DISABILITY, SOCIAL POLICY, AND CITIZENSHIP

MODELS OF DISABILITY AND THE AMERICANS WITH DISABILITIES ACT

Richard K. Scotch *

I. INTRODUCTION

For nearly a decade, the Americans with Disabilities Act (ADA)[1] has been the main protection for people with disabilities against discrimination in employment, public accommodations, public transportation, and telecommunications.[2] The act, approved by bipartisan majorities of 377–28 and 91–6 in the House of Representatives and the Senate (respectively) in 1990,[3] is a comprehensive statement of public policy that people with disabilities should not be unfairly excluded from employment, public accommodations, and other aspects of public life, and that the federal government should act to protect them.[4]

One might expect that if the ADA represented a consensus in 1990, it

*The author would like to thank Marvin Dunson III for his comments and assistance in the preparation of this article.

171

would still enjoy widespread support today, and in fact, there have been no serious attempts in Congress to repeal or legislatively limit the act. However, while popular criticism of the ADA persists,[5] the legal system has become the primary arena for challenges to the ADA's broad focus and underlying assumptions. Complaints filed under the ADA have been making their way through the administrative agencies responsible for implementation and the courts for several years now. In early 1999, the Supreme Court heard five ADA cases, and a major issue in several of these cases was the act's definition of disability.[6]

In this article, I suggest that much of the larger disagreement over the Americans with Disabilities Act can be characterized as a clash of perspectives about the meaning of disability. I do not address the specifics of statutory interpretation . . . rather, I suggest how underlying assumptions about disability frame the current debate over the ADA.

II. DISABILITY AS A SOCIOPOLITICAL CONSTRUCT

Opinions about the Americans with Disabilities Act depend to a large extent on how one defines disability and the nature of the problems faced by people who have disabilities. The ADA was the culmination of a two-decade shift in federal disability policy.[7] For over a hundred years, disability has been defined in predominantly medical terms as a chronic functional incapacity whose consequence was functional limitations assumed to result from physical or mental impairment.[8] This model assumed that the primary problem faced by people with disabilities was the incapacity to work and otherwise participate in society.[9] It further assumed that such incapacity was the natural product of their impairments, and to some extent their own "secondary" psychological reactions to their impairments. The corollary to this assumption was that the role of government in assisting people with disabilities was both to provide financial support to this deserving group, who could not support themselves through no fault of their own, and to help in the repair and rehabilitation of their damaged bodies and minds and any psychosocial incapacity accompanying the damage.[10]

In the late 1960s, a fundamental transformation occurred in federal disability policy that rejected a primarily medical/clinical model of disability and substituted a sociopolitical or minority group model.[11] Under this model, people with disabilities may be seen as a minority group subject to unfair discrimination, and the role of government is to protect their civil rights to political, economic, and social participation by eliminating that discrimination.[12] In such a formulation, the opportunities of people with disabilities are limited far more by a discriminatory environment than by their impairments.

In the sociopolitical model, disability is viewed not as a physical or mental impairment, but as a social construction shaped by environmental factors, including physical characteristics built into the environment, cultural attitudes and social behaviors, and the institutionalized rules, procedures, and practices of private entities and public organizations. All of these, in turn, reflect overly narrow assumptions about what constitutes the normal range of human functioning.[13]

Thus, the consequences of physical and mental impairments for social participation are shaped by the expectations and attitudes of the larger society. Michael Oliver, a leading British disability studies scholar, writes:

> All disabled people experience disability as social restriction, whether those restrictions occur as a consequence of inaccessibly built environments, questionable notions of intelligence and social competence, the inability of the general population to use sign language, the lack of reading material in [B]raille or hostile public attitudes to people with non-visible disabilities.[14]

Assumptions about how people perform everyday tasks, or about what people can and cannot do without assistance, are built into human environments in ways that can create barriers for those who do not conform to such expectations. If architecture and technology are based on limited images of "normal" physical functioning, they constrain individuals who must pursue alternative ways of performing various tasks. Stairs can limit the entry of people who use wheelchairs; printed words limit those who are blind. Similarly, organizational routines and public policies may limit participation through their assumptions about "normal" functioning. Fixed work schedules may exclude people whose conditions make it difficult for them to start work at 8 a.m., or who must take more frequent time off. Eligibility requirements for public assistance may assume that potential beneficiaries either are disabled and cannot work, or can work and therefore are not disabled. Thus, people with disabilities are frequently marginalized by the constraints of a constructed social environment in which assumptions of the inability to participate become self-fulfilling prophecies.

Building on this social model of disability is the assertion that, because they collectively occupy a stigmatized social position, people with disabilities occupy a social status analogous to that of racial and ethnic minorities.[15] People with disabilities share many of the stigmatizing experiences and characteristics of other groups commonly recognized as minorities. They are subject to prejudiced attitudes, discriminatory behavior, and institutional and legal constraints that parallel those experienced by African Americans and other disadvantaged and excluded groups.[16] People with disabilities are victimized by negative stereotypes that associate physical or mental impairments with assumed dependence on others and a general incapacity to perform social and economic activities.[17] Such stigmatizing assumptions can result in exclusion and social isolation, including lack of access to employment, public facilities, voting, and other forms of civic involvement.[18] Because of these factors, people with disabilities are denied the opportunity to fully participate in society, a form of exclusion which public policy has defined as discrimination.[19] Using the Civil Rights Act of 1964 as its legislative model, the ADA seeks to eliminate this discrimination.[20] The sociologist Paul Higgins writes of the broad goals of the ADA:

> Rather than (primarily) looking to individual characteristics to understand the difficulties experienced by people with disabilities, rights encourage us, even require us, to evaluate our practices that may limit people with disabilities. Rights empower people with disabilities. With rights, people with disabilities may legitimately contest what they perceive to be illegitimate treatment of them. No longer must they endure arrangements that disadvantage them to the advantage of nondisabled citizens.[21]

The ADA can be seen as more than a specific protection from discrimination—it is also a policy commitment to the social inclusion of people with disabilities. In 1986, the National Council of the Handicapped, a presidentially appointed advisory body, issued a report entitled *Toward Independence* that helped lay the groundwork for the development of the ADA.[22] The report stated that:

> [Preceding] handicap nondiscrimination laws fail to serve the central purpose of any human rights law—providing a strong statement of a societal imperative. An adequate equal opportunity law for persons with disabilities will seek to obtain the voluntary compliance of the great majority of law-abiding citizens by notifying them that discrimination against persons with disabilities will no longer be tolerated by our society.[23]

Similarly, in the introduction to her authoritative, edited volume written immediately after the ADA's passage, Jane West wrote:

> The ADA is a law that sends a clear message about what our society's attitudes should be toward persons with disabilities. The ADA is an orienting framework that can be used to construct a comprehensive service-delivery system. . . . The ADA is intended to open the doors of society and keep them open.[24]

III. THE CONSEQUENCES OF A SOCIOPOLITICAL MODEL OF DISABILITY

Because of the ADA's reliance on a sociopolitical model of disability, it does not employ a simple conception of who is to be considered to have a disability and under what circumstances the treatment given a person with a disability should be considered discriminatory. The sociopolitical model provides a complex view of disability and disability-related discrimination by focusing upon the relationship between an individual's impairment and the nature of the environment in which that individual must function. For example, the employment provisions of the ADA define a qualified person with a disability in terms of her ability to perform the essential functions of a job with or without reasonable accommodation.[25] This definition relies on an analysis of the characteristics of the job as well as the characteristics of the person seeking the job.[26] As the statute is applied, the perceptions and expectations associated with disability and work help to shape judgments about the capacity of persons with a disability to perform adequately within specific environments.

Because of this reliance upon knowledge of the environment, the application of the ADA to specific situations may not embody a clear, abstract, behavioral standard of differential treatment. While the statute provides a number of specific examples of disability-related discrimination[27] and of reasonable accommodation,[28] the complexity of disability[29] and of workplaces[30] may mean that the ADA will lead to a wide variety of resolutions based on specific combinations of individual impairments, potential environmental obstacles, and possible adaptations by the person with the impairment. The application of ADA criteria will almost inevitably vary among individuals and across various social settings, and may pose unusual problems of interpretation for federal regulators and the courts. Paul Hearne, the director of the National Council on Disability from 1988 to 1989, writes that "[t]he required type of accommodation will obviously vary with the individual employee, the requirements—and the purposes—of a particular job, and the environment of each workplace."[31]

Applying the requirements of the ADA was intended by its framers to change assumptions about how specific physical or mental impairments affect functioning.[32] Yet if the marginalization of people with disabilities is the result of social processes that are embedded in our culture, then it is not surprising that governmental and legal institutions as well have employed a traditional medical model of disability based on incapacity that focuses on the limitations of plaintiffs with disabilities in their application of the ADA.[33] Public officials and the courts frequently mirror well-established limiting assumptions about people with disabilities.[34] The statute's broad definitions of who has a legitimate disability, what constitutes discrimination on the basis of disability, and what remedies are appropriate in countering such discrimination may be at odds with popular understandings of who should be treated as "truly" disabled, what their problems are, and what protections they deserve from regulators and the courts.

Further, the flexibility written into the statute may have led to a greater reliance on popular and limited conceptions of what people with various impairments can and should be allowed to do. Donald O. Parsons wrote shortly after the ADA's passage:

> The human factor is likely to affect judicial behavior. . . . Cases that are either factually ambiguous or highly emotional are likely to be determined primarily by judicial preference. . . . How a judge views such cases will vary from judge to judge.[35]

IV. THE CONSERVATIVE CRITIQUE: ECONOMIC AND MORAL DIMENSIONS OF DISABILITY

Critics in Congress, academia, and the media have attacked the ADA's mandates, expressing skepticism over the validity of the claims of those seeking protection from discrimination related to disability and the efficacy of a civil rights (as opposed to a market) approach to improving the status of people with disabilities.[36] To critics, the ADA is a case of ill-considered social engineering in which an overly broad category of putative victims claimed unreasonable accommodations from society. For example, Dick Armey, Republican House Majority Leader [1995–2003], has called the ADA "a disaster," predicting that, "Under my majority leadership, the disabilities act will be revisited and will be written properly so its focus and intent goes to people with genuine disabilities."[37]

As discussed above, the medical model of disability characterizes people with disabilities as having pathological individual attributes, typically linked to incapacity and dependence, which in turn may lead to social and economic isolation. This model can accommodate recognition of discrimination as a problem associated with disability, but it emphasizes that people with disabilities must "overcome" the limitations of their impairments in order to function in society. By focusing on adaptations required from people with disabilities, the medical model implies far less from employers or other social gatekeepers in terms of accommodation since the environment is taken as given.[38] With regard to employment, the model suggests that people with disabilities ought to adapt themselves to the demands of productivity set in the marketplace. Efficiency concerns of firms should outweigh claims of disabled job applicants, despite any social costs (or in the language of economics, negative externalities) that might be generated for society at large. One leading critic, Carolyn Weaver, has written of the ADA:

> The legislation thus includes in the protected population people who, in an economic sense, are not as productive or do not make the same contribution to the profitability of the firm as other people with the same qualifications. (These are the people who can perform only the essential functions of the job and who can do so only with accommodation.) While promoting the employment of this much broader group may be a highly desirable social goal, the antidiscrimination-reasonable accommodation approach is a costly and inefficient way of doing so and is likely to have highly undesirable distributional consequences.[39]

The conservative critique of the ADA is not solely based on grounds of economic efficiency, however. Beyond the issue of productivity is a recurrent concern about the moral legitimacy of claims made by individuals with disabilities on employers and public officials. The issue of moral basis for disability policy is a recurrent historical theme in American social welfare policy. Deborah Stone writes that the popular conception of disability "is best understood as a moral notion. . . . Disability . . . is an essential part of the moral economy."[40] Similarly, Theda Skocpol writes, "Institutional and cultural oppositions between the morally 'deserving' and the less deserving run like fault lines through the entire history of American social provision."[41]

Political conservatives have traditionally expressed concerns in social policy debates that "undeserving" people might benefit from public programs.[42] The ADA's legislative history of the ADA establishes a broad and comprehensive definition of disability, including people with HIV/AIDS, alcoholism, most psychiatric conditions, and those with a history of substance abuse.[43] Conservative critics have expressed great discomfort with this broad definition. For example, a publication of the Republican National Committee has included the ADA's regulations among those that are well-intentioned but spiraling "out of control," at least in part because of their inclusion of "drug abusers, the obese and the 'emotionally disturbed'" among those protected.[44]

Frequently there is a moral dimension to this concern. Individuals who have conditions which are associated with engaging in morally questionable behavior or who are perceived as representing a lack of self-control or poor character may be seen as unworthy of public support. Even for some within the disability community, individuals with these conditions are not considered to be in the same moral category as people with visual or hearing impairments, or those who use wheelchairs. Some critics would even question the legitimacy of coverage for individuals with back problems, the impairment (along with spinal conditions) most often cited in early ADA complaints,[45] since the diagnosis of such problems is often based on self-reports of pain and the inability to perform certain tasks.[46]

Similar doubts may be raised about the moral legitimacy of the ADA by complaints that are based on conditions which some may perceive as frivolous expressions of self-indulgent victimhood such as obesity or chemical sensitivity. While people portrayed in media accounts as sad, angry, or troubled may have bona fide disabling conditions under the ADA's definitions, there may be little public sympathy for their claims. Media coverage of individuals claiming discrimination because they are fat, or phobic, or sensitive to environmental chemicals may color public perceptions of disability discrimination, regardless of the legal validity of the complaints or their ultimate disposition. The focus of criticism and stories in the media may create an image among the public about who benefits from the law that may overshadow the empirical reality of the great majority of disability discrimination and its victims.[47]

Do such concerns, based on perceptions shaped by the lenses of a limited, skeptical, and stigmatizing model of disability, constitute a backlash to the

Americans with Disabilities Act? The act is still in place, unamended and still intact, and there has been no serious attempt to repeal it, even at the zenith of conservative power in Congress. Similarly, there have been media accounts which cast a skeptical light on the act,[48] but these may be no worse than traditional coverage of disability rights issues. A few media horror stories have not led to any major public outcry against the ADA or people with disabilities.

From a larger social standpoint, there may be a reservoir of good will toward the concepts underlying the ADA and toward protecting people with disabilities from discrimination and unfair treatment. Despite some high-profile grumbling from political conservatives, the Americans with Disabilities Act appears to be in fairly good health as it approaches its tenth birthday. Nevertheless, one might ask whether the ADA has had its intended effect of rooting out discrimination and improving the social position of people with disabilities. I will conclude with a brief consideration of this question.

V. CIVIL RIGHTS AND SOCIAL CHANGE

The Americans with Disabilities Act is a potentially crucial protection for people with disabilities. Beyond the specific outcomes of legal proceedings, the ADA's mandates have led to significant expansion of access to the social, economic, and political mainstream by raising awareness about disability issues and by providing incentives to businesses and other covered entities to do the right thing. However, whatever legal protection from discrimination has been gained, it would be very difficult to argue that people with disabilities have achieved social or economic parity as the result of the ADA, or that having a disability is no longer a relevant factor in the life chances of many individuals.

But that might be far too much to expect from a civil rights law. People with disabilities face a variety of barriers to social participation, including limited human capital, social isolation, and cultural stereotypes.[49] While all of these can be directly linked to discrimination, none of them will be easily changed by an act of Congress. Fundamental and far-reaching social change will be necessary for people with disabilities to enjoy full access to American society.

The experience of African Americans has implications for the potential of civil rights statutes to serve as vehicles for overcoming social disadvantage. While Jim Crow laws and legal segregation have been abolished, the research community is divided on the effects of equal opportunity policy for

African Americans' incomes and access to employment.[50] Poorly educated African Americans as a group are relatively worse off in terms of earnings or employment then they were thirty years ago, and the state of black-white relations remains far short of the goals of the civil rights movement of the 1960s.[51] In fact, one of the most contentious issues in the current debate over race relations is affirmative action. The concept of affirmative action requires employers and others to take positive steps to overcome the historic disadvantages experienced by members of minority groups and women. In some ways, the concept is analogous to the positive accommodations needed to make employment, education, public accommodations, and other institutional spheres truly accessible to Americans with disabilities.

Just as the economic and social challenges facing many African Americans are not likely to be resolved by civil rights laws alone, the social exclusion of people with disabilities will not be resolved by the ADA on its own. Access to good jobs, health insurance, personal assistance, community-based services, and accessible technologies will be enhanced, but not guaranteed, by laws such as the ADA. Antidiscrimination laws may be necessary, but not sufficient, for major institutional change.

Might we then expect that the ADA can at least end overt discrimination committed on the basis of disability? If the social model of disability is correct, even this may be too great a burden to place on the legal system. The stigma associated with disability is so embedded and reinforced within our culture and social structure that it will take tremendous efforts to root out.[52] As we have experienced in race and gender equity issues, changing cultural values and social relationships that have become institutionalized in the informal patterns of everyday life may be beyond the capacity of statutory mandates. As Donald L. Horowitz has pointed out, the courts have a built-in emphasis on formal relationships, and may lack the capacity to alter informal patterns of behavior.[53] Such an effort may be a more appropriate task for a broadly based social and political disability movement than for a law dependent on judicial and regulatory enforcement. Interpersonal contacts may help to break down pernicious stereotypes and arbitrary limitations on people with disabilities. Grassroots advocates may be better able to educate communities about the nature of the barriers faced by people with disabilities and how the participation of people with disabilities can be achieved with beneficial results. Legal protections from discriminatory practice are probably indispensable, but such guarantees cannot be the only strategy toward ending the discrimination and social exclusion faced by Americans with disabilities.

NOTES

1. 42 U.S.C. § 12101 (1994).

2. A brief overview of the impact of the ADA is given in Fred Pelka, *The ABC-CLIO Companion to the Disability Rights Movement* (Santa Barbara, CA: ABC-CLIO, 1997), pp. 18–22.

3. Richard K. Scotch, *From Good Will to Civil Rights: Transforming Federal Disability Policy* (Philadelphia: Temple University Press, 1984).

4. See Jane West, "The Social and Policy Context of the Act," in *The Americans with Disabilities Act: From Policy to Practice*, ed. Jane West, 3, 21 (New York: Milbank Memorial Fund, 1991).

5. See, e.g., Cary LaCheen, "Achey Breaky Pelvis, Lumber Lung and Juggler's Despair: The Portrayal of the Americans with Disabilities Act on Television and Radio," *Berkeley Journal of Employment and Labor* 21 (2000): 223.

6. See Joan Biskupic, "Five Cases at Supreme Court Could Affect Disabilities Law," *Washington Post*, February 21, 1999, A3.

7. For a discussion of this transformation, see Scotch, *From Good Will to Civil Rights*.

8. See Harlan Hahn, "Towards a Politics of Disability: Definition, Disciplines, and Policies," *Social Science Journal* (October 1985): 87, 88–89. For a discussion of the historical roots of disability as a clinical concept in public policy, see Deborah A. Stone, *The Disabled State* (Philadelphia: Temple University Press, 1984), pp. 90–117. For an extended summary and critical discussion of the medical model of disability, see Gary L. Albrecht, *The Disability Business: Rehabilitation in America* (Newbury Park, CA: Sage, 1992), pp. 67–90.

9. See, e.g., Robert A. Scott, *The Making of Blind Men* (New York: Russell Sage Foundation, 1969), pp. 6–8.

10. For a history of the federal vocational rehabilitation system, see Edward D. Berkowitz, *Disabled Policy: America's Programs for the Handicapped* (Cambridge: Cambridge University Press, 1987).

11. See Scotch, *From Good Will to Civil Rights*, pp. 8–9. For a general discussion of the minority group model, see Harlan Hahn, "Introduction: Disability Policy and the Problem of Discrimination," *American Behavioral Scientist* 28 (1985): 293.

12. See Hahn, "Towards a Politics," pp. 93–96.

13. For a discussion of the consequences of a mismatch between natural human variation and the limited expectations built into social environments, see Richard K. Scotch and Kay Schrimer, "Disability as Human Variation: Implications for Policy," *Annals of the American Academy of Political and Social Science* 549, no. 1 (1997): 148, 154–57.

14. Michael Oliver, "The Politics of Disablement: A Sociological Approach,"

quoted in "Disability and the Necessity for a Socio-Political Perspective," ed. Len Barton et al., in *World Rehabilitation Fund Monograph* 5 (International Exchange of Experts and Information in Rehabilitation [IEEIR], 1992).

15. See Hahn, "Disability Policy," pp. 300–301.

16. See generally Frank Bowe, *Handicapping America: Barriers to Disabled People* (New York: Harper & Row, 1978); John Gliedman and William Roth, *The Unexpected Minority* (New York: Harcourt Brace Jovanovich, 1980); Louis Harris and Associates, Inc., *ICD Survey of Disabled Americans: Bringing Disabled Americans into the Mainstream* (1986); National Council on the Handicapped, *Toward Independence: An Assessment of Federal Laws and Programs Affecting Persons with Disabilities—With Legislative Recommendations* (1986).

17. For an extensive review of stereotypes commonly associated with disability and their consequences, see Alan Gartner and Tom Joe, eds., *Images of the Disabled, Disabling Images* (New York: Praeger, 1987).

18. Ibid.

19. For a discussion of how the civil rights framework became associated with the status of people with disabilities, see Scotch, *From Good Will to Civil Rights*.

20. Ibid., pp. 51–52.

21. Paul C. Higgins, *Making Disability: Exploring the Social Transformation of Human Variation* (Springfield, IL: C. C. Thomas, 1992), pp. 199–200.

22. See *Toward Independence*, pp. 18–21; see also National Council on Disability, *Equality of Opportunity: The Making of the Americans with Disabilities Act* (1997) (providing an account of the policy development process culminating in the enactment of the ADA).

23. *Toward Independence*, p. 18.

24. Jane West, "The Social and Policy Context of the Act," pp. 3, 22.

25. 42 U.S.C. § 12111 (8) (1994).

26. See, e.g., Chai R. Feldblum, "Employment Protections," in *The Americans with Disabilities Act: From Policy to Practice*, ed. Jane West, 81, 88–90 (New York: Milbank Memorial Fund, 1991).

27. Ibid., p. 90.

28. Ibid., p. 93.

29. Scotch and Schrimer, "Disability as Human Variation," pp. 154–57.

30. Ibid., pp. 157–58.

31. Paul G. Hearne, "Employment Strategies for People with Disabilities: A Prescription for Change," in *The Americans with Disabilities Act: From Policy to Practice*, ed. Jane West, 111, 124 (New York: Milbank Memorial Fund, 1991).

32. See Jane West, "Introduction—Implementing the Act: Where to Begin," in *The Americans with Disabilities Act: From Policy to Practice*, ed. Jane West, xi, xi–xii (New York: Milbank Memorial Fund, 1991).

33. See Robert L. Burgdorf Jr., "'Substantially Limited' Protection from Disability Discrimination: The Special Treatment Model and Misconstructions of the Definition of Disability," *Villanova Law Review* 42 (1997): 409.

34. For a discussion of the need for a reconsideration of the assumptions built into law and public administration, see Hahn, "Disability Policy," p. 315.

35. Donald O. Parsons, "Measuring and Deciding Disability," in *Disability & Work: Incentives, Rights, and Opportunities*, ed. Carolyn L. Weaver, 72, 73 (Washington, DC: AEI Press; Lanham, MD: Distributed by University Press of America, 1991).

36. See generally Carolyn L. Weaver, ed., *Disability & Work: Incentives, Rights, and Opportunities*; see also LaCheen, "Achey Breaky Pelvis, Lumber Lung and Juggler's Despair." Infra text accompanying note 37.

37. Barbara Vobejda, "Disabled People See Budget-Cutting Fervor as Threat, New Attitude," *Washington Post*, August 3, 1995, A12.

38. See Hahn, "Towards a Politics," p. 89.

39. Carolyn L. Weaver, "Incentives versus Controls in Federal Disability Policy," in *Disability & Work*, pp. 6–7.

40. Stone, *The Disabled State*, p. 143.

41. Theda Skocpol, *Protecting Soldiers and Mothers: The Political Origins of Social Policy in the United States* (Cambridge, MA: Belknap Press of Harvard University Press, 1992), p. 149.

42. See, e.g., Edward Berkowitz and Kim McQuaid, *Creating the Welfare State: The Political Economy of Twentieth-Century Reform*, 2nd ed. (New York: Praeger, 1988), p. 12.

43. See Feldblum, "Employment Protections," pp. 85–87.

44. Vobejda, "Disabled People See Budget-Cutting Fervor as Threat, New Attitude."

45. See Nancy R. Mudrick, "Employment Discrimination Laws for Disability: Utilization and Outcome," *Annals of American Academy of Political and Social Science* 549 (1997): 67.

46. For a discussion of the difficulty of scientifically measuring pain and subjective accounts of incapacity as eligibility criteria, see Stone, *The Disabled State*, pp. 134–39.

47. For an analysis of employment discrimination complaints under the ADA and comparable state statutes, see Mudrick, "Employment Discrimination Laws for Disability: Utilization and Outcome."

48. See LaCheen, "Achey Breaky Pelvis, Lumber Lung and Juggler's Despair."

49. For a discussion of the barriers faced by people with disabilities, see Hahn, "Disability Policy," pp. 304–309. For a discussion of barriers related to expanding employment for people with disabilities, see generally Edward H. Yelin, "The

Employment of People with and without Disabilities in an Age of Insecurity," *Annals of American Academy of Political and Social Science* 549 (1997): 117, and William G. Johnson, "The Future of Disability Policy: Benefit Payments or Civil Rights?" *Annals of American Academy of Political and Social Science* 549 (1997): 160.

50. See, e.g., Paul Burstein, *Discrimination, Jobs, and Politics: The Struggle for Equal Employment Opportunity in the United States since the New Deal* (Chicago: University of Chicago Press, 1985), p. 182.

51. Among the best recent overviews of the persistence of economic and social disadvantage among African Americans are William Julius Wilson, *The Truly Disadvantaged: The Inner City, the Underclass, and Public Policy* (Chicago: University of Chicago Press, 1987) and William Julius Wilson, *When Work Disappears: The World of the New Urban Poor* (New York: Knopf, 1996).

52. See Scotch and Schrimer, "Disability as Human Variation: Implications for Policy," p. 152.

53. See Donald L. Horowitz, *The Courts and Social Policy* (Washington, DC: Brookings Institution, 1977), pp. 255–98.

THE HISTORY OF THE AMERICANS WITH DISABILITIES ACT

A Movement Perspective

Arlene Mayerson

The history of the ADA did not begin on July 26, 1990, at the signing ceremony at the White House. It did not begin in 1988 when the first ADA was introduced in Congress. The ADA story began a long time ago in cities and towns throughout the United States when people with disabilities began to challenge societal barriers that excluded them from their communities, and when parents of children with disabilities began to fight against the exclusion and segregation of their children. It began with the establishment of local groups to advocate for the rights of people with disabilities. It began with the establishment of the independent living movement, which challenged the notion that people with disabilities needed to be institutionalized and which fought for and provided services for people with disabilities to live in the community.

The ADA owes its birthright not to any one person, or any few, but to the many thousands of people who make up the disability rights movement—

Originally published in 1992. We thank the Disability Rights Education and Defense Fund for permission to reprint this article. Visit www.dredf.org.

people who have worked for years organizing and attending protests, licking envelopes, sending out alerts, drafting legislation, speaking, testifying, negotiating, lobbying, filing lawsuits, being arrested—doing whatever they could for a cause they believed in. There are far too many people whose commitment and hard work contributed to the passage of this historic piece of disability civil rights legislation to be able to give appropriate credit by name. Without the work of so many—without the disability rights movement—there would be no ADA.

The disability rights movement, over the last couple of decades, has made the injustices faced by people with disabilities visible to the American public and to politicians. This required reversing the centuries-long history of "out of sight, out of mind" that the segregation of disabled people served to promote. The disability rights movement adopted many of the strategies of the civil rights movements before it.

Like the African Americans who sat in at segregated lunch counters and refused to move to the back of the bus, people with disabilities sat in federal buildings, obstructed the movement of inaccessible buses, and marched through the streets to protest injustice. And like the civil rights movements before it, the disability rights movement sought justice in the courts and in the halls of Congress.

From a legal perspective, a profound and historic shift in disability public policy occurred in 1973 with the passage of Section 504 of the 1973 Rehabilitation Act. Section 504, which banned discrimination on the basis of disability by recipients of federal funds, was modeled after previous laws which banned race, ethnic origin, and sex-based discrimination by federal fund recipients.

For the first time, the exclusion and segregation of people with disabilities was viewed as discrimination. Previously, it had been assumed that the problems faced by people with disabilities, such as unemployment and lack of education, were inevitable consequences of the physical or mental limitations imposed by the disability itself. Enactment of Section 504 evidenced Congress's recognition that the inferior social and economic status of people with disabilities was not a consequence of the disability itself, but instead was a result of societal barriers and prejudices. As with racial minorities and women, Congress recognized that legislation was necessary to eradicate discriminatory policies and practices.

Section 504 was also historic because for the first time people with disabilities were viewed as a class—a minority group. Previously, public policy had been characterized by addressing the needs of particular disabilities by category based on diagnosis. Each disability group was seen as separate, with differing needs. Section 504 recognized that while there are major physical and mental variations in different disabilities, people with disabilities as a group faced similar discrimination in employment, education, and access to society. People with disabilities were seen as a legitimate minority, subject to discrimination and deserving of basic civil rights protections. This "class status" concept has been critical in the development of the movement and advocacy efforts. The coalition of people with disabilities has been constantly put to the test by attempts to remove protections for particular groups. The history of the ADA is a testament to the movement's commitment to solidarity among people with different disabilities.

After Section 504 established the fundamental civil right of non-discrimination in 1973, the next step was to define what nondiscrimination meant in the context of disability. How was it the same or different from race and sex discrimination? The Department of Health, Education and Welfare (HEW) had been given the task of promulgating regulations to implement Section 504, which would serve as guidelines for all other federal agencies. These regulations became the focus of attention for the disability rights movement for the next four years. During this time the movement grew in sophistication, skill, and visibility. The first task was to assure that the regulations provided meaningful antidiscrimination protections. It was not enough to remove policy barriers   it was imperative that the regulations mandated affirmative conduct to remove architectural and communication barriers and provide accommodations.

The second step was to force a recalcitrant agency to get the regulations out. All over the country people with disabilities sat-in at HEW buildings. The longest sit-in was in San Francisco, lasting twenty-eight days. A lawsuit was filed, hearings before Congress were organized, testimony was delivered to Congressional committees, negotiations were held, and letters were written. The disability community mobilized a successful campaign using a variety of strategies, and on May 4, 1977, the Section 504 regulations were issued. It is these regulations which form the basis of the ADA. In the early 1980s the disability community was called upon to defend the hard-fought-for Section 504 regulations from attack. After taking office President Reagan established the Task Force on Regulatory Relief under the leadership of then Vice President George Bush. The mission of the task force was to "de-regulate" regulations which were burdensome on businesses. The Section 504 regulations were chosen for "de-regulation." This news sent a current throughout the disability movement across the country, which quickly mobilized a multi-tier strategy to preserve the regulations.

For two years, representatives from the disability community met with administration officials to explain why all of the various de-regulation proposals must not be adopted. These high-level meetings would not have continued or been successful without the constant bombardment of letters to the White House from people with disabilities and parents of children with disabilities around the country protesting any attempt to de-regulate Section 504.

After a remarkable show of force and commitment by the disability community, the administration announced a halt to all attempts to de-regulate Section 504. This was a tremendous victory for the disability movement. Those two years proved to be invaluable in setting the stage for the ADA. Not only were the Section 504 regulations, which form the basis of the ADA, preserved, but it was at this time that high officials of what later became the first Bush administration received an education on the importance of the concepts of nondiscrimination contained in the Section 504 regulations in the lives of people with disabilities.

During much of the 1980s, the disability community's efforts in Washington were focused on reinstating civil rights protections which had been stripped away by negative Supreme Court decisions. The longest legislative battle was fought over the Civil Rights Restoration Act (CRRA), first introduced in 1984 and finally passed in 1988. The CRRA sought to overturn *Grove City College v. Bell*, a Supreme Court decision that had significantly restricted the reach of all the statutes prohibiting race, ethnic origin, sex, or disability discrimination by recipients of federal funds. Because the court decision affected all of these constituencies, the effort to overturn the decision required a coalition effort. For the first time, representatives of the disability community worked in leadership roles with representatives of minority and women's groups on a major piece of civil rights legislation.

Working in coalition again, in 1988, the civil rights community amended the Fair Housing Act (FHA) to improve enforcement mechanisms, and for the first time disability antidiscrimination provisions were included in a traditional civil rights statute banning race discrimination. During these years working on the CRRA and the FHA, alliances were forged within the civil rights community that became critical in the fight for passage of the ADA. Because of its commitment to disability civil rights, the Leadership Conference on Civil Rights played an important leadership role in securing passage of the ADA.

During the 1980s, it also became clear to the disability community that it should play a very active role in Supreme Court litigation under Section 504. The first Section 504 case which was decided by the Supreme Court in 1979, *Southeastern Community College v. Davis*, 442 U.S.397, revealed at best, a lack of understanding, and at worst, a hostility toward even applying the concept of discrimination to exclusion based on disability. In that case, a hearing-impaired woman was seeking admission to the nursing program of Southeastern Community College. The court found that Ms. Davis's hearing impairment rendered her unqualified to participate in the program because she would not be able to fully fulfill all of the clinical requirements. However, the Court did not limit itself to the fate of Ms. Davis, but included within the decision several very broad negative interpretations of Section 504. In fact, the Davis decision cast doubt on whether those entities covered by Section 504 would be required to take any affirmative steps to accommodate the needs of persons with disabilities. Contrary to established Court doctrine, the Section 504 regulations that had been issued by the Department of Health, Education and Welfare (HEW) were given little deference by the Court. Ironically the Court attributed this lack of deference to the fact that HEW had been recalcitrant in issuing the regulations.

After the Davis decision it was clear that the Supreme Court needed to be educated on the issue of disability based discrimination and the role that it plays in people's lives. Moreover, it was clear to the disability community that the focus of its efforts in any future Supreme Court litigation must be to reinforce the validity of the 1977 HEW regulations. In the next case to be granted review by the Supreme Court, *Consolidated Rail Corporation v. Darrone*, 465 U.S.624 (1984), the disability community focused its efforts on educating the Court and bolstering the validity of the HEW regulations interpreting Section 504. The issue in *Consolidated Rail Corporation* was whether employment discrimination was covered by the antidiscrimination provisions of Section 504. In order to educate the court on the pervasive role of discrimination in the unemployment and underemployment of persons with disabilities, the Disability Rights Education and Defense Fund filed an amicus brief on behalf of sixty-three national, state, and local organizations dedicated to securing the civil rights of persons with disabilities. This amicus brief served not only to educate the courts on discriminatory employment policies and practices, but also to demonstrate to the Court that these issues concern the millions of Americans who were affiliated with the organizations that filed the brief. DREDF also worked very closely with the lawyer representing the disabled person in the lawsuit in order to present to the Court the very best legal arguments on the validity of the 1977 HEW regulations which had found that employment discrimination was covered by provision of Section 504. The decision in *Consolidated Rail Corporation v. Darrone* marked a significant victory for the disability rights community. The court found that employment discrimination was in fact prohibited by Section 504, but equally importantly the Court found that the regulations issued in 1977 by HEW were entitled to great deference by the courts. It is these regulations which were elevated by the Court in *Consolidated Rail Corporation* which formed the basis of the ADA.

The disability community continued its active involvement in Section 504 cases in the Supreme Court throughout the 1980s. In 1987, the Court was presented with the issue of whether people with contagious diseases are covered by Section 504. Although the case involved a woman with tuberculosis, it became clear throughout the country that the Court's decision in this case would be critical for protection against discrimination by people with HIV infection. The disability rights community worked closely with the lawyers representing the woman with tuberculosis as well as filing numerous amicus briefs in the Supreme Court. The Supreme Court's decision in *School Board of Nasar County v. Airline*, 480 U.S.273 (1987), became the foundation for coverage of people with AIDS under Section 504 and the ADA. Working on the Airline case also provided a critical opportunity for lawyers in the disability rights community and lawyers in the AIDS community to work closely together and form alliances that would carry through and prove to be critical in the battle to secure passage of the ADA.

During the 1980s the disability community was also successful in overturning by legislation several disability-specific negative Supreme Court rulings. Legislation was passed to reinstate the coverage of antidiscrimination provisions to all airlines, the right to sue states for violations of Section 504, and the right of parents to recover attorney fees under the Education for Handicapped Children's Act (now called IDEA). These legislative victories further advanced the reputation of the disability community and its advocates in Congress. The respect for the legal, organizing, and negotiations skills gained during these legislative efforts formed the basis of the working relationships with members of Congress and officials of the administration that proved indispensable in passing the ADA. Whether by friend or foe, the disability community was taken seriously—it had become a political force to be contended within Congress, in the voting booth, and in the media.

The ADA, as we know it today, went through numerous drafts, revisions, negotiations, and amendments since the first version was introduced in 1988. Spurred by a draft bill prepared by the National Council on Disability, an independent federal agency whose members were appointed by President Reagan, Senator Weicker and Representative Coelho introduced the first version of the ADA in April 1988 in the 100th Congress.

The disability community began to educate people with disabilities about the ADA and to gather evidence to support the need for broad anti-discrimination protections. A national campaign was initiated to write "discrimination diaries." People with disabilities were asked to document daily instances of inaccessibility and discrimination. The diaries served not only as testimonials of discrimination, but also to raise consciousness about the barriers to daily living which were simply tolerated as a part of life. Justin Dart, Chair of the Congressional Task Force on the Rights and Empowerment of People with Disabilities, traversed the country holding public hearings which were attended by thousands of people with disabilities, friends, and families documenting the injustice of discrimination in the lives of people with disabilities.

In September 1988, a joint hearing was held before the Senate Subcommittee on Disability Policy and the House Subcommittee on Select Education. Witnesses with a wide variety of disabilities, such as blindness, deafness, Down's syndrome, and HIV infection, as well as parents of disabled children testified about architectural and communication barriers and the pervasiveness of stereotyping and prejudice. A room which seated over seven hundred people overflowed with persons with disabilities, parents, and advocates. After the hearing, a commitment was made by Senator Kennedy, Chair of the Labor and Human Resources Committee, Senator Harkin, Chair of the Subcommittee on Disability Policy, and Representative Owens of the House Subcommittee on Select Education, that a comprehensive disability civil rights bill would be a top priority for the next Congress. At the same time, both presidential candidates, Vice President Bush and Governor Dukakis, endorsed broad civil rights protections for people with disabilities. The disability community was determined to assure that President Bush would make good on his campaign promise, and reinvoked it repeatedly during the legislative process.

On May 9, 1989, Senators Harkin and Durrenberger and Representatives Coelho and Fish jointly introduced the new ADA in the 101st Congress. From that moment, the disability community mobilized, organizing a multilayered strategy for passage. A huge coalition was assembled by the Consortium for Citizens with Disabilities (CCD), which included disability organizations, the Leadership Conference on Civil Rights (LCCR), and an array of religious, labor, and civic organizations

A team of lawyers and advocates worked on drafting and on the various and complex legal issues that were continually arising; top-level negotiators and policy analysts strategized with members of Congress and their staffs; disability organizations informed and rallied their members; a lobbying system was developed using members of the disability community from around the country; witnesses came in from all over the country to testify before Congressional committees; lawyers and others prepared written answers to the hundreds of questions posed by members of Congress and by businesses; task forces were formed; networks were established to evoke responses from the community by telephone or mail; protests were planned—the disability rights movement coalesced around this goal: passage of the ADA. From the beginning the "class" concept prevailed—groups representing specific disabilities and specialized issues vowed to work on all of the issues affecting all persons with disabilities. This commitment was constantly put to the test. The disability community as a whole resisted any proposals made by various members of Congress to exclude people with AIDS or mental illness or to otherwise narrow the class of people covered. Even at the eleventh hour, after two years of endless work and a Senate and House vote in favor of the act, the disability community held fast with the AIDS community to eliminate an amendment which would have excluded food-handlers with AIDS, running the risk of indefinitely postponing the passage or even losing the bill. Likewise, all of the groups, whether it was an issue particularly affecting their constituencies or not, held fast against amendments to water down the transportation provisions. The underlying principle of the ADA was to extend the basic civil rights protections extended to minorities and women to people with disabilities. The 1964 Civil Rights Act prohibited employment discrimination by the private sector against women and racial and ethnic minorities, and banned discrimination against minorities in public accommodations. Before the ADA, no federal law prohibited private sector discrimination against people with disabilities, absent a federal grant or contract.

The job of the disability rights movement during the ADA legislative process was to demonstrate to Congress and the American people the need for comprehensive civil rights protections to eradicate fundamental injustice

—to demonstrate not only how this injustice harms the individual subjected to it, but also how it harms our society.

The first hearing in the 101st Senate on the new ADA was a historic event and set the tone for future hearings and lobbying efforts. It was kicked off by the primary sponsors talking about their personal experiences with disability. Senator Harkin spoke of his brother who is deaf, Senator Kennedy of his son, who has a leg amputation, and Representative Coelho, who has epilepsy, spoke about how the discrimination he faced almost destroyed him.

The witnesses spoke of their own experiences with discrimination. A young woman who has cerebral palsy told the senators about a local movie theater that would not let her attend because of her disability. When her mother called the theater to protest that this attitude "sounded like discrimination," the theater owner stated "I don't care what it sounds like." This story became a symbol for the ADA and was mentioned throughout the floor debates and at the signing. The members and the president related this story to demonstrate that America "does care what it sounds like" and will no longer tolerate this type of discrimination.

A Vietnam veteran who had been paralyzed during the war and came home using a wheelchair testified that when he got home and couldn't get out of his housing project, or on the bus, or off the curb because of inaccessibility, and couldn't get a job because of discrimination, he realized he had fought for everyone but himself—and he vowed to fight tirelessly for passage of the ADA. The president of Gallaudet College gave compelling testimony about what life is like for someone who is deaf, faced with pervasive communication barriers. The audience was filled with Gallaudet students who waved their hands in approval.

The committee also received boxes loaded with thousands of letters and pieces of testimony that had been gathered in hearings across the country the summer before from people whose lives had been damaged or destroyed by discrimination.

A woman testified that when she lost her breast to cancer, she also lost her job and could not find another one as a person with a history of cancer. Parents whose small child had died of AIDS testified about how they couldn't find any undertaker that would bury their child.

At this Senate hearing and in all the many hearings in the House, members of Congress heard from witnesses who told their stories of discrimination. With each story, the level of consciousness was raised and the level of tolerance to this kind of injustice was lowered. The stories did not end in the hearing room. People with disabilities came from around the country to talk to members of Congress, to advocate for the bill, to explain why each provision was necessary, to address a very real barrier or form of discrimination. Individuals came in at their own expense, slept on floors by night and visited Congressional offices by day. People who couldn't come to Washington told their stories in letters, attended town meetings, and made endless phone calls.

And it was a long haul. After the spectacular Senate vote of 76 to 8 on September 7, 1989, the bill went to the House, where it was considered by an unprecedented four committees. Each committee had at least one sub-committee hearing, and more amendments to be explained, lobbied, and defeated. Grassroots organizing became even more important because by this time many business associations had rallied their members to write members of Congress to oppose or weaken the bill. The perseverance and commitment of the disability movement never wavered. Through many moments of high stress and tension, the community stayed unified. For every hearing the hearing room was full and for every proposed amendment to weaken the bill letters poured in and the halls of Congress were canvassed. ... With the passage of the ADA, for the first time in the history of our country, or the history of the world, businesses had to stop and think about access for people with disabilities. If the ADA means anything, it means that people with disabilities will no longer be out of sight and out of mind. The ADA is based on a basic presumption that people with disabilities want to work and are capable of working, want to be members of their communities, and are capable of being members of their communities, and that exclusion and segregation cannot be tolerated. Accommodating a person with a disability is no longer a matter of charity but instead a basic issue of civil rights.

While some in the media portray this new era as falling from the sky unannounced, the thousands of men and women in the disability rights movement know that these rights were hard fought for and are long overdue. The ADA is radical only in comparison to a shameful history of outright exclusion and segregation of people with disabilities. From a civil rights perspective the Americans with Disabilities Act is a codification of simple justice.

20 WHO LOST THE ADA?

Douglas Lathrop

Welcome to Post-ADA America. We hope you've enjoyed your flight. Before leaving, please be sure to check the area around your seat for any civil rights or scraps of human dignity you may have managed to keep us from stealing. Thank you for flying with us—and remember, if you feel your rights have been violated, you're required by law to wait ninety days before suing us. Have a nice day.

The death of the Americans with Disabilities Act—if it is in fact dead—did not occur suddenly. Rather, the Supreme Court has subjected it to the judicial equivalent of the Death of a Thousand Cuts. No single ruling by the high court could be considered fatal, but cumulatively they—especially in the sections of the ADA pertaining to employment—have narrowed the scope of the act so drastically that only a small number of the estimated 54 million disabled Americans remain covered. As Sarah Triano, an advocate with Access Living Chicago and a person with an immune system disorder, says, "I'm not even protected by the ADA anymore."

Reprinted by permission from the disability lifestyle magazine *New Mobility*, September 2003. www
.newmobility.com.

So far, Title III of the ADA—which requires access to public accommodations such as restaurants, stores, and movie theaters—has escaped the Supreme Court's attention. Here, however, it's the United States Congress that seems eager to put on the executioner's hood. In February 2000 the so-called "ADA Notification Act" was tossed into the Congressional hopper, and it has been reintroduced in the current session. Under the Notification Act, a person with a disability wishing to file suit against an inaccessible business will have to wait an additional ninety days to do so—presumably to give the ghosts of Christmases Past, Present, and Future enough time to visit the business owner and shame him or her into rushing to comply with a law that has already been on the books for thirteen years.

"I don't think we dare let any more [ADA] cases come before this Supreme Court," says Lucy Gwin, editor of *Mouth* magazine. For over ten years Gwin's rousing, in-your-face style has typified the magazine she calls "The Voice of the Disability Nation"—yet when asked if the ADA is dead, she answers with an unqualified yes. "It's unenforceable. . . . That's no law at all."

ANGER MANAGEMENT

When I think about what has happened to the ADA, I feel angry. And dejected. And betrayed.

Like a lot of people with disabilities on July 26, 1990, I felt a huge sense of triumph when I heard the act had been signed. I was too young to have taken part in the disability rights struggles of the preceding two decades, but each of the movement's victories had affected me profoundly. After sixth grade, thanks to the Individuals with Disabilities Education Act, I had the right to graduate from a segregated "special" elementary school into the same junior high that my brothers and sister had attended. My parents bought me a membership in the California Association of the Physically Handicapped (now known as Californians for Disability Rights), and when the organization's monthly newsletter arrived in the mail, I'd devour every word of it. I wrote letters to my city councilman demanding curb cuts in my neighborhood so I could wheel to the corner store. When disability activists occupied the San Francisco offices of the US Department of Health, Education and Welfare to demand implementation of Section 504 of the Rehabilitation Act, I cheered them on—and when a 1979 *Newsweek* article described disability as America's next great civil rights movement, I spent an entire lunch period in the school library looking for a copy of it. Times were changing, and even my pimply fourteen-year-old self felt like a part of it.

In high school and college my interest in disability rights waned (replaced by sex, beer, science fiction, and punk rock, in no particular order) but it never completely faded. When deaf students at Gallaudet University took over the campus in 1988 to protest the appointment of a non-hearing-impaired chancellor, I felt a certain amount of pride even though I'm not deaf. And in July 1990 that pride all came rushing back. To this day, I still can't look at that photo of Justin Dart looking over President George H. W. Bush's shoulder without getting goose bumps.

When I think about the years since that photo was taken, however, I end up asking: *What the hell happened?*

And then: *Where the hell was the disability movement while it was happening?*

Anger is like fire. Unchecked, it can burn you up from the inside and then destroy everything around you. But, channeled and controlled, it can become a useful tool—or a powerful weapon. I've decided to channel my anger into finding out why the disability movement never achieved the critical mass expected back in the 1970s. There's no way a single magazine article can provide an in-depth historical analysis of the disability rights movement—and no one without a PhD in history would want to read it anyway   but it can ask some important, outside-the-party-line questions:

Could the disability rights movement have done more to protect the ADA?

Are we up to the task of salvaging what's left?

Do we need to start thinking beyond the ADA and finding new ways to bring about equality and inclusion for people with disabilities?

In these post-ADA, post-September 11, civil-rights-averse times, is it all our movement can do simply to keep from becoming irrelevant?

THE MEDIA MISS THE MESSAGE

"The biggest problem," says Cyndi Jones, "is that the movement isn't moving."

I'm sitting with Jones and her husband, Bill Stothers, at a café next door to the San Diego offices of the Center for an Accessible Society—a national organization designed to focus public attention on disability and independent living issues. It's in a quaint old part of town, whose Victorian and Craftsman houses are largely inaccessible but whose sidewalks—most of them, anyway—have curb cuts.

If anyone can help me find some answers, these two can. It was they—as the editors of *Mainstream*—who gave me some of my first assignments as a freelance writer, when no one else was buying stories about disabled people who weren't climbing El Capitan or pimping for Jerry's Kids.

I start the interview with the question of the day, the same one I asked Lucy Gwin: Is the ADA dead?

"No," Stothers says. "I don't think it's dead. Everybody focuses on the court rulings, but the fact is that access is happening." Although disability rights laws from the ADA on down remain underenforced, equality and integration for people with disabilities have slowly percolated through the larger culture—particularly when it comes to public facilities. In the United States, a disabled person will encounter many more ramps, accessible restrooms, Braille signage, and closed-captioned television broadcasts in an average day than they would in comparably wealthy countries such as France, Germany, the United Kingdom, or Canada—no matter how much more socially progressive those nations may otherwise be. "There's this change of attitude that's more powerful than the law itself," says Jones, "and that . . . is what causes things to happen."

Signs of this attitudinal shift have also appeared even in organizations usually viewed with suspicion by disability rights activists. While the Jerry Lewis MDA Telethon still draws protests, and MDA itself has come under fire for alleged discrimination, groups like United Cerebral Palsy, the National Multiple Sclerosis Society, and the American Diabetes Association have quietly included civil rights issues among their traditionally medical, research-and-treatment-oriented concerns. Says UC San Francisco historian Paul Longmore, PhD, "If you go to their Web sites, you'll find sections that address issues of public policy that don't have to do with medical research, but have to do with civil rights, [as well as] information about individuals confronting prejudice and discrimination." What's more, he adds, in recent years there has been a marked change in the American people's expectations for the role people with disabilities play in society. "They expect to see people with disabilities participating. . . . They're shocked and appalled when they learn about work disincentives. They support us, and when things are reported to them, they agree with us."

The problem is, so many of the issues facing us—the reasons that we need an ADA in the first place—have gone unreported. We haven't insisted that they be reported. The campaign for the ADA's passage is notable for its lack of any attempt by the disability movement to engage the media or public in the debate surrounding it, or in any broader discussion of disability rights and what they might mean for American society. You'd think that a movement so grounded in the ideals of previous civil rights struggles would have recognized the crucial importance of public support and sympathy; yet in our case, disability activists preferred to work behind the scenes with elected officials and did not seek the attention of the voters who elected them. "Most other civil rights legislation has come with broad, deep public support," Stothers says. "People demanded that it happen—they saw those police dogs chasing [civil rights workers] in Alabama and there was outrage. That's never happened with disability."

According to Mary Johnson—editor of *Ragged Edge*, codirector (with Jones and Stothers) of the Center for an Accessible Society, and author of *Make Them Go Away: Clint Eastwood, Christopher Reeve and the Case Against Disability Rights*—the lobbyists working on Capitol Hill perceived, correctly, that it would be easier to sell the ADA directly to Congress without getting bogged down in lengthy public debate or dealing with the media. "As a short-range 'get a law passed' strategy it was very good," Johnson says. "But . . . in the long term you create a backlash when you don't get the public on board with you. The epigram that begins my book says it all for me: 'A law cannot guarantee what a culture will not give.'"

If a Congressperson submitted a bill in the House requiring African Americans to wait ninety days before suing a business for race discrimination, the airwaves and op-ed pages of the nation would instantly be filled with calls for his or her political head. For instance, gay and lesbian activists were highly vocal in their denunciations of Senator Rick Santorum for remarks that they perceived as anti-gay. So why hasn't the disability community mounted a similar response to attacks on the ADA? In the words of Bob Dole, where's the outrage?

"We don't publicize our programs, our ideas," Johnson says. "Over and over again, I come back to that as our essential problem. The public only knows about the disability rights movement from the high-profile stories by the likes of John Stossel—they think it's a bunch of whiny opportunists complaining about every little thing and refusing to take responsibility. . . . We [could] show them that disability rights is about helping everyone to get the access and accommodation they need to live a decent life. But we don't frame things like this. We could, we should. But we don't."

LOSING CONSCIOUSNESS

We don't connect with other crips, either. For me, the idea of my disability as a political and not just a medical issue took hold early on—but my experience is the exception that proves the rule. According to Longmore, the majority of disabled Americans "never got politicized about disability." That would certainly explain why, more often than not, when I first meet other people with disabilities and use names or concepts that folks in the movement take for granted—Section 504, IDEA, ADAPT, even New Mobility—they'll give me the blankest of blank stares.

Says Johnson, "Wade Blank [the founder of ADAPT] many, many years ago made a point about how the way to get new people into a movement was to do things publicly that would draw people to you." If more disability rights groups took this approach—filing high-profile suits against inaccessible businesses, holding press conferences constantly, engaging in the sort of confrontational street theater for which ADAPT is well known—"folks would start knowing about disability rights and . . . some young folks—the ones who have an activist bent—would start coming forward."

In Gwin's opinion, the disability community should replicate the consciousness-raising sessions that formed the foundation for the modern-day feminist movement. "The women's movement jumped on those—there was this huge buzz around the country because women were running off to meet other women . . . talking to each other about their civil rights for the first time in history. This is the kind of person-to-person organizing that we have to do now."

It sounds good in theory. But it also makes us sound as if we're stuck in the '60s. The leadership of the disability movement is not getting any younger—either it brings in some new blood, or it eventually becomes extinct. If we shut out everyone not old enough to remember Woodstock, how do we expect to attract the Warped Tour crowd?

People like Sarah Triano are just the type of up-and-coming leaders that the disability movement needs. As one of the founders of the National Disabled Students Union, Triano has worked to mobilize young people with disabilities on college campuses around the country. She, too, sees a desperate need for consciousness raising within the disability community: "The greatest obstacle [we] face today is our own sense of internalized oppression and shame. What good is an ADA, an IDEA or a Section 504 if people with disabilities are too ashamed to even admit they have a disability?" Socialized by nondisabled society to think of themselves as worthless, many disabled Americans are too demoralized to lay claim to the legislated rights they already have. "I call it cultural terrorism—that's what's been inflicted on us."

However, any outreach to young people with disabilities is going to have to come from young activists. Within the disability movement there persists a wide—and often unacknowledged—generation gap. "The first centers for independent living . . . were started by very young activists," Triano says. "But they've aged. And the view is that as you age you get more conservative. . . . A lot of the students in the NDSU don't see [older] leaders with disabilities as very radical."

On the other side, movement veterans often view younger generations— X, Y, Z, whatever—as either unaware or unappreciative of the effort and risk that went into earlier disability rights battles. "A lot of young people seem to assume that they will have the same kinds of life opportunities as their nondisabled peers," Longmore says. "I think they will, at some point, hit a glass ceiling, and I hope that that will politicize them." As someone who falls in the middle of this generational divide (either a young Boomer or an old GenXer, depending on where you draw the line), I suspect that the mistrust on both sides is at least partially justified. But when it comes to the issue of consciousness raising—or lack thereof—the argument is also irrelevant. By definition, the disability community is cross-generational, and no one age group holds a monopoly on apathy and ignorance. If we truly want the disability movement to be more than a historical flash in the pan, we ultimately must set aside these kinds of differences and figure out how to mobilize our people across the board—with new perspectives, new ideas, and a renewed sense of our own unity.

LIGHTS, CAMERA . . .

It's also no longer enough to confine our activities to the courts, the Centers for Independent Living, and the marble-lined corridors of policy wonkdom. Disabled people "have too long relied on courts to provide fundamental human justice, and not enough on popular action to demand it," says Marta Russell. The author of *Beyond Ramps: Disability at the End of the Social Contract*, Russell has written extensively not just on disability rights, but on labor issues, radical politics, and the impact of economic globalization. "After the Supreme Court showed its colors regarding employment, for instance, we should have [demonstrated] against Toyota, Chevron, every corporation that displaced a disabled worker instead of making reasonable accommodations."

That kind of high-visibility, in-your-face action requires media savvy and the ability to mobilize large numbers of people—qualities that the disability rights movement has sorely lacked. Of the established disability organizations, only ADAPT has made street protest a regular part of its modus operandi—and while it typically stages at least two demonstrations a year, the number of attendees seems to have plateaued and the actions rarely make more than a brief blip on the media's radar screen.

Of course, part of the problem with mobilizing the disabled masses is a logistical one. It can be just plain *hard* for a person with a disability to travel from one city to another. Finding accessible transportation and lodging, arranging for attendant services on the road, dealing with broken wheelchair parts or sudden medical emergencies—all of these things can frustrate the hell out of just one disabled individual. Multiply them by seven figures—for a "Million Crip March" on Washington, DC, say—and you have a logistical nightmare of apocalyptic proportions.

For this reason, some in the disability movement have begun to emphasize smaller-scale action at the local level over big, splashy—and overly ambitious—national spectacles. "You have to mobilize people locally—this is how democracy works," Gwin says. "You can't do it from a sitting position at home in front of the television. . . . People have to see the faces of their organizers."

Johnson agrees. "Our real strength is in the grass roots. We need to do local stuff, constantly and consistently, that gets ordinary people to understand that they have [rights]. If we can do that consistently . . . getting ourselves into the public eye as a local movement that *benefits everyone*, we will be doing a heck of a lot."

Whether it's local or national, mobilizing effectively is going to require each of us to recognize the common ground we share with those whose disabilities are different from ours—in other words, no more griping from us wheelchair users about how people with hidden disabilities aren't "really disabled"—and with other communities working to achieve their own civil rights goals. During the 504 protests, the people occupying HEW received active support from African Americans, gays and lesbians, organized labor—all of whom recognized that they were fighting the same basic battle. But now, after more than two decades' worth of "identity politics" (also known as "multiculturalism," "political correctness," and "I'm a bigger victim than you are"), the civil rights landscape is as fragmented as a map of the former Yugoslavia. "Identity politics means that groups compete for 'our' agenda or 'our' piece of a reduced pie, whether economic, social or political," Russell says. "What we need to do is demand a transformation that delivers a different pie—one big enough for all of us. . . . We do not need to abandon 'our issues' but we do need to integrate our struggles with other struggles."

That's not easy to do, though—not when "progressive" organizers shut out people with disabilities by holding events at inaccessible venues, or disability activists pepper their discussions with racist or homophobic jokes that drive away interested people from other communities. "The disability rights movement can't be insular," Triano says. "We have African-Americans, we have women, we have gays and lesbians already in our movement . . . [but] I don't think there's enough coalition building."

British folk singer Johnny Crescendo—a polio survivor active in the disability movement in the United Kingdom—once said that there can be no integration without power; once we have power, we can choose to integrate with whomever we want. However, doesn't it also work the other way? If we separate ourselves from the larger community, how can we possibly attain the power?

HISTORY NEVER ENDS

A few years after the ADA became law, I attended a disability event in Los Angeles. Billed as a "Chautaqua," the event was designed to bring disabled writers, artists, and activists together to exchange ideas and educate ourselves about the experience and culture we had in common. One of the projects was a detailed timeline of important events in the history of disability. Some—such as the 504 protests—were well known to me, while others—such as the turn-of-the-century "Ugly Laws" in Chicago, which barred people with visible physical deformities from going out in public—came as a shock. The timeline began in biblical times and continued across the millennia to July 26, 1990—where it abruptly stopped. As if getting the president to sign his name to a piece of paper were the pinnacle of what we could hope to achieve.

At the time I thought to myself, "What self-congratulatory bullshit! Yeah, we got a law passed, and that's great, but that's not the end of it. We're sitting here patting each other on the ass like football players who've just scored a touchdown, and meanwhile the rest of the game is being rigged against us."

In retrospect, I probably overreacted. But then 1994 came around—the year of the Gingrich Revolution, the "Contract with America," and the first of many vocal attacks on the ADA from the media and the halls of Congress. The ensuing backlash against disability rights did not come as a shock to everyone. Says Longmore, "I had expected it long before it finally did occur"—but the movement as a whole was utterly gobsmacked by it, and it has never regained its momentum.

So maybe I wasn't overreacting after all.

On the other hand, the African American civil rights movement didn't end with Martin Luther King Jr.'s "I Have a Dream" speech. It didn't begin there, either—nor did it begin with Rosa Parks, who had received intensive training as a civil rights organizer long before she refused to give up her seat on that bus. There's something to be said for the old saying about what happens when the going gets tough.

"This is the best time [for the disability movement] to be relevant," Jones says. "When things are easy, you get complacent. When things get difficult, that's when you need to come out and fight. . . . But that means you have to go out and do the organizing. It's not going to get any easier in fifty years."

Nor is the battle going to go away—not in fifty years or a century. That's the tragic burden accepted by anyone who believes in civil rights: Whatever your vision of equality looks like, chances are that you won't live to see it. Sometimes change happens with surprising swiftness, sometimes it becomes glacial, stops, or even moves backwards—but one human lifespan is never long enough. True success, then, comes in taking a view that transcends generations and laying the foundation for a movement that will outlive all of us.

The timeline never ends. Not unless the world ends with it.

21

CITIZENSHIP AND DISABILITY

Michael Bérubé

n the six years since I published a book about my son Jamie, *Life as We Know It*, a great deal has changed in Jamie's life—starting with his realization that there is a book about him. When I completed the book Jamie was only four, and had not yet entered the public K-12 system. But I did not stop serving as Jamie's recorder and public representative when I finished that book: I still represent him all the time, to school officials, camp counselors, babysitters and friends, to academic audiences, and to Down Syndrome associations. I take it as one of my tasks to watch for important things he's never done before, as a way of charting and understanding the irreplaceable and irreducible little person he is, especially as he gets less and less little, and more and more capable of representing himself.

Jamie is now in his sixth year of school, having entered kindergarten in 1997–1998. In the intervening years he has not continued to perform at grade level (he is repeating fourth grade, at age eleven), and he has occasionally

From Michael Bérubé, "Citizenship and Disability," *Dissent Magazine*, Spring 2003. Reprinted by permission of the publisher.

presented his schoolmates with some eccentric behavior. On the other hand, he has learned to read, to do two- and three-digit addition and subtraction, to multiply two-digit numbers, and most recently to do division by single numbers, with and without remainders. My wife, Janet, and I did not teach him these things, but the minute it became clear that he could do them in school, we picked up the ball and ran with it. We've tried to make every available use of his startlingly prodigious memory, and we've learned that when he tells us that such and such bird is not a parrot but is instead a scarlet macaw, he's usually right. He has some idiosyncrasies that do not serve him well in school or in testing situations: at one point he memorized the numbers on the wrong side of his flash cards, the serial numbers that indicate each card's place in the deck. He likes to pretend that he does not know left from right, referring instead (with perverse delight) to his "left foot" and his "other foot." He is a stubborn ignatz, as people find whenever they try to get him to do something he has no interest in, or whenever his teachers or aides try to make him move from one task to another. For a while he tried to put off unpleasant tasks by telling his teachers or therapists, "Let's do that tomorrow"; before long he realized that this didn't work, and began saying instead, "We did that yesterday"—a ruse with which he has had some success.

His conversational skills are steadily improving, but unless you're talking to him about one of the movies he's seen or one of the routines he's developed at school or at home, you'll find that his sense of the world is sometimes unintelligible, sometimes merely a bit awry. He recently received an invitation to a classmate's birthday party (his third such invitation since we moved to central Pennsylvania sixteen months ago: we count and cherish each one), and Janet asked him what the birthday boy looked like: "he's a small boy," said Jamie, holding his hand around his shoulder level.

"What color is his hair?" she asked.

"Black," Jamie replied.

"What color are his eyes?"

"Blue."

"Does he wear glasses?" (Jamie has worn glasses for about five years.)

"No," Jamie said, "just eyes."

But then, Janet and I did not expect him to be able to describe his classmates at all. Nor did we expect him to be so talented a mimic; he can imitate both of us, just as he can imitate break dancers and gymnasts and snakes and lemurs. We did not expect him to be able to do multiplication or division; we did not expect him to open books and ask us to "read and tell all the things";

we did not expect him to be able to ask us "why" questions, as when he asked me why I could not leave him alone in a hotel room while I went to park the car. We did not expect him to win a spelling award in second grade for maintaining an average above 90 on his spelling tests for the year. We did not expect him to be designated by his classmates in third grade as the kid with the best sense of humor.

Over eleven years, then, we've come to expect that Jamie will defeat or exceed our expectations when we least expect him to. And from this I draw two points. One, he's a child. Two, and this is a somewhat more elaborate conclusion, although it can be derived from point one: it might be a good idea for all of us to treat other humans as if we do not know their potential, as if they just might in fact surprise us, as if they might defeat or exceed our expectations. It might be a good idea for us to check the history of the past two centuries whenever we think we know what "normal" human standards of behavior and achievement might be. And it might be a very good idea for us to expand the possibilities of democracy precisely because democracy offers us unfinished and infinitely revisable forms of political organization that stand the best chance, in the long run, of responding adequately to the human rights of the unpredictable creatures we humans are. That might be one way of recognizing and respecting something you might want to call our human dignity.

Jamie is, of course, one reason why I am drawn to the question of disability rights and their relation to democracy: every morning I take him to school, I know how very fortunate he is to be living under a social dispensation that entitles him to a public education alongside his nondisabled peers. But beyond my immediate interest in forwarding Jamie's interests, I want to argue that disability issues are—or should be—central to theories of social justice in a much broader sense. Nancy Fraser's account of the "politics of recognition" and the "politics of redistribution" (*Adding Insult to Injury: Social Justice and the Politics of Recognition*), for example, offers a theory that tries to accommodate what were the two major strands of American progressive–left thought in the 1990s, multiculturalism and democratic socialism (in all their varieties)—or what Richard Rorty, in *Achieving Our Country*, termed the "cultural left" and the "reformist left," the former concerned primarily with combating social stigma and the latter concerned primarily with combating greed. Fraser has shown convincingly that the politics of recognition and redistribution offer a productive way to think about feminism: cultural politics with regard to body images or sexual harassment, for example, are not to be understood as distractions from "real" politics that address comparative worth or the minimum wage. Rather, recognition politics have consequences for the redistribution of social goods and resources even though they cannot be reduced to their redistributive effects. And since many left intellectuals in the 1990s were all too willing to think of politics as a zero-sum game in which any attention paid to multiculturalism had to come at the expense of democratic socialism and vice versa, Fraser's work seems to offer a way for the left to champion a progressive tax code and an end to racial profiling at the same time.

It is striking, nonetheless, that so few leftists have understood disability in these terms. Disability is not the only area of social life in which the politics of recognition are inseparable from the politics of redistribution; other matters central to citizenship, such as immigration, reproductive rights, and criminal justice, are every bit as complex. Nonetheless, our society's representations of disability are intricately tied to, and sometimes the very basis for, our public policies for "administering" disability. And when we contemplate, in these terms, the history of people with cognitive and developmental disabilities, we find a history in which "representation" takes on a double valence: first, in that people who were deemed incapable of representing themselves were therefore represented by a sociomedical apparatus that defined—or, in a social-constructionist sense, created—the category of "feeblemindedness"; and second, in the sense that the visual and rhetorical representations of "feebleminded" persons then set the terms for public policy. One cannot plausibly narrate a comprehensive history of ideas and practices of national citizenship in the post–Civil War United States without examining public policy regarding disability, especially mental disability, all the more especially when mental disability was then mapped onto certain immigrant populations who scored poorly on intelligence tests and were thereby pseudoscientifically linked to criminality. And what of reproductive rights? By 1927, the spurious but powerful linkages among disability, immigration, poverty, and criminality provided the Supreme Court with sufficient justification for declaring involuntary sterilization legal under the Constitution.

There is an obvious reason why disability rights are so rarely thought of in terms of civil rights: disability was not covered in the Civil Rights Act of 1964. And as Anita Silvers points out, over the next twenty-five years, groups covered by civil rights law sometimes saw disability rights as a dilution of civil rights, on the grounds that people with disabilities were constitutively incompetent, whereas women and minorities faced discrimination merely on the basis of social prejudice. Silvers writes, "[t]o make disability a category that activates a heightened legal shield against exclusion, it was objected, would alter the purpose of legal protection for civil rights by transforming the goal from protecting opportunity for socially exploited people to providing assistance for naturally unfit people." The passage of the Americans with Disabilities Act (ADA) in 1990 did add disability to the list of stigmatized identities covered by antidiscrimination law, but thus far the ADA has been interpreted so narrowly, and by such a business-friendly judiciary, that employers have won over 95 percent of the suits brought under the act.

Perhaps if plaintiffs with disabilities had won a greater number of cases over the past thirteen years, the conservative backlash against the ADA—currently confined to a few cranks complaining about handicapped parking spaces and a wheelchair ramp at a Florida nude beach—would be sufficiently strong as to spark a movement to repeal the law altogether. But then again, perhaps if the law were read more broadly, more Americans would realize their potential stake in it. In 1999, for instance, the Supreme Court ruled on three lower-court cases in which people with "easily correctable" disabilities—high blood pressure, nearsightedness—were denied employment. In three identical 7–2 decisions, the Court found that the plaintiffs had no basis for a suit under the ADA precisely because their disabilities were easily correctable. As disability activists and legal analysts quickly pointed out, this decision left these plaintiffs in the ridiculous situation of being too disabled to be hired but somehow not disabled enough to be covered by the ADA; or, to put this another way, plaintiffs' "easily correctable" disabilities were not so easily correctable as to allow them access to employment. One case involved twin sisters who were denied the opportunity to test as pilots for United Airlines on the grounds that their eyesight did not meet United's minimum vision requirement (uncorrected visual acuity of 20/100 or better without glasses or contacts) even though each sister had 20/20 vision with corrective lenses (*Sutton v. United Airlines, Inc.*); another involved a driver/mechanic with high blood pressure (*Murphy v. United Parcel Service*); the third involved a truck driver with monocular vision (20/200 in one eye) who in 1992 had received a Department of Transportation waiver of the requirement that truck drivers have distant visual acuity of 20/40 in each eye as well as distant binocular acuity of 20/40 (*Albertson's, Inc. v. Kirkingburg*). Because, as Silvers argues, "litigation under the ADA commonly turns on questions of classification rather than access," all three plaintiffs were determined to have no standing under the law. The question of whether any of them was justly denied employment was simply not addressed by the Court. Indeed, in writing her opinion for the majority, Justice Sandra Day O'Connor explicitly refused to consider the wider question of "access," noting that 160 million Americans would be covered by the ADA if it were construed to include people with "easily correctible" disabilities (under a "health conditions approach"), and since Congress had cited the number 43 million in enacting the law, Congress clearly could not have intended the law to be applied more widely. "Had Congress intended to include all persons with corrected physical limitations among those covered by the Act, it undoubtedly would have cited a much higher number of disabled persons in the findings," wrote O'Connor. "That it did not is evidence that the ADA's coverage is restricted to only those whose impairments are not mitigated by corrective measures."

It is possible to object that O'Connor's decision was excessively literalist, and that the potential number of Americans covered by the ADA is, in any case, quite irrelevant to the question of whether a woman can fly a plane when she's got her glasses on. But I've since come to believe that the literalism of the decision is an indirect acknowledgment of how broad the issues at stake here really are. If the ADA were understood as a broad civil rights law, and if it were understood as a law that potentially pertains to the entire population of the country, then maybe disability law would be understood not as a fringe addition to civil rights law but as its very fulfillment.

Rights can be created, reinterpreted, extended, and revoked. The passage of the ADA should therefore be seen as an extension of the promise of democracy, but only as a promise: any realization of the potential of the law depends on its continual reinterpretation. For the meaning of the word, just as Wittgenstein wanted us to believe (in order that we might be undeceived about how our words work), lies in its use in the language. Similarly, the Individuals with Disabilities Education Act of 1975 (originally the Education for All Handicapped Children Act) was not some kind of breakthrough discovery whereby children with disabilities were found to be rights-bearing citizens of the United States after all, and who knew that we'd had it all wrong for 199 years? On the contrary, the IDEA invented a new right for children with disabilities, the right to a "free and appropriate public education in the least restrictive environment." And yet the IDEA did not wish that right into being overnight; the key terms "appropriate" and "least restrictive" had to be interpreted time and again, over the course of fifteen years, before they were understood to authorize "full inclusion" of children with disabilities in "regular" classrooms. Nothing about the law is set in stone. The only philosophical "foundation" underlying the IDEA and its various realizations is our own collective political will, a will that is tested and tested again every time the act comes up for reauthorization. Jamie Bérubé currently has a right to an inclusive public education, but that right is neither intrinsic nor innate. Rather, Jamie's rights were invented, and implemented slowly and with great difficulty. The recognition of his human dignity, enshrined in those rights, was invented. And by the same token, those rights, and that recognition, can be taken away. While I live, I promise myself that I will not let that happen, but I live with the knowledge that it may: to live any other way, to live as if Jamie's rights were somehow intrinsic, would be irresponsible.

Of course, many of us would prefer to believe that our children have intrinsic human rights and human dignity no matter what; irrespective of any form of human social organization; regardless of whether they were born in twentieth-century Illinois or second-century Rome or seventh-century central Asia. But this is just a parent's—or a philosophical foundationalist's—wishful thinking. For what would it mean for Jamie to "possess" rights that no one on earth recognized? A fat lot of good it would do him. My argument may sound either monstrous or all too obvious: if, in fact, no one on earth recognized Jamie's human dignity, then there would in fact be no human perspective from which he would be understood to possess "intrinsic" human dignity. And then he wouldn't have it, and so much the worse for the human race.

In one respect, the promise of the IDEA, like the promise of the ADA, is clear: greater inclusion of people with disabilities in the social worlds of school and work. But in another sense the promise is unspecifiable; its content is something we actually cannot know in advance. For the IDEA does not merely guarantee all children with disabilities a free appropriate public education in the least restrictive environment. Even more than this, it grants the right to education in order that persons with disabilities might make the greatest possible use of their other rights—the ones having to do with voting, or employment discrimination, or with life, liberty, and the pursuit of happiness.

IDEA is thus designed to enhance the capabilities of all American children with disabilities regardless of their actual abilities—and this is why it is so profound a democratic idea. Here again I'm drawing on Nancy Fraser, whose theory of democracy involves the idea of "participatory parity," and the imperative that a democratic state should actively foster the abilities of its citizens to participate in the life of the polity as equals. Fraser's work to date has not addressed disability, but as I noted above, it should be easy to see how disability is relevant to Fraser's account of the politics of recognition and the politics of redistribution. This time, however, I want to press the point a bit harder. Fraser writes as if the promise of democracy entails the promise to enhance participatory parity among citizens, which it does, and she writes as if we knew what "participatory parity" itself means, which we don't. (This is why the promise of disability rights is unspecifiable.)

Let me explain. First, the idea of participatory parity does double duty in Fraser's work, in the sense that it names both the state we would like to achieve and the device by which we can gauge whether we're getting there. For in order to maintain a meaningful democracy in which all citizens participate as legal and moral equals, the state needs to judge whether its policies enhance equal participation in democratic processes. Yet at the same time, the state needs to enhance equal participation among its citizens simply in order to determine what its democratic processes will be. This is not a meta-theoretical quibble. On the contrary, the point is central to the practical workings of any democratic polity. One of the tasks required of democrats is precisely this: to extend the promise of democracy to previously excluded individuals and groups some of whom might have a substantially different understanding of "participatory parity" than that held by previously dominant groups and individuals.

Could anything make this clearer than the politics of disability? Imagine a building in which political philosophers are debating, in the wake of the attacks of September 11, 2001, the value and the purpose of participatory parity over against forms of authoritarianism or theocracy. Now imagine that this building has no access ramps, no Braille or large-print publications, no American Sign Language interpreters, no elevators, no special-needs paraprofessionals, no in-class aides. Contradictory as such a state of affairs may sound, it's a reasonably accurate picture of what contemporary debate over the meaning of democracy actually looks like. How can we remedy this? Only when we have fostered equal participation in debates over the ends and means of democracy can we have a truly participatory debate over what "participatory parity" itself means. That debate will be interminable in principle, since our understandings of democracy and parity are infinitely revisable, but lest we think of deliberative democracy as a forensic society dedicated to empyreal reaches of abstraction, we should remember that debates over the meaning of participatory parity set the terms for more specific debates about the varieties of human embodiment. These include debates about prenatal screening, genetic discrimination, stem-cell research, euthanasia, and, with regard to physical access, ramps, curb cuts, kneeling buses, and buildings employing what is now known as universal design.

Leftists and liberals, particularly those associated with university humanities departments, are commonly charged with being moral relativists, unable or unwilling to say (even after September 11) why one society might be "better" than another. So let me be especially clear on this final point. I think there's a very good reason to extend the franchise, to widen the conversation, to democratize our debates, and to make disability central to our theories of egalitarian social justice. The reason is this: a capacious and supple sense of what it is to be human is better than a narrow and partial sense of what it is to be human, and the more participants we as a society can incorporate into the deliberation of what it means to be human, the greater the chances that that deliberation will in fact be transformative in such a way as to enhance our collective capacities to recognize each other as humans entitled to human dignity. As Jamie reminds me daily, both deliberately and unwittingly, most Americans had no idea what people with Down syndrome could achieve until we'd passed and implemented and interpreted and reinterpreted a law entitling them all to a free appropriate public education in the least restrictive environment. I can say all this without appealing to any innate justification for human dignity and human rights, and I can also say this: Without a sufficient theoretical and practical account of disability, we can have no account of democracy worthy of the name.

Perhaps some of our fellow citizens with developmental disabilities would not put the argument quite this way; even though Jamie has led me to think this way, he doesn't talk the way I do. But those of us who do participate in political debates, whether about school funding in a specific district or about the theory and practice of democracy at its most abstract, have the obligation to enhance the abilities of our children and our fellow citizens with disabilities to participate in the life of the United States as political and moral equals with their nondisabled peers—both for their own good, and for the good of democracy, which is to say, for the good of all of us.

V

DISABILITY AND PHYSICIAN-ASSISTED SUICIDE

NATIONAL COUNCIL ON DISABILITY POSITION PAPER ON DISABILITY AND PHYSICIAN-ASSISTED SUICIDE* ISSUED IN 1997 AND REAFFIRMED IN 2005

Executive Summary

Physician-assisted suicide and related issues have garnered much judicial, media, and scholarly attention in recent months. Two cases presently pending before the United States Supreme Court raise the issue of the legality of state laws prohibiting physician-assisted suicide. As the principal agency within the federal government charged with the responsibility of providing cross-disability policy analysis and recommendations regarding government programs and policies that affect people with disabilities, the National Council on Disability is issuing this position paper in the hope of presenting a coherent and principled stance on these issues drawn from the input and viewpoints of individuals with disabilities.

In the body of this position paper, the Council examines a number of insights derived from the experiences of people with disabilities focusing on the following topics:

---

*Written for the National Council on Disability by Professor Robert L. Burgdorf Jr., University of the District of Columbia Law School.

217

1. The Paramount Issue—Rights, Services, and Options
2. The Reality and Prevalence of Discrimination
3. Deprivation of Choices and the Importance of Self-Determination
4. Others' Underestimation of Life Quality
5. Fallibility of Medical Predictions
6. Eschewing the Medical Model of Disabilities
7. The Impact of Onset of Disability upon Emotional State and Decision Making
8. The Reality of Living with Pain and Bodily Malfunction
9. Divergent Interests of Those Involved in Assisted Suicide Decisions

Based upon these insights from those who have experienced disabilities and upon the existing legal framework, the National Council on Disability has formulated its position on the issue of physician-assisted suicide for persons with imminently terminal conditions as follows: The benefits of permitting physician-assisted suicide are substantial and should not be discounted; they include respect for individual autonomy, liberty, and the right to make one's own choices about matters concerning one's intimate personal welfare; affording the dignity of control and choice for a patient who otherwise has little control of her or his situation; allowing the patient to select the time and circumstances of death rather than being totally at the mercy of the terminal medical condition; safeguarding the doctor/patient relationship in making this final medical decision; giving the patient the option of dying in an alert condition rather than in a medicated haze during the last hours of life; and, most importantly, giving the patient the ability to avoid severe pain and suffering.

The Council finds, however, that at the present time such considerations are outweighed by other weighty countervailing realities. The benefits of physician-assisted suicide only apply to the small number of people who actually have an imminently terminal condition, are in severe, untreatable pain, wish to commit suicide, and are unable to do so without a doctor's involvement. The dangers of permitting physician-assisted suicide are immense. The pressures upon people with disabilities to choose to end their lives, and the insidious appropriation by others of the right to make that choice for them are already prevalent and will continue to increase as managed healthcare and limitations upon healthcare resources precipitate increased "rationing" of healthcare services and healthcare financing.

People with disabilities are among society's most likely candidates for ending their lives, as society has frequently made it clear that it believes they would be better off dead, or better that they had not been born. The experience in the Netherlands demonstrates that legalizing assisted suicide generates strong pressures upon individuals and families to utilize that option, and leads very quickly to coercion and involuntary euthanasia. If assisted suicide were to become legal, the lives of people with any disability deemed too difficult to live with would be at risk, and persons with disabilities who are poor or members of racial minorities would likely be in the most jeopardy of all.

If assisted suicide were to be legalized, the only way to ward off the most dire ramifications for people with disabilities would be to create stringent procedural prerequisites. But, to be effective, such procedural safeguards would necessarily sacrifice individual autonomy to the supervision of medical and legal overlords to an unacceptable degree—the cure being as bad as the disease.

For many people with disabilities, it is more often the discrimination, prejudice, and barriers that they encounter, and the restrictions and lack of options that this society has imposed, rather than their disabilities or their physical pain, that cause people with disabilities' lives to be unsatisfactory and painful. The notion that a decision to choose assisted suicide must be preceded by a full explanation of the programs, resources, and options available to assist the patient if he or she does not decide to pursue suicide strikes *many* people with disabilities as a very shallow promise when they know that all too often the programs are too few, the resources are too limited, and the options are nonexistent. Society should not be ready to give up on the lives of its citizens with disabilities until it has made real and persistent efforts to give these citizens a fair and equal chance to achieve a meaningful life.

For these reasons, the Council has decided that at this time in the history of American society it opposes the legalization of assisted suicide. Current evidence indicates clearly that the interests of the few people who would benefit from legalizing physician-assisted suicide are heavily outweighed by the probability that any law, procedures, and standards that can be imposed to regulate physician-assisted suicide will be misapplied to unnecessarily end the lives of people with disabilities and entail an intolerable degree of intervention by legal and medical officials in such decisions. On balance, the current illegality of physician-assisted suicide is preferable to the limited benefits to be gained by its legalization. At least until such time as our society provides a comprehensive, fully-funded, and operational system of assistive living services for people with disabilities, this is the only position that the National Council on Disability can, in good conscience, support.

23

AUTONOMY BOARD POSITION STATEMENT
ON PHYSICIAN-ASSISTED SUICIDE

M embers of the Board of AUTONOMY strongly disagree with the October Bulletin "opposing legalizing assisted suicide" from the National Council on Disability (NCD).

Paul Spiers, AUTONOMY Board Chairman responds, "NCD fails to represent the political, religious and ethnically diverse views of persons with disabilities. Polls show a majority of the disability community favors passage of laws providing choice at the end of life." He added, "AUTONOMY encourages leaders of other disability organizations to adopt a neutral stance on the Oregon law and on legislative efforts to provide a compassionate choice at life's end for their constituents. It is important for these organizations to realize that a vocal few do not speak for a majority of the disability community. Persons with disabilities are, in fact, far more vulnerable in states where the transparency enshrined in the Oregon law does not exist."

Politics and Activism AUTONOMY Press Release, November 22, 2005. Available at http://www
.disthis.com.

Alan Toy of UCLA, AUTONOMY's Board Secretary comments, "The issue of physician assisted dying is more about personal choice than disability rights. Personal choice is something the disability community is unanimously in favor of when it comes to living. Well, I would ask NCD, isn't making a well-controlled choice to die a bit sooner in the face of a terminal illness, an independent choice made by the living? How dare we take away their choice, based on our fear of being devalued as human beings? We devalue them and ourselves by presuming to make that choice for them."

The Oregon law authorizes an adult to obtain a lethal prescription to hasten their impending death when two physicians agree that a mentally competent person is terminally ill. Anecdotal information provided by the Oregon Hospice Association and Compassion & Choices, a public interest organization providing clinical services to terminally ill patients, shows that not a single person using the law has done so for the sole purpose of escaping a preexisting disability.

According to Karen Hwang, EdD, an author and counseling psychologist who serves on the AUTONOMY Board, and who is herself quadriplegic, "Many of us believe the vulnerability argument is inherently discriminatory because it denies our capacity for informed consent, and makes blanket assumptions about the entire disability population's perception of life and death—exactly what proponents of vulnerability decry in the current medical and social establishment."

AUTONOMY represents the interests of people with disabilities who wish to be able to exercise choice in all aspects of life, including choice at the end of life. Other AUTONOMY board members include James Werth, PhD from the University of Akron, Cornelius Baker, former Executive Director of the Whitman-Walker Clinic, and Louis Hall, a disability rights advocate living in Oregon.

24

GALLAGHER AND BATAVIA ON PHYSICIAN-ASSISTED SUICIDE

An Open Letter to People with Disabilities

Drew Batavia and Hugh Gregory Gallagher

W e write to you because we believe certain persons and organizations who claim to speak for persons with disabilities may have seriously misrepresented the views of many of us.

Public attention in recent years has focused on issues surrounding end-of-life care. We believe this is all to the good. Death, like birth, is part of the life process, neither to be feared nor denied. In truth, the end of life can be a time of expressing and sharing love, forgiveness, and thankfulness. We believe end-of-life choices are a private matter. Interest groups, legislators, judges, and publicity seekers have no business interfering with the decision-making autonomy of the dying patient.

We wish to make clear that we do not support the practices of Jack Kevorkian any more than we support the objectives of those who would deny us the right to control our lives, either during the prime or at the end.

People with disabilities know all too well what it is like to lose personal autonomy—this is what the fight for self-determination and disability rights is all about. We do not think that people with disabilities, who have struggled for many years to have control over their own lives and bodies, would or should give up this decision-making autonomy at the end of life.

A DECLARATION OF DISABILITY RIGHTS

WE BELIEVE the disability rights movement is based fundamentally on the autonomy and self-determination of people with disabilities, and that individuals with disabilities should be allowed to control all aspects of their lives.

WE BELIEVE people with disabilities, including individuals with terminal illnesses, should have access to adequate healthcare services, and should not be discriminated against in gaining such access.

WE BELIEVE informed consent must be obtained before any healthcare practitioner may provide treatment, and the patient must always have the right to refuse treatment, including refusal of extraordinary efforts to sustain his or her life.

WE BELIEVE medical treatment must never be denied or withdrawn solely because a patient has a disability, and may only be denied or withdrawn as a result of the express desire of the individual (or someone appropriately authorized to decide on the individual's behalf).

WE BELIEVE an individual's "quality of life" can only be judged by that individual (or by a person assigned by that individual in the event that he or she becomes incompetent), and others such as physicians and hospital administrators have no moral authority to make such judgments.

WE BELIEVE persons in the final stage of a terminal disease should have access to hospice care, as well as access to as much pain medication as they need for comfort.

WE BELIEVE persons with disabilities in the end stage of terminal disease determined to end their lives should have access to competent counseling on the issue.

WE BELIEVE people with disabilities—being of sound mind, in pain at the end stage of terminal disease—who are determined to take their lives should have access to the medication and assistance necessary to achieve their objectives.

25

PHYSICIAN-ASSISTED DEATH

Are We Asking the Right Questions?

Barry Corbet

It's so deceptive, this one simple question: Should we make it legal for people to secure a doctor's assistance in hastening death? Yes or no? Ask, and you might get a definitive answer. Ask why, and what you'll get is slippery, contentious, anything but definitive. Yet we hold to our polarized answers and we do, by God, love them. In our crowd, to take a renegade position is to invite our own public beheading. The wise stay out of it. But we can't. Since virtually all people who request hastened death have old or new disabilities, we're essential to the debate. Death-with-dignity laws are about us.

The discord begins with a name—whatever we're going to call death requested by a patient and facilitated by a physician. The most commonly used term is physician-assisted suicide, or PAS. In disability circles, that acronym stands for personal assistance services, so it is rejected here. Not Dead Yet, a major player in the debate, prefers physician-induced death, or

PID. It has undertones of medical murder so is rejected on the basis of bias. For this discussion, I've compromised with physician-assisted death, or PAD.

Some background: Suicide is legal in every state, as is passively attending a suicide. Euthanasia, actively helping someone end his or her life, is illegal in every state. PAD, a physician providing a lethal dose for a patient to take without further assistance, is legal only in Oregon.

Two disability rights–based organizations have formed to address the PAD question: Not Dead Yet, which opposes PAD and the Oregon law, and AUTONOMY, which endorses both. The Hemlock Society has been given much weight because it is the country's oldest and largest group supporting PAD and often incurs NDY's and AUTONOMY's wrath.

In attempting to understand PAD, I've viewed it from three perspectives, each raising progressively harder questions: PAD as personal preference, PAD as a disability issue, and PAD as public policy. The categories overlap, but they guide us toward asking the right questions.

PAD AS PERSONAL PREFERENCE

As president of the Hemlock Society, Faye Girsh (now vice president), asked me what seems like a reasonable question: "Why can't those who don't want hastened death live out their full lifespans and those who do want it have this humane option available to them?" Girsh meant the question innocently, but is it truly benign? Not if it's the alpha and omega of the discussion. It sweeps way too many valid concerns under the rug, even on a personal level.

You may feel comfortable in your decision that under certain circumstances you want PAD. You've talked to your family, doctor, and hospital, and given everyone copies of your advance directives, the legal documents that state your wishes. You've entrusted your medical power of attorney to someone close. But did you know how easily your advance directives, and therefore your life-and-death choices, can change or be completely ignored?

"In an ideal world, advance directives include individual decisions based on personal consultation with a physician," says Lauri Yablick, a Tucson psychologist who works with people with disabilities. "How can there be informed consent without that?"

Yet by law, on admission to a hospital or nursing home, you must be asked if you have, or want to create, advance directives. At each readmission, the question is repeated. That means an untrained clerical worker often solicits a life-or-death decision from a sick or forgetful patient, an uninformed relative, or a court-appointed guardian. Just sign the orange form, honey, and we'll get you in bed.

"Each new admission brings the potential for a surrogate decision-maker to override the pre-existing directive," Yablick says. "I've found inconsistent advance directives on more charts than you can imagine. And the options are pared to a dichotomy. No matter what your advance directive says, your chart says 'full code' [save me no matter what] or 'DNR' [do not resuscitate]. No one's considering clauses like 'meaningful chance for recovery.'" We should find this unsettling. If advance directives can change, how can we have PAD and feel confident that we're following the person's wishes?

But you're a take-charge person, you can make things happen your way. Or can you? You may be unconscious when the time comes, or demented, declared incompetent, or taken to an unfamiliar hospital. Your appointed surrogate may have died or your doctor retired. Dozens of things can change, and you aren't in charge anymore.

And how realistic are our ideas of what is acceptable health in the future? "Before your accident would you, fairly, have been able to project yourself into the life you've led since your injury?" Yablick asks. Not a chance. We may say we are not willing to live with certain physical or mental states, but do we really know what we're afraid of? Sometimes the fear is disproportionate to the reality.

What about the limited solace of any plan to get out before the going gets too tough? If you've laid in a supply of barbiturates to take before you fade into dementia, you have to act while you're still mentally and physically capable. You could wait too long or you could make a preemptive strike too early, losing valued months or years. I confess to a painful preoccupation with this point. My mother and maternal grandmother both had Alzheimer's disease, and neither enjoyed it. Three generations of our family didn't either, and I don't want to follow that path myself or subject my children and grandchildren to its furies. I have a vested interest in PAD.

Yet with or without such concerns, you might find powerful comfort in having that bottle of Nembutal in the cabinet whether you use it or not. No matter how much you love life now, you can still hope to control how and when you depart.

PAD AS A DISABILITY ISSUE

Not Dead Yet

Here's another reasonable-sounding question, this time from the late Drew Batavia: "Disability rights are about autonomy and self-determination. Why shouldn't that freedom of choice extend to end-of-life decisions?"

Because, NDY might say, the current state of institutionalized prejudice against people with disabilities turns that choice into no choice. Because nondisabled people seem to fear disability more than death. Because doctors are fallible in diagnosing and treating depression and estimating life expectancy. Because the current rush to cut healthcare costs conflicts with our need for lifelong care. Because PAD can be seen as the ultimate sanction, the ultimate form of discrimination.

Our PAD "choices" may, in fact, be subtly conditioned. "The problem is that our desires are so malleable and manipulable," says Harriet McBryde Johnson, a disability rights attorney from Charleston, South Carolina, and a supporter of NDY. "You know how easy it is to internalize other people's expectations, how exhausting it can be to oppose them, especially when you're sick. What we confront usually isn't homicidal hate, it's that pervasive assumption that our lives are inherently bad. That attitude can wear us down to the point where we want to be killed."

Can't we build ironclad safeguards into the law?

"Safeguards as presently proposed," counters Johnson, "are about defining a class whose desire to die may be presumed rational, because of illness or disability so 'bad' that no 'reasonable' person would want to endure it. That whole veneer of beneficence. The law has the power to validate and structure prejudice. These [PAD] laws tell suicidal newbies that yes, it really is as bad as it feels, and don't expect it ever to get better. They tell the larger society that disability and illness equal misery, so there's no need to bother about making our lives good. There's an easy way out."

Johnson acknowledges the possibility of individual situations where assisting a suicide or looking the other way might be morally right. "But I wouldn't try to objectively define those situations and build law around them," she says. "It just can't be done. Killing is too serious to manage by checklist."

And what of our physical vulnerability? "We are living the lives that others fear," says Johnson. "I depend on others to keep me alive every day. If I'm lucky, I get them to honor my requests—and keep me alive—on the strength of my paychecks and my charms. But money and charms are transient and, at bottom, we need people to know they're stuck with us no matter what and that they'll see us through those days when we feel bad about the pressures we put them under or when we get tired of all the complications."

With PAD, insurers may be less inclined to see us through. As a class, we're both poor and expensive; beer income, champagne needs. We're the medically unattractive. Of course we fear that insurers will deny us expensive treatment options while holding out the carrot of "a peaceful and dignified death." The cheapest care is no care.

If eligibility for PAD is based on health status, then what is health status? It's a construct grounded in the medical model, and doctors are its arbiters. Yet doctors have a singularly vivid sense of how rotten our lives are. According to several studies, they underrate our quality of life and overestimate our depression, and those perceptions do affect the treatments they prescribe and the advice they give. Given both PAD and prospective payment, will they be too quick to write us off?

We may help them do it. All it will take is one sympathetic healthcare worker reporting our ambivalence, however momentary, about staying alive. Then the wheels can turn, doctors can agree that our lives are unendurable, and we can be hustled off to hospice amid a nauseating chorus of people saying we're dying the way we wanted to. With absurd ease, we can be put out of our "misery" with no malice on the part of any segment of the healthcare system. It happens now. Is this freedom of choice?

AUTONOMY

"We are not a right-to-die group," wrote Drew Batavia, the president of AUTONOMY until his death in January. "We are a disability-rights organization that supports our right to decide issues of our lives. The unifying theme is choice and control."

Batavia and Hugh Gallagher cofounded AUTONOMY partly to fight Attorney General John Ashcroft's efforts to nullify Oregon's Death With Dignity Act, partly as a reaction to NDY. Batavia felt that while the leadership of many disability rights groups opposes PAD and presumes to speak for all of us, many of the rank and file support it.

He may be right. In a 2001 Harris Poll, 68 percent of people with disabilities polled nationwide favored PAD. A small study by Pamela Faden shows a fairly even split, but she warns against using her survey to quantify consensus. Her study does show that many members of disability rights groups fear criticism if they speak out in favor of PAD.

Batavia—but not necessarily AUTONOMY—saw personal autonomy as the primary goal, and solving social issues that surround PAD as secondary. This is not to say Batavia ignored such issues. To the contrary, his fingerprints are all over key legislation to remedy them.

"Assisted suicide," he wrote, "cannot be held responsible for the consequences of our society's failure to provide adequately for the needs of many people with disabilities." Jack Kevorkian? "Kevorkian demonstrated why laws like the Oregon Act are necessary. He operated without standards." People with nonterminal conditions? "I admit to some ambivalence about this issue," Batavia wrote in 1999, but he included only terminal conditions when speaking for AUTONOMY. And always, Batavia returned the discussion to choice. "Our overall mission," he said, "is to provide a full range of options for people with disabilities." And elsewhere: "Our positions are based fundamentally on the value of autonomy."

Gallagher, like NDY, objects to Hemlock's use of the word "hopeless" as a criterion for hastened death in much of its literature. "A sense of hopelessness is a call for help in living, not dying," he says. He emphasizes that AUTONOMY wants personal control during the dying process, not hastened death for people struggling with life.

Do the Oregon law's guidelines, as Johnson suggests, simply define a class considered better off dead? "Absolutely not," Gallagher says. "The Oregon law is reactive, not proactive. . . . It has the support of a large majority of its citizens. It's an insult to say Oregonians believe their terminally ill loved ones are better off dead. It cheapens and polarizes a serious moral issue."

Gallagher is not looking for conflict. "This is not a game of one team opposing another. Different people, cultures and religions hold different positions. These positions must be respected. AUTONOMY believes it should be up to the individual. Our whole purpose is to reduce the vulnerability of disabled persons to outside influence. We are grown-ups and we don't need Ashcroft telling us what we can or cannot do."

And Gallagher sets out his own credo: "I have fought hard to live my life as I choose to live it, to make my own life decisions. I will not give up this autonomy of decision making on my deathbed."

THE HEMLOCK SOCIETY USA

Since Hemlock is headquartered in Denver, I know several of its principals. They are good, intelligent people who wonder why we demonize them and, equally, why we don't see that they promote choice, not coercion.

They don't want to kill people with disabilities. They don't want to kill anyone. They don't provide physical assistance in hastening death. They do provide counseling, information, and support. They do support PAD legislation. They want all possible supports at the end of life, and oppose suicide for emotional or financial reasons. They say they address the agonies of dying, not the tribulations of living.

At Hemlock's heart is its Caring Friends program. Caring Friends, trained and certified by the national office, respond when a member asks for help in hastening death. The Caring Friend visits the member and family, then refers the case to Denver for evaluation.

"When the Caring Friends Program accepts a case," says Girsh, "it is with medical records and a great deal of assessment. Since each case is decided on its own merits, there is often disagreement on the committee about the cases it will accept. This becomes especially difficult when we have people 85 and older asking for our assistance because they have macular degeneration, arthritis or other ailments that make them miserable but will not cause death."

Some will see red flags in this statement, which reflects the Caring Friends program's policy of assisting people who are "suffering from an irreversible physical condition that severely compromises his or her quality of life."

All disabled people have irreversible physical conditions. Most nondisabled people think these conditions compromise our quality of life. In contrast, Compassion in Dying, another mainstream right-to-die group and a key force behind Oregon's Death With Dignity Act, supports PAD only for people who are terminal.

"We go a little further," says Girsh. "We assist in both terminal and hopeless cases." She points out that Hemlock does not use "hopeless" as a criterion in proposed legislation, yet its Web site is riddled with the word— hopeless, hopeless, hopeless.

I ask the obvious question. "So why not provide hope? Why not target the hopelessness?" "We provide hope," she says.

Hemlock provides information on two methods of "self-deliverance," barbiturates and helium—the latter for those who can't get barbiturates and are willing to place a bag over their heads and inhale gas from a tank. Helium has its advantages; it's quick, certain, and available.

I mention to Girsh that an old friend, a retired physician and Caring Friend, recently attended the death from helium inhalation of a woman with "relentlessly progressive multiple sclerosis which had left her essentially immobile." He was impressed with the thoroughness and sensitivity of Hemlock's counseling and the speed and peaceful nature of her death, but had one misgiving. "She wasn't truly terminal," he said. "I had a very slight concern as to how much of her motivation was related to her parents, whose lives had been totally turned upside down for four years of 24-hour caregiving. But there was certainly no compulsion and, to the contrary, much love."

Girsh is familiar with the case and knows the family. "So what should we have done?" she asks. "Money isn't the problem. Love isn't the problem. Care isn't the problem." I say something weak about community supports but I really don't know what might have helped short of a turnaround in how our society views disability.

"Truly," says Girsh, "I would like an answer from our critics. Why can't some organizations fight to make life better for people with disabilities and others deal with the reality that death is coming to all of us and it needn't be brutal, lonely or agonizing?"

Yet Hemlock, through conflicting statements by its leaders, has been largely responsible for the copious ill will that exists between the disability community and the right-to-die movement.

Derek Humphry, Hemlock's founder, has taken heat for advocating "justified suicide by a handicapped person," and there's this oft-quoted chestnut from Janet Good, founder of Michigan Hemlock: "Pain is not the reason we want to die. It's the indignity. It's the inability to get out of bed or get onto the toilet, let alone drive a car or go shopping without another's help. . . . Most of them say, 'I can't stand my mother—my husband—wiping my butt.' That's why everybody in the movement talks about dignity. People have their pride."

They do, but are driving, shopping, continence, and self-buttwiping prerequisites?

A recent public-relations disaster occurred when Hemlock invited Philip Nitschke to address its national conference in San Diego. Nitschke, an Australian campaigner for euthanasia, advocates making "rational suicide" available to everyone from troubled teenagers to lonely old people. At the conference, he called Kevorkian a hero and offended many Hemlock members by his immoderate zeal for suicide. Hemlock, for the record, has distanced itself from Kevorkian, and may now be edging away from Nitschke.

It hasn't helped that Nitschke receives funding from Hemlock to design machines people can use to kill themselves, or that he assisted in the very public death—twenty-one family members and friends attended—of euthanasia advocate Nancy Crick, who reportedly was dying from a recurrence of bowel cancer. A postmortem found no sign of cancer, and Nitschke later admitted he was aware of Crick's cancer-free state.

But organizations can learn and change, and there are signs that Hemlock is doing just that. Paul Spiers, a T6 paraplegic who will take office as board chair in July, says he's committed to improving communication and healing wounds.

PAD AS PUBLIC POLICY

A good friend with Parkinson's disease killed himself some years ago. He had talked to his inner circle, giving most of us a chance to talk him out of it, and we failed him utterly.

Once he'd decided to die, he tried to direct the exhaust of his car into his house. Neighbors kept walking by, and he decided the effort was entirely too public. He slit his wrists, but didn't bleed fast enough. "It's like *The Three Stooges Commit Suicide*," he wrote in his journal. Finally he succeeded in hanging himself. It was awful for him, awful for his friends.

Most unassisted suicides tend to be grotesque. They're violent or fail or create new disabilities. They exclude loved ones at a time when closure is needed. Wouldn't the option of PAD be better than that?

"I think it ought to remain difficult and messy," says Harriet Johnson, "something you'd think about pretty hard before doing. I don't see every suicide as irrational or even tragic. However, I have no trouble following NDY in toto when it comes to the law, which is what NDY is really about. Killing should remain a criminal act. When it's discovered, we should prosecute. But the law isn't the same as justice and never will be. It serves too many conflicting purposes to represent any kind of ideal."

So to serve justice, at times, we should ask someone to bend or break the law for us? That's hard on the someone else.

"As it ought to be. Gut-wrenching, bone-chilling agony."

My friend was very far from terminal, which raises another sticky question: Johnson thinks Oregon's restriction of its PAD law to people with six months to live is suspect. "It's really illogical to give them, and only them, the right to a quick and easy out. I agree with Kevorkian that if anyone 'needs' death services it's people with a long life expectancy who are miserable. I don't quite understand why the lines are drawn the way they are. But then, I reject the whole idea of line-drawing."

So we should offer PAD to everyone or no one?

"To no one."

"I believe that whether or not to continue living is as personal a choice as anyone could make," says Lauri Yablick, "and that helping people die is potentially as valid a role for healthcare providers as helping them live." But legalizing PAD? "No. Not here, not now, and given our healthcare system, not for a long time. This is such a complicated issue and people want to treat it so simply."

Yablick questions the Oregon law's lack of consistency and inclusion. "The Oregon Act excludes most people with mental conditions. Who sold the myth that we can make a clear, reliable and objective determination of competency and emotional stability? Where's the logic in excluding people with depression and other serious mental illness—groups with the highest rates of suicide—from the sanctioned version? Won't people with progressive dementias still feel pressured to act prematurely? Who decided that physical suffering trumps emotional suffering?

"Another great fallacy is that regulations prevent abuses," she says. "[The] Ten Commandments didn't bring a loving and peaceful world. More laws didn't bring fewer prisons. And the regulations intended to prevent other healthcare abuses have failed miserably. I know in every finger, toe and split end that widespread acceptance [of PAD] will result in further abuse."

Yablick points to how easily health professionals can encourage someone to die. "The way I see this playing out if PAD is added to the mix is that, in the midst of an outburst, some disinhibited pain-in-the-ass substance-abusing patient exclaims, 'I'd just rather be dead!' He suddenly gets the individual attention he's been craving in this understaffed pit, and is lovingly coached to his rightful place.

"The law has to be crafted for the most vulnerable members of society," Yablick reminds us. "The law is for everybody. How can we support hastened death under these circumstances? It's a choice I want available for me and for everyone I love, but it's just too damn costly."

PERSONAL REDUX

The law is for everybody. Viewed through that framework, some of the pieces shift into place and some go skittering off the puzzle board. What you make of PAD is your business, but here's where I landed after I made it mine:

After all the discussion, suicide remains a personal matter. Individuals, not organizations, commit suicide. We shouldn't moralize or psychologize after the fact.

Suicide aided by laypeople who provide knowledge and support—Hemlock's sort of assistance—raises the ante. More people participate and coercion, by others or by circumstance, becomes a greater concern. Yet Hemlock and other programs like it provide an alternative to PAD, and perhaps a better one. They enable facing death peacefully in the home, after the goodbyes are said, with friends and family present.

If we really want the option of hastening death, and if Hemlock were to drop its advocacy for PAD and concentrate on what it already does—take the P out of PAD—I'd be tempted to say it's the best way we can provide some autonomy in end-of-life decisions without opening the door to systemic abuse.

True, utilizing Hemlock's help can send a terrible message about disability, but it's a gentler message than legalizing PAD. And what message do we send if we allow ourselves to linger through intractable pain, dementia, through it all, whatever we've got, into nothing? Won't people say, "I wouldn't want to die that way"? Is it so bad to end a good life with a good death?

PAD is an enormous escalation from suicide, either solitary or in the company of others. It makes our end-of-life choices the province of law, medicine, and economics, as implemented by a deeply flawed healthcare system. My fear is that PAD will become a constant presence in healthcare settings, a big friendly mutt that lays its head in our laps and wags its lethal invitation whenever we doubt our ability to go on.

Readers with long memories may recall that I've been kinder to PAD in the past. I said I wanted the option available for myself and couldn't bring myself to distrust my doctors or hospitals. I feel the same now, but was wrong to think my preference was relevant to PAD legislation. It's relevant only to me.

NDY's arguments do seem relevant. They no longer strike me as paranoid and shrill, but as reasoned reflections of horrors already seen. With all my faith in my healthcare providers, I have seen them. And NDY, more than other organizations, addresses the complexity of the issue.

AUTONOMY's arguments are tight, attractive, and easy to grasp. That's its strength and its weakness—all its philosophical eggs in one basket. Personal autonomy is a worthy goal, but it's only one factor in lawmaking and, for that matter, disability rights. It offers no guarantee of benefit to society.

In the diffuse light of complexity, I see PAD inviting excess—eugenics resurrected by fetal DNA testing, for example, or Nitschke's vision of one-way euthanasia cruises, burial at sea included. Kevorkian's posturing as a savior. Peter Singer's promotion of infanticide for disabled newborns.

I'm left with too many inconsistencies that smell fishy. Why limit PAD to people who are terminal? Don't the nonterminal suffer? Why is PAD wrong in the presence of depression? Is it not part of the suffering that needs relief, and must we disqualify anyone whose depression cannot be cured? Why a waiting period for PAD requests? Whose asses and assets are we covering? Why offer PAD to people who are physically capable of taking their own lethal dose, and deny it to those who are not? Why aren't we better at the long-term and palliative care that might make PAD less attractive? Why do we "respect" the suicidal wishes of disabled people, yet treat the same wishes of nondisabled people as cries for help? Why would we make trusted doctors speed our passage to eternity? Why do so many people want PAD only because they're afraid of becoming like us?

There are good answers to some of these questions. But until they all, and many more, are part of the debate, we don't understand the issue.

There may come a time when PAD will make sense in this country. I cautiously hope so. But PAD now? I don't think so.

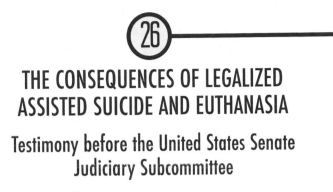

THE CONSEQUENCES OF LEGALIZED ASSISTED SUICIDE AND EUTHANASIA

Testimony before the United States Senate Judiciary Subcommittee

Diane Coleman

INTRODUCTION: PERSONAL HISTORY

Mr. Chairman, vice-chairman, members, thank you for the opportunity to address this subcommittee. My name is Diane Coleman. I have a juris doctorate and masters in business administration from the University of California at Los Angeles, and am a member of the California bar, on inactive status. During the last twenty-four years, I have been employed first as an attorney for the state of California, then as codirector of an assistive technology center in Nashville, Tennessee, and now I am the executive director of Progress Center for Independent Living in Forest Park, Illinois, a nonprofit nonresidential service and advocacy center operated by and for people with disabilities.

I have had a neuromuscular disability since birth, and have used a motorized wheelchair since the age of eleven. From 1987 through 1995, I volunteered as a national organizer for ADAPT, also known as the American Dis-

Testimony from May 25, 2006.

abled for Attendant Programs Today. I continue to advocate, speak, and guest lecture on long-term care issues within Illinois.

When I was six years old, my doctor told my parents that I would not live past the age of twelve. A few years later, the diagnosis changed and so did my life expectancy. Over time, I learned that respiratory issues would probably develop. I have friends who've used nighttime ventilators for years, so I knew what symptoms to watch for, and four years ago, started using a breathing machine at night. I had two other friends, one in her thirties and one in her fifties, who needed the same thing. But their doctors discouraged them from it, reinforcing their fears, and either didn't know or didn't disclose what the medical journals said would happen as a result. At an early age, they each went into respiratory distress, and died within a month from infections. A number of my other friends have been pressured by hospital employees to sign do-not-resuscitate orders and other advance directives to forego treatment, coupled with negative statements about how bad it would be if they became more disabled. Frankly, I'm becoming worried about what might happen to me in a hospital if I have a heart attack or other medical crisis. I have appointed my healthcare proxy, but will the decisions I have entrusted to him be followed by my healthcare providers? I am not at all convinced that decisions to live are any longer treated with the same respect by healthcare providers as decisions to die. In fact, I am sure they are not.

NOT DEAD YET

Ten years ago, I was on my way to testify before the House Constitution Subcommittee about the opposition to legalized assisted suicide coming from national disability rights organizations. Many of us were worried about Jack Kevorkian, whose body count was 70 percent people with nonterminal disabilities, and we were worried about two circuit courts declaring assisted suicide a constitutional right. Kevorkian even had a legal defense fund provided by the Hemlock Society, later renamed "End-of-Life Choices" and now merged with "Compassion in Dying" to form "Compassion and Choices." In 1996, disability activists had begun to think that we needed a street action group like ADAPT to address the problem (see www.adapt.org), and it was actually the head of ADAPT, Bob Kafka, who thought of our name, taken from a running gag in *Monty Python and the Holy Grail*, "Not Dead Yet." From our viewpoint, assisted suicide laws would create a dangerous double standard for society's response to suicidal expressions, an unequal response depending on one's health or disability status, with physicians as gatekeepers. That sounds like deadly discrimination to us and, frankly, we've been disappointed that the US Department of Justice didn't use our civil rights law, the Americans with Disabilities Act, instead of the Controlled Substances Act, to challenge the Oregon assisted suicide law. Like other minority groups, we feel that discrimination is best addressed on the federal level, and states' rights have too often meant states' wrongs.

THE PROBLEM OF THE CULTURE WAR

The first thing I want to emphasize is that I'm sick and tired of the hypocrisy on both sides of the culture war in this debate.

During the primary election campaigns this year, I still heard of candidates using the Schiavo case to fuel the culture war. My personal hero during that crisis has been conveniently forgotten. Senator Tom Harkin raised the legitimate concerns of people with disabilities. In a press conference held on March 18, 2005, he said:

> Where there is a genuine dispute to what the desires of the incapacitated person really are, then there ought to be at the end some review by a federal court outside of state jurisdiction. You might say, "Why a federal court?" State courts vary in their evidentiary proceedings and in their process—fifty different ones. . . . Every review of that, up through the state courts, is basically on the procedure, not upon the first facts. In a case like this, where someone is incapacitated and their life support can be taken away, it seems to me that it is appropriate—where there is a dispute, as there is in this case—that a federal court come in, like we do in habeas corpus situations, and review it and make another determination.

I'm sick and tired of our opponents on this issue, often our liberal or progressive allies on other issues, who oversimplify the dangers facing disabled people who depend on others for basic needs. Court-appointed and statutory guardians have potential conflicts of interest. The most common are the spouse and adult child, who are also the most common perpetrators of elder abuse. If we were talking about child abuse, everyone would admit that there is a legitimate role for government intervention, carefully balanced against privacy rights. Do people in guardianship deserve less? Nor can we trust state courts as the final word. If we were talking about death penalty cases, most would admit that the courts are far from infallible, and that a right of federal review is an important protection for the constitutional rights of the accused. Do people in guardianship deserve less?

I'm also sick and tired of our allies on this issue, often our conservative opponents on other issues, who see assisted suicide and euthanasia as violating their principles, but see no contradiction as they slash budgets for the healthcare we need to survive. The Republican governor of Missouri has cut Medicaid funding for feeding tubes and ventilators, establishing a difficult procedure to get these devices, with most who try to use it reportedly failing to get what they need. Jeb Bush just cut Medicaid coverage for the food that goes in the feeding tube by adding similar burdensome procedures. The irony is not lost on us, but media exposure in Florida put this action on hold. This is nothing less than back door euthanasia. And let's face it, much of the struggle at the state level flows from federal cuts. Backdoor euthanasia.

Disability rights groups have a unique perspective, informed by both our principles and our experiences. Our principles embrace nondiscrimination, civil rights, and self-determination. Our collective experiences include monumental struggles against the crushing oppression of a healthcare system that devalues us and a society that fears significant disability as a fate worse than death. We are consumers on the front lines of the healthcare system, facing your worst fears with grace and dignity, yet we have been pushed to the margins and even excluded outright from the debate on these issues.

I am sick and tired of our opponents who claim that Not Dead Yet represents only a few. Twenty-six national disability groups strongly questioned the use of conflicted evidence to justify Terri Schiavo's euthanasia by starvation and dehydration. Since then, thirty-seven organizations have adopted a Statement of Common Principles, affirming the civil and constitutional rights of people with disabilities, whatever our age or type of disability, but especially those under the decision-making authority of a third party.

I am even more sick and tired of our opponents who falsely claim that Not Dead Yet is a puppet of the Christian right, or funded by pro-life groups (which our bylaws prohibit). One blogger, Working For Change columnist Bill Berkowitz, recently claimed that our attorneys on our three Schiavo amicus briefs were "foot soldiers" of the religious right and funded by conservative foundations. But our attorneys never received a penny for their services on behalf of Not Dead Yet and the sixteen national disability rights groups that joined our briefs, and these attorneys work for a prominent disability rights organization in Chicago, Access Living.

Why are our opponents so intent on misleading people about who we are? Perhaps they think that is the best way to stop people from hearing what we have to say. We will never be silenced. But who will question the simplistic rhetoric and decide to listen?

The topic of this hearing is broad, and could include five areas of concern to us: [1] assisted suicide, [2] passive euthanasia based on a surrogate's decision to withhold treatment, [3] passive euthanasia based on a physician's decision to withhold treatment (aka futility judgments), [4] active euthanasia, and [5] denial of healthcare by a health plan or government insurer (aka back door euthanasia).

[1] ASSISTED SUICIDE

What's It Got to Do with Disability?

Assisted suicide is supposedly about terminal illness, not disability, so many question the legitimacy of disability groups "meddling" and trying to "take away" what they see as the general public's right to choose assisted suicide, some say when they're terminally ill, others say when they're suffering. The stated criteria vary between Compassion and Choices and Final Exit Network, among others, and some people switch group affiliations and eligibility criteria depending on the audience.

The disability experience is that people who are labeled "terminal," based on a medical prediction that they will die within six months, are—or will become—disabled.

The real issue is the reasons people ask for assisted suicide. Although intractable pain has been sold as the primary reason for enacting assisted suicide laws, it's really a "bait-and-switch" situation. The reasons doctors actually report for issuing lethal prescriptions are the patient's "loss of autonomy," "loss of dignity," and "feelings of being a burden."

Those feelings often arise when a person acquires physical impairments that necessitate relying on other people for help in tasks and activities formerly carried out alone. Those are disability issues. In a society that prizes physical ability and stigmatizes impairments, it's no surprise that previously able-bodied people equate disability with loss of dignity.

Studies of patient attitudes toward assisted suicide and euthanasia confirm that "[p]atients' interest in physician-assisted suicide appeared to be more a function of psychological distress and social factors than physical factors." "When patients ask for death to be hastened," another study concluded, "the following areas should be explored: the adequacy of symptom control; difficulties in the patient's relationships with family, friends, and health workers; psychological disturbances, especially grief, depression, anxiety. . . . ." And another study exploring psychosocial factors provided the following analysis:

> The desire for euthanasia or assisted suicide resulted from fear and experience of two main factors: disintegration and loss of community. These factors combined to give participants a perception of loss of self. . . . Symptoms and loss of function can give rise to dependency on others, a situation that was widely perceived as intolerable for participants: "I'm inconveniencing, I'm still inconveniencing other people who look after me and stuff like that. I don't want to be like that. I wouldn't enjoy it, I wouldn't, I wouldn't. No, I'd rather die."
>
> Participants frequently used the notion of dignity to describe the experiences associated with disintegration: . . . "You've become a bag of potatoes to be moved from spot to spot, to be rushed back and forth from the hospital, to be carried to your doctors' appointments or wheeled in a wheelchair, and it really does take away any self-worth, any dignity, or any will to continue to live."
>
> . . . Loss of community entailed the progressive diminishment of desire and opportunities to initiate and maintain close personal relationships, owing to loss of mobility, exclusion and alienation by others, and self-isolating actions by participants. . . .
>
> Participant: "I think we should all be allowed to die with our dignity intact."
> Interviewer: "OK and what do you mean by dignity?"
> Participant: "Um, the ability to perform simple things like, you know, going to the bathroom on your own and not through a bag, um, breathing with your own lungs. . . . I used to be somebody, but now, like I mean, you know, I'm no better than like a doll, somebody has to dress me and feed me and I guess it's uh, I don't know how to explain it, really."

These are common words for newly disabled people.

Disability groups, however, object to the implicit claim that any of us need to die to have dignity. Needing help in dressing, bathing, and other intimate daily tasks does not rob a person of autonomy and dignity. Unfortunately, popular culture has done virtually nothing to educate the public about how people with severe disabilities actually live autonomous and dignified lives. Our lives are portrayed as tragedies or sensationalized as heroism, but the real life issues and coping styles that most people will need if they live long enough are left out of the picture. No wonder people who acquire disabilities so often see death as the only viable solution.

But studies show that whether or not they are terminally ill, people who ask for assisted suicide or euthanasia usually change their minds.

The Problem of Physicians as Gatekeepers of Assisted Suicide

The disability rights movement has a long history of healthy skepticism toward medical professionals, and there's an established body of research demonstrating that physicians underrate the quality of life of people with disabilities compared with our own assessments. Our skepticism has grown into outright distrust in our profit-driven healthcare system.

It should be noted that suicide, as a solitary act, is not illegal in any state. Disability concerns are focused on the systemic implications of adding assisted suicide to the list of "medical treatment options" available to seriously ill and disabled people. The Oregon law grants civil and criminal immunity to physicians providing lethal prescriptions based on a stated claim of "good faith" belief that the person was terminal, acting voluntarily, and that other statutory criteria were met. This is the lowest culpability standard possible, even below that of "negligence," which is the minimum standard theoretically governing other physician duties.

As the Oregon reports on physician-assisted suicide make clear, the state has not been able to assess the extent of nonreporting or noncompliance with the law's purported safeguards, but only obtains brief interviews with physicians who file their paperwork. There are no enforcement provisions in the law, and the reports themselves demonstrate that nonterminal people are receiving lethal prescriptions. As the *Oregonian* newspaper stated on March 8, 2005, in "Living with the Dying 'Experiment,'" examining the case of David E. Prueitt who woke from his assisted suicide after two weeks and did not try again, "The rest of us . . . still need an answer from a system that seems rigged to avoid finding one."

This is the system that controls eligibility for assisted suicide under the Oregon law. Physicians decide who's terminal and who isn't, despite well-known problems with prediction. Physicians decide what "feasible alternatives" to disclose to the individual. I can't help but note, however, that these same doctors have never been required to disclose any financial conflicts of interest they might have in determining what course of treatment to recommend. We're all supposed to take it on faith that no doctor will be influenced by the financial terms of his or her health plan contracts in the information and advice they give. Physicians also decide if the individual's judgment is impaired, if the desire to die seems rational to them.

The Oregon law immunizes physicians from being accountable for each of these decisions.

The reasons doctors actually report for issuing lethal prescriptions are the patient's "loss of autonomy" (86 percent), "less able to engage in activities" (85 percent), "loss of dignity" (83 percent), and "feelings of being a burden" (37 percent). People with disabilities are concerned that these psychosocial factors are being widely accepted as sufficient justification for assisted suicide, with most physicians not even asking for a psychological consultation (14 percent) or the intervention of a social worker familiar with home- and community-based services that might alleviate these feelings. The societal message is "so what?" or "who cares?"

The primary underlying practical basis for the physician's determination that the individual is eligible for assisted suicide is the individual's disabilities and physical dependence on others for everyday needs, which is viewed as depriving them of what nondisabled people often associate with "autonomy" and "dignity," and may also lead them to feel like a "burden." This establishes grounds for physicians to treat these individuals completely differently than a physically able-bodied suicidal person would be treated.

In effect, the Oregon law gives physicians the power to judge whether a particular suicide is "rational" or not based on his or her evaluation, or devaluation, of the individual's quality of life, and then to actively assist certain suicides based on that judgment. The Oregon Death With Dignity Act authorizes and empowers physicians to discriminate in their response to a patient's expression of the wish to die based on the patient's disability. This should be viewed as a violation of the Americans with Disabilities Act, which prohibits such discrimination.

The Impact of Assisted Suicide Laws on Others

But perhaps the most important question is not whether the rights of the few people who request assisted suicide and get it have been compromised, though that is a concern, but whether legalizing these individual assisted suicides has a broader social impact. Does it matter that a society accepts the disability-related reasons that people give for assisted suicide, declares the suicide rational, and provides the lethal means to complete it neatly? Does it harm people who are not deemed eligible for assisted suicide under the current version of the law, but nevertheless experience severe illnesses and newly acquired disabilities as a loss of dignity and autonomy?

To assess that, I think we should look at the fact that Oregon has the fourth-highest elder suicide rate in the country. From the disability rights perspective, this is not surprising. In the face of constant social messages over nearly two decades that needing help in everyday living robs one of dignity and autonomy, makes one a burden, and justifies state-sponsored suicide, maybe Oregon's elders have taken this disgusting and prejudicial message to heart.

What looks to some like a choice to die begins to look more like a duty to die to many disability activists. I have yet to see an article in which the Oregon health authorities who profess concern about the high elder suicide rates go so far as to even mention the Oregon Death With Dignity Act, much less examine the social message behind it. From a disability rights perspective, the potential connection seems obvious.

[2] THE EROSION OF PROTECTIONS FOR PEOPLE IN GUARDIANSHIP

Assisted suicide laws and practices do not stand in isolation, but arise in the context of a larger healthcare system that also includes substitute decision making affecting the lives of people who are deemed "incompetent" or not capable of making and communicating their own decisions. Determinations of "incompetence" are made both formally through the courts, and informally, depending on state laws and healthcare provider policies. A competent individual may direct his or her future medical care during a potential period of incompetence through the use of an advance directive. An advance directive can specify the medical treatments that an individual would accept or refuse in various circumstances. In addition or in the alternative, an advance directive can designate a substitute or proxy whom the individual trusts to weigh the complex information and factors that may be involved in a specific healthcare decision.

Healthcare decisions for people deemed incompetent are generally governed by state laws. Substitute decision-makers may be proxies chosen by the individual while competent, or surrogates appointed according to a priority list established in state law (the list usually beginning with the spouse and ending with the public guardian). Surrogate decisions are supposed to be based on what the individual's wishes would have been, if competent.

However, most states have laws permitting healthcare providers to avoid compliance with advance directives. When the provider refuses to withhold or withdraw treatment the patient doesn't want (a rarity these days), these provisions are referred to as "conscience clauses" and usually require some effort to transfer the patient to another provider. When the provider refuses to provide desired care (common these days), these provisions are called "futile care" policies.

Several court cases have arisen from family disputes involving people who became incompetent without executing an advance directive. Before the well-known case of Terri Schiavo in Florida, there was the case of Robert Wendland in California. Both Mr. Wendland's wife and mother agreed that he was not in a "persistent vegetative state," and that he had not left clear and convincing evidence of his wishes. Nevertheless, his wife argued that she should be able to remove his tube feeding anyway. A state statute, based on a national model healthcare decisions code, gave her the right to starve and dehydrate him even if he had expressly requested food, and forty-three bioethicists filed a friend of the court brief in agreement, under the authorship of Jon Eisenberg.

Ten disability rights organizations filed in support of the mother's view, and against the general presumption that no one would want to live with his disabilities, which was being used to justify lowering constitutional protections of his life. Ultimately, the California Supreme Court agreed that Mr. Wendland's life could not be taken without clear and convincing evidence of his wishes. Unfortunately, this ruling was issued three weeks after he died from pneumonia, having been deprived of antibiotics.

By the time the Schiavo case reached major national attention in 2003, twenty-six national disability organizations had taken a position that Terri Schiavo should receive food and water, due to the highly conflicting evidence of her wishes and the fact that she had not chosen her own guardian. We were deeply disturbed to see court after court uphold questionable lower court rulings. This time, Jon Eisenberg and fifty-five bioethicists supported the removal of food and water. Disability rights groups were also disturbed that the court allowed most of Terri Schiavo's rehabilitation funds to be spent on her husband's lawyers, that she was denied a properly fitted wheelchair, a swallowing test and therapy, the potential for oral feeding, speech therapy, and the freedom to leave the hospice with her parents, even temporarily. Despite media reports to the contrary, the autopsy report was not inconsistent with a finding that she was in a minimally conscious state and could have benefited from these things. And we were concerned that adult protective services did not intervene, and the state protection and advocacy agency tried but proved powerless.

It would appear that the prevalent prejudice that no one would want to live like Terri Schiavo translated into her guardian's unfettered right to treat her at best as a prisoner, at worst as though she was already dead. Too many of us have been told by someone that he or she could not stand to live the way we are. Too many of us have been forced into institutions and locked away.

Nevertheless, the perspectives of such prominent national groups as the Arc of the United States (formerly the Association for Retarded Citizens), the National Spinal Cord Injury Association, the National Council on Independent Living, and many others were consistently ignored by most of the press, as well as the courts.

Unfortunately, the anecdotal evidence suggests that Terri Schiavo's case may be the tip of a very large and almost fully submerged iceberg. I've been a healthcare advocate for a couple of decades, often joining street protests against government health cuts. One mission of the end-of-life care movement is a good one, to educate health care providers about how to provide good palliative care, but another mission is to shape public policy on healthcare. It appears that a certain line of thought in bioethics has pretty much taken over the policy-making work. This line of thought involves a lifeboat approach, deciding who gets thrown out.

This week, I received a phone call from a woman with three children and an ex-husband who died Sunday. She had found Not Dead Yet on the Internet. Her ex-husband, age thirty-five, had been in a car wreck on April 2. She said that he had been on a ventilator until two weeks ago, but had been weaned from it. She described ways in which he seemed to be slowly improving in responsiveness. But from the beginning, the doctors in Peoria, Illinois, had urged the man's mother and all of his family to withhold treatment. Last Thursday, they finally persuaded his mother to remove his food and fluids. Had he survived until Monday, a lawyer was set to go into court and argue that the mother should not have been guardian due to alcoholism and other factors that made her susceptible to pressure, but too late. I'm getting too many calls like this from people being pressured.

For the last three decades, mainstream bioethicists have told the press and the public that euthanasia is about "compassionate progressives" versus the "religious right" and have equated their proposals with "patient autonomy" and the "right to die." Nevertheless, these bioethicists are actually talking about the legal parameters for statutory guardians and healthcare providers to medically end the lives of people with disabilities, especially cognitive disabilities, on a discriminatory, nonvoluntary and involuntary basis. Based on their well-funded policy work, it often takes more documentation to dispose of our property than to dispose of our lives. This affects people with brain damage resulting from birth injuries, accident or trauma, strokes and dementia, and other causes.

One of the leaders of the end-of-life care movement, Dr. Ira Byock, was interviewed by *Ragged Edge Magazine*, a leading disability rights publication. He stated that Partnership for Caring and Last Acts, national leaders in the movement until they disappeared under a cloud late in 2004, had excluded the disability perspective, and that this exclusion was "deliberate and irresponsible." What's especially disturbing is that they had fifteen years and hundreds of millions in funding from prominent foundations, and set up surrogate decision-making protocols to end the lives of people with intellectual disabilities, without seeking the input of such individuals and the established organizations that address issues of self-determination for people who have less typical ways of receiving, processing, and communicating information.

What might other disability groups have brought to the discussion table? There are many journal articles about the problems with advanced directives. A consistent finding in several funded studies is that people change their minds about what treatments they want, and what level of disability they will accept, as they move through the experience of having increasing disabilities. The disability community has a response to that, to use a popular phrase, "well, duh."

And you may have seen reports of an Alzheimer's study in 2004. It confirmed previous studies that caregivers have a lower opinion of their relative's quality of life with Alzheimer's than the persons themselves have, and found an explanation for the discrepancy. The caregivers project their own feelings about the burden of care-giving onto the person they care for. Once again, the disability community response is "well, duh." And these are the very caregivers who make life-ending decisions.

Policies on removal of food and water have serious and far-reaching implications. Many people in nursing homes are on feeding tubes not because they cannot eat orally, but because there are not enough staff to help them eat. One study also found that in for-profit nursing homes, African Americans with dementia are taken off hand feeding and put on a feeding tube sooner in the disease process than their white counterparts. Abracadabra, the individual is then on "life support," the kind that can be removed by a third-party decision-maker.

Another key issue for protection of people in guardianship is the problem of state guardians, who may have an inherent conflict of interest due to the state's role in Medicaid. The Kentucky Supreme Court ruled in 2004 that a public guardian may deprive life-sustaining treatment from a man labeled mentally retarded, despite the financial conflict of interest for a state guardian of a ward on Medicaid. Another state guardian case involved Haleigh Poutre, an eleven-year-old girl in Massachusetts who was allegedly beaten into a coma by her stepfather and whom the state wanted to remove from life support earlier this year. The resulting legal dispute bought a little time. The court agreed to remove life support, but by then Ms. Poutre defied physician pronouncements, woke up, and was transferred to rehabilitation.

[3] FUTILITY

Now, increasingly, another type of third-party medical decision threatens older and disabled people, decisions by physicians in open opposition to the patient, their surrogate, or their advance directive, i.e., futility. A big part of many futile care policies is an ethics committee that holds meetings to persuade the family that they should agree with the doctor and thereby avoid the potential for litigation. This was the strategy suggested in a 1999 article in the *Journal of the American Medical Association*. But if the doctor can't convince the surrogate to withhold treatment, then they may overrule the surrogate.

Futile care policies provide that a doctor may overrule a patient or their authorized decision-maker in denying wanted life-sustaining treatment. Futile care policies do not generally require that the treatment be objectively futile, but allow doctors to use subjective criteria such as quality of life judgments as grounds for denying treatment.

Studies consistently demonstrate that physicians and other healthcare providers rate the quality of life of people with significant disabilities and illnesses significantly below the individual's rating of their own quality of life. These healthcare providers may also be financially penalized for providing too much healthcare (contracts call it "over-utilization"). We've learned that lawyers rarely take wrongful death cases involving people with significant illnesses, because damages are generally calculated based on lost earnings, and cause of death may be hard to prove. So there's very little protection for consumers with expensive needs.

Recently, a Texas futility case received some media attention. Andrea Clark, a conscious heart surgery patient in Houston was sentenced to die before her time in Texas under its "Futile Care" statute. An "ethics committee" told her family that life support would be removed ten days after they were given notice. The Texas law allows the ethics committee to give only forty-eight hours' notice for a meeting, but HIPAA (Health Insurance Portability and Accountability Act) allows providers seventy-two hours before medical records must be provided to the family. Both before her surgery and when not drugged into unconsciousness afterward, Ms. Clark herself made her wishes in favor of treatment very clear. She had reportedly been declared terminal five years earlier and repeatedly survived her predicted demise. Through massive efforts, including protests and legal wrangling, the hospital relented and Ms. Clark spent an extra week with her family, including her twenty-three-year-old son, before she died. But why did her family have to fight for her wishes to be honored?

Disability rights leader Bob Kafka said of the Texas law, "The essence of the futility law embraces involuntary euthanasia. The ability of a doctor to overrule both the patient and their surrogate in withdrawing life-sustaining treatment is a violation of the principle of patient autonomy. This law can't be fixed, it needs to be killed—or euthanized."

[4] ACTIVE EUTHANASIA

My colleague Dr. Carol Gill, a disabled psychologist, delivered a keynote address at a 2001 conference, sponsored by Neiswanger Institute for Bioethics and Health Policy, at Loyola University of Chicago. She detailed the events leading up to the death of her mother-in-law, who had become increasingly disabled over a seven-year period, and lived in an assisted-living facility. A daughter was the woman's guardian. The mother was hospitalized after a stroke. Though she had not had a swallowing test, the mother was on a feeding tube. At one point, the guardian/daughter and doctor withheld feeding for four days without the agreement of the rest of the family, but mother kept asking for ice cream, so they relented. But by then she was weakened, and soon seemed to be nearing the end of her life. One morning, the daughter asked the doctor to get it over with, so her morphine dose was increased until she died. I thought about Dr. Gill's story when I heard the news about a new law in Colorado.

On April 4, the governor signed a bill pushed by the pro-assisted suicide advocacy group Compassion and Choices. Senate Bill 102 protects doctors and caregivers from being prosecuted under the manslaughter statute for giving palliative care to the terminally ill. According to one of the bill's proponents, "No Colorado physician delivering palliative-care medications has been charged with manslaughter, but many physicians have hesitated to prescribe painkillers to terminally ill patients out of fear of prosecution." Now, I always thought they were afraid of prosecution under drug laws, not manslaughter statutes.

Why didn't they seek immunity from drug laws? What is the motivation for manslaughter immunity? What group besides doctors could be powerful enough to get a statute to protect them from a nonexistent problem of prosecution just because they wrongfully deny patients pain relief? How is it that the medical profession is afforded such lack of accountability?

Years ago, Kathryn Tucker of Compassion and Choices wrote about a case involving nonvoluntary withholding of food and water, and concluded that "a wide chasm exists between the requirements of Washington state law and medical practice" when it comes to healthcare decisions. There are two ways to respond to that problem. One is to enhance consumer protection by increasing the accountability of healthcare providers. The other is to rewrite the laws to correspond to actual practice. This is already being done for surrogacy laws and futility laws. Is the Colorado statute another example of the same phenomenon, ensuring that doctors won't risk prosecution for active euthanasia of people who have agreed to palliative care?

[5] BACK DOOR EUTHANASIA—RATIONING AND BUDGET CUTS

Back before the patient autonomy movement of the 1970s and 1980s, doctors did make all the life and death decisions. Now, some doctors think that patients and their families have gone too far in demanding medical treatment for people who are too old and have advanced chronic health impairments. Some physicians and lawyers think that healthcare resources need to be rationed, and that physicians know best who should receive healthcare.

These lifeboat bioethicists seem to think of themselves as progressives, but oddly they never spend much energy on ways to cut unnecessary costs before cutting lives. My sister recently started a new career as a medical assistant at a practice with twenty-five doctors in Michigan. She said that four days out of five, she doesn't have to buy lunch because it's catered in by pharmaceutical companies. Marketing costs. But rather than spending all that professional brain power on conquering the waste and inhumanity of a profit-driven healthcare system, these bioethicists are pushing new health-care decision laws to kill disabled people who aren't going to die soon enough for their taste without a little push.

In the face of these developments, the disability rights movement has expertise to bring. But we also have an attitude about disability that diverges from the mainstream, especially the mainstream of bioethics. Frankly, I think that's why we were deliberately excluded from the last decade of policy-making conducted off the public radar screen, why the right-wing-left-wing script was so important to these bioethicists, no matter how untrue and exclusionary.

Basically, the bioethicists have warped the palliative care movement into a life-ending movement. They've had hundreds of millions of dollars to work with, and they've used it to build a steamroller that's decimating the civil and constitutional rights of people whose lives are viewed as too marginal to merit support. This affects more than the disability community of today, it affects everyone, directly or through family, sooner or later. A privileged few are making the rules for who lives and who dies, but it's happening behind closed doors and has not been subject to public discussion. The Texas chapter of Not Dead Yet just resigned from a Texas Advance Directives Coalition, calling for just such a public discussion. But this is relevant in all states and at the federal level as well.

If the bioethics debate can't hold up to open public scrutiny, then how can it legitimately determine what our nation's healthcare policies will be?

While disagreeing with mainstream bioethics, the conservatives have their own way of rationing healthcare. Instead of basing it on the person's health status, they base it on their economic status. For those who depend on publicly funded healthcare, especially in this aging society, federal and state budget cuts pose a very large threat.

I can't help but note that much of the power of the end-of-life movement has come from the fact that Medicare did not cover prescription drugs, including pain relievers. It was pure extortion to require people to agree to forego curative treatment in order to get pain relief, and I've been terribly disturbed to see that the new Medicare prescription drug coverage does not include the primary pain-relieving medications, continuing the pattern of extortion that forces people to agree to hospice, refuse curative treatment, and accept a potentially premature death in order to receive pain relief.

HOW CAN FEDERAL LEGISLATORS HELP?

OPEN PUBLIC DISCUSSION

Foster open public discussion of these policies. At this point, people find out about futility when a family member is denied treatment he or she wants. We think that futility policies are unconstitutional, but the wider public needs to know before policy actions can be formulated. And disability rights groups must be included.

MEANINGFUL FEDERAL REVIEW

Under Medicare and Medicaid law, you could provide for meaningful federal review of contested third-party decisions to withhold treatment in the absence of an advance directive or personally appointed surrogate. Uphold a clear and convincing evidence standard with teeth in it. Uphold a presumption for food and fluids.

CONGRESSIONAL STUDY

Ever since the Cruzan decision in 1990, people with disabilities, old and young, have been starved and dehydrated based on surrogate or health provider decisions, but we don't know who, why, how, or what factors were involved. We also know that physicians are overruling patient autonomy and denying treatment under futility policies. You could ask for all hospitals to send you their futility policies. Congressional examination of the impact of existing policies is necessary.

STATE-BY-STATE REVIEW OF LAWS AND POLICIES

Funding for a disability rights–based state-by-state review of guardianship and healthcare decision laws is needed, along with comprehensive efforts to develop reforms to safeguard against nonvoluntary and involuntary euthanasia.

PUBLIC EDUCATION BY PEOPLE WITH DISABILITIES

There should be funding for public education about the perspectives of people living with significant disabilities on the difference between end-of-life decisions and decisions to end the lives of disabled people who are not otherwise dying.

OLMSTEAD IMPLEMENTATION, PASSAGE OF MiCASSA

The civil rights of people with disabilities to long-term supports in the community under the US Supreme Court decision in Olmstead should be implemented. We call for passage of the Medicaid Community Attendant Services and Supports Act, which would allow people receiving Medicaid funding to have a life in the community instead of being forced into a nursing home. This bill also includes consumer-directed options that maximize personal responsibility and reduce costs.

SUSTAIN GOVERNMENT-FUNDED HEALTHCARE PROGRAMS

Conservatives who honestly supported efforts to protect the life of Terri Schiavo should work on a bipartisan basis with moderates and liberals to ensure continued appropriate funding of Medicare and Medicaid.

CONCLUSION

To conclude, regardless of our abilities or disabilities, none of us should feel that we have to die to have dignity, that we have to die to be relieved of pain, or that we should die to stop burdening our families or society. Cognitive abilities must not be allowed to determine personhood under the laws of the United States. Reject the script you have been given by the right-to-die and the right-to-life movements. Instead, listen to the disability rights movement. We are your advance guard, in anticipation of the aging of our society, with decades of experience in living with disability and on the front lines of the healthcare system. We offer a very different vision, as well as the practical know-how and leadership to help build a society that respects and welcomes everyone.

SUICIDE INTERVENTION FOR PEOPLE WITH DISABILITIES

A Lesson in Inequality

Carol J. Gill

The American commitment to equality, which affirms the value of all individuals and their entitlement to the pursuit of a good life, is by no means a "hands off" ethic. It is backed by a determination to support and protect vulnerable individuals (and, as we have seen recently, even nations) during hardship. America's prominence in suicide prevention is certainly consistent with this tradition.

A different belief system—one that weighs the value of human life in terms of its costs, that idealizes mental and physical superiority, and that endorses termination of weak individuals in the name of "mercy"—is one we tend to associate with other cultures in other places. In reality, we know these beliefs, too, are part of America's history. Some argue that social Darwinism and the eugenics movement are becoming as influential in American thinking currently as when they flourished early in this century.[1]

When a culture values human life conditionally, suicide intervention becomes selective. Devalued populations fail to receive rigorous protection, assessment, and treatment.[2] Already at heightened risk from their oppressed status, devalued people are further endangered by deprivation of psychological support. Current research indicates that unaddressed social stress factors (not any inherent physiological or racial defect) account for high rates of depression and suicide in certain minority groups in the United States.[3]

People with disabilities compose a minority group for which little suicide data have been collected. A great deal is known, however, about the virulent social oppression endured by this population. In employment, interpersonal acceptance, economic stability, freedom of mobility, and community access—all variables thought to have a significant bearing on suicide potential—people with disabilities are among the most disadvantaged.[4] Moreover, current research indicates people with disabilities experience more environmentally induced depression than average,[5] suggesting an increased potential for preventable suicide.

Ironically, this population, on whose behalf so little suicide research has been conducted, is subject to a burgeoning number of legal and medical decisions concerning the management of intentions to die. Critical life and death precedents and policies are being established at alarming speed, with little concern for the facts and gaps existing in our understanding of disability and suicide.

Often in psychology, the precursor to sound research documentation is careful clinical observation. In the area of disability and suicide, I have endeavored to make such observations on the basis of specialized training and practice in psychological crisis-intervention (including suicide treatment), thousands of therapy hours working with disabled people in rehabilitation and individual practice, and more than three decades of personal experience living in the world as a disabled person actively involved with other people with disabilities.

Over the years of my "continuing education" and clinical experience with disabled individuals, I have heard their problems, fears, needs, and desires with growing force and clarity. At the same time, I have become increasingly concerned by the dearth of resources available to support their impressive efforts to pursue a good life in a frustrating, unwelcoming environment. Particularly alarming is the current trend to deny basic suicide prevention services to individuals who are severely disabled, those most exposed to high-risk factors.

IDENTIFICATION

The discriminatory treatment of disabled people who express a desire to die begins with the initial interpretation and labeling of that desire. When a nondisabled person reveals a desire to die, ordinarily it is categorized as "suicidal," and the individual is treated accordingly. For persons with severe disabilities, however—particularly persons who use a respirator, feeding assistance, or other life aids—the desire to die has acquired labels such as "refusal of treatment," a wish to avoid prolonged suffering or dying, a desire to let a terminal disease take its natural course (used in cases of long-term disability lacking any evidence of terminal illness!), and "not committing suicide."[6] The implication is that there is something natural, reasonable, or proper about a disabled person's dying as opposed to a nondisabled person's dying.

Complicating matters is the fact that disabled persons' communications of suicidal intent are frequently confounded by their own negative statements regarding disability. The public misunderstands "right to die" cases in which the troubled individual laments the disability itself or the need for "life supports." Lacking an informed perspective and harboring intense fears of becoming disabled, the public, including judges, ethicists, and media reporters, takes such complaints at face value and looks no further for their significance. Such people readily conclude that the disabled person's wish to die is reasonable because it agrees with their own preconception that the primary problem for such individuals is the unbearable experience of a permanent disability (and/or dependence on life aids). If permanent disability is the problem, death is the solution. In this analysis, the wish to die is transformed into a desire for freedom, not suicide. If it is suicide at all, it is "rational" and, thereby, different from suicides resulting from emotional disturbance or illogical despair.

These assumptions betray a faulty understanding of both living with disability and considering suicide. Addressing the latter, Edwin Shneidman, pioneering researcher and clinician in American suicide prevention, has described suicide as "a multidimensional malaise in a needful individual who defines an issue for which the suicide is seen as the best solution."[7] He explains that any deliberate act of self-annihilation is suicide, even if effected through the acts of others (e.g., when individuals ask to be killed by others) or coerced (e.g., when captives are forced to kill themselves by the brutality of others). He emphasizes that all suicidal behavior is motivated by need, not reason alone. Although the choice of dying seems logical to the suicidal individual, it is a logic distorted by need, distress, and constricted perception. According to Shneidman and other suicidologists, every suicide, no matter how calm and rational on the surface, involves emotional distress or "perturbation."[8] By this definition, disabled people's requests to die are, indeed, suicidal. Furthermore, they are emotional. While some suicides seem to make more sense to us than others, none is exclusively based on reason without an element of untidy, irrational, human distress.

It is impossible to appreciate the suicidal aspect of many right to die cases unless one understands not only suicide but the realities of living with a disability. The fact is, with sufficient time and support, people generally adjust to disabilities. People of all kinds buck social prejudice regarding disability and gradually change their perspectives on quality of life.[9] They learn to use human and technological assistance to enhance life, integrating the use of such things as respirators, attendant services, urinary devices, and assisted feeding—all referred to in this article as life aids—into their daily routines as gracefully as many people have adjusted to their need for computers and fax machines. Social attitudes notwithstanding, people with disabilities generally feel neither heroic nor tragic because they use life aids. They view such assistance as a mundane aspect of their lifestyle.

When an individual with disabilities expresses intolerance of life aids or living with a disability, then, it is symptomatic. Such distress may arise from a variety of factors. Often it represents an unresolved adjustment reaction to either a new disability or a change in an existing disability. With appropriate support, information, and time, the distress usually diminishes.

Other times, the distress signals underlying emotional illness, particularly acute or chronic depression. People who struggle to survive in a thwarting environment occasionally despair or "burn out." Before assisted suicide for people with disabilities became popular, severely disabled Lynn Thompson carefully engineered her own death after learning she would lose her independent-living funding. Her recorded message left no doubts about the cause of her despair. The threatened cut in her support funds was, she said, "the straw that broke the camel's back."[10]

For people with disabilities, as for anyone else, bouts of depression may lead to suicidal impulses. Depression and psychopathology of long standing may also be expressed indirectly in somatic complaints, including complaints about disability. Research on depression indicates a tendency in troubled individuals toward global negative thinking and internalization.[11] For people with disabilities, this suggests that when depressed for any reason, they are more likely to "internalize" society's rejection and devaluation of disability. More vulnerable, at such points, to the negative regard they sustain on a daily basis, they express the depression as a global disdain for the disabled self. Any features of the individual's life that represent disability or "abnormality," e.g., life aids, become intolerable.

For some persons with disabilities, the distress they express regarding life aids is particularly misleading because it is expressed in the service of a secondary goal. This occurs when an individual selects discontinuance of life aids as a *method* of suicide precisely because it is likely, these days, to elicit a cooperative response from the environment. For example, if I am a respirator user and I have decided to commit suicide because of a romantic breakup, it would make strategic sense for me to convince others that I can no longer tolerate the respirator. They might not support my death over a romantic loss, but they might accept it—even assist in it—if I present it as an escape from disability. If I receive approval or assistance to commit suicide, not only is the result guaranteed, but I am also relieved of the usual tension of sole responsibility for making the decision and implementing it. People with severe disabilities characteristically are master survivalists. They learn by necessity how to influence others to assist them. It is an essential, creative skill that, unfortunately, can also be applied consciously or unconsciously for self-destruction.

In the special matter of requests by institutionalized disabled persons for discontinuance of life aids, an element of self-destructive anger may be operating that is dangerously overlooked.[12] The underlying psycho-logic of such requests may be: "If people won't help me live my life the way I wish, at least I'll make them help me die." When disability activists and other supportive individuals intervened to prevent quadriplegic Larry McAfee's death, for example, it released his considerable anger towards people and policies responsible for his institutionalization.[13]

The point is, whether a nonterminal disabled person's request to discontinue life aids results from a disability adjustment crisis, an internalized rejection of the disabled self during depression, anger turned inward, or solely an attempt to solicit environmental assistance in performing the suicidal act, such requests are clearly pathological and clearly suicidal. To view them otherwise is to deny the dignity and value of ordinary life with disability and those who live it.

DISABILITY AND SUICIDE IN CLINICAL PRACTICE

The tendency on the part of the public and the legal system to deny the suicidal intent of disabled persons requesting death assistance could possibly be attributed to lack of information. It is more difficult to comprehend this behavior in medical and mental health professionals. Yet in publicized right to die cases involving disabled people, medical experts have been guilty of a striking denial of suicide risk and depressive disorder in the face of significant evidence of psychopathology.

According to the *Diagnostic and Statistical Manual of the American Psychiatric Association* (DSM-III-R), a major depressive episode is characterized by depressed mood, a loss of interest in usual activities, or both. For definitive diagnosis, there must be a significant number of symptoms from a list that includes appetite disturbance, sleep disturbance, psychomotor agitation or retardation, loss of energy, feelings of worthlessness, difficulty thinking or concentrating, and thoughts of dying. Additional features may include withdrawal from friends and family, soft or slowed speech, guilt, suicide attempts, panic attacks, preoccupation with physical problems, irritability, antisocial behavior, and abuse of drugs or alcohol. The average onset is in early adulthood. There is interference in social and occupational functioning; in severe cases the individual may be incapable of self-feeding, dressing, and personal hygiene. Psychosocial stressors, such as the death of a loved one, marital separation, and childbirth, can precipitate a major depressive episode. The manual alerts practitioners to suicide as the most serious complication in this disorder.[14]

A brief review of two famous cases exemplifies how professionals sometimes abandon medical diagnostic guidelines, such as those just described, when confronted with disability. At age twenty-six, Elizabeth Bouvia, a woman with cerebral palsy, expressed the wish to die after a series of severe losses, including a miscarriage and marital separation. Essentially homeless and impoverished, she voluntarily entered the hospital, anorexic and seeking narcotics. Her verbalizations focused narrowly on somatic complaints and death. She had a plan to bring about her death. She made demands for support and care from the hospital staff. She said she was unable to feed herself, a fact that people who knew her disputed. In sum, she presented more than the necessary number of signs to qualify for a diagnosis of depression with suicide risk of moderate lethality. Yet, several professionals pronounced her free of disorder and labeled her plan reasonable.[15]

In an interview videotaped before his death from respirator disconnection, David Rivlin, a man with quadriplegia, presented classic symptoms of depression.[16] He was tearful, his speech slow and flat, his affect consistently depressed. He talked about being sad and fearful. He expressed anger at society for its attitudes toward people with disabilities. He said he could no longer tolerate life in an institution and asked the public to "reach out to others before they lose hope." Records indicate that Mr. Rivlin had been increasingly isolated in his last year and that he had withdrawn from past interests.[17] He indicated reluctance to die but said he saw no alternative. In the face of this evidence, it is difficult to imagine how mental health professionals could have overlooked his depression and suicide potential. Mr. Rivlin died with the assistance of a physician he barely knew following a farewell party in which he saw friends and family who had failed to visit him for years.[18] The assisting physician lauded his death as "a beautiful event" and "good medicine."[19]

DISCRIMINATORY TREATMENT OF SUICIDAL PERSONS WITH DISABILITIES

Suicide treatment involves several activities or strategies that are thought to be crucial steps in helping individuals at risk.[20] They can be summarized as follows: (1) Conceptualizing the problem for which the individual has chosen death as the solution; (2) Identifying and treating the individual's urgent needs; (3) Offering alternate solutions to break through the individual's constrictive thinking; (4) Supporting and reinforcing the life preserving side of the suicidal ambivalence; and (5) Preventing death. Examining each step in the treatment process while referring to recent right to die cases will, hopefully, illustrate the problems of discriminatory suicide intervention for people with disabilities.

Conceptualizing the Problem

It is in the identification of the problem, perhaps, where the unequal treatment of people with disabilities is most blatant. In all the public right to die cases involving conscious nonterminal disabled persons, there is scant evidence of anyone looking beyond the obvious, the disability, as the cause of distress. In fact, there has been a tendency to discount readily available clues leading to other suicide precipitants. Dismissed have been predisposing historical factors such as multiple losses, family dysfunction, childhood abuse or neglect, current stresses (e.g., work, finances, housing, romance), alcohol or drug problems, isolation, loss of control over lifestyle, and low self-regard.

David Rivlin repeatedly expressed despair and anger over his confinement to a nursing facility. He talked about his death as the only avenue to freedom from the imprisonment of institutionalization. Apparently, his signals of distress were in vain. No professional ever identified his institutionalization as the problem to be addressed. No one helped him find a way to live independently with assistance (as many with similar disabilities do) or to live at all. Kenneth Bergstedt stated his problem so clearly that no one could miss it.[21] Physicians, reporters, and judges all agreed that Bergstedt wanted to die because he was afraid—afraid of losing his ill father, afraid no one would look after his needs.[22] No one treated Bergstedt's fear or despair. No professional even suggested helping him accomplish a healthy separation from his father or teaching him the skills of living he needed to survive. Professionals trained to help and heal allowed Kenneth Bergstedt to be suffocated by his father, as if assenting to a primitive right of filicide.

Physicians and mental health practitioners who hastily conclude in such cases that disability itself is the problem violate their most basic responsibility to conduct a thorough examination. They allow personal bias to distort their grasp of the problem, thereby precluding the quality of assessment required for appropriate intervention.

Addressing Needs

Without an accurate view of the problem, it is impossible for helping professionals to guide desperate persons with disabilities in fulfilling critical needs. A person exhausted by the struggle to live in a world of frustrating barriers may need a variety of things, some concrete, others more spiritual: money, equipment, a place to live, an attendant, nurturance, control over lifestyle, outside stimulation, creative outlets, love, work, or validation of personal worth. However, if permanent disability itself is the only problem acknowledged, the need to escape the disability receives undue emphasis. A therapeutic response that focuses on one impossible need while neglecting all others may be more detrimental than no response at all. It reinforces the individual's own sense of hopelessness that life can be fulfilling enough to justify living. Rivlin and McAfee needed a way to conduct their lives outside an institution. Kenneth Bergstedt needed to secure quality attendant services as well as support to cope without his father. Elizabeth Bouvia needed many things, but, perhaps above all, she needed time—time to heal and re-emerge as she had during past crises in her life.

Offering Alternative Solutions

One of the most dangerous aspects of despair is the development of rigid, constrictive thinking, sometimes referred to as tunneling. When death seems like the only solution, death is likely to follow. Here, the task of the therapist is to present as many alternatives as possible, seeking help and information as needed from family members, agencies, and other professionals.

All too often, however, persons with disabilities are offered few viable alternatives to death. The professionals assigned to help them are frequently as afflicted by tunnel vision regarding disability as their clients! Unfortunately, most physicians, nurses, psychologists, and even rehabilitation staff know little beyond the medical facts about living day to day with a disability.[23] Disability and quality living seem antithetical to many. This bias prevents many professionals from realizing they lack information that their clients deserve. The fatal error, literally, is their failure to consult disability advocates for advice and resource information, thus cutting their clients off from a world of possible solutions.

Siding with Life

In the management of suicidal ambivalence, people with disabilities have been treated with striking discrimination. Suicide experts explain that in despairing individuals the desire to die and the desire to find life worth living teeter in balanced opposition until something tilts the equilibrium. A central tenet of suicide treatment is that the helping person must ally with the life-desiring side of the dilemma.[24] Quite the opposite occurred for Bouvia, Rivlin, McAfee, and Bergstedt. Ambivalence went unrecognized. Doctors, judges, and family members agreed with the self-destructive impulse, calling it "rational," "courageous," and "the solution." Clearly, people with disabilities find the scale of ambivalence heavily weighted on the side of death.

People with disabilities who have been suicidal often tell us how important it was in their recovery to receive unwavering opposition to their death wishes from key people in the environment. In her account of how she coped with suddenly acquiring quadriplegia, "Tough Love" co-founder Phyllis York describes her battle with initial depression. Her husband and close friends adamantly protested her desire to die. She writes:

People who tell me they understand my wanting to commit suicide are not helpful. They say that they have been in bad places, too, and can understand my desire. But I hear them silently telling me to do it—that I'm such a mess I shouldn't want to live. People who tell me to shut up make me angry, but at least they don't sanction my death.[25]

Preventing Death

The most basic policy of suicide prevention is to protect the client from dying. Not only are disabled individuals often denied this protection, increasingly they are given assistance in committing the act. In the *Bouvia* case, the ACLU (American Civil Liberties Union) actually intervened to restrain Riverside General Hospital from treating Ms. Bouvia as it would a nondisabled person in similar circumstances.[26] In the cases of Rivlin,[27] McAfee,[28] and Bergstedt,[29] courts sanctioned their deaths without even ordering suicide assessment or treatment from professionals qualified to work with disabled clients. . . .

RECOMMENDATIONS

To address the problem of discrimination in suicide prevention for people with disabilities, the following recommendations are offered. They are not intended to be complete. They are listed in the hope that they will underscore the urgency of this problem and stimulate concern, discussion, and action from other quarters.

Better Scrutiny of Disabled Persons' Intentions to Die

When a person with disabilities wants to die, the most appropriate response (and, sadly, these days, the most neglected) is, "Why?" The death request of a person with disabilities should be explored as rigorously and objectively as it would be for anyone else, including the specific reasons behind it and possible solutions. Mental health professionals who work with people in crisis are trained to be meticulous sleuths. They are taught not only to hear their clients' obvious complaints but also to look further in order to uncover latent problems. Unfortunately, this process is commonly abbreviated or bypassed when the client is severely disabled, with dire results.

Millions of people live with disabilities. Disability is no more a sufficient or acceptable reason for wanting to die than romantic failure would be for an adolescent. Both losses may seem, at times, like the end of the world to those who experience them; but if important people in the environment address this sense of hopelessness rather than acquiesce to it, the individual has a fighting chance of mastering despair.

The Evaluation and Treatment of Disabled Persons Who Wish to Die Should Be Conducted by Professionals with Disability Expertise

Standards of practice in mental health enjoin professionals from practicing beyond the limits of their training and experience. Particularly, practitioners are cautioned against treating minority clients before obtaining adequate education regarding their clients' minority cultural experience. This dictum has been egregiously violated in the treatment of people with disabilities. Basic medical training by itself is grossly insufficient for dealing with the daily socioeconomic/political problems of disability. Professionals with little appreciation of the complexities of the disability lifestyle mishandle the needs of disabled clients in despair. Disabled people who want to die deserve to be seen by therapists who speak their language and understand their experience.

Persons Reacting to New or Changing Disabilities Should Be Given Sufficient Time and Support for Adjustment

When the suicidal wish derives from a troubled adjustment to disability, it should be treated as aggressively as any other kind of crisis. Suicide prevention should be implemented. Additionally, the support of family, friends, and community organizations should be enlisted for problem solving to enhance life quality. This may ultimately require education and treatment for the family to correct prejudices that could sabotage the adjustment of the disabled individual.

Persons Experiencing "Disability Burn-Out" Should Be Treated for Stress

Disabled individuals who are exhausted by their struggles with economic, social, and structural barriers in the environment need protection and time to recover. They need guidance to comprehend and rechannel their feelings and an astute counselor who neither downplays their struggle nor shares their temporary loss of hope. They also need to connect with disability advocates to help them through the barriers ahead.

Psychological Disorder Contributing to Suicidality in Persons with Disabilities Should Be Treated

This recommendation may seem too obvious to warrant listing. It should be beyond question that a person with disabilities who is suffering from depression, situational crisis, panic, and other disorders is as entitled to the full range of therapeutic interventions as a nondisabled person in distress. However, the personalities and emotional problems of people with disabilities are often overlooked when helpers fixate on their physical status. Equal treatment includes not only suicide prevention and, when needed, psychiatric hospitalization, but also the option of continuing long-term treatment for any remaining disorder or life problems once the crisis phase has passed.

Legal Protections Must Remain in Place

In a society that fears and rejects life with disability, people with disabilities need laws and the courts to safeguard their equal access to suicide prevention. In cases such as Bouvia's and McAfee's, the time delays and argument inherent in the court process itself may have permitted their change of heart. Many right to die proponents argue for the private right of families (with physicians' consultation) to make expedient life and death decisions for incompetent loved ones. This is a misguided position. Any therapist who has worked with disabled people has heard tragic stories of harm inflicted by loving, well-meaning family members making decisions on their behalf. The commonness of such recollections reminds us that loving someone with a disability does not naturally confer insight or even immunity from prejudice. Moreover, society does little to encourage families in their efforts to support the lives of relatives with disabilities. Consequently, families of people with disabilities often function under considerable economic and emotional strain. They are bombarded with dim assessments of potential life quality from others, including the media and the medical professionals who advise them. Unquestionably, the most caring families can make mistakes. Their authority in life and death decisions must remain amenable to the checks and balances of the legal process.

Disability Experts Must Be Involved

The views of many parties—physicians, family members, attorneys, religious advocates, politicians, ethicists, civil libertarians, right to die proponents, and journalists—have been well represented in court and in the media when persons with disabilities have asked to die. Less often heard and rarely heeded has been the voice of the disability community. Briefs filed by disability advocacy groups have been virtually unacknowledged in court proceedings. Views of experts who are disabled are rarely sought or recognized by the legal system, medical establishment, or media. One might wonder if people with disabilities have credibility only when asking to die! An extreme example of the neglect of the disability perspective is the Bergstedt case, in which the court sanctioned the death of a conscious, nonterminal adult without even speaking directly with him. He was represented, in part, by a parent in questionable mental health and by a doctor who acknowledged but saw no need to treat Bergstedt's depression.[30] Disability advocates were allowed no opportunity to intervene. The only instance in which disability activists and others familiar with disability issues managed to intervene was in the McAfee case. Here the disability perspective dramatically altered the course of events, and a life was saved.

To guarantee nondiscriminatory treatment of disabled persons who are suicidal, right to die proceedings must be informed by disability awareness. No assistance in dying should ever be considered without evaluation and intervention by qualified professionals and advocates who either have personal disability experience or extensive familiarity with disabled people and their life issues. Competency training for professionals should be developed incorporating key contributions and monitoring by disabled professionals, consumers, and advocates. Physicians, allied medical personnel, suicide prevention staff, hotline workers, and psychiatric intake workers should receive such training to sensitize them to the social dynamics of disabled people's despair.

LAST WORDS

For a country that purports to embrace human diversity, citizens with disabilities constitute the acid test. Our integration into American culture would involve radical changes in such concepts as independence, normality, and quality of life. The belief that life with a severe disability, including the use of life aids, is untenable rudely rejects the culture—the customs and ways of living—of people with disabilities. Reminiscent of the days when many people preferred to "be dead than Red," current opinion reflects an overwhelming public preference for death to disability.[31] Tragically, this sentiment is only too apparent in the lack of suicide prevention services offered to people with disabilities.

As long as society supports suicide prevention services for anyone, it is morally and legally obligated to extend these services to people who are disabled. To accept a suicide is to encourage it. Encouraging the self-destructive urges of persons with disabilities who despair is not merciful or compassionate. It is dangerous for those individuals, for all disabled people as a devalued group, and ultimately for a society founded on equality. Persons with disabilities demonstrate that they value their lives a great deal more than others do.[32] Those who give up on life do so only after struggling with the very human pain of unmet needs. Society must not silence those needs by death but by assisting in their fulfillment. That is the authentic compassionate response.

NOTES

1. Nat Hentoff, "Are Handicapped Infants Worth Saving?" *Village Voice*, January 8, 1991, 18; Richard J. Neuhaus, "The Return of Eugenics," *Commentary*, April 1988, 15–26.

2. Robert Kastenbaum and Ruth Aisenberg, *The Psychology of Death* (New York: Spring, 1972), pp. 426, 463.

3. George H. Colt, *The Enigma of Suicide* (New York: Summit Books, 1991), pp. 251–58; "Culture Blamed for Women's Depression," *Chicago Tribune*, December 6, 1990, § 1, 9; Herbert Hendin, *Suicide in America* (New York: Norton, 1982), pp. 88–93; Kastenbaum and Aisenberg, *The Psychology of Death*, p. 463.

4. Harlan Hahn, "Disability Policy and the Problem of Discrimination," *American Behavioral Scientist* 28 (1985): 293–318.

5. R. Jay Turner and Morton Beiser, "Major Depression and Depressive Symptomatology among the Physically Disabled," *Journal of Nervous and Mental Disease* 178 (1990): 343, 345–46.

6. Mary Johnson, "Suicide Lessons," *Disability Rag*, January/February 1990, 25, 27 (quoting Judge Edward H. Johnson).

7. Edwin S. Shneidman, *Definition of Suicide* (New York: Wiley, 1985), p. 203.

8. H. S. Olin, "The Third Wish," in *What We Know about Suicidal Behavior and How to Treat It*, ed. S. Lesse, 77–84 (Northvale, NJ: Aronson, 1988); K. Siegel, "Psychosocial Aspects of Rational Suicide," *American Journal of Psychotherapy* 40 (1986): 405–18; Shneidman, *Definition of Suicide*, p. 208.

9. R. Stensman, "Severely Mobility-Disabled People Assess the Quality of Their Lives," *Scandinavian Journal of Rehabilitative Medicine* 17 (1985): 87–99.

10. See *60 Minutes*, CBS television broadcast, October 1, 1977.

11. S. Deutscher and P. Cimbolic, "Cognitive Processes and Their Relationship to Endogenous and Reactive Components of Depression," *Journal of Nervous and Mental Disease* 178 (1990): 351, 352, 356.

12. Paul G. Quinnett, *Suicide: The Forever Decision* (New York: Continuum, 1987), p. 53; P. Tridon et al., "Abandon ou refus therapeutique: rite de passage chez l'adolescent handicape et malade chronique," *Neuro-Psychiatrie de L'Enfance et de L'adolescence* 31 (1983): 407–408.

13. Larry McAfee touched off a public controversy in 1989 when he filed for judicial permission to have his ventilator disconnected to cause his death. He had been injured by a motorcycle accident and as a result had lost the use of his arms and legs. He required constant care. Eventually the Georgia Supreme Court affirmed his right to refuse ventilation. See *State v. McAfee*, 385 S.E.2d 651 (Ga. 1989); see also Peter Applebome, "Judge Rules Quadriplegic Can Be Allowed to End Life," *New York Times*, September 7, 1989, 10. During and after the court proceedings, McAfee befriended and then was assisted by numerous individuals to obtain job training and secure independent living outside the nursing home environment. These developments persuaded McAfee to reverse his decision to die and instead continue to live. See Peter Applebome, "An Angry Man Fights to Die, Then Tests Life," *New York Times*, February 7, 1990, A1.

14. American Psychiatric Association, *Diagnostic and Statistical Manual of Mental Disorders*, 3rd rev. ed. (Washington, DC: American Psychiatric Association, 1987), pp. 218–24.

15. Stanley S. Herr et al., "No Place to Go: Refusal of Life-Sustaining Treatment by Competent Persons with Physical Disabilities," *Issues in Law and Medicine* 8 (1992): 3, 9.

16. *The Life of David Rivlin*, WDIV, Detroit, television broadcast, August 6, 1989.

17. *People Magazine*, August 7, 1989, 58.

18. Before his death, Rivlin had sought judicial approval to have his life support withdrawn. Petition for Removal of Life-Sustaining Apparatus and Incidental Relief, *In re* Rivlin (Mich. Cir. Ct. 1989) (No. 89369904). In an oral ruling, however, Judge Hilda R. Gage of the Michigan Circuit Court of Oakland County held that the court lacked subject matter jurisdiction because Rivlin's petition was un-

opposed and the case failed therefore to present a justiciable controversy. The court would not issue a declaratory judgment unless the petitioner amended his petition to plead an actual dispute. Rivlin declined to do so. Apparently, the court was of the opinion that Rivlin's case was not a right to die action but a right to refuse medical treatment action. Thus, no court order was issued approving or restricting the intended refusal. See letter from Bruce Brakel, law clerk for Judge Hilda R. Gage, to Theresa Kealy, staff counsel, National Legal Center for the Medically Dependent and Disabled, Inc., September 27, 1989, characterizing on ruling issued from bench by Judge Gage; on file with the National Legal Center litigation office.

19. Statements made by John W. Fin, MD, WMUZ Detroit, radio broadcast, March 2, 1990 (direct quote from broadcast), and *The Life of David Rivlin* (direct quote from broadcast).

20. Shneidman, *Definition of Suicide*, pp. 225–35.

21. The father of Kenneth Bergstedt, a twenty-two-year-old person with quadriplegia and dependent on a ventilator, petitioned the Nevada courts for authority to remove his son's ventilator. Though Kenneth died before the case was resolved, the Nevada Supreme Court went on to rule that he had a right to refuse life support and that such action would not constitute suicide, nor assisting suicide if carried out by others. *McKay v. Bergstedt*, 801 P.2d 617 (Nev. 1990).

22. Mary Johnson, "Unanswered Questions," *Disability Rag*, September/October 1990, 19.

23. H. G. Gallagher, *By Trust Betrayed: Patients, Physicians, and the License to Kill in the Third Reich* (New York: Holt, 1990), pp. 40–41; Carol J. Gill, "A New Social Perspective on Disability and Its Implications for Rehabilitation," in *Sociocultural Implications in Treatment Planning in Occupational Therapy*, 49–55 (New York: Haworth, 1987).

24. Edwin S. Shneidman et al., *The Psychology of Suicide* (1976), p. 430.

25. Phyllis York, *Getting Strong in All the Hurting Places* (New York: Rawson Associates, 1989), p. 208.

26. See Diane Coleman, "Withdrawing Life-Sustaining Treatment from People with Severe Disabilities Who Request It: Equal Protection Considerations," *Issues in Law and Medicine* 8 (1992): 55.

27. See note 18.

28. *State v. McAfee*, 385 S.E.2d 651 (Ga. 1989).

29. *McKay v. Bergstedt*, 801 P.2d 617 (Nev. 1990).

30. Affidavit of Jack A. Jurasky, MD, *Bergstedt v. McKay* (Nev. Dist. Ct. 1990) (No. A281607).

31. Barbara Brotman, "Ruling Prompts Paper Chase to Get Affairs in Order," *Chicago Tribune*, July 6, 1990, § 5, 1.

32. N. Weinberg and J. Williams, "How the Physically Disabled Perceive Their Disabilities," *Journal of Rehabilitation* (July 1978): 31–33.

FREEING CHOICES

Nancy Mairs

A September Sunday morning, still and hot. George [my husband] and I munch our ritual scones with strawberry jam as we leaf through the *New York Times* and half listen to Weekend Edition on NPR. An interview comes on that I begin to heed more closely: a discussion of the increasingly common practice of using amniocentesis to determine the sex of a fetus, followed by abortion if the parents don't want the sort they've begun. What they generally want, as parents have done from time immemorial, is a boy.

The person being interviewed plainly shares my distaste for sexual selectivity. But the way she articulates it brings me up short. "Sex," she tells her interlocutor emphatically, "is not a birth defect."

"That sort of statement strikes a chill straight through my heart," I say to George, who has begun to listen more closely, too. He looks puzzled for a moment and then responds: "Oh. Yes. I can see how it might. I never thought of it that way."

Not very many people would. The implicit argument appears self-evident: the use of abortion to fulfill the desire for a male (or female) child is impermissible, but the same use to prevent an imperfect one is not merely legitimate but, many would argue, socially responsible. As a defective myself, however, I have some doubts.

Although mine was not a birth defect, some evidence suggests a genetic predisposition toward MS, and one day—perhaps even quite soon—this may be detectable. What then? What if, I find myself wondering, such a test had been devised more than half a century ago? Suppose a genetic counselor had said to my mother, "Your baby will be born healthy, and she will probably remain so throughout childhood. But at some point, perhaps in her twenties, she is likely to develop a chronic incurable degenerative disease of the central nervous system. She may go blind. She may not be able to speak. Her bladder and bowels may cease to function normally. She may become incapable of walking or even of moving at all. She could experience tingling, numbness, or intractable pain. In the end, she might have to be fed, bathed, dressed and undressed, turned over in bed, as helpless as an infant." What would Mother have done then? What should she have done?

I don't know. Morally, I feel a lot more confident asking questions than answering them. What I do know, from my own circumstances, is that I am glad Mother never faced the option to "spare" me my fate, as she might have felt obliged to do. I simply cannot say—have never been able to say, even at my most depressed, when I have easily enough wished myself dead—that I wish I had never been born. Nor do I believe that MS has poisoned my existence. Plenty of people find my life unappealing, I know. To be truthful, it doesn't altogether appeal to me. But a good scone with a cup of hot coffee does much to set things right.

I know I am lucky. There are conditions crueler than MS, including many birth defects, and some of these are already detectable by amniocentesis and ultrasound. Suppose—and I'm being far less speculative here than I was in imagining my own mother—that a woman learns that her fetus has spina bifida. The degree of disability may be impossible to predict, but the risks, she is told, include intellectual impairment, bladder and bowel dysfunction, repeated infections, and the inability to walk. Bright, healthy, and active herself, the woman strains to imagine what quality a life thus impaired might possess. Such a child can adapt to her circumstances, of course, and grow into an energetic and resourceful woman like my friend Martha, now in her sixties, married, and the moderator of her own show.

Even if persuaded of this potentiality, the mother still must decide whether she is emotionally and financially equipped for such an undertaking, with access to medical care and educational programs, reliable assistance from the child's father, a supportive community, a flexible attitude toward surprises and obstacles, and an indefatigable sense of humor. You can't decide that you're in the middle of a great book, and anyway you're sick unto death of the four-hour catheterization schedule, and the kid's bladder can damned well wait a couple of hours till you're more in the mood. Caring for children, even undamaged ones, never ceases, and in our society mothers are customarily expected to provide or arrange it. Much as I admire the mothers of variously disabled children I have known—and much as I believe their extraordinary qualities to derive, at least in part, from the rigors of their lives—I could not blame a woman who chose not to test her mettle in this way.

If I make her appear to be choosing in a social vacuum, I do so because, in a society where the rearing of even a healthy child is not viewed as a community undertaking, where much-touted "family values" are always ascribed to the nuclear and not the human family, the parents of a disabled child will find themselves pretty much on their own. If they are lucky enough to have health insurance, the insurer, whose goal is to maximize shareholders' profits rather than the well-being of patients, is not about to spring for a $7,000 power wheelchair that would enable a child with muscular dystrophy to mingle independently with his classmates on an almost equal "footing," though it might provide $425 for a manual wheelchair to be pushed by an attendant (which it would not pay for). A school system, underfunded by screaming taxpayers, is not likely to procure a Kurtzweil machine that would permit its blind students to "read" their own textbooks. Unless they are wealthy, Mom and Dad do the pushing, the reading, and whatever other extra duties are required, on top of their jobs and their care for any other children in the family.

"Eric and I plan to have only a couple of children," my daughter tells me, contemplating the start of a family. "Why should we expend our resources on a damaged one?" A plausible point, as I have come to expect from this most clearheaded of young women. And in fact, as she knows, her father and I took great care to avoid conceiving another child after her younger brother was born in distress because of Rh incompatibility. After a couple of blood exchanges, he recovered, but we were told that another baby would likely be damaged, perhaps gravely, by the antibodies in my blood. I was no more eager to raise a deformed or retarded child than Anne is. I might have chosen an abortion if contraception had failed.

But then I think of my godson, the product of contraceptive failure, who shares with his sister a possibly unique genetic condition that has caused severe visual impairment in them both. Many seeing people have a dread of blindness so overwhelming that they might well consider abortion if such a defect could be detected (as it could not in this case). But these are otherwise ideal children—healthy, smart, funny, confident, affectionate—and I think they're going to become terrific adults. The problem is that if you eliminate one flaw, you throw out the whole complicated creature, and my world would be a poorer place without Michael and Megan.

Obviously, I don't have an unambiguous answer to this dilemma. I don't think one exists. I do feel certain, in view of the human propensity for exploiting whatever techniques we can devise with virtually no regard for consequences, that more and more people will choose, either for their own reasons or in response to the social pressure not to produce "unnecessary" burdens, to terminate pregnancies so as to avoid birth defects (and to select for sex as well). This development won't eradicate people with disabilities, of course: birth trauma, accidental injury, and disease will continue to create them from those who started out as even the healthiest fetuses. What it will do is to make their social position even more marginal by emphasizing that no one with the power to choose would ever have permitted them to exist. Their own choice to survive will seem suspect. *We're doing everything we can to exterminate your kind*, the social message will read, *and we'd get rid of you too if only we knew how*. No one will ever say this. No one will have to.

This mute message—that one is an accident that ought not to have happened—is communicated again, in the issues surrounding the other end of life, by the current movement to legally protect the "right to die." This phrase always strikes me as a little odd, since the right to do a thing presupposes the option not to do it. Although one's conception and birth are chancy at best (will a sperm reach the egg, and if so, which one? will the egg implant? will the fetus reach viability?), one's death is absolutely not; and legislation in such matters seems wildly inappropriate. Human beings have never been able to leave one another's bodies alone, however, but seem compelled to regulate even their most private moments, and so I suppose it is inevitable that some of them are going to set out to protect one's legal right to do what one can't help doing anyway.

The phrase "right to die" is shorthand, of course, and seems considerably less reductive when spelled out: what is generally being called for by right-to-die advocates is the protection of one's freedom to choose the time and circumstances of one's own death and to receive assistance from willing accomplices if necessary. I am as adamantly pro-choice in this matter as I am with regard to abortion; but as with abortion, the question of "choice" here is vastly more complex than politicians, legislators, and religious fundamentalists make it. Their (self-)delegated task is to reduce the rich ambiguities of life to a set of binaries—us/them, law/transgression, right/wrong. The labels vary but the underlying aim is constant—so that we can all stretch out on the couch every Saturday afternoon in front of some quintessentially binary sports contest rather than on a moral rack. Just as your team wins or loses, you either vote for a candidate or you don't, who upon election either does or does not enact certain promised laws, which you either break or obey, and in the end, depending on the choices made, both you and your representative go to Heaven or to Hell.

For absolutists, the "right to die" issue is as indisputable as abortion: killing oneself, or helping another to die, is murder; although the first act is humanly unpunishable, the second ought to be penalized to the full extent of the law, which, in most states, requires that the perpetrator receive assistance in dying by electrocution, suffocation, or lethal injection. Oh well, "a foolish consistency is the hobgoblin of little minds," and all that. Absolutists come in more than one stripe, however (though such a pluralistic view would be repudiated by absolutists themselves), and some of those who crusade to pass legislation permitting assisted suicide seem just as scarily single-minded as their opponents: Jack Kevorkian, "Dr. Death," the principle figure among them.

My own relationship to suicide renders this an unusually vexed topic for me. I have suffered from clinical depression for several decades now, and although not all depressives become suicidal during an episode, I do. I have tried to kill myself more than once, and the last time I so nearly succeeded, taking an overdose of antidepressant medication, that I am unlikely to fail another time. Thus, I must monitor myself ceaselessly for symptoms that signal a downward spiral in order to seek timely treatment. I have spent a good deal of my life struggling to deny myself the death to which activists would like to guarantee me the right.

To complicate matters, I am as vulnerable as the next person to the ordinary situational depression that surges in response to painful life events. The triggers vary from person to person—a broken friendship, a miscarriage, divorce, the departure of children, even a failed exam or the death of a pet—but almost all of us have endured at least brief periods of sleeplessness, loss of appetite, panic attacks, distractibility, or ill-defined malaise following some personal catastrophe. Although my own situation gladdens more than it pains me, it does contain some grimmish elements, especially the threat of my husband's death. And because I am a suicidal depressive, I respond to this threat by wanting to kill myself.

A couple of years ago, George began to experience severe bowel problems, and because his melanoma had last recurred in his small bowel, these strongly suggested a relapse. Although I have always known that this may happen at some point, knowledge is no proof against terror, and I went instantly into a tailspin that very nearly carried me over the precipice of panic into the eternal abyss. I procured twice the amount of the medication that had nearly killed me the last time, and I began to plan: "Some afternoon while George is still teaching, so as to have plenty of time," I wrote in my journal. "Drink a beer to relax. Spread out an underpad to avoid soiling the bed. Lie down on it. That way I can't chicken out—once down, I can't get up again. Put on the white-noise machine. Go to sleep forever." Fortunately, I've been in the depression business long enough now to remain a little skeptical about my urges. "It would be stupid to die for no reason," I noted, "so I suppose I should wait until the tumor has been located." That shred of rationality held me back long enough to learn that this time George had not cancer but an antibiotic-induced colitis, and we have both lived to tell the tale.

My intimacy with self-destructive urges leads me to question the term "rational" suicide, which right-to-die proponents use supposedly to distinguish the death they have in mind from the one I have approached so closely. Suicide appears imperative only when one loses sight of all other alternatives (and there is always at least one other). Since hopelessness is a distinctive symptom of depression, which is an emotional disorder, actions carried out in a despairing state seem to me intrinsically irrational. This last time I clung to some shreds of reason, which saved me.

I also remembered my son-in-law's words during a family discussion of the precarious future, his voice flat and slightly muffled as it can get with strong feeling: "I think it would be very inconsiderate of you to kill yourself." If there's anything that chagrins me, it's acting stupid or inconsiderate. Better I should stay alive.

Seriously, consideration for others is one of the motives often expressed by people who argue for the license to end their own lives: the desire, sometimes quite desperate, not to be a "burden" on others. Perhaps as a legacy of the rugged individualism that fueled colonial settlement, our society has developed a peculiar structure, in which we create small units that, after a certain amount of time, break and expel even smaller fragments who will form their own similarly friable units: children can't wait to escape their parents, who sometimes can't wait to be escaped, and have families of their "own." The parent who becomes more than a peripheral part of the new constellation, especially one who because of incapacity requires a child's assistance, is considered an intrusion.

Shucking the previous generation in this way doesn't appear to have a practical basis. I mean, we hardly live under the conditions that forced the Eskimos to float their aged and ill off on ice floes in order to conserve scarce resources. The hardships entailed in keeping three or even four generations under one roof are, I think, psychological rather than material. And, as our staggering divorce rate makes clear, we are not, as a society, tolerant of the kind of psychological hardship I have in mind, caused by the tensions that inevitably arise between people living in intimacy. Our notion of satisfactory relationships is incurably romantic in the least wholesome sense of the phrase. We are so bombarded in the media by various and garbled messages about intimate interactions—from the pictorial rapture of a perfume advertisement to the pop-psych-speak of experts on television talk shows to horrific newspaper accounts of domestic abuse—that instead of accepting ordinary conflict as one of the fixed, though less agreeable features, of the human condition, we label it "bad," "sick," and damp it down as best we can, sticking the latest Arnold Schwarzenegger movie into the VCR, pouring a drink or popping a Prozac, heading out for a day at the mall, filing for divorce, whatever it takes to disengage from the maddening other. Or we explode, savaging or even killing the source of irritation.

No wonder the presence of another can seem a burden. No wonder some people would rather die than play such a role.

Many years ago, when I first became active in securing low-income housing for my community, I asked a friend from Israel, whose descriptions of various social programs there had impressed me, about housing for the elderly. He looked a little puzzled, and thinking he didn't understand the term, though his English was excellent, I explained the concept.

"Yes, I understand," he said. "We don't have any."

"What do you do with your old people, then?"

"They live with their families."

This notion was hardly foreign to me, since my grandmother had lived with us from the time I was nine; but the idea that an entire society could accept such an arrangement seemed strange indeed. Even though my own experience proved the contrary, I assumed that each generation naturally desired to be quit of the other, except perhaps at holidays, as soon as possible.

The horror of functioning as one of Job's afflictions can be so overwhelming that it obscures the needs and desires of others. That day years back when, panic stricken at George's impending death, I told my neurologist that I didn't want my children to take care of me because "that's not who I want to be in their lives," Dr. Johnson merely nodded, and we went on to discuss home help, Meals on Wheels, assisted-living arrangements in retirement communities, and other alternatives to the nursing home that evokes dread in just about all of us. I had then, and still have, no idea whether Anne (and now her husband) would consider taking me into their lives, and how burdensome they would find me if they did, but that's just the point: *I have no idea.* Anne was sitting right there, but I blurted what I thought she'd be relieved to hear—that she'd never be saddled with me—without taking the time to ask. At that moment, in the presence of a woman we scarcely knew, both of us distraught over George's illness, we could hardly have delved into the matter. But I could have said, should have said, something open-ended: "I don't know about living with my children. We haven't yet talked about it." Instead, I played Boss Mom, as I have done all too often, decreeing that only what I wanted could be done.

What I wanted—and what I think all of us want who demand the right to die on our own terms—was to maintain a sense of control. Even more than the dread of becoming a burden, helplessness triggers in us a manic terror that things are slipping from our grasp, and I was feeling more impotent than I had ever felt before. A few months earlier, a severe fall had signaled the dreaded end of my walking days. Since then, I had watched George's flesh melt mysteriously away, and now the bony remains huddled like jetsam on a hospital bed, tubes in his arms, his nose, his penis, and nothing I could do would bring him back. These circumstances struck me as intolerable, and I wanted the right to refuse them permanently and irreversibly.

I still do. I want to be the one in charge of my life, including its end, and I want to be able to enlist someone to help me terminate it if I choose "rational" suicide. I have a friend, a doctor whom I admire deeply, who has told me about assisting a patient, irreversibly ill and on a ventilator, to die: listening carefully to the man's clear and repeated requests, calling together his family for their last good-byes, administering a shot of morphine to ease his passage, turning off the ventilator, remaining with him until he had gone. I would hope to find someone as brave and compassionate if I were to make a similar appeal.

But I would not seek out Dr. Kevorkian or any other crusader for euthanasia, because people who act on principle are likely to sacrifice the individual for the agenda, which is frequently shaped by their own, often deeply buried, presuppositions about what constitutes an acceptable life. Doctors despise disease, or else they wouldn't become doctors, and I have heard of those who couldn't bring themselves to tell a patient she or he had multiple sclerosis because the diagnosis seemed too horrible to bear. Isn't a doctor suffering from this kind of anxiety all too likely to tell me: "You have MS? Of course you want to die! Here, let me write prescription so you can peacefully end it all."

In other words, the social construction of disability which makes me uneasy about urging abortion to prevent defective children disturbs me here, too. Behind the view of death as a "right" to be seized and defended lurks the hidden assumption that some lives are not worth living and that damaged creatures may be put out of their misery. True, all kinds of safeguards would be put into place to ensure that only the person doing the dying could make the ultimate decision; but no amount of regulation can eliminate the subtle pressure to end a life perceived by others to be insufferable. If, ideally, I ought never to have born, and if my dependent existence creates a burden on those who must care for me, then don't I have not merely the right but the obligation to die? How can I honorably choose otherwise?

My purpose in raising questions about abortion and euthanasia is not to condemn these procedures, which I believe ought to be freely available, in strict privacy, to any fully informed person who elects them. In fact, I would educate doctors more, and regulate them less, so that they and their patients could explore options, reach decisions, and take action without intrusion. My concern is that these issues be confronted in such a way as to create a social climate in which people with disabilities perceive life to be an honorable choice. And that means sending the social message that disabled people are valued and valuable, precious even, by investing, financially and emotionally, in institutions and practices that help them out.

Everybody, well or ill, disabled or not, imagines a boundary of suffering and loss beyond which, she or he is certain, life will no longer be worth living. I know that I do. I also know that my line, far from being scored in stone, has inched across the sands of my life: at various times, I could not possibly do without long walks on the beach or rambles through the woods; use a cane, a brace, a wheelchair; stop teaching; give up driving; let someone else put on and take off my underwear. One at a time, with the encouragement of others, I have taken each of these (highly figurative) steps. Now I believe my limit to lie at George's death, but I am prepared to let it move if it will. When I reach the wall, I think I'll know. Meanwhile, I go on being, now more than ever, the woman I once thought I could never bear to be.

I cannot excuse or condemn those women with MS, less crippled than I, who sought out Dr. Kevorkian's services. They had their lines. They may have lacked adequate support: familial, medical, psychological, spiritual. I can, however, defend the human right to choose actions that the nondisabled find unfathomable and perhaps even indecent. If a woman, upon learning that her fetus has spina bifida, may choose abortion, then she ought also to feel free to decide, without apology, to bear and rear the child, certain that she will have the same access to medical care and educational programs that a nondisabled child enjoys. If, after consulting with family, spiritual counselors, and medical personnel, a diabetic with gangrenous legs may ask for an easeful death, he should also be fully supported in his decision to live on as an amputee, confident that he can continue to work, shop, attend church, take his wife out for dinner and a movie, just as he has always done. Only in a society that respects, and enables, these choices are atrocities against the disabled truly unthinkable.

"But provisions for these people cost *money*," fiscal conservatives squeal, "and why should *I* pay for someone else's misfortune?" Because that's what human beings do: take care of one another. "But we can't *afford* it." In my experience, this argument is most commonly made by those who mean they can't afford both high taxes or charitable donations and membership in the country club or a winter home in Florida, but never mind. The perception of scarcity is highly subjective, and if you believe yourself on the doorsill of the poorhouse, nothing I say can comfort your fears (though, as Thomas Friedman once pointed out in an editorial in the *New York Times*, a short trip to Africa might have a salutary effect).

Let me point out, instead, being something of a fiscal conservative myself, that we're not talking huge amounts here, nothing like the billions squandered on Star Wars and the B-2 stealth bomber, which plenty of people believed we could afford. If the money is spent wisely, it will constitute not a drain but an investment. Thousands of people with disabilities are already productive citizens; with adequate funds for medical care and research into preventable equipment, we can create thousands more. They will support themselves! They will pay taxes! They will make charitable donations! Their potential contributions to culture are impossible to gauge. (Alexander Pope and Toulouse-Lautrec were hunchbacks, after all; Milton went blind; Beethoven, deaf, and so on, and so on. We can ill afford to kill off our geniuses, and every live birth holds such promise.) They will weave into the social fabric important strands of tenacity, patience, and ingenuity. We will all be glad they were born, I think. We will be glad they chose to live on.

VALUES AT STAKE IN DISABILITY DEBATES

Moral and Religious Issues

A DEFENSE OF GENOCIDE

—●— *Cal Montgomery*

Although [Peter] Singer is best known for his work on animal liberation, it is important to understand the consequences of his ethical theories for people with disabilities, especially since he argues that our lives are not always worth protecting.

WHO SHOULD LIVE?

Singer's understanding of whose life should be protected comes from a moral theory called "preference utilitarianism." According to this theory, you should behave so that the result of your behavior is, to the greatest extent possible, in accordance with the preferences of those who will be affected by it, whether directly or indirectly.

When you kill someone who wants to stay alive, you make it impossible for any of her preferences for the future to be realized—this is what makes killing a particularly bad thing. But it may be morally praiseworthy to kill someone who wants to be killed. And killing someone whose preferences are likely to be frustrated even if she stays alive may be less blameworthy than killing someone whose preferences are likely to be fulfilled.

But not everyone, Singer thinks, is capable of wanting to be alive. He argues that in order to have an interest in staying alive, you have to be a thinking, self-aware being and have an understanding of yourself as a being which endures through time. Following philosophical tradition, he calls such beings "persons," in order, as he says in his 1993 book, *Practical Ethics*, "to capture those elements of the popular sense of 'human being' that are not covered by 'member of the species Homo sapiens.'" Only persons, he says, can be said to have an interest in living and a right not to be killed; non-persons, by definition, cannot.

Obviously, wherever Singer's ideas are accepted as the basis for policy, it becomes a vitally important thing to be seen as a person. Infants, for example, are seen as non-persons. According to Singer they may therefore be killed with far less justification than would be required if they were understood to be persons. Certain adults to whom labels such as "persistent vegetative state" (PVS), "profound mental retardation," and "dementia" are attached may also be killed with less justification, according to Singer.

It would be okay, for example, to kill a "non-person" if you did it because everyone else's preferences would be more likely to be fulfilled if that individual were removed from their lives: that's one justification Singer gives for letting parents kill newborns expected to become disabled children. If parents, freed of responsibility for the disabled infant, were able to try again, says Singer, both they and the nondisabled child they'd ultimately raise could expect to live happier lives.

"We know," he says in his 1994 book, *Rethinking Life and Death*, "that once our children's lives are properly underway, we will become committed to them; for that very reason, many couples do not want to bring up a child if they fear that both the child's life and their own experience of child-rearing will be clouded by a major disability."

Another justification Singer offers for killing a "non-person" is that it frees "persons," or society, from what they may see as the "burden" imposed by the life of a "non-person." In *Practical Ethics*, which is often used as a textbook, Singer advocates making it legal to kill disabled infants up to twenty-eight days after birth as well as older "non-persons with disabilities."

Singer's work suggests a number of questions:

Is there a meaningful distinction between human persons and human non-persons?

If so, is there a reason to believe that personhood or lack thereof is a judgment that can reliably be made?

Are disabled people (and our families) really less likely than non-disabled people (and their families) to have happy lives?

If so, what is the appropriate public response?

PROVING PERSONHOOD

The distinction between "persons" and "non-persons" has led to Singer's prominence within the animal liberation movement. He argues that it is mere "speciesism" (the prejudice that membership in the right species is what earns beings moral consideration) leading us to believe that all human lives are of equal value. Singer wants us to recognize that many nonhuman animals should be treated with the same respect with which we believe humans should be treated.

But his theory also allows that some humans can be treated less well.

While his attack on speciesism has gained him a reputation as a progressive in some circles, he has been attacked in other circles for "intelligism" and "ableism" (prejudices that perceived intelligence or lack of disability is what earns beings moral consideration).

In his 1995 article, "The Proof of the Vegetable," published in the *Journal of Medical Ethics*, Australian disability advocate Chris Borthwick discusses ethicists' interest in "the distinction between those beings who are accorded the privileges of humanity and those who should be. The identification of a class of people who are 'humans' but not human, if any such could be found, would therefore be central."

Borthwick argues that a diagnosis of PVS is not enough to conclude that someone is unconscious or that she will not recover consciousness. He points out that a great deal of the judgment that someone has PVS depends upon her failure to react in ways that seem to doctors to demonstrate consciousness. We should give anyone who appears unconscious the benefit of the doubt, says Borthwick, pointing out that 58 percent of people judged to be permanently unconscious in one study were considered conscious within three years.

Whether or not one accepts the idea of "non-persons," says Borthwick, we've shown we cannot reliably identify such individuals.

But Singer assumes that we can. In *Rethinking Life and Death*, he quotes his own words, originally from a 1983 article in *Pediatrics*, that

> If we compare a severely defective human infant with a nonhuman animal, a dog or a pig, for example, we will often find the nonhuman to have superior capacities, both actual and potential, for rationality, self-consciousness, communication, and anything else that can plausibly be considered morally significant.

He then goes on to say that this assertion is "not only true, but obviously true."

Borthwick shows, though, that we cannot truly be sure even that it is true. At best, we are making assumptions based on current theories of neurology and practices of intelligence testing, and treating those assumptions as if they were fact. Far from being obvious, this presumed inferiority is founded on uncertain assumptions.

"If the discipline of ethics cannot cope with uncertainty, it is useless in the real world. If it persists in attempting to deny the existence of uncertainty, it may also be dangerous," says Borthwick.

What Singer is advocating is that we create a class of human beings whose "capacities, both actual and potential," are "obviously" rather than uncertainly inferior, and whose members must therefore demonstrate, to the satisfaction of nondisabled testers, their personhood in order to be accorded the same rights given everyone else. Singer seems willing to give the benefit of the doubt to nonhumans like pigs and dogs who haven't mastered our communication system. He is less willing to extend the same courtesy to humans whose disabilities impact communication.

FRUSTRATED LIVES?

Is life with a disability any more "clouded," as Singer terms it, than life without a disability? And if so, what should we do about it?

Several studies focusing primarily on people with severe, stable disabilities suggest that people who have been disabled long enough to become accustomed to it rate their quality of life similarly to nondisabled people. The medical professionals treating them, though, tend to underestimate their subjective quality of life.

"Many people assume that living with cerebral palsy means that I am endlessly confronted by my body's limitations," writes human services consultant Norman Kunc in a 1995 article with his wife, Emma Van der Klift. "Actually, this is not my experience. Having cerebral palsy means living a life in which innovation, improvisation, creativity and lateral thinking are essential." The description of his life that Kunc offers readers makes it sound more like a dance than a diminishment. While some people with disabilities do attribute significant frustration to disability, it is clear that frustration is by no means a necessary consequence of impairment.

People with disabilities do often find their preferences frustrated in ways that people without disabilities do not. But that frustration is not inherent in their impairments. Rather, it arises from an environment—physical or social—which is not designed to accommodate all members of the human race.

What, then, ought we do about that frustration? To offer a parallel: Is the selective infanticide of daughters in societies where boys are offered many more opportunities than are girls an acceptable practice? The girls' lack of opportunity is not intrinsically connected with being born female; nonetheless, the parents and the child they will eventually raise can expect better prospects if daughters are "replaced" by sons. Singer's theory could, therefore, be used to justify the practice of killing off infant girls, thus guaranteeing sons to parents who want them. To date he has not offered that justification.

"I question whether Princeton would hire a faculty member who argued that parents should be permitted to kill their infant daughters so that they could have a son," says National Council on Disability chairperson Marca Bristo. And yet prejudice against people with disabilities is so much more pervasive and unquestioned than sexism that promoting identical methods directed against us raises no concern.

Edward Stein of Yale University, in a recent paper on genetic screening and sexual orientation published in *Bioethics*, argues convincingly that choosing only to have children with characteristics valued by society—such as heterosexuality—reinforces the social preference for that characteristic. If this is the case, then choosing to have only sons—or only children without apparent disabilities—produces moral consequences far beyond the effect it will have on one's own family.

Such choices have an effect on all of us, Bristo told Princeton students. "Singer's core vision—that the life of a person with a disability is worth less than the life of a person without a disability, and therefore it is okay to kill infants with disabilities if that is what the parent wants to do—amounts to a defense of genocide."

TOLERANCE AND SPEECH

Because Singer advocates the killing of disabled infants up to twenty-eight days after birth, Christopher Benek of Princeton Students against Infanticide argues that his hiring violates Princeton's "Commitment to Community" policy, which warns that "Abusive or harassing behavior, verbal, or physical, which demeans, intimidates, threatens, or injures another because of his or her personal characteristics or beliefs is subject to University disciplinary sanctions."

Benek has called for Princeton either to rescind the appointment or abandon the policy on tolerance. He maintains that there is an essential difference between limiting Singer's speech, which Benek is not proposing, and not offering Singer a privileged position from which to speak.

Bristo agrees. "Princeton University does not condone hate," she told an audience at a PSAI-sponsored rally this spring. "Princeton University does not abide racism or anti-Semitism or homophobia. Princeton University should not abide Peter Singer."

30

UNSPEAKABLE CONVERSATIONS

Harriet McBryde Johnson

He insists he doesn't want to kill me. He simply thinks it would have been better, all things considered, to have given my parents the option of killing the baby I once was, and to let other parents kill similar babies as they come along and thereby avoid the suffering that comes with lives like mine and satisfy the reasonable preferences of parents for a different kind of child. It has nothing to do with me. I should not feel threatened.

Whenever I try to wrap my head around his tight string of syllogisms, my brain gets so fried it's . . . almost fun. Mercy! It's like *Alice in Wonderland*.

It is a chilly Monday in late March, just less than a year ago. I am at Princeton University. My host is Professor Peter Singer, often called—and not just by his book publicist—the most influential philosopher of our time. He is the man who wants me dead. No, that's not at all fair. He wants to legalize the killing of certain babies who might come to be like me if allowed to live. He also says he believes that it should be lawful under some circumstances to kill, at any age, individuals with cognitive impairments so severe

From the *New York Times*, February 16, 2003. Reprinted by permission of the author.

that he doesn't consider them "persons." What does it take to be a person? Awareness of your own existence in time. The capacity to harbor preferences as to the future, including the preference for continuing to live.

At this stage of my life, he says, I am a person. However, as an infant, I wasn't. I, like all humans, was born without self-awareness. And eventually, assuming my brain finally gets so fried that I fall into that wonderland where self and other and present and past and future blur into one boundless, formless all or nothing, then I'll lose my personhood and therefore my right to life. Then, he says, my family and doctors might put me out of my misery, or out of my bliss or oblivion, and no one count it murder.

I have agreed to two speaking engagements. In the morning, I talk to 150 undergraduates on selective infanticide. In the evening, it is a convivial discussion, over dinner, of assisted suicide. I am the token cripple with an opposing view.

I had several reasons for accepting Singer's invitation, some grounded in my involvement in the disability rights movement, others entirely personal. For the movement, it seemed an unusual opportunity to experiment with modes of discourse that might work with very tough audiences and bridge the divide between our perceptions and theirs. I didn't expect to straighten out Singer's head, but maybe I could reach a student or two. Among the personal reasons: I was sure it would make a great story, first for telling and then for writing down.

By now I've told it to family and friends and colleagues, over lunches and dinners, on long car trips, in scads of e-mail messages and a couple of formal speeches. But it seems to be a story that just won't settle down. After all these tellings, it still lacks a coherent structure; I'm miles away from a rational argument. I keep getting interrupted by questions—like these:

Q: Was he totally grossed out by your physical appearance?
A: He gave no sign of it. None whatsoever.

Q: How did he handle having to interact with someone like you?
A: He behaved in every way appropriately, treated me as a respected professional acquaintance and was a gracious and accommodating host.

Q: Was it emotionally difficult for you to take part in a public discussion of whether your life should have happened?
A: It was very difficult. And horribly easy.

Q: Did he get that job at Princeton because they like his ideas on killing disabled babies?

A: It apparently didn't hurt, but he's most famous for animal rights. He's the author of *Animal Liberation*.

Q: How can he put so much value on animal life and so little value on human life?

That last question is the only one I avoid. I used to say I don't know; it doesn't make sense. But now I've read some of Singer's writing, and I admit it does make sense—within the conceptual world of Peter Singer. But I don't want to go there. Or at least not for long.

So I will start from those other questions and see where the story goes this time.

That first question, about my physical appearance, needs some explaining.

It's not that I'm ugly. It's more that most people don't know how to look at me. The sight of me is routinely discombobulating. The power wheelchair is enough to inspire gawking, but that's the least of it. Much more impressive is the impact on my body of more than four decades of a muscle-wasting disease. At this stage of my life, I'm Karen Carpenter thin, flesh mostly vanished, a jumble of bones in a floppy bag of skin. When, in childhood, my muscles got too weak to hold up my spine, I tried a brace for a while, but fortunately a skittish anesthesiologist said no to fusion, plates and pins—all the apparatus that might have kept me straight. At fifteen, I threw away the back brace and let my spine reshape itself into a deep twisty S-curve. Now my right side is two deep canyons. To keep myself upright, I lean forward, rest my rib cage on my lap, plant my elbows beside my knees. Since my backbone found its own natural shape, I've been entirely comfortable in my skin.

I am in the first generation to survive to such decrepitude. Because antibiotics were available, we didn't die from the childhood pneumonias that often come with weakened respiratory systems. I guess it is natural enough that most people don't know what to make of us.

Two or three times in my life—I recall particularly one largely crip, largely lesbian cookout halfway across the continent—I have been looked at as a rare kind of beauty. There is also the bizarre fact that where I live, Charleston, South Carolina, some people call me Good Luck Lady: they consider it propitious to cross my path when a hurricane is coming and to kiss my head just before voting day. But most often the reactions are decidedly negative. Strangers on the street are moved to comment:

> I admire you for being out; most people would give up.
> God bless you! I'll pray for you.
> You don't let the pain hold you back, do you?
> If I had to live like you, I think I'd kill myself.

I used to try to explain that in fact I enjoy my life, that it's a great sensual pleasure to zoom by power chair on these delicious muggy streets, that I have no more reason to kill myself than most people. But it gets tedious. God didn't put me on this street to provide disability awareness training to the likes of them. In fact, no god put anyone anywhere for any reason, if you want to know.

But they don't want to know. They think they know everything there is to know, just by looking at me. That's how stereotypes work. They don't know that they're confused, that they're really expressing the discombobulation that comes in my wake.

So. What stands out when I recall first meeting Peter Singer in the spring of 2001 is his apparent immunity to my looks, his apparent lack of discombobulation, his immediate ability to deal with me as a person with a particular point of view.

Then, 2001. Singer has been invited to the College of Charleston, not two blocks from my house. He is to lecture on *Rethinking Life and Death*. I have been dispatched by Not Dead Yet, the national organization leading the disability rights opposition to legalized assisted suicide and disability-based killing. I am to put out a leaflet and do something during the Q and A.

On arriving almost an hour early to reconnoiter, I find the scene almost entirely peaceful; even the boisterous display of South Carolina spring is muted by gray wisps of Spanish moss and mottled oak bark.

I roll around the corner of the building and am confronted with the unnerving sight of two people I know sitting on a park bench eating veggie pitas with Singer. Sharon is a veteran activist for human rights. Herb is South Carolina's most famous atheist. Good people, I've always thought—now sharing veggie pitas and conversation with a proponent of genocide. I try to beat a retreat, but Herb and Sharon have seen me. Sharon tosses her trash and comes over. After we exchange the usual courtesies, she asks, "Would you like to meet Professor Singer?"

She doesn't have a clue. She probably likes his book on animal rights. "I'll just talk to him in the Q and A."

But Herb, with Singer at his side, is fast approaching. They are looking at me, and Herb is talking, no doubt saying nice things about me. He'll be saying that I'm a disability rights lawyer and that I gave a talk against assisted suicide at his secular humanist group a while back. He didn't agree with everything I said, he'll say, but I was brilliant. Singer appears interested, engaged. I sit where I'm parked. Herb makes an introduction. Singer extends his hand.

I hesitate. I shouldn't shake hands with the Evil One. But he is Herb's guest, and I simply can't snub Herb's guest at the college where Herb teaches. Hereabouts, the rule is that if you're not prepared to shoot on sight, you have to be prepared to shake hands. I give Singer the three fingers on my right hand that still work. "Good afternoon, Mr. Singer. I'm here for Not Dead Yet." I want to think he flinches just a little. Not Dead Yet did everything possible to disrupt his first week at Princeton. I sent a check to the fund for the fourteen arrestees, who included comrades in power chairs. But if Singer flinches, he instantly recovers. He answers my questions about the lecture format. When he says he looks forward to an interesting exchange, he seems entirely sincere.

It *is* an interesting exchange. In the lecture hall that afternoon, Singer lays it all out. The "illogic" of allowing abortion but not infanticide, of allowing withdrawal of life support but not active killing. Applying the basic assumptions of preference utilitarianism, he spins out his bone-chilling argument for letting parents kill disabled babies and replace them with nondisabled babies who have a greater chance at happiness. It is all about allowing as many individuals as possible to fulfill as many of their preferences as possible.

As soon as he's done, I get the microphone and say I'd like to discuss selective infanticide. As a lawyer, I disagree with his jurisprudential assumptions. Logical inconsistency is not a sufficient reason to change the law. As an atheist, I object to his using religious terms ("the doctrine of the sanctity of human life") to characterize his critics. Singer takes a note pad out of his pocket and jots down my points, apparently eager to take them on, and I proceed to the heart of my argument: that the presence or absence of a disability doesn't predict quality of life. I question his replacement-baby theory, with its assumption of "other things equal," arguing that people are not fungible. I draw out a comparison of myself and my nondisabled brother Mac (the next-born after me), each of us with a combination of gifts and flaws so peculiar that we can't be measured on the same scale.

He responds to each point with clear and lucid counterarguments. He proceeds with the assumption that I am one of the people who might rightly have been killed at birth. He sticks to his guns, conceding just enough to show himself open-minded and flexible. We go back and forth for ten long minutes. Even as I am horrified by what he says, and by the fact that I have been sucked into a civil discussion of whether I ought to exist, I can't help being dazzled by his verbal facility. He is so respectful, so free of condescension, so focused on the argument, that by the time the show is over, I'm not exactly angry with him. Yes, I am shaking, furious, enraged—but it's for the big room, two hundred of my fellow Charlestonians who have listened with polite interest, when in decency they should have run him out of town on a rail.

My encounter with Peter Singer merits a mention in my annual canned letter that December. I decide to send Singer a copy. In response, he sends me the nicest possible e-mail message. Dear Harriet (if he may) . . . Just back from Australia, where he's from. Agrees with my comments on the world situation. Supports my work against institutionalization. And then some pointed questions to clarify my views on selective infanticide.

I reply. Fine, call me Harriet, and I'll reciprocate in the interest of equality, though I'm accustomed to more formality. Skipping agreeable preambles, I answer his questions on disability-based infanticide and pose some of my own. Answers and more questions come back. Back and forth over several weeks it proceeds, an engaging discussion of baby killing, disability prejudice, and related points of law and philosophy. Dear Harriet. Dear Peter.

Singer seems curious to learn how someone who is as good an atheist as he is could disagree with his entirely reasonable views. At the same time, I am trying to plumb his theories. What has him so convinced it would be best to allow parents to kill babies with severe disabilities, and not other kinds of babies, if no infant is a "person" with a right to life? I learn it is partly that both biological and adoptive parents prefer healthy babies. But I have trouble with basing life-and-death decisions on market considerations when the market is structured by prejudice. I offer a hypothetical comparison: "What about mixed-race babies, especially when the combination is entirely nonwhite, who I believe are just about as unadoptable as babies with disabilities?" Wouldn't a law allowing the killing of these undervalued babies validate race prejudice? Singer agrees there is a problem. "It would be horrible," he says, "to see mixed-race babies being killed because they can't be adopted, whereas white ones could be." What's the difference? Preferences based on race are unreasonable. Preferences based on ability are not. Why? To Singer, it's pretty simple: disability makes a person "worse off."

Are we "worse off"? I don't think so. Not in any meaningful sense. There are too many variables. For those of us with congenital conditions, disability shapes all we are. Those disabled later in life adapt. We take constraints that no one would choose and build rich and satisfying lives within them. We enjoy pleasures other people enjoy, and pleasures peculiarly our own. We have something the world needs.

Pressing me to admit a negative correlation between disability and happiness, Singer presents a situation: imagine a disabled child on the beach, watching the other children play.

It's right out of the telethon. I expected something more sophisticated from a professional thinker. I respond: "As a little girl playing on the beach, I was already aware that some people felt sorry for me, that I wasn't frolicking with the same level of frenzy as other children. This annoyed me, and still does." I take the time to write a detailed description of how I, in fact, had fun playing on the beach, without the need of standing, walking, or running. But, really, I've had enough. I suggest to Singer that we have exhausted our topic, and I'll be back in touch when I get around to writing about him.

He responds by inviting me to Princeton. I fire off an immediate maybe. Of course I'm flattered. Mama will be impressed.

But there are things to consider. Not Dead Yet says—and I completely agree—that we should not legitimate Singer's views by giving them a forum. We should not make disabled lives subject to debate. Moreover, any spokesman chosen by the opposition is by definition a token. But even if I'm a token, I won't have to act like one. And anyway, I'm kind of stuck. If I decline, Singer can make some hay: "I offered them a platform, but they refuse rational discussion." It's an old trick, and I've laid myself wide open.

My invitation is to have an exchange of views with Singer during his undergraduate course. He also proposes a second "exchange," open to the whole university, later in the day. This sounds a lot like debating my life— and on my opponent's turf, with my opponent moderating, to boot. I offer a counterproposal, to which Singer proves amenable. I will open the class with some comments on infanticide and related issues and then let Singer grill me as hard as he likes before we open it up for the students. Later in the day, I might take part in a discussion of some other disability issue in a neutral forum. Singer suggests a faculty-student discussion group sponsored by his department but with cross-departmental membership. The topic I select is "Assisted Suicide, Disability Discrimination and the Illusion of Choice: A Disability Rights Perspective." I inform a few movement colleagues of this turn of events, and advice starts rolling in. I decide to go with the advisers who counsel me to do the gig, lie low, and get out of Dodge.

I ask Singer to refer me to the person who arranges travel at Princeton. I imagine some capable and unflappable woman like my sister, Beth, whose varied job description at a North Carolina university includes handling visiting artists. Singer refers me to his own assistant, who certainly seems capable and unflappable enough. However, almost immediately Singer jumps back in via e-mail. It seems the nearest hotel has only one wheelchair-accessible suite, available with two rooms for $600 per night. What to do? I know I shouldn't be so accommodating, but I say I can make do with an inaccessible room if it has certain features. Other logistical issues come up. We go back and forth. Questions and answers. Do I really need a lift-equipped vehicle at the airport? Can't my assistant assist me into a conventional car? How wide is my wheelchair?

By the time we're done, Singer knows that I am twenty-eight inches wide. I have trouble controlling my wheelchair if my hand gets cold. I am accustomed to driving on rough, irregular surfaces, but I get nervous turning on steep slopes. Even one step is too many. I can swallow purées, soft bread, and grapes. I use a bedpan, not a toilet. None of this is a secret; none of it cause for angst. But I do wonder whether Singer is jotting down my specs in his little note pad as evidence of how "bad off" people like me really are.

I realize I must put one more issue on the table: etiquette. I was criticized within the movement when I confessed to shaking Singer's hand in Charleston, and some are appalled that I have agreed to break bread with him in Princeton. I think they have a very good point, but, again, I'm stuck. I'm engaged for a day of discussion, not a picket line. It is not in my power to marginalize Singer at Princeton; nothing would be accomplished by displays of personal disrespect. However, chumminess is clearly inappropriate. I tell Singer that in the lecture hall it can't be Harriet and Peter; it must be Ms. Johnson and Mr. Singer.

He seems genuinely nettled. Shouldn't it be Ms. Johnson and Professor Singer, if I want to be formal? To counter, I invoke the ceremonial low-country usage, Attorney Johnson and Professor Singer, but point out that Mr./Ms. is the custom in American political debates and might seem more normal in New Jersey. All right, he says. Ms./Mr. it will be.

I describe this awkward social situation to the lawyer in my office who has served as my default lunch partner for the past fourteen years. He gives forth a full-body shudder.

"That poor, sorry son of a bitch! He has no idea what he's in for."

Being a disability rights lawyer lecturing at Princeton does confer some cachet at the Newark airport. I need all the cachet I can get. Delta Airlines has torn up my power chair. It is a fairly frequent occurrence for any air traveler on wheels.

When they inform me of the damage in Atlanta, I throw a monumental fit and tell them to have a repair person meet me in Newark with new batteries to replace the ones inexplicably destroyed. Then I am told no new batteries can be had until the morning. It's Sunday night. On arrival in Newark, I'm told of a plan to put me up there for the night and get me repaired and driven to Princeton by 10 a.m.

"That won't work. I'm lecturing at 10. I need to get there tonight, go to sleep and be in my right mind tomorrow."

"What? You're lecturing? They told us it was a conference. We need to get you fixed tonight!"

Carla, the gate agent, relieves me of the need to throw any further fits by undertaking on my behalf the fit of all fits.

Carmen, the personal assistant with whom I'm traveling, pushes me in my disabled chair around the airport in search of a place to use the bedpan. However, instead of diaper-changing tables, which are functional though far from private, we find a flip-down plastic shelf that doesn't look like it would hold my seventy pounds of body weight. It's no big deal; I've restricted my fluids. But Carmen is a little freaked. It is her first adventure in power-chair air travel. I thought I prepared her for the trip, but I guess I neglected to warn her about the probability of wheelchair destruction. I keep forgetting that even people who know me well don't know much about my world.

We reach the hotel at 10:15 p.m., four hours late.

I wake up tired. I slept better than I would have slept in Newark with an unrepaired chair, but any hotel bed is a near guarantee of morning crankiness. I tell Carmen to leave the TV off. I don't want to hear the temperature.

I do the morning stretch. Medical people call it passive movement, but it's not really passive. Carmen's hands move my limbs, following my precise instructions, her strength giving effect to my will. Carmen knows the routine, so it is in near silence that we begin easing slowly into the day. I let myself be propped up to eat oatmeal and drink tea. Then there's the bedpan and then bathing and dressing, still in bed. As the caffeine kicks in, silence gives way to conversation about practical things. Carmen lifts me into my chair and straps a rolled towel under my ribs for comfort and stability. She tugs at my clothes to remove wrinkles that could cause pressure sores. She switches on my motors and gives me the means of moving without anyone's help. They don't call it a power chair for nothing.

I drive to the mirror. I do my hair in one long braid. Even this primal hairdo requires, at this stage of my life, joint effort. I undo yesterday's braid, fix the part and comb the hair in front. Carmen combs where I can't reach. I divide the mass into three long hanks and start the braid just behind my left ear. Section by section, I hand it over to her, and her unimpaired young fingers pull tight, crisscross, until the braid is fully formed.

A big polyester scarf completes my costume. Carmen lays it over my back. I tie it the way I want it, but Carmen starts fussing with it, trying to tuck it down in the back. I tell her that it's fine, and she stops.

On top of the scarf, she wraps the two big shawls that I hope will substitute for an overcoat. I don't own any real winter clothes. I just stay out of the cold, such cold as we get in Charleston.

We review her instructions for the day. Keep me in view and earshot. Be instantly available but not intrusive. Be polite, but don't answer any questions about me. I am glad that she has agreed to come. She's strong, smart, adaptable, and very loyal. But now she is digging under the shawls, fussing with that scarf again.

"Carmen. What are you doing?"

"I thought I could hide this furry thing you sit on."

"Leave it. Singer knows lots of people eat meat. Now he'll know some crips sit on sheepskin."

The walk is cold but mercifully short. The hotel is just across the street from Princeton's wrought-iron gate and a few short blocks from the building where Singer's assistant shows us to the elevator. The elevator doubles as the janitor's closet—the cart with the big trash can and all the accouterments is rolled aside so I can get in. Evidently there aren't a lot of wheelchair people using this building.

We ride the broom closet down to the basement and are led down a long passageway to a big lecture hall. As the students drift in, I engage in light badinage with the sound technician. He is squeamish about touching me, but I insist that the cordless lavaliere is my mike of choice. I invite him to clip it to the big polyester scarf.

The students enter from the rear door, way up at ground level, and walk down stairs to their seats. I feel like an animal in the zoo. I hadn't reckoned on the architecture, those tiers of steps that separate me from a human wall of apparent physical and mental perfection, that keep me confined down here in my pit.

It is five before ten. Singer is loping down the stairs. I feel like signaling to Carmen to open the door, summon the broom closet, and get me out of here. But Singer greets me pleasantly and hands me Princeton's check for $500, the fee he offered with apologies for its inadequacy.

So. On with the show.

My talk to the students is pretty Southern. I've decided to pound them with heart, hammer them with narrative, and say "y'all" and "folks." I play with the emotional tone, giving them little peaks and valleys, modulating three times in one forty-five-second patch. I talk about justice. Even beauty and love. I figure they haven't been getting much of that from Singer.

Of course, I give them some argument too. I mean to honor my contractual obligations. I lead with the hypothetical about mixed-race, nonwhite babies and build the ending around the question of who should have the burden of proof as to the quality of disabled lives. And woven throughout the talk is the presentation of myself as a representative of a minority group that has been rendered invisible by prejudice and oppression, a participant in a discussion that would not occur in a just world.

I let it go a little longer than I should. Their faces show they're going where I'm leading, and I don't look forward to letting them go. But the clock on the wall reminds me of promises I mean to keep, and I stop talking and submit myself to examination and inquiry.

Singer's response is surprisingly soft. Maybe after hearing that this discussion is insulting and painful to me, he doesn't want to exacerbate my discomfort. His reframing of the issues is almost pro forma, abstract, entirely impersonal. Likewise, the students' inquiries are abstract and fairly predictable: anencephaly, permanent unconsciousness, eugenic abortion. I respond to some of them with stories, but mostly I give answers I could have e-mailed in.

I call on a young man near the top of the room.

"Do you eat meat?"

"Yes, I do."

"Then how do you justify—"

"I haven't made any study of animal rights, so anything I could say on the subject wouldn't be worth everyone's time."

The next student wants to work the comparison of disability and race, and Singer joins the discussion until he elicits a comment from me that he can characterize as racist. He scores a point, but that's all right. I've never claimed to be free of prejudice, just struggling with it.

Singer proposes taking me on a walk around campus, unless I think it would be too cold. What the hell? "It's probably warmed up some. Let's go out and see how I do."

He doesn't know how to get out of the building without using the stairs, so this time it is my assistant leading the way. Carmen has learned of another elevator, which arrives empty. When we get out of the building, she falls behind a couple of paces, like a respectful chaperone.

In the classroom there was a question about keeping alive the unconscious. In response, I told a story about a family I knew as a child, which took loving care of a nonresponsive teenage girl, acting out their unconditional commitment to each other, making all the other children, and me as their visitor, feel safe. This doesn't satisfy Singer. "Let's assume we can prove, absolutely, that the individual is totally unconscious and that we can know, absolutely, that the individual will never regain consciousness."

I see no need to state an objection, with no stenographer present to record it; I'll play the game and let him continue.

"Assuming all that," he says, "don't you think continuing to take care of that individual would be a bit—weird?"

"No. Done right, it could be profoundly beautiful."

"But what about the caregiver, a woman typically, who is forced to provide all this service to a family member, unable to work, unable to have a life of her own?"

"That's not the way it should be. Not the way it has to be. As a society, we should pay workers to provide that care, in the home. In some places, it's been done that way for years. That woman shouldn't be forced to do it, any more than my family should be forced to do my care."

Singer takes me around the architectural smorgasbord that is Princeton University by a route that includes not one step, unramped curb, or turn on a slope. Within the strange limits of this strange assignment, it seems Singer is doing all he can to make me comfortable.

He asks what I thought of the students' questions.

"They were fine, about what I expected. I was a little surprised by the question about meat eating."

"I apologize for that. That was out of left field. But—I think what he wanted to know is how you can have such high respect for human life and so little respect for animal life."

"People have lately been asking me the converse, how you can have so much respect for animal life and so little respect for human life."

"And what do you answer?"

"I say I don't know. It doesn't make a lot of sense to me."

"Well, in my view—"

"Look. I have lived in blissful ignorance all these years, and I'm not prepared to give that up today."

"Fair enough," he says and proceeds to recount bits of Princeton history. He stops. "This will be of particular interest to you, I think. This is where your colleagues with Not Dead Yet set up their blockade." I'm grateful for the reminder. My brothers and sisters were here before me and behaved far more appropriately than I am doing.

A van delivers Carmen and me early for the evening forum. Singer says he hopes I had a pleasant afternoon.

Yes, indeed. I report a pleasant lunch and a very pleasant nap, and I tell him about the Christopher Reeve Suite in the hotel, which has been remodeled to accommodate Reeve, who has family in the area.

"Do you suppose that's the $600 accessible suite they told me about?"

"Without doubt. And if I'd known it was the Christopher Reeve Suite, I would have held out for it."

"Of course you would have!" Singer laughs. "And we'd have had no choice, would we?"

We talk about the disability rights critique of Reeve and various other topics. Singer is easy to talk to, good company. Too bad he sees lives like mine as avoidable mistakes.

I'm looking forward to the soft vegetarian meal that has been arranged; I'm hungry. Assisted suicide, as difficult as it is, doesn't cause the kind of agony I felt discussing disability-based infanticide. In this one, I understand, and to some degree can sympathize with, the opposing point of view—misguided though it is.

My opening sticks to the five-minute time limit. I introduce the issue as framed by academic articles Not Dead Yet recommended for my use. Andrew Batavia argues for assisted suicide based on autonomy, a principle generally held high in the disability rights movement. In general, he says, the movement fights for our right to control our own lives; when we need assistance to effect our choices, assistance should be available to us as a matter of right. If the choice is to end our lives, he says, we should have assistance then as well. But Carol Gill says that it is differential treatment—disability discrimination—to try to prevent most suicides while facilitating the suicides of ill and disabled people. The social-science literature suggests that the public in general, and physicians in particular, tend to underestimate the quality of life of disabled people, compared with our own assessments of our lives. The case for assisted suicide rests on stereotypes that our lives are inherently so bad that it is entirely rational if we want to die.

I side with Gill. What worries me most about the proposals for legalized assisted suicide is their veneer of beneficence—the medical determination that, for a given individual, suicide is reasonable or right. It is not about autonomy but about nondisabled people telling us what's good for us.

In the discussion that follows, I argue that choice is illusory in a context of pervasive inequality. Choices are structured by oppression. We shouldn't offer assistance with suicide until we all have the assistance we need to get out of bed in the morning and live a good life. Common causes of suicidality—dependence, institutional confinement, being a burden—are entirely curable. Singer, seated on my right, participates in the discussion but doesn't dominate it. During the meal, I occasionally ask him to put things within my reach, and he competently complies.

I feel as if I'm getting to a few of them, when a student asks me a question. The words are all familiar, but they're strung together in a way so meaningless that I can't even retain them—it's like a long sentence in Tagalog. I can only admit my limitations. "That question's too abstract for me to deal with. Can you rephrase it?"

He indicates that it is as clear as he can make it, so I move on.

A little while later, my right elbow slips out from under me. This is awkward. Normally I get whoever is on my right to do this sort of thing. Why not now? I gesture to Singer. He leans over, and I whisper, "Grasp this wrist and pull forward one inch, without lifting." He follows my instructions to the letter. He sees that now I can again reach my food with my fork. And he may now understand what I was saying a minute ago, that most of the assistance disabled people need does not demand medical training.

A philosophy professor says, "It appears that your objections to assisted suicide are essentially tactical."

"Excuse me?"

"By that I mean they are grounded in current conditions of political, social and economic inequality. What if we assume that such conditions do not exist?"

"Why would we want to do that?"

"I want to get to the real basis for the position you take."

I feel as if I'm losing caste. It is suddenly very clear that I'm not a philosopher. I'm like one of those old practitioners who used to visit my law school, full of bluster about life in the real world. Such a bore! A once-sharp mind gone muddy! And I'm only forty-four—not all that old.

The forum is ended, and I've been able to eat very little of my puréed food. I ask Carmen to find the caterer and get me a container. Singer jumps up to take care of it. He returns with a box and obligingly packs my food to go.

When I get home, people are clamoring for the story. The lawyers want the blow-by-blow of my forensic triumph over the formidable foe; when I tell them it wasn't like that, they insist that it was. Within the disability rights community, there is less confidence. It is generally assumed that I handled the substantive discussion well, but people worry that my civility may have given Singer a new kind of legitimacy. I hear from Laura, a beloved movement sister. She is appalled that I let Singer provide even minor physical assistance at the dinner. "Where was your assistant?" she wants to know. How could I put myself in a relationship with Singer that made him appear so human, even kind?

I struggle to explain. I didn't feel disempowered; quite the contrary, it seemed a good thing to make him do some useful work. And then, the hard part: I've come to believe that Singer actually is human, even kind in his way. There ensues a discussion of good and evil and personal assistance and power and philosophy and tactics for which I'm profoundly grateful.

I e-mail Laura again. This time I inform her that I've changed my will. She will inherit a book that Singer gave me, a collection of his writings with a weirdly appropriate inscription: "To Harriet Johnson, So that you will have a better answer to questions about animals. And thanks for coming to Princeton. Peter Singer. March 25, 2002." She responds that she is changing her will, too. I'll get the autographed photo of Jerry Lewis she received as an MDA poster child. We joke that each of us has given the other a "reason to live."

I have had a nice e-mail message from Singer, hoping Carmen and I and the chair got home without injury, relaying positive feedback from my audiences—and taking me to task for a statement that isn't supported by a relevant legal authority, which he looked up. I report that we got home exhausted but unharmed and concede that he has caught me in a generalization that should have been qualified. It's clear that the conversation will continue.

I am soon sucked into the daily demands of law practice, family, community, and politics. In the closing days of the state legislative session, I help get a bill passed that I hope will move us one small step toward a world in which killing won't be such an appealing solution to the "problem" of disability. It is good to focus on this kind of work. But the conversations with and about Singer continue. Unable to muster the appropriate moral judgments, I ask myself a tough question: am I in fact a silly little lady whose head is easily turned by a man who gives her a kind of attention she enjoys? I hope not, but I confess that I've never been able to sustain righteous anger for more than about thirty minutes at a time. My view of life tends more toward tragedy.

The tragic view comes closest to describing how I now look at Peter Singer. He is a man of unusual gifts, reaching for the heights. He writes that he is trying to create a system of ethics derived from fact and reason, that largely throws off the perspectives of religion, place, family, tribe, community, and maybe even species—to "take the point of view of the universe." His is a grand, heroic undertaking.

But like the protagonist in a classical drama, Singer has his flaw. It is his unexamined assumption that disabled people are inherently "worse off," that we "suffer," that we have lesser "prospects of a happy life." Because of this all-too-common prejudice, and his rare courage in taking it to its logical conclusion, catastrophe looms. Here in the midpoint of the play, I can't look at him without fellow-feeling.

I am regularly confronted by people who tell me that Singer doesn't deserve my human sympathy. I should make him an object of implacable wrath, to be cut off, silenced, destroyed absolutely. And I find myself lacking a logical argument to the contrary.

I am talking to my sister, Beth, on the phone. "You kind of like the monster, don't you?" she says.

I find myself unable to evade, certainly unwilling to lie. "Yeah, in a way. And he's not exactly a monster."

"You know, Harriet, there were some very pleasant Nazis. They say the SS guards went home and played on the floor with their children every night."

She can tell that I'm chastened; she changes the topic, lets me off the hook. Her harshness has come as a surprise. She isn't inclined to moralizing; in our family, I'm the one who sets people straight.

When I put the phone down, my argumentative nature feels frustrated. In my mind, I replay the conversation, but this time defend my position.

"He's not exactly a monster. He just has some strange ways of looking at things."

"He's advocating genocide."

"That's the thing. In his mind, he isn't. He's only giving parents a choice. He thinks the humans he is talking about aren't people, aren't 'persons.'"

"But that's the way it always works, isn't it? They're always animals or vermin or chattel goods. Objects, not persons. He's repackaging some old ideas. Making them acceptable."

"I think his ideas are new, in a way. It's not old-fashioned hate. It's a twisted, misinformed, warped kind of beneficence. His motive is to do good."

"What do you care about motives?" she asks. "Doesn't this beneficent killing make disabled brothers and sisters just as dead?"

"But he isn't killing anyone. It's just talk."

"Just talk? It's talk with an agenda, talk aimed at forming policy. Talk that's getting a receptive audience. You of all people know the power of that kind of talk."

"Well, sure, but—"

"If talk didn't matter, would you make it your life's work?"

"But," I say, "his talk won't matter in the end. He won't succeed in reinventing morality. He stirs the pot, brings things out into the open. But ultimately we'll make a world that's fit to live in, a society that has room for all its flawed creatures. History will remember Singer as a curious example of the bizarre things that can happen when paradigms collide."

"What if you're wrong? What if he convinces people that there's no morally significant difference between a fetus and a newborn, and just as disabled fetuses are routinely aborted now, so disabled babies are routinely killed? Might some future generation take it further than Singer wants to go? Might some say there's no morally significant line between a newborn and a three-year-old?"

"Sure. Singer concedes that a bright line cannot be drawn. But he doesn't propose killing anyone who prefers to live."

"That overarching respect for the individual's preference for life—might some say it's a fiction, a fetish, a quasi-religious belief?"

"Yes," I say. "That's pretty close to what I think. As an atheist, I think all preferences are moot once you kill someone. The injury is entirely to the surviving community."

"So what if that view wins out, but you can't break disability prejudice? What if you wind up in a world where the disabled person's 'irrational' preference to live must yield to society's 'rational' interest in reducing the incidence of disability? Doesn't horror kick in somewhere? Maybe as you watch the door close behind whoever has wheeled you into the gas chamber?"

"That's not going to happen."

"Do you have empirical evidence?" she asks. "A logical argument?"

"Of course not. And I know it's happened before, in what was considered the most progressive medical community in the world. But it won't happen. I have to believe that."

Belief. Is that what it comes down to? Am I a person of faith after all? Or am I clinging to foolish hope that the tragic protagonist, this one time, will shift course before it's too late?

I don't think so. It's less about belief, less about hope, than about a practical need for definitions I can live with.

If I define Singer's kind of disability prejudice as an ultimate evil, and him as a monster, then I must so define all who believe disabled lives are inherently worse off or that a life without a certain kind of consciousness lacks value. That definition would make monsters of many of the people with whom I move on the sidewalks, do business, break bread, swap stories, and share the grunt work of local politics. It would reach some of my family and most of my nondisabled friends, people who show me personal kindness and who sometimes manage to love me through their ignorance. I can't live with a definition of ultimate evil that encompasses all of them. I can't refuse the monster-majority basic respect and human sympathy. It's not in my heart to deny every single one of them, categorically, my affection and my love.

The peculiar drama of my life has placed me in a world that by and large thinks it would be better if people like me did not exist. My fight has been for accommodation, the world to me and me to the world.

As a disability pariah, I must struggle for a place, for kinship, for community, for connection. Because I am still seeking acceptance of my humanity, Singer's call to get past species seems a luxury way beyond my reach. My goal isn't to shed the perspective that comes from my particular experience, but to give voice to it. I want to be engaged in the tribal fury that rages when opposing perspectives are let loose.

As a shield from the terrible purity of Singer's vision, I'll look to the corruption that comes from interconnectedness. To justify my hopes that Singer's theoretical world—and its entirely logical extensions—won't become real, I'll invoke the muck and mess and undeniable reality of disabled lives well lived. That's the best I can do.

31

SHOPPING AT THE GENETIC SUPERMARKET

Peter Singer

Consider . . . the issue of genetic engineering. Many biologists tend to think the problem is one of design, of specifying the best types of persons so that biologists can proceed to produce them. Thus they worry over what sort(s) of person there is to be and who will control this process. They do not tend to think, perhaps because it diminishes the importance of their role, of a system in which they run a "genetic supermarket," meeting the individual specifications (within certain moral limits) of prospective parents. . . . This supermarket system has the great virtue that it involves no centralized decision fixing the future of human type(s).

—Robert Nozick, *Anarchy, State and Utopia*

1. THE GENOCIDE OF DEAF CULTURE?

Nozick's genetic supermarket has arrived on the wings of angels brought to us by Ron Harris, the founder of ronsangels.com. How should we respond

From *Bioethics in Asia in the 21st Century*, ed. Song Sang-yong, Koo Young-Mo, and Darryl R. J. Macer (Christchurch, New Zealand: Eubios Ethics Institute, 2003), pp. 143–56. Copyright © 2003 Peter Singer. Reprinted by permission of the author.

to this and other options that will soon be beckoning? To assist us in answering these questions, I shall begin by considering a technique that has been with us for some time, but has the effect of changing the nature of children. Understanding the basis on which this technique can be supported may help us to grapple with the more difficult question of what we should do about newer options that also change the nature of our children. It is not, however, my aim here to deal with all the objections that could be urged against these options. My purpose is the narrower one of developing a clear understanding of the central values at stake.[1]

In the deaf community there has, for some years now, been a debate over attempts to alleviate some of the effects of deafness by the provision of cochlear ear implants in children. Although this is not a technique that makes use of genetics, the issues raised are in many respects similar to those that would be raised by the discovery of a genetic marker for congenital deafness. Cochlear implants do not restore normal hearing; instead they transform speech and other sounds into electrical impulses, and transmit these impulses to auditory nerve fibres in the inner ear. When implanted in children below the age of three, they make it possible for them to grow up "hearing" speech and thus to be able to take part in the speaking community as if they could hear.[2] In children who have been deaf from birth, the implants are less successful when implanted at a later age.

The scientists who first developed cochlear implants assumed that they would be enthusiastically embraced by the deaf community, and especially by the parents of congenitally deaf infants. Some parents of deaf children do have exactly this response. But others have a very different response, as the following statement indicates:

THE GENOCIDE OF DEAF CULTURE
FACT: The law says that genocide is the destruction of an ethnic group.
FACT: The law says that an ethnic group is "a set of individuals whose identity is distinctive in terms of common cultural traditions or heritage."
FACT: Deaf people are "a set of individuals whose identity is distinctive in terms of common cultural traditions or heritage."
=====> Cochlear implants are an attempt to eliminate the trait of Deafness.
=====> Eliminating the trait of Deafness will destroy "a set of individuals whose identity is distinctive in terms of common cultural traditions or heritage." (That "set" of individuals will no longer exist.)
=====> THEREFORE—COCHLEAR IMPLANTS ARE GENOCIDE[3]

Though extreme in its language, this is not an isolated point of view. A significant number of deaf parents are refusing to allow their deaf children to have the implants. They argue that the implants will cut them off from the Deaf community and from Deaf culture, which survives because of its distinctive language and its separation from the world of hearing people. (The Deaf community expresses the idea that it has a distinctive culture by the use of capitalization. To be Deaf is to be part of a culture [like being French or Jewish] whereas to be deaf is to be unable to hear.) As one parent said: "If somebody gave me a pill to make me hear, would I take it? No way. I want to be deaf."[4]

Something similar is happening among people with the short, stocky body shape known as achondroplasia, or dwarfism, since the discovery of the gene for this condition raised the prospect of prenatal diagnosis and selective termination. Little People of America, an association for those with short stature, has issued a position statement asserting that some of its members fear "genetic tests such as these will be used to terminate affected pregnancies and therefore take the opportunity for life away from children such as ourselves and our children." In response, they remind the rest of us that they are productive members of society who "face challenges, most of them are environmental (as with people with other disabilities)" and "value the opportunity to contribute a unique perspective to the diversity of our society . . ." They have "a common feeling of self-acceptance, pride, community and culture."[5]

For a final example, consider the contrasting views taken of Down's syndrome. At least 90 percent of women in both the United States and the United Kingdom will terminate a pregnancy after prenatal diagnosis shows that they are carrying a child with Down's Syndrome.[6] Yet others have described people with Down's Syndrome as "stars in an increasingly materialistic world," "without exception magic children," and capable of "unconditional love." One parent has said:

> Those of us with a Down's Syndrome child (our son, Robert, is almost 24) often wish that all our children had this extraordinary syndrome, which deletes anger and malice, replacing them with humour, thoughtfulness and devotion to friends and family.[7]

Consistently with this view, Diane Beeson has opposed present practices of prenatal diagnosis on the grounds that:

> The central assumption behind the deployment of prenatal diagnosis is that life with a disability is not worthwhile and is primarily a source of suffering. . . . From a disability-rights perspective, prenatal testing for fetal anomalies gives a powerful message that we seek to eliminate future persons with disabilities, fails to recognize the social value of future persons with disabilities, and conveys a devaluation of those now living with disability. . . . By focusing so many resources on the elimination of potential persons with disability, we are drifting toward a eugenic resurgence that differs only superficially from earlier patterns. In the process we are seriously distorting the historical purpose of medicine as healing. We are creating a society in which disability is becoming increasingly stigmatised; with the result that human imperfection of all kinds is becoming less tolerated and less likely to be accepted as normal human variation.[8]

The cochlear ear implant, the discovery of the gene for achondroplasia, and the use of selective abortion to prevent the birth of children with Down's syndrome serve to test the outer limits of our support for the politics of equality and diversity. We say that we believe that all humans are equal, and we value diversity. Does our belief in equality go so far that we hesitate to say that it is better not to have a disability than to have one? Does the value we place on diversity mean that we should oppose any measures that might weaken Deaf culture, or reduce the number of people born with Down's syndrome or achondroplasia? Should we stop the use of public funds for prenatal diagnosis or cochlear ear implants?

To assess this criticism of prenatal diagnosis, it will help to think for a moment about two related questions. First, how important is it to most parents to give their child the best possible start in life? Second, how serious a reason does a woman need in order to be justified in ending her pregnancy?

The answer to the first question is that, for most parents, giving their child the best possible start in life is extremely important. The desire to do so leads pregnant women who have smoked or drunk heavily to struggle to kick the addiction; it sells millions of books telling parents how to help their child achieve her or his potential; it causes couples to move out to suburbs where the schools are better, even though they then have to spend time in daily commuting; and it stimulates saving so that later the child will be able to go to a good college.

The answer to the second question must begin with the fact that, in accordance with the decision in *Roe v. Wade*, a woman in the United States can, in the first and second trimesters, or at least until the fetus is viable, terminate her pregnancy for any reason whatsoever. This does not, of course, mean that she is ethically justified in doing so. Some say that she is never ethically justified in terminating her pregnancy, and others that she is justified in doing so only to save her own life, or in cases of rape and incest. Beeson and many others who are concerned about prenatal diagnosis, however, do not rest their argument on opposition to abortion. So rather than argue this point in detail here, I shall simply state that, as I have argued elsewhere, I do not think that a fetus is the kind of being that has a right to life.[9] Hence it is not hard to justify terminating a pregnancy. For example, suppose that a couple plan to have children, but an unplanned pregnancy has occurred before they feel ready to do so—let's say that at present they are sharing a studio apartment and cannot afford anything larger, but in five years they will be able to move to a larger home. In my view, they would not be acting unethically if they decide to obtain an abortion.

Now think about a couple who are told that the child the woman is carrying will have a disability, let's say, Down's syndrome. Like most parents, the couple thinks it important to give their child the best possible start in life, and they do not believe that having Down's syndrome is the best possible start in life. Is it true that this couple must be making the assumption that "life with a disability is not worthwhile and is primarily a source of suffering"? There is no more reason to believe that these parents make that assumption, than there is to believe that parents who terminate a pregnancy because they can't afford a larger apartment believe that "life as a child in one room with one's parents is not worthwhile and is primarily a source of suffering." In both cases, all that the parents need assume is that it would be better to have a child without Down's syndrome, or to have a child who can have a room of her own. After all, in neither case are the parents choosing whether or not to have a child at all. They are choosing whether to have this child or another child that they can, with reasonable confidence, expect to have later, under more auspicious circumstances.[10]

Thus it is possible to justify abortion in these circumstances while accepting Beeson's claims that people with congenital disabilities "often achieve the same high levels of life satisfaction as non-disabled persons." A couple may reasonably think that "often" is not good enough. They may also accept—as I do—that people with Down's syndrome often are loving, warm people who live happy lives. But they may still think that this is not the best they can do for their child. Perhaps they just want to have a child who will, eventually, come to be their intellectual equal, someone with whom they can have good conversations, someone whom they can expect to give them grandchildren, and to help them in their old age. Those are not unreasonable desires for parents to have.

What of the "powerful message that we seek to eliminate future persons with disabilities" that Beeson tells us is sent by prenatal diagnosis and abortion to people with disabilities? Her concern seems highly selective. She has surely noticed that every bottle of alcoholic beverage sold in the United States bears the words: **GOVERNMENT WARNING:** (1) ACCORDING TO THE SURGEON GENERAL, WOMEN SHOULD NOT DRINK ALCOHOLIC BEVERAGES DURING PREGNANCY BECAUSE OF THE RISK OF BIRTH DEFECTS.

Does not that warning—much more visible to ordinary Americans than prenatal diagnosis—send out a "powerful message" that we should prevent the birth of children with defects? What about the message sent by programs that immunize girls against rubella? Is anyone seriously proposing to withdraw such government warnings, or end such immunization programs?

The Surgeon General's desire that women should not, through alcohol consumption, give birth to people with disabilities, does not in any way imply that he has less concern for the interests of people living with disabilities than he has for those without disabilities. As I have argued elsewhere, we can and should have equal consideration for the interests of all beings that have interests.[11] Although this is, in my view, the fundamental basis of equality both within our own species and between our species and beings of other species that have interests, for that very reason it may not satisfy the advocates of people with disabilities. But what other defensible sense can we give to the idea of equal worth?

Ani Satz has argued that measures to prevent the birth of people with disabilities are compatible with regarding people with disabilities as having equal worth, because these practices do not imply any judgments about the value of life with a disability:

> The obese are not devalued by overweight individuals who join Jenny Craig on the belief that obesity detracts from quality of life.... Organizations actively try to prevent workplace, automobile, household, and sporting accidents, contributors to disabling conditions. These precautions do not judge the moral worth of disabled individuals. To argue otherwise would be to assume, reductio absurdum, that industrial workers or rock concert-goers who wear earplugs are indicating that membership in the deaf community would be of less value than membership in the hearing community.[12]

We should distinguish two different kinds of judgment that are in danger of being conflated in this passage: judgments about "the moral worth of disabled individuals" and judgments about the general quality of life, or even the value of life, with a given disability. The moral worth of individuals is not dependent on their abilities, except where they have very limited intellectual capacities; but the reductio with which Satz ends her argument in the passage quoted above is, in my view, not at all *absurdum*. If I take precautions to prevent deafness, I do so on the grounds that I think life with the ability to hear is, in general, better than life without the ability to hear. Is this perhaps just because I have been able to hear for the first fifty years of my life, and would have difficulty in making the adjustment to being a member of the Deaf community? That may be part of the story, but it is not the whole story. Imagine that shortly after the birth of our child, a doctor tells us that it has an ear infection, which unless treated will cause deafness. Fortunately, the doctor adds, there is an antibiotic that will clear up the infection in a few days. Would we contemplate for a moment saying: "Wait a minute, Doctor, we need to think about whether we value membership of the hearing community more highly than membership of the Deaf community"? Obviously not: but the reason we would not is not that we are not judging membership in the Deaf community to be less desirable than membership in the hearing community, but because we take it for granted that it is less desirable.

To get this point correct, we need to be very precise in our language. Jonathan Glover has said: "Medical treatment presupposes that health is better than sickness, but those who believe in it are able to treat sick people as their equals."[13] That is true, of course, but the sense in which the sick are our equals needs to be specified. As Glover himself has pointed out, if we do not have enough resources to treat all the sick, we have to decide whom to treat. He has supported the view that in making this decision we should take into account both the expected life span of the sick person, and the quality of that person's life, at least when it is clear that it is not worth living.[14] So while we treat the sick as our equals, socially, morally, and politically, when it comes to tough decisions about saving their lives, some of the sick are less equal than others.

The same point applies to a claim made by Allen Buchanan:

> We devalue disabilities because we value the opportunities and welfare of the people who have them—and it is because we value people, all people, that we care about limitations on their welfare and opportunities. We also

know that disabilities, as such, diminish opportunities and welfare, even when they are not so severe that the lives of those who have them are not worth living. Thus, there is nothing incoherent or disingenuous in our saying that we devalue the disabilities and wish to reduce their incidence and that we value all existing persons with disabilities—and value them equally to those who are not disabled.[15]

The argument of this passage is compelling, until we get to the word "equally" in its final clause. Suppose that there are two infants in the neonatal intensive care unit, and we have the resources to save only one of them. We know nothing about either of them, or their families, except that one infant has no disabilities, and the other has one of the disabilities that Buchanan mentions—a disability that will limit the child's "welfare and opportunities." In these circumstances, it seems rational, for precisely the reasons Buchanan gives, to save the life of the child without disabilities—but this shows that there is a clear sense in which we do not value both children equally.[16]

In our very commendable concern to give equal consideration and respect to every member of our community, and to avoid the least appearance of bias against those with disabilities, we are in danger of going to what is a truly absurd conclusion: that the abilities we have—to hear, to see, to walk, to speak, to understand and reflect upon information given to us—are of no value. We must not deny the obvious truth that most people, disabled or not, would prefer to be without disabilities, and would prefer to have children without disabilities. There may be some members of the Deaf community and some people with achondroplasia who disagree, and of course there are many people with intellectual disabilities who are incapable of expressing an opinion, but to the best of my knowledge advocates for people in wheelchairs accept that they would be better off if they could walk; at least I am not aware of them ever calling for governments to stop wasting their taxes by supporting research into ways of overcoming paralysis.

If the use of cochlear implants means that there are fewer Deaf people, is this "genocide"? Does our acceptance of prenatal diagnosis and selective abortion mean that we are "drifting toward a eugenic resurgence that differs only superficially from earlier patterns." If the use of the term "genocide" is intended to suggest a comparison with the Holocaust, or Rwanda, it overlooks the crucial fact that cochlear implants do not have victims. On balance, it seems that they benefit the people who have them; if this judgment is contestable, it is at least not clear that they are worse off for having the implant. Imagine a minority ethnic group in which all the parents reach separate decisions that their children will be better off if they marry a member of the majority group, and hence urge them to do so. Is this encouraging "genocide"? If so, it is genocide of such a harmless form that the term should be divorced from all its usual moral associations.

Similarly, if Diane Beeson's reference to "earlier patterns" of eugenics is a veiled reference to Nazi policies that led to the murder of tens of thousands of disabled people, she is guilty of overlooking the vast moral gulf between what happened then and what is happening now. No state is ordering anyone's death; no one who wants to go on living is being murdered; no children whose parents want them to survive are being killed. The Nazi program was based on the interests of the *Volk*, and utter indifference to the interests of the individuals most involved, including both the victim and his or her family. Even if Beeson has in mind not Nazism but American eugenics in the first half of the twentieth century, the differences are profound. That eugenics movement used compulsory sterilization of criminals, introduced an immigration policy based on belief in the superiority of the Northern European races, and became, as Dan Kevles puts it, a facade for "advocates of race and class prejudice, defenders of vested interests of church and state, Fascists, Hitlerites, and reactionaries generally."[17] There is no comparison between such state sponsored, coercive policies and the use of prenatal diagnosis and selective abortion by couples that choose to avail themselves of this option.

Even if cochlear implants are not genocidal, and prenatal diagnosis combined with selective abortion is not at all like past eugenic practices, they might be considered wrong. But consider the following principle: For any condition X, if it would be a form of child abuse for parents to inflict X on their child soon after birth, then it must, other things being equal, at least be permissible to take steps to prevent one's child having that condition.

I propose this not as a self-evident truth, nor as a derivation from any particular moral foundation, but as something that might appeal to many people, irrespective of the foundations of their moral views. The "preventive principle" as I shall call it, requires us to reject the view that the fact that something is the outcome of the genetic lottery is enough to make it right. Why would anyone believe that? Only, I suggest, if somewhere deep down, they think of the genetic lottery as no lottery at all, but rather the workings of a divine Providence. If that were the case, then we might think it wrong to interfere with the natural order of things. But let us put that view aside, for lack of supporting evidence, and assume that the genetic lottery really is a lottery. Then, if there is no moral barrier that says we must not interfere with the way things are, the preventive principle seems sound.

Now let us apply the preventive principle to the cases we have been considering. Suppose that a Deaf couple give birth to a daughter who can hear normally. Because they value very highly their membership of the Deaf community, and they fear that their daughter will not be a part of the Deaf community, they make arrangements with a sympathetic surgeon to destroy the child's hearing. The operation, performed under general anesthesia, causes the child no pain, but achieves its goal. The child will now be permanently deaf. Is this a case of child abuse? I suggest that it is. What the parents have done ensures that their child will never be able to hear Beethoven, or a babbling brook, or listen to lectures and debates delivered in spoken languages, except in translation. The child will also be at a disadvantage in countless other ways in getting through life. Admittedly, we must also take into account the benefits that the child will get from being part of the Deaf community, especially when being a part of the Deaf community means that the child grows up in the community to which her parents already belong. But that does not justify what they have done.

If you respond to this example in the way I do, and accept the principle I stated above, it follows that it must at least be permissible, other things being equal, for parents to take steps to ensure that their child will not be deaf.

This argument does raise the difficulty of where to draw the line. Strictly, I could avoid this difficulty by pointing out that the preventive principle simply says that prenatal diagnosis and selective termination are permissible if they are a way of avoiding a condition that it would be child abuse to inflict on one's child. So the question could be answered with another question: would it be child abuse for a couple to ensure that their child would be a homosexual? In whatever way you answer that question, you should also answer the question whether the couple should be allowed to terminate a pregnancy on the basis of prenatal diagnosis that the child will be homosexual.

I will, however, try to say a little more on this topic. Andrew Solomon has written:

> Being Deaf is a disability and a culture in modern America; so is being gay; so is being black; so is being female; so even, increasingly, is being a straight white male. So is being paraplegic, or having Down syndrome. What is at issue is which things are so "cultural" that you wouldn't think of "curing"

them, and which things are so "disabling" that you must "cure" them—and the reality is that for some people each of these experiences is primarily a disability experience while for others it is primarily a cultural one.[18]

Is being black a disability? Is being gay a disability? The racial case is easy to distinguish from the case of deafness, because although it may be true deaf people must contend with some socially constructed barriers, it is also indisputable that they lack the ability to hear. African Americans do not lack any ability that people of other races possess. There are only patterns of discrimination or prejudice. Hence being black is not a disability.

What about being gay? While gays and lesbians lack the ability to be sexually attracted to the opposite sex, straight people lack the ability to be sexually attracted to their own sex. This line of argument implies that unless we are bisexual we are suffering from an erotic disability. Is it possible to argue that homosexuals are disabled because they cannot enjoy "normal" sexual intercourse, involving a penis and a vagina? That would require an argument to the effect that this mode of sexual intercourse is superior to others that are available to gays and lesbians, and I do not know how, in the absence of an argument from "natural law," such an argument could be grounded. Nor do I think that a natural law grounding would be satisfactory.[19]

Stephen Macedo has suggested a more plausible ground for seeing homosexuality as a disability:

> Even if we were to wipe away all the prejudice in the world and even if homosexuals had all of the same opportunities as heterosexuals—including marriage and adoption—homosexuality would still be a misfortune: a misfortune resembling marriage to a sterile partner. Sterility is properly regarded as a misfortune (though not, it should be stressed, an especially grave one) and homosexuality can likewise be regarded as one, insofar as some of the great goods of marriage—the shared participation in pregnancy and new life—are not fully available to homosexual couples.

In a footnote, Macedo adds: ". . . Because some gays and lesbians are likely to take (unjustified, I believe) offense on this score, I should emphasize that to the extent that there is misfortune here, it is a misfortune that I share."[20]

If infertility is a disability, it is one that seems likely to be overcome very soon for lesbians, at least, as we learn how to mix gametes from same-sex partners and inject them into a denucleated egg. Male homosexuals would still have to find a surrogate willing to carry the child for them. But perhaps at present, infertility-within-the-relationship does mean that homosexuality remains a disability, though as Macedo says, not an especially grave one.

2. SHOPPING FOR BEAUTY AND BRAINS

In February 1999, advertisements in newspapers in some of America's most prestigious universities offered $50,000 to an egg donor who was athletic, had scored extremely well in scholastic aptitude tests, and was at least 5' 10" tall.[21] Later in the same year ronsangels.com opened with a splash of publicity. At the time of writing, it features eight "models," offering "beauty and brains to the highest bidder." Visitors to the site can see a photograph of each model, together with her vital statistics, the ages of her mother and grandmother, a brief biography, and an indication of the minimum bid required to obtain an egg, which ranges from $15,000 to $90,000. To provide some gender balance, the site also has a "sperm auction" featuring a well-muscled man in a brief bathing suit. His sperm is available for a minimum bid of $15,000.

The "Ron" in Ron's Angels is Ron Harris, no mere egg and sperm auctioneer but also something of a philosopher, as an "Editorial" that he has added to the site reveals:

> It is human nature to strive to improve everything. From fruits and vegetables, to medicine, and even to plant and animal genes, we modify everything to produce the best we can. Now, modern science presents the miraculous possibility of improving ourselves. Currently, our means is in vitro fertilization, wherein your eggs or sperm are combined with the eggs or sperm of superior genetic background. . . . Of course, there are no guarantees that the children produced from superior genes combined with your own will result in similarly superior children—but our striving reflects the determination to pass every advantage possible along to our descendants.

It is not our intention to suggest that we make a super society of only beautiful people. This site simply mirrors our current society, in that beauty usually goes to the highest bidder. There are of course many other attributes that impart an advantage in our increasingly competitive society: intelligence, talent, personality, and social skills. . . . This is the first society to truly comprehend how important beautiful genes are to our evolution. Just watch television and you will see that we are only interested in looking at beautiful people. From the network anchors, to supermodels that appear in most advertisements, our society is obsessed with youth and beauty. As our society grows older, we inevitably look to youth and beauty. . . . If you could increase the chance of reproducing beautiful children, and thus giving them an advantage in society, would you?

Any gift such as beauty, intelligence, or social skills, will help your children in their quest for happiness and success.

There is, admittedly, something a little suspect about ronsangels.com. The models and bids went unchanged for months. Bids were listed, but none exceed the specified minimum. When I began work on this paper, the auctions had closing dates, some of which had already passed. Subsequently the closing dates disappeared from the site, but the models offering their eggs have not changed. A clue to why this may be the case can be found in a link that takes you, in two clicks, to another Ron Harris site, where the interest in women is explicitly sexual rather than reproductive. Another click takes you to Harris's very candid advice on "how to make money with an adult web site." Prominent here is the injunction to: "GET TRAFFIC, ANY WAY YOU CAN! . . . Do whatever you have to do to get traffic. Traffic is the e-porn industries' currency. The more you have the more money you'll make."

Even if his egg sales are just a way of getting people to visit his porn site, ronsangels.com is a test case for the view that the market knows best. The United States is exceptional among the industrialized nations in allowing a free market in human gametes. There are already other commercial operations selling gametes, and there can be little doubt that, unless such activities are prohibited, there will soon be more, offering couples ever more technologically sophisticated ways of improving their odds of having tall, slim children with above-average beauty, health, intelligence, and athletic, musical, and artistic talent.

There are many grounds on which we might find the ideas behind Ron's Angels distasteful, or worse. We could argue that they indicate a warped sense of how to think about one's future child, a sense shaped by a society that puts too high a premium on beauty and success. That may be, but what should we do about it? There is credible evidence suggesting that many of the things that parents look for in their children have a genetic component: physical appearance, including height and body shape, intellectual aptitude, many athletic skills, and longevity. As we have already noted, parents already do their best to influence the environmental factors that undoubtedly also play a part in shaping these characteristics. They can now influence genetic factors as well as environmental ones, in one of three ways. By using in vitro fertilization, they can have the embryo screened before implantation; they can use prenatal diagnosis and selective abortion; and they can obtain eggs, sperm, or embryos from people they regard as genetically superior. All of these techniques have disadvantages. The first is costly, inconvenient, and does not always lead to a pregnancy. The second involves an abortion, which is not a pleasant procedure for a woman, irrespective of her views about the moral status of the fetus. The third means that the child will not be a biological child of the couple, but will carry the genes of at least one other person. Probably within the next two decades, however, we will have a fourth option: genetic enhancement of our own embryos.

Ron Harris asks: "If you could increase the chance of reproducing beautiful children, and thus giving them an advantage in society, would you?" He is doubtless correct in his assumption that most of us will answer that question affirmatively. We go to so much effort to shape our children's environment to give them the best possible start in life, that once we gain the ability to select their genes, we are unlikely to reject it. What might restrain some potential parents are factors like risk, cost, and whether the children will still be their own children, in a biological sense. The last of these has up to now been a constraint on the number of couples willing to use donor eggs and sperm. But our rapidly increasing knowledge of human genetics will soon make it possible for us to have children who are genetically our own, and yet who are genetically superior to the children we would produce if we left it to the random process of normal reproduction. This will come initially through increasingly sophisticated genetic screening of in vitro embryos. Before very long, however, it will become possible to insert new genetic material safely into the in vitro embryo. Both of these techniques will enable couples to have a child whose abilities are likely to be superior to those offered by the natural lottery but who will be "theirs" in the sense of having their genes, not the genes of only one of them, or the genes of a third person, except (when genetic modification rather than simply genetic selection is used) to the extent necessary to produce the specific desired characteristics.

Many people say that they accept selection against serious diseases and disabilities, but not for enhancement above what is normal. There is, however, no bright line between selection against disabilities and selection for positive characteristics. From selecting against Huntington's disease it is no great step to selecting against genes that carry a significantly elevated risk of breast or colon cancer, and from there it is easy to move to giving one's child a better-than-average genetic health profile. Similarly, if almost all of us are willing to abort a fetus that has Down's syndrome, most of us will also be willing to abort one with genes that indicate other intellectual limitations, for example, genes that correlate with IQ scores below 80. But why stop at 80? Why not select for at least average IQ? Or a bit above average? The existing market in human eggs suggests that some people will also select for height, which in turn correlates to some extent with income. Then, as Harris points out, there is beauty, and we will not reject the opportunity to ensure that our children are beautiful.

3. CHOICES, PRIVATE AND PUBLIC

How should we react to the scenario that extrapolates beyond Ron's Angels? We could treat it as a slippery slope argument, one that proves that we must act now to stop prenatal screening, because otherwise we are heading towards a nightmarish future in which children are made to order, and wanted for their specifications, not loved for what they are. But taking the argument that way forces us either to reject something—current practices of prenatal diagnosis—that most people regard as a great boon, or to show that we can stop somewhere short of permitting the choices I have described. Neither is a convincing option. A second possibility is to say that the future just sketched is no nightmare, but a better society than we now have, one full of healthier, more intelligent, taller, better-looking—perhaps even more ethical?—people. There is, therefore, no "slippery slope," because the slope [is] not down to an abyss, but upward to a higher level of civilization than we have achieved so far.

Nozick's words cited at the head of this paper suggest a third possible answer: it is not up to us to judge whether the outcome of this process will be better or worse. In a free society, all we can legitimately do is make sure that the process consists of freely chosen individual transactions. Let the genetic supermarket rule—and not only the market, but also altruistic individuals, or voluntary organizations, anyone who wishes, for whatever reason, to offer genetic services to anyone who wants them and is willing to accept them on the terms on which they are offered.

That the United States should allow a market in eggs and sperm which goes some way towards fulfilling Nozick's prophecy is no accident. In other countries a practice that threatens to turn the child of a marriage into an item of commerce would meet powerful opposition from both conservative "family values" politics and from left of center groups horrified at the idea of leaving to the market something as socially momentous as the way in which future generations are conceived. In the United States, however, that leftist attitude is restricted to groups on the margins of political life, and the conservatives who dominate Congress show their support for family values merely by preventing the use of federal funds for ends that they dislike; in all other respects, they allow their belief that the market always knows best to override their support for traditional family values.

There are strong arguments against state interference in reproductive decisions, at least when those decisions are made by competent adults. If we follow Mill's principle that the state is justified in interfering with its citizens only to prevent harm to others, we could see such decisions as private ones, harming no one, and therefore properly left to the private realm.[22] For who is harmed by the genetic supermarket? Having the healthier, handsomer, and more intelligent children whom they want does not harm the parents. Are the children harmed? In an article on the practice of buying eggs from women with specific desired characteristics like height and intelligence, George Annas has commented: "What's troubling is this commodification, this treating kids like products. Ordering children to specification can't be good for the children. It may be good for adults in the short run, but it's not good for kids to be thought of that way."[23]

But to say that this is "not good" for these children forces us to ask the question: not good compared with what? The children for whom this is supposed not to be good could not have existed by any other means. If the egg had not been purchased, to be fertilized with the husband's sperm, that child would not have been alive. Is life going to be so bad for this child that he or she will wish never to have been born? That hardly seems likely. So on one reading of what the standard of comparison should be, it is clearly false that the purchase of these eggs is not good for the kids.[24]

Suppose that we read "not good for kids" as meaning "not the best thing for the next child of this couple." Then whether the purchase of the egg is or is not good for the kid will depend on a comparison with other ways in which the couple could have had a child. Suppose, to make the comparison easier, they are not infertile—they bought an egg only in order to increase their chances of having a tall, athletic child who would get into a very good university. If they had not done so, they would have had a child in the normal way, which would have been their genetic child. Was it bad for their child to buy the egg? Their child may have a more difficult life because he or she was "made to order," and perhaps will disappoint his or her parents. But perhaps their own child would have disappointed them even more, by being less likely to be any of the things that they wanted their child to be. I don't see how we can know which of these outcomes is more likely. So I do not think we have grounds for concluding that a genetic supermarket would harm either those who choose to shop there, or those who are created from the materials they purchase.

If we switch from an individualist perspective to a broader social one, however, the negative aspects of a genetic supermarket become more serious. Even if we make the optimistic assumption that parents will select only genes that are of benefit to their children, there are at least three separate grounds for thinking that this may have adverse social consequences. The first is that some of the traits that people seek to ensure for their children will be advantageous for them only in comparative, not absolute terms. To increase one's children's longevity is good for them, whether or not everyone else's longevity has been increased by a similar amount. To increase one's children's height, however, is beneficial only if it also moves them up relative to the height of others in their society. There would be no disadvantage in being 5 feet tall, if the average height in the community were 4' 9" and there will be no advantage in being 6'3" if the average height is 6'6". Arguably, it would be better if everyone were shorter, because we would require less food to sustain us, could live in smaller houses, drive smaller, less powerful cars, and make a smaller impact on the environment. Thus being able to select for height—something couples are already doing, on a small scale, by offering more for the eggs of tall women—could start the human equivalent of the peacock's tail—an escalating "height race" in which the height that distinguishes "tall" people from those who are "normal" increases year by year, to no one's benefit, at considerable environmental cost, and perhaps eventually even at some health cost to the children themselves.[25]

The second ground for objecting to a genetic supermarket is the fear that it would mean less diversity among human beings. Not all forms of diversity are good. Diversity in longevity is greater when there are more people with genes that doom them to an early death. The loss of this diversity is welcome. But what about the loss of the merely unusual, or eccentric? Antony Rao, a specialist in behavioral therapy in children, finds that many middle- and upper-class parents come to him when their children behave in unusual ways, wanting them to be medicated, because "they fear that any deviation from the norm may cripple their child's future."[26] If this is true of behavioral abnormalities that for many children are merely a passing phase, it is likely to be even truer of genetic abnormalities. It is easy to imagine genetic screening reports that indicate that the child's genes are unusual, although the significance of the abnormality is not well understood (usually medical shorthand for "We don't have a clue."). Would many parents decide to terminate the pregnancy in those circumstances, and if so, would there be a loss of diversity that would leave human society a less rich place, and perhaps even, in the long run, reduce the species' capacity to adapt to changing circumstances?

The third and in my view most significant ground for objecting to a genetic supermarket is its threat to the ideal of equality of opportunity. John Schaar has written: "No policy formula is better designed to fortify the dominant institutions, values, and ends of the American social order than the formula of equality of opportunity, for it offers *everyone* a fair and equal chance to find a place within that order."[27] It is, of course, something of a myth to believe that equality of opportunity prevails in the United States, because wealthy parents already give their children enormous advantages in the race for success. Nevertheless, the Ron's Angels slogan of "beauty and brains to the highest bidder" points to a future in which the rich have beautiful, brainy, healthy children, while the poor, stuck with the old genetic lottery, fall further and further behind. Thus inequalities of wealth will be turned into genetic inequalities, and the clock will be turned back on centuries of struggle to overcome the privileges of aristocracy. Instead the present generation of wealthy people will have the opportunity to embed their advantages in the genes of their offspring. These offspring will then have not only the abundant advantages that the rich already give their children, but also whatever additional advantages the latest development in genetics can bestow on them. They will most probably therefore continue to be wealthier, longer-lived, and more successful than the children of the poor, and will in turn pass these advantages on to their children, who will take advantage of the ever more sophisticated genetic techniques available to them. Will this lead to a *Gattaca* society in which "Invalids" clean toilets while "Valids" run the show and get all the interesting jobs?[28] Lee Silver has pictured a United States a millennium hence in which the separation between "Gene-enriched" humans and "Naturals" has solidified into separate species.[29] That is too far in the future to speculate about, but Maxwell Mehlman and Jeffrey Botkin may well be right when they predict that a free market in genetic enhancement will widen the gap between the top and bottom strata of our society, undermine belief in equality of opportunity, and close the "safety valve" of upward mobility.[30]

Suppose that we do not wish to accept this situation: what choices do we have? We can ban all uses of genetic selection and genetic engineering that go beyond the elimination of what are clearly defects. There are some obvious difficulties with this course of action:

1. Are we violating Mill's principle, and if so, can we justify doing so? We could claim that although individual reproductive decisions appear only to affect the parties to the decision, and the child who develops from it, this appearance is deceptive. Reproduction of the kind described will change the nature of society by taking away the age-old dream that anyone can make it to the top. This is, arguably, a "harm to others" serious enough to justify the intervention of the state.

2. Who will decide what is clearly a defect? Presumably, a government panel will be assigned the task of keeping abreast with relevant genetic techniques, and deciding which are lawful and which are not. This allows the government a role in reproductive decisions, which some may see as even more dangerous than the alternative of leaving them to the market.

3. There are serious questions about whether a ban on genetic selection and engineering for enhancement purposes could be made to work across the United States, given that matters regulating conception and birth are in the hands of the states, rather than the federal government. In the case of surrogacy, attempts by various states of the United States to make the practice illegal, or to make surrogacy contracts void, have had little effect because Arkansas, California, and Ohio are more friendly to surrogacy. Couples seeking a surrogate to bear a child for them are prepared to travel to achieve what they want. As Lee Silver remarks: "What the brief history of surrogacy tells us is that Americans will not be hindered by ethical uncertainty, state-specific injunctions, or high costs in their drive to gain access to any technology that they feel will help them achieve their reproductive goals."[31]

4. Assuming that we could get the US Congress to ban genetic selection and engineering when used for enhancement, persuade the Supreme Court that the legislation violates neither the rights of the states to legislate in this area, nor any constitutional rights to privacy in reproduction, and effectively enforce the ban within the United States, we would still have to deal with the fact that we now live in a global economy. A small impoverished nation might be tempted to allow enhancement genetics, thus setting up a niche industry serving wealthy couples from the United States and other countries that have banned enhancement. Moreover, in view of the competitive nature of the global economy, it may even pay industrialized nations to encourage

enhancement genetics, thus giving them an edge over those that do not. On Singapore's National Day, in 1983, Prime Minister Lee Kuan Yew gave a speech about the heritability of intelligence, and its importance for Singapore's future. Shortly afterwards, the government introduced measures explicitly designed to encourage university graduates to have more children.[32] Had genetic enhancement been available to Lee Kuan Yew at the time, he might well have preferred it to the government-sponsored computer dating services and financial incentives on which he was then forced to rely.

If a ban in the United States turns out to be unattainable, ineffective, or contrary to the vital interests of the US economy, a bolder strategy could be tried. Assuming that the objective is to avoid a society divided in two along genetic lines, genetic enhancement services could be subsidized, so that everyone can afford them. But could society afford to provide everyone with the services that otherwise only the rich could afford? Mehlman and Botkin propose an ingenious solution: the state should run a lottery in which the prize is the same package of genetic services that the rich commonly buy for themselves. Tickets in the lottery would not be sold; instead every adult citizen would be given one. The number of prizes would relate to how many of these packages society could afford to pay for, and thus would vary with the costs of the genetic services, as well as with the resources available to provide them. To avoid placing a financial burden on the state, Mehlman and Botkin suggest, the use of genetic technologies could be taxed, with the revenue going to fund the lottery.[33] Clearly universal coverage would be preferable, but the use of a lottery would at least ensure that all have some hope that their children will join ranks of the elite, and taxing those who are, by their use of genetic enhancement for their own children, changing the meaning of human reproduction seems a fair way to provide funds for it.

Thus shopping at the genetic supermarket has taken us to the surprising conclusion that the state should be directly involved in promoting genetic enhancement. The justification for this conclusion is simply that it is preferable to the most probable alternative—leaving genetic enhancement to the marketplace.

NOTES

1. For further discussion of other objections, see Lynn Gillam, "Prenatal Diagnosis and Discrimination against the Disabled," *Journal of Medical Ethics* 25

(1999): 163–171; Allen Buchanan, "Choosing Who Will Be Disabled: Genetic Intervention and the Morality of Inclusion," *Social Philosophy and Policy* 13 (1996) 18–45; Christian Munthe, *The Moral Roots of Prenatal Diagnosis*, Royal Society for Arts and Sciences in Gothenburg, Studies in Research Ethics no. 7 (Gothenburg, Sweden, 1996); Dena Davis, "Genetic Dilemmas and the Child's Right to an Open Future," *Hastings Center Report* 27, no. 2 (1997) 7–15.

2. "Cochlear Implants in Adults and Children," NIH Consensus Statement Online 13, no. 2 (May 15–17, 1995): 1–30.

3. Brice Alden, http://hometown.aol.com/scarter11/gdc.htm.

4. Sally Weale, "Hearing Both Sides," *Guardian*, October 6, 1999, p. 10.

5. http://web.syr.edu/~sndrake/lpgen.htm.

6. Arie Drugan, Anne Greb, et al., "Determinants of Prenatal Decisions to Abort for Chromosome Abnormalities," *Prenatal Diagnosis* 10, no. 8 (1990): 483–90; E. Alberman, D. Mutton, et al., "Down's Syndrome Births and Pregnancy Terminations in 1989 to 1993: Preliminary Findings," *British Journal of Obstetrics and Gynaecology* 106, no. 6 (1995): 445–47. Cited by Rayna Rapp, *Testing Women, Testing the Fetus: The Social Impact of Amniocentesis in America* (London: Routledge, 1999), p. 223.

7. Quoted from Ann Bradley, "Why Shouldn't Women Abort Disabled Fetuses?" first published in *Living Marxism* 82 (September 1995), available at http://www.informinc.co.uk/LM/LM82/LM82_Taboos.html.

8. Diane Beeson, "Social and Ethical Challenges of Prenatal Diagnosis," *Medical Ethics Newsletter* (Lahey Clinic), Winter 2000, p. 2; for similar claims, see Christopher Newell, "Critical Reflections on Disability, Difference and the New Genetics," in *Goodbye Normal Gene: Confronting the Genetic Revolution*, ed. Gabrielle O'Sullivan, Everlyn Sharman, and Stephanie Short (Annandale, New South Wales: Pluto Press, 1999), p. 68; Adrienne Asch, "Prenatal Diagnosis and Selective Abortion: A Challenge to Practice and Policy," *American Journal of Public Health* 89 (1999): 1649–57, esp. p. 1650.

9. See my *Practical Ethics*, 2nd ed. (Cambridge: Cambridge University Press, 1993), ch. 5.

10. Allen Buchanan makes the same point, using the example of a woman who postpones having a child because she is living in a refugee camp, in his "Choosing Who Will Be Disabled: Genetic Intervention and the Morality of Inclusion," *Social Philosophy and Policy* 13 (1996): 18–45, at p. 29.

11. Peter Singer, *Animal Liberation*, 2nd ed. (New York: New York Review/Random House, 1990), ch. 1.

12. Ani Satz, "Prenatal Genetic Testing and Discrimination against the Disabled: A Conceptual Analysis," *Monash Bioethics Review* 18, no. 4 (October 1999): 16.

13. Jonathan Glover, "Gene Mapping, Gene Therapy and Equality of Respect," in *Advances in Biotechnology: Proceedings of an International Conference Organized by the Swedish Council for Forestry and Agricultural Research and the Swedish Recombinant DNA Advisory Committee*, Sollentuna, Sweden, March 11–14, 1990, p. 2.

14. Jonathan Glover, *Causing Death and Saving Lives* (Harmondsworth, Middlesex: Penguin, 1977), pp. 220–24.

15. Buchanan, "Choosing Who Will Be Disabled," p. 33.

16. The World Health Organization is currently attempting to measure the global burden of disease. Its analysis holds that it is equally valuable to extend life by a finite period—say, one year—irrespective of whether the person whose life is saved has a disability—say, blindness—and that it can be justifiable to spend health-care resources to prevent a disability such as blindness, even at the cost of not extending some lives that could be extended by those resources. It seems doubtful that these positions can be reconciled. [Information from Dan Wikler, "Measuring the Global Burden of Disease: Are All Lives of Equal Worth?" a lecture presented to the DeCamp Bioethics Seminar, Princeton University, April 18, 2000.]

17. Daniel Kevles, *In the Name of Eugenics: Genetics and the Uses of Human Heredity* (New York: Knopf, 1985), p. 164.

18. Andrew Solomon, "Defiantly Deaf," *New York Times Magazine*, August 28, 1994, p. 38.

19. See Peter Singer and Deane Wells, *Making Babies* (New York: Scribner, 1985), pp. 24–29.

20. Stephen Macedo, "Homosexuality and the Conservative Mind," *Georgetown Law Journal* 84, no. 2 (December 1995): 269, and note 122 at p. 292.

21. Gina Kolata, "$50,000 Offered to Tall, Smart Egg Donor," *New York Times*, March 3, 1999, p. A10.

22. See J. S. Mill, *On Liberty*, various editions.

23. Lisa Gerson, "Human Harvest," *Boston Magazine*, May 1999, www.bostonmagazine.com/highlights/humanharvest.shtml.

24. On the difficult issue of whether we can benefit a child by bringing it into existence, see Derek Parfit, *Reasons and Persons* (Oxford: Clarendon, 1984), p. 367, and Peter Singer, *Practical Ethics*, 2nd ed. (Cambridge: Cambridge University Press, 1993), pp. 123–25.

25. Helena Cronin, *The Ant and the Peacock* (Cambridge: Cambridge University Press, 1991), ch. 5.

26. Jerome Groopman, "The Doubting Disease," *New Yorker*, April 10, 2000, p. 55.

27. John Schaar, *Legitimacy in the Modern State* (New Brunswick, NJ: Transaction Books, 1981), p. 195; cited in Maxwell Mehlman and Jeffrey Botkin, *Access*

to the Genome: The Challenge to Equality (Washington, DC: Georgetown University Press, 1998), p. 100.

28. *Gattaca*, written and directed by Andrew Niccol, 1997.

29. Lee Silver, *Remaking Eden* (New York: Avon, 1998), p. 282.

30. Mehlman and Botkin, *Access to the Genome*, ch. 6.

31. Silver, *Remaking Eden*, p. 177.

32. Chan Chee Khoon and Chee Heng Leng, "Singapore 1984: Breeding for Big Brother," in *Designer Genes: I.Q., Ideology and Biology*, ed. Chan Chee Khoon and Chee Heng Leng (Selangor, Malaysia: Institute for Social Analysis [Insan], 1984), pp. 4–13.

33. Mehlman and Botkin, *Access to the Genome*, pp. 126–28.

32

THE UNCERTAIN RATIONALE FOR PRENATAL DISABILITY SCREENING

David Wasserman and Adrienne Asch

On November 10, 2005, an article in the *New England Journal of Medicine* reported the increasing accuracy of first trimester screening for Down syndrome. The introduction of first trimester tests for the condition was heralded in 1998 by the National Institute of Child Health and Human Development (NICHHD) as reducing complications for women who choose abortion. NICHHD reportedly spent $15 million on the study—presumably to fulfill its mission "to ensure that every person is born healthy and wanted." Of course, few children with trisomy 21 detected in the first trimester are likely to be born at all. NICHHD's mission is also "to ensure that women suffer no harmful effects from reproductive processes," and that goal may also have provided a rationale for funding the research—many women might see the birth of a child with Down syndrome as a "harmful effect" of their pregnancy. We suggest that *it is difficult to justify prenatal screening for disability on either of these grounds, as protecting the health of the fetus or child or as protecting women from harmful effects of reproduction.*

From *Virtual Mentor* 8, no. 1 (January 2006): 53–56. Reprinted by permission of the American Medical Association.

Prenatal diagnosis—through amniocentesis, chorionic villus sampling, or preimplantation genetic diagnosis (PGD) for Down syndrome, cystic fibrosis, female gender, or blue eyes—needs to be seen for what it is, or more important, what it is not. It is not a medical procedure—that is, a procedure intended to protect or restore an individual's physical or mental health. Rather, it is typically a procedure to identify unwanted organisms. Occasionally, testing is sought to guide the management of delivery and labor. But far more often its purpose is to provide information about fetal characteristics so a woman can decide whether or not to continue her pregnancy.

To say that prenatal testing and any resulting abortion are not medical procedures is not to say that they are wrong or that a doctor is wrong to perform them. A pregnancy test for an unmarried adolescent who does not want a child is not a medical procedure either, nor is the abortion that may follow positive pregnancy test results. We may regard that test and abortion as justifiable, and regard a doctor as the appropriate agent to carry them out, without believing that they serve to protect or restore the health of an individual patient. If doctors can properly perform a nonhealing intervention in aborting the unwanted fetus carried by a teenager, can they do so in enabling parents to prevent the birth of a child with Down syndrome?

The answer will depend on whether there is a distinct justification for the intervention that is not based on protecting or restoring the health of individual patients. Two rationales are often given for the use of prenatal testing, and both gain spurious strength from their conflation with stronger rationales for different practices. The first is the public health rationale of reducing the incidence of genetic disease and "defects." This rationale elides the striking difference between prenatal testing and true medical preventive measures: for the foreseeable future, prenatal testing can prevent disease and disabilities only by preventing the existence of people who would bear them. Prevention by prenatal screening lacks the obvious justification of most public health measures: preventing medical harm to existing people. While it may be reasonable to treat the incidence of disability among existing people as, in part, a public health problem, it is problematic to treat the existence of future people with disabilities that way. A policy of prevention-by-screening appears to reflect the judgment that lives with disabilities are so burdensome to the disabled child, her family, and society that their avoidance is a health-care priority—a judgment that exaggerates and misattributes many or most of the difficulties associated with disability.

We believe the principal difficulties faced by people with disabilities and their families are caused or exacerbated by discriminatory attitudes and practices that are potentially remediable by social, legal, and institutional change—in much the same way that many of the difficulties associated with being African American or female in America have been ameliorated. A policy that promotes selection against embryos and fetuses with disabling traits conveys the strong impression that the problem is the disability itself rather than the society that could do so much more to welcome and include all its members.

The second rationale offered in support of prenatal screening is the enhancement of parental autonomy. The justification for enabling a woman to decide *whether* to have a child is stronger than the justification for enabling her to decide *what kind* of child she will have. Pregnancy makes massive demands on a woman's body; parenthood involves an enormous, open-ended commitment. To treat the difference between having a disabled and a nondisabled child as being of a similar magnitude as the difference between having and not having a child greatly exaggerates the burden of disability and ignores the source of so much of that burden.

We recognize that people with disabilities and their families face difficulties in our present society and that perhaps some of those difficulties would remain even after comprehensive social reform. But we maintain that few disabilities are so undesirable that they provide good reason for abandoning a parental project, for declining to become a parent to the child who would develop from the diagnosed fetus. Given the difficulties that a disabled child is likely to face in our present society, a prospective parent may have good reason not to *cause* disability, but that is not reason enough to *select against* a fetus with a disability. In creating families, prospective parents should aspire to an ideal of unconditional welcome; an ideal opposed to the exercise of selectivity through prenatal testing. If a child develops a disease or disability—diabetes or attention deficit disorder—loving parents incorporate the challenges posed by that condition into the project of raising and nurturing him. We do not believe that parents should reject those challenges in bringing future children into their families. (It is important to recognize that most disabilities are caused by accidents or disease, not by genetic variations.)

If, however, we accept the use of biomedical technology to give parents greater choice in the kind of children they have, we should not limit that choice to the avoidance of genetic impairment; we should facilitate testing for any conditions parents might find burdensome or desirable. And even if we are comfortable with such parental selectivity, enhancing it clearly should not enjoy the priority given to measures that protect the choice about whether to become a parent in the first place.

On the other hand, if we object to such unfettered choice as corrupting or debasing the parental role, we should not make an exception for disability. To do so is to treat disabilities as uniquely burdensome, in the face of strong contrary evidence from research on families with disabled children.[1] To assume that most genetically detectable disabilities impair the prospects for individual and family flourishing in a way that other potentially detectable characteristics do not is truly to stigmatize disability. While such stigmatization is understandable when it is displayed by anxious couples awaiting a life-transforming event, it should not guide the public funding of reproductive research or the formulation of reproductive policy.

Given the difficulties in justifying the public funding of research and development in prenatal screening, the money spent for that purpose might be better used for research on improving the health, functioning, and longevity of children with genetically based disabilities.

NOTE

1. C. Baxter, K. Poonia, L. Ward, and Z. Nadirshaw, "A Longitudinal Study of Parental Stress and Support: From Diagnosis of Disability to Leaving School," *International Journal of Disability, Development, and Education* 42 (1995): 125–36; B. M. Cahill and L. M. Gidden, "Influence of Child Diagnosis on Family and Parental Functioning: Down Syndrome versus Other Disabilities," *American Journal on Mental Retardation* 101 (1996): 149–60; P. M. Ferguson, "Mapping the Family: Disability Studies and the Exploration of Parental Response to Disability," in *Handbook of Disability Studies*, ed. G. L. Albrecht, K. D. Seelman, and M. Bury (Thousand Oaks, CA: Sage Publications, 2001); R. Gallimore, T. S. Weisner, S. Z. Kaufman, and L. P. Bernheimer, "The Social Construction of Ecocultural Niches: Family Accommodation of Developmentally Delayed Children," *American Journal of Mental Retardation* 94 (1989): 216–30; and K. W. Krauss, "Child-Related and Parenting Stress: Similarities and Differences between Mothers and Fathers of Children with Disabilities," *American Journal of Mental Retardation* 97 (1993): 393, 404.

SUGGESTED READING

A. Asch, "Disability, Equality and Prenatal Testing: Contradictory or Compatible?"
Florida State University Law Review 30 (2003): 315–42.

D. Wasserman and A. Asch, "Where Is the Sin in Synecdoche: Prenatal Testing and
the Parent-Child Relationship," in *Quality of Life and Human Difference:
Genetic Testing, Health Care, and Disability*, ed. D. Wasserman, R. Wachbroit,
and J. Bickenbach (New York: Cambridge University Press, 2005).

LIVING AND DYING WITH DIGNITY

An Alternative Perspective*

S. Kay Toombs

INTRODUCTION

As a person living with progressively debilitating neurological disease (multiple sclerosis) and significant disability, I have a particular interest in the debate concerning dignity and end-of-life decision making.[1] Recent statistics from Oregon show that the rate of physician-assisted suicide among patients with neurological disease (ALS) is substantially higher than among patients with other illnesses—a finding that is confirmed in the experience of physician-assisted suicide and euthanasia in the Netherlands.[2] Moreover, several of those who killed themselves under the direction of Jack Kevorkian suffered from MS. Having experienced what it means to live with serious neurological dysfunction, I feel a certain uncomfortable kinship with these patients. I know how difficult it can be for the incurably ill to retain a sense

---

*This essay was originally published under the title "Living and Dying with Dignity: Reflections on Lived Experience." Copyright © 2004 by *Journal of Palliative Care*. Reprinted from *Journal of Palliative Care* 20, no. 3 (September 2004): 193–200. Reprinted by permission of the publisher.

of personal dignity in the context of prevailing cultural attitudes about such things as health, independence, physical appearance, and mortality, and in light of the almost "magical" confidence we have in the curative power of medicine.[3]

While there may be philosophical debate about the meaning of the term "dignity," in everyday life the notion of dignity is equated with self-worth. To be treated with dignity is to be treated with respect, to be considered worthy of the regard of others. To lose one's dignity is to feel that one's value as a person is irreparably diminished.

One of the most powerful barriers to retaining a sense of dignity in illness is the prevailing cultural perspective on autonomy (an ideal that, as Agich has noted, represents the "mainstream" model of autonomy and that "prominently features the attributes and values of self-reliance, personal preference, and self assertion" and that "implies a robust independent individual capable of acting without help").[4] Since self-reliance "involves the capacity to provide for one's own needs without another's help,"[5] there is a strong cultural message that we should be able to "stand on our own two feet," "look after ourselves." Dependence on others is perceived as weakness. Furthermore, since the attributes and values of personal preference and self-assertion "focus on the absence of obstacles to choice" and the "requirement that being free necessarily involves the active pursuit of the fulfillment of one's own desire,"[6] connected to this mainstream notion of autonomy is the sense that persons should be able "to do their own thing," without a sense of limits. Consequently, when we have to ask for help, we feel ashamed and presume we are a burden to others.

Given this view of autonomy, society places inordinate value on independence and self-determination. Thus, the act of "giving," of serving another, is negatively equated with self-denial.[7] Full-time care giving (whether it be of children in the home, of elderly parents, or of a sick person) is deemed less valuable than pursuing activities that will bring individual fulfillment—a fulfillment that is almost exclusively measured in terms of professional and economic markers that signify "success" according to societal values. Thus, none of my female university students could imagine self-fulfillment as full-time homemakers and mothers, elderly parents constantly worry that they will end up being a "burden" to their children who "have their own lives to live," and there is a widespread presumption that those with disabilities are a drain on the lives of their able-bodied partners.[8] When care giving is conceived as a purely negative form of self-sacrifice, this inevitably arouses feelings of resentment on the part of the caregiver and incalculable feelings of guilt and self-recrimination on the part of the person receiving care. In this cultural climate, it is perhaps not surprising that the fear of "being a burden to others" features prominently as a rationale for requesting physician-assisted suicide. Indeed, so ingrained are these societal attitudes that the incurably ill may unwittingly feel that, by killing themselves, they are acting unselfishly in the best interests of others and, furthermore, that they are—in some sense—obligated to do so. In the year 2000, 63 percent of those whose suicides were reported under the Oregon "Death with Dignity Act" said they feared becoming burdens on their families, friends, and caregivers. Every year this concern has consistently been shown to be a significant factor in the decision to request physician-assisted suicide.[9]

Thus, the prevailing cultural view of autonomy has a paradoxical effect. In stressing that individuals have the "right" to live their own lives, to make personal choices that are minimally constrained by the values or desires of others, this attitude may, on the one hand, influence an individual's decision to end his or her life *out of a sense of obligation to spare others* (not to "put them through that") or, on the other hand, accord one the "right" to end one's own life *solely as an act of self-determination without regard to the wishes of others.*[10] Thus, the regulations of the Oregon "Death with Dignity Act," do not require the notification of family members, despite the fact that the act of suicide is devastating for those closely associated with a person who commits suicide.[11]

An important barrier to retaining dignity in debilitating illness is the cultural emphasis on "doing" as opposed to "being." A person's worth is judged according to his or her capacity to produce (to be useful) or his ability to achieve a certain professional status. When we say to our children, "You can *be* anything you want to be," what we mean is that you can achieve worth through *doing*. Consequently, when activities are curtailed and roles inevitably change, there is a profound loss of self-esteem. Given this cultural attitude, a person who is unable to "do" not only feels diminished by the inability to continue projects that are deemed meaningful according to societal markers of "success," but he or she also feels no longer able to contribute anything of worth to others. Furthermore, the cultural emphasis on self-fulfillment takes little account of the fragility of physical existence and mortality. People find it hard to accept that there are certain givens, inherent limitations that may well "derail" even the most carefully constructed life plan.

Recognizing the difference between "being" and "doing" can be an important step in preserving self-worth. As a woman with Parkinson's disease told me, "I always imagined that when I became a grandmother, I would *do* a lot with my grandchildren. Then I got Parkinson's. However, now I realize that I can just *be* for my grandchildren." This was a very empowering realization for her. Of course, the attitude of others is also a determining factor in enhancing the ability to retain dignity in the face of increasing debility. If, by your actions, you demonstrate that I am worthy of regard, no matter what the circumstances, then you affirm me in a powerful manner.

The loss of bodily control is also a prominent cause of loss of dignity.[12] Indeed, this is one of the three most commonly mentioned reasons for requesting physician-assisted suicide.[13] Accepting the loss of bodily control is particularly difficult in the context of prevailing cultural attitudes regarding health, autonomy, and death, and in light of the almost boundless confidence we have in the curative power of medicine.

In our culture "health" is equated with an unrealistic ideal of complete physical integrity and the absence of bodily (or mental) limitation, a view that carries with it the expectation that cure, good health, and happiness are a personal right. Given this view incurable illness is an affront. We seem to have lost the ability to accept illness, aging, and death as a natural part of life. This is partly due to the undeniable successes of modern technological medicine—successes that have caused us to harbor unrealistic expectations about the power of medicine to "fix" medical problems and to keep us alive. In this context, to discover that one's condition cannot be cured is to experience the most elemental loss of control. I remember well my own sense of helplessness at discovering I had an incurable disease.[14]

Furthermore, given the cultural perspective on autonomy and self-determination, there is an expectation that one has (or should have) absolute control over one's life without the imposition of limits. Incurable illness concretely shatters this illusion, profoundly threatening the sense of self-integrity. Consequently, many see the availability of physician-assisted suicide and euthanasia as a means to regain control in what is an essentially uncontrollable situation. (Paradoxically, the advances of medical technology also add to the profound sense of loss of control in another manner: people fear that this technology will be used to keep them alive against their wishes.)

For many, the loss of bowel and bladder control represents the most grievous experience of loss of dignity. Since I live with both types of dysfunction, I can indeed attest to the powerful feelings of degradation that these particular disorders can arouse. Not only is it the case that one feels oneself reduced to the status of an infant (with the accompanying sense that, as an adult, one really "ought" to be able to exercise control) but there is the ever-present threat of public humiliation. This threat of humiliation can be overwhelming in the face of cultural attitudes that treat such disorders with contempt. Indeed, so harrowing is the possibility of public disgrace that many patients withdraw from social interaction. Some decide to end their lives on the grounds that incontinence robs them of all personal dignity.[15]

In living with MS, I have found that certain practical strategies help me cope with the loss of bodily control. First, it is helpful to recognize there is always some level of control that one can exercise—even in the face of increasingly disruptive symptoms. Patients are much less likely to feel helpless if they can develop concrete strategies that permit even minimal control.[16] I have also found that distancing oneself from the body is imperative in dealing with the "mess" of sickness and the degradations that inevitably arouse feelings of shame and self-loathing. If one can recognize that the body's failings are purely mechanical problems for which one is not personally responsible, then one can deal with them in a dispassionate manner. Of course, it is vital that others show by their actions and responses that they are not repulsed by the loss of bodily control. If you can demonstrate to me that my illness does not degrade my worth as a person, that it is not beneath *your* dignity to care for me, you affirm me in a powerful manner.

No discussion of loss of dignity would be complete without noting how cultural attitudes make it extraordinarily difficult for people with disabilities to retain a sense of self-worth. We live in a culture that places inordinate value on appearance, promoting unrealistic ideals of "beauty" and physical fitness that inevitably devalue those who do not meet these ideals. These negative cultural attitudes are difficult to ignore. (Each time I have had to adopt a new way of getting around—first a cane, then crutches, then a walker, then a wheelchair—I have felt shame.) The loss of self-esteem that accompanies changes in appearance can be profound. Chochinov notes that patients who suffer from conditions that highly disfigure the body are among those most likely to commit suicide in the face of terminal illness.[17]

In the eyes of the able-bodied, there is the widespread assumption that disability is incompatible with living a meaningful life. When strangers observe I am in a wheelchair, they make the immediate judgment that my situation is an essentially negative one, that I am unable to engage in professional activities, and that I am wholly dependent on others. On many occasions strangers have said to me, "Aren't you *lucky* to have your husband?"

This is not so much a comment about my husband's character, as it is a perception that my relationship with him is purely one of burdensome dependence. In observing my physical incapacities, strangers assume that my intellect is likewise affected. People address questions to my companion and refer to me in the third person: "Where would *she* like to sit?" Such common responses are demeaning and reinforce the perception that disability reduces personal and social worth. Furthermore, as many have noted, people with disabilities are needlessly handicapped by social structures and practices.[18] Since, for the nondisabled, acceptable quality of life is measured almost exclusively according to "ableist" norms that do not accurately reflect the lived experience of disability, there is the widespread presumption that it is *prima facie* rational for a person with severe disabilities to express the desire to die rather than to live with limitation.[19]

If one is to afford respect to those with disabilities, one must look beyond the stereotype to the person. People who live with disability are people—simply that—people first and foremost. If you focus only on my disability, then you essentially make *me* invisible. In attending to the *person* and not the disability, others indicate that physical or mental limitation does not denigrate personal worth. It is also vitally important that, as a society, we focus as much attention on promoting conditions that allow people to live with dignity (regardless of their physical or mental state), as we do on debating death with dignity.

ENHANCING DIGNITY

Reflections on Lived Experience in a Christian Community

My purpose in this section of the paper is to share my lived experience of incurable debilitating illness in the context of the practices and values of a nondenominational Christian community, and to show how these particular values and practices are dignity enhancing. It is not possible in the context of this paper to provide a detailed account of the vision, roots, and cultural position of our community (nor is it the appropriate place to do so). I should perhaps explain that we draw probably the greatest portion of our beliefs and lifestyle and values from the Anabaptist tradition, although there have been additional major influences such as Pietism and others. I recognize, of course, that our lived community is unique in some respects but my intent is to show how the countercultural core values of our community of Christians consistently enhance dignity, even in the face of debilitating illness and death. What I have written should not be construed as a judgment on the merits or demerits of the experience of others who live in other cultural contexts. Nor should it be taken as implying that these are the only practices that can enhance dignity in the care of the terminally ill.

My reflections on loss of dignity have grown out of my personal experience of neurological disease in the context of prevailing cultural values. I would now like to share how becoming a Christian seven years ago has broadened my understanding of these issues. In particular, I want to suggest that authentic Christian community may offer an alternative culture with a radically different value system—one that enhances personal dignity.

As I have noted, a major barrier to the preservation of dignity in illness is the cultural emphasis on independence and self-determination. A problem with this focus is that it disregards the importance of relationship. Living in a nondenominational Christian community has taught me that self-sufficiency is illusory and not a goal to which we should strive. As Christians, we are called to a radically different understanding of dependence. Rather than pursuing the goal of autonomy, we are called to live out our lives in relationship: relationship with God and with each other. In imitating the example of Jesus, the suffering servant, we are called to continually lay down our lives for one another: "Greater love has no one than this, that one lay down his life for his friends."[20] Since love, rather than self-determination, is the cardinal value, care giving (care of and for another) is not considered a negative form of self-sacrifice but, rather, it is the foundation of Christian community. Far from depriving the individual, such service becomes a means of developing the highest moral qualities of character.

Living in close relationship permits us to live out this ethic of service in very concrete ways. As an example, since I can no longer clean my house, three of the young mothers in our fellowship have volunteered to do this for me. Their gift of service is more than just a house cleaning. All of us are enriched by the opportunity to know one another better, especially as we are from different generations and very diverse backgrounds. When my husband and I had the flu, people prepared all our meals and served them to us, did our grocery shopping, and took care of all our household chores. When we moved house, so that we could bring my ninety-year-old mother to live with us, friends in the community helped me to pack up two houses, and moved all of our furniture and household effects to our new house. In fact, they moved our furniture while I was out of the country on a speaking engagement in Sweden. When we returned, our new home was ready for us! Such acts of service are not just valuable, in and of themselves (although they are surely that), but they are of inestimable worth in bringing us into ever-deepening relationships of love for one another. Indeed, we have found that one of the fruits of Christian community and the rejection of self-centered values is the breaking down of artificial social barriers that separate on the basis of age, economic status, education, ethnicity, culture, and appearance.

Another example of concrete service relates to the care of a forty-nine-year-old father of five who is dying of a brain tumor. Friends in the community prepare meals every day for his family (when they deliver the food, they take *their* families with them, so that both families can eat and spend time together); take his children to music lessons, dentist's appointments, and to play with friends; and assist his wife with home schooling and grocery shopping. Others take two-hour shifts to provide him with round-the-clock care (and to permit his family to attend church meetings and other events); three close friends attend to his personal needs (bathing, shaving, and so on). Others participate in a prayer chain from midnight to 6:00 a.m., seven days a week, to supplement the church's existing prayer chain for the sick. Also, as a token of love and respect, several are tithing monetary offerings to cover all the family's financial needs. Such concrete opportunities to lay down our lives for one another are not limited to responding to the needs of the sick, but are lived out daily in the commitment to meet *any* need that might arise in anyone's life. As we voluntarily make these sacrifices for those we love, we do not feel deprived or taken advantage of, but we feel thankful for the opportunity to become more like the One who made the ultimate sacrifice.

A central tenet of Christianity is that all human beings have intrinsic worth, regardless of any contingent circumstances. Since personal worth is independent of worldly criteria, it is not related to material success, physical condition, or to the individual's ability to produce. Consequently, Christian values turn the cultural perspective on the importance of "doing" versus "being" upside down. The emphasis for the Christian is not so much, "How do I define myself by my role?" but "How do I live out whatever role God has provided for me?" "What kind of a person am I?" Believers are called to be imitators of Christ.[21] Christian virtues have to do with character. As we put on the new self[22] and discard the values of the old, we remember that Jesus said blessed are the "poor in spirit," "the meek," those who "hunger and thirst for righteousness," the "merciful," the "pure in heart."[23] We are urged to clothe ourselves with compassion, kindness, humility, gentleness, and patience, not to be envious, boastful, self-seeking, or proud.[24] While these virtues are exercised through acts, they relate to a way of being in the world that is not dependent upon physical attributes or abilities and that does not look to the world's criteria of success.

When I think of the value of "being," I remember Perry, a member of our community who died from ALS at the age of thirty-five. Towards the end of his life, Perry could "do" nothing. Yet he was (and remains) a powerful influence in all our lives. Steadfast in faith, intelligent, thoughtful, funny, and full of joy, he was a loving father and husband who instilled lifelong values in his children. His struggles and victories in adversity encouraged all of us to persevere in our own trials. Perry did not meet the worldly ideal of physical beauty and strength. One day a saleswoman, eyeing his physical condition, said to his wife, "I can't believe you've stuck with him!" Yet the scriptures call us to a different standard of beauty: one that is inner rather than outer. Even the Messiah Himself was described as having "no form nor comeliness . . . and no beauty that we should desire him."[25] In judging Perry's worth solely on the basis of outward appearance, this woman completely missed the strength and beauty of his spirit. Since we are so dependent on visual perception, we all find it difficult to look beyond the physical manifestation of radical disfigurement or disability. Yet, unless we do, we may well miss a beautiful spiritual demeanor.

As Christians, we are also reminded that cultural attitudes that stress personal control and the postponement of death are, in fact, illusions. In recognizing that man is "but a breath," his days are like a "fleeting shadow," we comprehend the undeniable fact that there are certain givens in our lives.[26] We live always with the fragility of mortality. It is often hard for us to relinquish control in *all* areas of our lives—especially as these relate to our perception of what it means to be, say, a wife, a mother, or a breadwinner. When a dear friend became debilitated with cancer, she found it particularly hard to give up full responsibility for taking care of her own home. Yet she found that the act of relinquishing control in *that* area of her life, of submitting to her vulnerability and need, gave her the opportunity to experience depths of affection and thanksgiving that she had never felt before. If those of us who need help can come to recognize that our need is a form of communion with others (rather than a burdensome obligation that we are imposing on them), we can avoid the self-recrimination and guilt that poisons the gift of love. And if we are not willing to receive, we prevent someone from giving.

In a culture that views health and happiness as a personal right, suffering is an affront. Consequently, people tend to withdraw from the incurably ill. This enforced isolation contributes to the person's sense that he or she has become less worthy of regard. The meaning of suffering is very different from a Christian perspective where disease, pain, discomfort, and death are understood to be very much a part of what it means to be human. Thus, in my suffering, I do not feel set apart from others, quarantined (as it were) from the rest of the human race. Furthermore, I do not feel isolated because, as a Christian, I know I serve a God who shared in the experience of suffering, a God who was "despised and rejected by men, a man of sorrows, and *familiar with suffering*" or, as the King James translation has it, "a man acquainted with grief."[27] I am comforted in the knowledge that I am never expected to face suffering alone. The God of love is Immanuel (God with Us).[28] Nor am I alone in the very real sense that I am part of the Body of Christ. In living in a close relationship with a community of believers who follow the way of the cross, of Christ's suffering, I do not face trials alone.

Becoming a Christian has also reminded me that my knowledge is necessarily fragmentary, that I can never see the "whole" picture or plan for my life."[29] Indeed, the hardest truth and the profound mystery is that, along with pain, suffering, frustration, and loss, my illness has brought with it a unique opportunity to share the meaning of illness with doctors, nurses, medical students, and other caregivers. In my writing, speaking, and teaching, I have found a life's work that has been very meaningful.

This comment is not intended to deny that human lives are often beset with unfathomable tragedy. Christianity does not turn its face away from the agony of personal suffering. Central to its message is the stark reality of the cross. When I am tempted to despair, I am reminded of the Garden of Gethsemane, of the One in whom there was no sin, but who died on the cross for my transgressions. The Gospels record that in His agony, Jesus prayed until "His sweat was like drops of blood falling to the ground" asking, "My Father, if it is possible, may this cup be taken from me." But He finished his prayer with the words, "Yet not *my* will but *Thine*."[30] In those moments when it seems impossible to pray this prayer, I think of the apostle Paul, who prayed three times that the "thorn in his flesh" would be taken away, only to receive the promise, "My grace is sufficient for you, for my power is made perfect in weakness."[31]

The reality of the cross is at odds with the cultural understanding of autonomy.[32] In imitating Christ, believers are called to relinquish absolute control over their lives. Jesus' admonition is to "pick up your cross and follow Me," every single day.[33] Along the way, we may well have to face the burdens of illness, suffering, and disability, and inevitably we will experience the reductions of aging and death. These reductions do not diminish one's intrinsic worth as a human being. Furthermore, if I am to stay true to the example given by Jesus in Gethsemane, I cannot arbitrarily circumscribe the limits of the cross I am willing to bear. The desire to "limit the cross" is motivated by the wish to escape a "worst case scenario" that seems personally unendurable. (This is one reason people desire to exercise control over the manner of their death.) Yet, as Christians, we have found that one can experience supernatural grace even in these direst of circumstances. As she neared death, our dear friend Helen shared, "The *one thing* I don't want to happen is to feel that I'm suffocating." On the night she died, her worst fears were realized when she began to struggle for breath. Yet, as she gave herself to the prayer, "Not *my* will but *Thine*," she almost instantly experienced an overwhelming sense of peace. "I keep thinking of that song, 'God has been so good to me. Forever I will praise His name,'" she said. Then she smiled, whispered, "I love you," closed her eyes, and died.

As Christians, we believe that the cross is not the end of the story in God's eternal purposes. Our faith calls us to look beyond the present suffering to a future glory that will be revealed to us, if we are willing to stay the course. It also assures us that nothing—"tribulation, distress, persecution, famine, nakedness, peril or sword" nor "death, nor life, nor angels, nor principalities, nor powers, nor things present, nor things to come"—shall be able to separate us from the love of God.[34] We are encouraged, therefore, to persevere in the face of trials, trusting in God, and knowing that beyond the agony of Calvary lies the promise of the Empty Tomb. This promise is no illusion. We have a "cloud of witnesses"[35] who have gone before us and who have testified to its truth. I have space to share only one of many testimonies: At the time of his death, due to the ravages of ALS, Perry had been unable to talk for more than a year. He regained the ability to speak just moments before he died. In a clearly discernible voice, he used his dying breaths to tell those gathered with him to share with everybody that God would remain "faithful *all the way to the end*" in each of their lives too.

From an immanent perspective, perseverance in the face of suffering is meaningless. In a culture that celebrates autonomy as the cardinal value, life or death outside of personal control will be experienced as personally demeaning, alienating, and undignified.[36] From an eternal perspective, there is a larger wisdom that places disease, suffering, and death within the context of a cosmic narrative of the power of love overcoming even the power of death.

In conclusion, in reflecting on what it means to live in a Christian community, I am reminded of the centrality of the covenantal relationship in our lives as Christians: relationship with God and with each other. This covenantal relationship is built upon the foundation stone of self-sacrificial love—a love that is exemplified in the life and death of Jesus and which finds its fullest expression in the context of a body of believers, the Body of Christ. The values and practices that spring from this foundation of self-sacrificial love deliberately eschew the cultural perspective on autonomy and self-determination. Rather, the focus is on honoring and serving one another as an expression of the love of God. This ethic of love necessarily enhances human dignity.

I have been asked whether my experience of living in a Christian community has universal relevance. In this essay I stress that Christian community provides a different way of conceiving the values of independence, health, productivity, beauty, and mortality and, particularly, the way we think about the relationship between caregivers and those who need care. I would hope that, given my discussion regarding the ways in which prevailing cultural values directly contribute to loss of dignity in incurable illness, my description of this countercultural position may, at the very least, provide insights into explicit ways in which dignity may be enhanced in illness. Nevertheless, it is true that the full expression of this Christian perspective is grounded in the beliefs that our community holds in common with a long-standing Christian tradition, and rests on the vision, roots, and cultural position of our community—a context that allows us and others with a similar vision to concretely live out this perspective in very specific ways.

NOTES

1. I have lived with multiple sclerosis for over thirty years. Over the years my illness has affected my ability to see, to sense, to move, to stand up, to sit up, to maintain my balance, to walk, and to control my bowels and bladder. My disease has progressed to the point that I use a motorized wheelchair full time.

2. Physician-assisted suicide legislative statute and reports, 1998–2002, Oregon Department of Health Services, http://www.ohd.hr.state.or.us/chs/pas/ors.cfm.

3. I am thinking here of values that are prevalent in North American culture and in Western scientific medicine although, to the extent that these values have spread to other parts of the world, these comments apply to the meaning of illness in other cultures.

4. Agich notes that, although "autonomy is acknowledged by many authors to involve a family of meanings," the model of autonomy described in this paper is, in fact, the "standard," "mainstream" model whose "importance and pervasiveness can hardly be overestimated." See G. J. Agich, "Chronic Illness and Freedom" in *Chronic Illness: From Experience to Policy*, ed. S. K. Toombs, D. Barnard, and R. A. Carson (Bloomington: Indiana University Press, 1995), pp. 133, 136, 138.

Engelhardt points out that in a culture that celebrates autonomy as the cardinal value, the preservation of dignity is identified with self-determination or self-rule. See H. T. Engelhardt, *The Foundations of Christian Bioethics* (The Netherlands: Swets & Zeitlinger, 2000), pp. 43–44, 311, 312.

It is not my intent in this paper to provide a philosophical critique of the mainstream model of autonomy, or to provide an alternative model, as important as these tasks might be. Rather, I am limiting my comments to the ways in which this prevailing and culturally widespread notion of autonomy directly contributes to the loss of dignity experienced by those like myself who live with progressively debilitating illness and disability. I recognize that (as is the case with the concept of dignity) there is much philosophical debate about the definition of "autonomy" and its relevance in the context of medical ethics. See, for example, H. T. Engelhardt, *The Foundations of Bioethics* (New York: Oxford University Press, 1986); T. L. Beauchamp and J. F. Childress, *Principles of Biomedical Ethics* (New York: Oxford University Press, 2001); Engelhardt, *The Foundations of Christian Bioethics*. For a philosophical and sociohistorical critique of the prominence of the principle of autonomy in medical ethics, see E. D. Pellegrino and D. C. Thomasma, *For the Patient's Good: The Restoration of Beneficence in Health Care* (New York: Oxford University Press, 1988); H. Brody, *The Healer's Power* (New Haven, CT: Yale University Press, 1992). For a philosophical discussion of the implications of the principle of autonomy for chronic illness, see G. J. Agich, "Chronic Illness and Freedom," pp. 129–53.

5. G. J. Agich, "Chronic Illness and Freedom," p. 133.

6. Ibid.

7. Agich notes the mainstream view of autonomy "involves a view of persons as isolated and independent rational and competent decision makers who are, by definition, involved in the ceaseless pursuit of the fulfillment of their own preferences, for without such pursuit and fulfillment, autonomy would be a vacuous concept on this view." Ibid.

8. A. R. Robillard, *The Meaning of a Disability: The Lived Experience of Paral-*

ysis (Philadelphia: Temple University Press, 1999); M. Fine and A. Asch, eds., *Women with Disabilities: Essays in Psychology, Culture and Politics* (Philadelphia: Temple University Press, 1988).

9. Physician-assisted suicide legislative statute and reports, 1998–2002.

10. A dominant focus of standard accounts of autonomy is on choice. According to this model, if an individual is to be truly autonomous, he or she should be afforded "unrestricted" and "unfettered" choice from a given range of options—the crucial condition being that such choice is "not constrained in any way." G. J. Agich, "Chronic Illness and Freedom," p. 136.

11. Physician-assisted suicide legislative statute and reports, 1998–2002.

12. S. K. Toombs, *The Meaning of Illness* (The Netherlands: Kluwer Academic Publishers, 1992).

13. Physician-assisted suicide legislative statute and reports, 1998–2002.

14. S. K. Toombs, "Sufficient unto the Day: A Life with Multiple Sclerosis," in *Chronic Illness: From Experience to Policy*, ed. S. K. Toombs, D. Barnard, and R. A. Carson (Bloomington: Indiana University Press, 1995), pp. 3–23.

15. As a personal example, a close relative tragically cited this, and the fear of being a burden to others, as the primary reasons for taking his life.

16. It has been suggested to me that these personal examples of "developing concrete and appropriate strategies of control" hint at a more sophisticated notion of autonomy than the mainstream view. Such a notion would, of course, be very different from the prevailing model, in that it would have to allow for the realities of unavoidable limitation, dependence, and necessary restriction of choice—all of which denote the explicit loss of autonomy in the mainstream view. Such strategies do exemplify the exercise of control (albeit limited control) on the part of the patient—and this is an important aspect of enhancing dignity in palliative care settings.

17. H. Chochinov and M. Lander, "Desire for Death in the Terminally Ill," in *Topics in Palliative Medicine* (Secrets, Hanley and Belfus, Inc., 1999), pp. 185–87.

18. H. Hahn, "The Politics of Physical Differences: Disability and Discrimination. *Journal of Social Issues* 44 (1988): 39–47; M. Oliver, *Understanding Disability: From Theory to Practice* (New York: St. Martin's, 1996); S. K. Toombs, "Reflections on Bodily Change: The Lived Experience of Disability," in *Handbook of Phenomenology and Medicine*, ed. S. K. Toombs (The Netherlands: Kluwer Academic Publishers, 2001), pp. 247–61.

19. B. Corbet, "Physician Assisted Death: Are We Asking the Right Questions?" *New Mobility*, May 2003. [Essay is included in this volume.] Since euthanasia became legal in the Netherlands in 2002, there have been political moves to liberalize the laws to include those who are not terminally ill. See, for example, article at http://www.cnn.com/2002/WORLD/europe/04/01/netherlands.euthanasia. Among those organizations that advocate the legalization of PAS and euthanasia elsewhere,

there is support for including those who are not terminally ill. In 1992 the Dutch Pediatric Association issued guidelines for killing severely handicapped newborns. See article on euthanasia in the Netherlands, *International Task Force on Euthanasia and Assisted Suicide*, p. 4. http://www.internationaltaskforce.org/fctholl.htm.

20. John 15:13. The scriptural references in this section are included at the request of a reviewer. All are taken from the *New American Standard Bible* (California: Foundation Publications, Inc.), except where a different translation is noted in the text.

21. John 13:12–15; Ephesians 5:1–2.

22. Colossians 3.

23. Matthew 5:3–11.

24. 1 Corinthians 13:1–13; Colossians 3:12–15.

25. Isaiah 53:2.

26. Psalm 39:4–5; Psalm 144:4; James 4:14.

27. Isaiah 53:3–5.

28. Matthew 1:23; Isaiah 7:14.

29. Proverbs 3:5–7.

30. Matthew 26:39; Mark 14:33–36; Luke 22:41–44.

31. 2 Corinthians 12:7–9.

32. It has been suggested to me that, in voluntarily laying down His life, Jesus was "exercising a sort of transcendent self-determination," which exemplifies a kind of "autonomy." While I do not have space to fully respond to this suggestion in this context, I would interpret Jesus' example of self-sacrificial love, and His voluntary submission to God, and the givens in His life, as an example of freely relinquishing one's claims to absolute autonomy or self-rule—of setting aside the "active pursuit of fulfillment of one's own desire" and "the ceaseless pursuit of the fulfillment of [one's own] preferences," which characterize the exercise of autonomy in our culture (see notes 4, 7, and 10 above)—in submission to the rule of love. This is certainly the view that shapes my experience as a Christian and that informs our vision as a Christian community.

33. Matthew 10:38–39, 16:24–25; Mark 8:34–35; Luke 9:23–24, 14:27.

34. Romans 8:35–39.

35. Hebrews 12:1–2.

36. Engelhardt, *The Foundations of Christian Bioethics*, p. 312.

34

A CHRISTIAN APPROACH TO DISABILITY STUDIES

A Prolegomenon

Samuel Joeckel

I have the right when I go out and pay good money for a meal to enjoy it. The sight of a woman in a wheelchair with food running down her chin would make me throw up. I believe my rights should be respected as much as the rights of the person in the wheelchair . . . maybe even more so, because I am normal and she is not.

In my opinion, restaurants should have a special section for handicapped people—partially hidden by palms or other greenery so they are not seen by other guests.

Excerpts from two letters to Ann Landers, spring 1987[1]

What accounts for such charged responses to the sight of the disabled? Why is the repulsion expressed in the excerpted letters so visceral? Far more than a reaction against uncouth eating habits, the sentiments conveyed in the letters betray a deep-seated prejudice against the disabled that stems

From *Christian Scholar's Review* 35, no. 3 (Spring 2006). Reprinted by permission.

from socially encoded meanings ascribed to the disabled body. The disabled body possesses symbolic power that is embedded in cultural structures of meaning. To provide just one example of this symbolic power, Robert F. Murphy describes how the disabled body "contravene[s] the values of youth, virility, activity, and physical beauty that Americans cherish. . . ."[2] Consequently, the disabled are "subverters of an American Ideal, just as the poor are betrayers of the American Dream. And to the extent that [the disabled] depart from the ideal, [they] become ugly and repulsive to the able-bodied."[3] Transcribed as the "definitively Other, the disabled figure in cultural discourse assures the rest of the citizenry of who they are not while arousing their suspicions of who they could become."[4]

More recently, the spotlight on Terri Schiavo and the success of the 2004 film *Million Dollar Baby* (directed by Clint Eastwood) have galvanized similar responses to disability. Based upon the court-appointed death of the former and the four Oscars awarded to the latter,[5] what might we conclude about the legislative and cultural attitude toward those with disabilities? In both cases, the message seems to be that some of those with disabilities are better off dead and that it is not worthwhile to live with a disability: If you become disabled, the heroic and most humane course of action is suicide. In addition, neither the Schiavo case nor the film generated much realistic discussion about what living with a disability is truly like: that disability need not be merely tragic and that what often brings despair to those with disabilities is not impairment but the cultural prejudices that isolate them (prejudices present, though generally overlooked, in the film and in the popular response to Schiavo's death). Unfortunately, most Americans are unaware of this reality and, in fact, seem to subscribe to the message conveyed by both the Schiavo case and the film.[6]

How might one defuse this erroneous message? How might one disarm the sort of hate-filled responses in the letters above as well the destructive cultural meanings that underlie them, meanings that contribute to the oppression of the disabled? With the passage of the Americans with Disabilities Act (ADA) in 1990, scholars and activists have gained new momentum in reconceiving disability in order to accommodate the disabled into society. One catalytic agent for these efforts is the field of disability studies. The first part of this essay will map out the basic contours of disability studies. The second part will consider reasons why Christians have been slow to engage this burgeoning field. What Helen R. Betenbaugh wrote in 1995 is still too true today: "Why has the Church neglected to do its homework in the area of disability and chronic illness with respect to biblical studies, systematic, historical and practical theology, especially pastoral care, liturgy, and preaching? Why, in 1995 and several years post-ADA, are we just beginning to work on these issues? Worse, why has the Church resisted doing this work, and why does it continue to do so?"[7] The latter half of this essay will explore this question, serving as a prolegomenon for future Christian approaches to disability studies.[8]

TOWARD A DEFINITION OF DISABILITY STUDIES: AN OVERVIEW

Disability studies attempts to redress the wrongs occasioned by the sort of sociocultural conceptualizations of disability explained above. It interrogates and deconstructs these conceptualizations, unmasking their inhumane implications and replacing them with enfranchising models of disability theorized by those partisan to the disability community itself. Within the field, theory and advocacy thus go hand in hand.

Disability studies thus consists of two components, one scholarly and one political. The former, as Lennard Davis explains, involves the "act of assembling a body of knowledge owned by the disability community"; the latter entails deploying this knowledge to effect social change, "political actions involving the classroom, the workplace, the courts, the legislature, the media, and so on."[9] Disability has thus become not only a subject of scholarly investigation but a theoretical lens ("disability theory") by which other subjects are examined—a "subject of critical inquiry and a category of critical analysis."[10]

Both as subject and category, issues of disability have achieved a stronger presence in academia. Organizations like the Society for Disability Studies and the Committee for Disability Issues within the Modern Language Association, publications such as the *Disability Studies Quarterly*, Web sites such as DISC, "A Disability Studies Academic Community" (<http://www.mith2.umd.edu:8080/disc/index.html>), and graduate programs in disability studies represent the growing number of scholars and activists who re-position disability within theoretical frameworks that challenge traditional and often oppressive cultural inscriptions of disability.

DISABILITY STUDIES IN CONTEXT

Divine Disfavor and Heroically Overcome Obstacle

Disability studies developed as a response to prior culturally prescribed meanings of disability and disability issues. An overview of these meanings will thus help contextualize disability studies. Judeo-Christian cultures (especially those before the Enlightenment) have often viewed disability as a sign of divine punishment or, more generally, disfavor. Darrel Amundsen and Gary Ferngren assert that the Old Testament often portrays a God who promises "health and prosperity for the covenant people if they are faithful to him, and disease and other suffering if they spurn his love."[11] To some degree, this portrayal of God continues in the New Testament and is still adhered to by Christians today. (I will analyze this paradigm in more detail later in the essay.)

The divine-disfavor model uneasily coexists in the eighteenth century with a paradigm that sees disability as a tragedy with the potential to be triumphantly overcome, or, as Helen Deutsch puts it, an obstacle "to be heroically conquered by a randomly afflicted individual."[12] Representations of disability bounce between these two discursive categories—divine disfavor and triumphant overcoming—during the eighteenth century. As Deutsch writes, "The eighteenth century, then, was torn in its representations of disability between two ideas of agency—one divine and insurmountable, one human and exceptional. In one model the body is a sign for God to write on, in the other the body is rendered significant by individual attempts to overcome it."[13] Loosed from religious moorings, the latter model figures disability as "random, impersonal, and something over which the individual sufferer triumphs."[14]

The Medical Model

A third paradigm of disability wields considerable discursive power today. It is also the paradigm against which disability studies offers the most resistance. As Paul Longmore defines it, the "medical model assumes that pathological physiological conditions are the primary obstacle to disabled people's social integration."[15] According to the medical model, the disabled body is a defective body that requires repair through medical procedures.[16]

While the other paradigms invest disability with a cosmic significance or associate disability with the resiliency of the human spirit, the medical model approaches disability as impairment to be medically ameliorated. In this transition, the "clinical gaze . . . replaces the stare of wonder."[17]

Critiquing the medical model may seem counterintuitive. After all, when illness comes, who doesn't seek medicine? When the body becomes impaired, who wouldn't seek the aid of a physician with expert knowledge of the physiology of the body? How can one deny that medical research and practice are the disabled community's strongest allies? As Simi Linton affirms, "It may seem foolish to take issue with [the medical model's] agenda. After all, isn't reduction of disability everyone's aim?"[18] Linton's answer strikes at the heart of a guiding principle of disability studies: "Maybe not. What I find most troubling about the impulse to eliminate, cure, or contain disability is the ascendancy of that idea over accommodation and integration. The impulse to control disability rather than to stop oppression is the theme throughout the social science literature that is most problematic and most in need of problematizing."[19]

In other words, while persons with disabilities may be thankful for medical care, the medical model paradoxically victimizes and disempowers persons with disabilities. The medical model perpetuates the misnomer that the root problem of disability lies in the disabled body rather than in the social forces that stigmatize and marginalize persons with disabilities. To use Linton's words, the medical model advocates a method that "'treat[s]' the condition and the person with the condition rather than 'treating' the social processes and policies that constrict disabled people's lives."[20] In fact, the medical model can contribute to oppressive social practices. As Irving Zola explains, when doctors fail to provide cures for the disabled, the anger directed toward the disability spills over to the bearers of the disability. "In this context," he writes, "the physically handicapped become objects, permanent reminders of a lost and losing struggle, symbols of a past and continuing failure."[21]

In addition, the medical model sees impairment as the central defining characteristic of an individual with a disability, thereby stripping the individual of agency. Analyzing illness narratives, Arthur W. Frank identifies the medical model as a component of a modernist milieu that authoritatively imposes medicalized meanings upon individual experiences of illness; those imposed meanings subsequently shape those very experiences, wresting narrative control away from those who seek to order their own lives in the face of illness or disability. He writes, "I understand this obligation of seeking medical care as a narrative surrender and mark it as the central moment in modernist illness experience. The ill person not only agrees to follow physical regimens that are prescribed; she also agrees, tacitly but with no less implication, to tell her story in medical terms."[22]

In fact, the medical model enables an epistemology of disability that privileges "objective" medical truth claims while accounts of disability rendered from within the disabled perspective itself are discounted as "subjective." As Paul Redding notes, "From the doctor's theoretically grounded diagnostic and therapeutic perspective . . . the specific complaints of the patient are downgraded as forms of knowledge."[23]

Frank thus looks beyond a modernist framework for a more enabling narrative epistemology: "The postmodern experience of illness begins when ill people recognize that more is involved in their experiences than the medical story can tell."[24] According to Frank, the postmodern turn marks the moment when persons with illnesses/disabilities reclaim their voices and their stories from the medical model and its structures of meaning. For these reasons, disability theorists look with suspicion upon the medical model of disability. Linton registers this concern when she explains how the "health and occupational therapy programs' appropriation of 'Disability Studies' compromises the integrity of a field designed to explicate disability as a social, political, and cultural phenomenon."[25]

TOWARD A DEFINITION OF DISABILITY STUDIES: THEORY, PRAXIS, AND GENRE

Disability studies shares a theoretical kinship with minority models of otherness. As Longmore observes, "For the vast majority of people with disabilities, prejudice is a far greater problem than any impairment; discrimination is a bigger obstacle for them to 'overcome' than any disability."[26] Rosemarie Garland-Thomson seeks to "move disability from the realm of medicine into that of political minorities, to recast it from a form of pathology to a form of ethnicity."[27] Recasting disability as a form of ethnicity underscores how cultural attitudes often hinder the disabled from full participation in society; applying a minority model of otherness to disability can show how body difference generates prejudice. In addition, applying a minority model can restore agency to individuals with disabilities.

Theory and Praxis

In making this move, most disability theorists acknowledge the politicization and cultural construction of subjectivities. That is, identity does not refer to an ontologically given entity but instead refers to a cultural process whereby competing prescriptive meanings vie for discursive ascendancy. Dominant ideologies that are invested with significant cultural power possess strong potential to imprint their meanings upon group identities. In this way, identity is culturally constructed. Far from an essentialistic entity, identity is forged in the crucible where culture negotiates meaning. Michel Foucault reveals how the body has historically been the site of often violent cultural struggles over meaning, identity, and, of course, power. He attests how the body is "directly involved in a political field; power relations have an immediate hold upon it; they invest it, train it, torture it, force it to carry out tasks, to perform ceremonies, to emit signs."[28] The notion of the body as source of multiple significations, all culturally constructed, constitutes an important theoretical premise of disability studies. In fact, one might identify cultural constructionism as the dominant epistemology of disability studies.[29]

Why is this the case? For one, the epistemology of cultural constructionism provides the theoretical fuel that generates the transition from a medical model of disability to disability studies; that is, it enables the paradigm that views disability less in terms of physical impairment and more in terms of social injustice. As Mark Jeffreys explains, cultural constructionism "makes possible the argument that disability is itself not so much a pathological or even biological condition as it is a cultural condition, a marginalized group identity that has a history of oppression and exclusion, a stigmatized category created to serve the interests of the dominant ideology and its privileged classes."[30] Or, as G. Thomas Couser puts it, "[R]ecognizing disability as a cultural construct enables us to understand and deconstruct the procedures by which some bodies are privileged over others."[31] Cultural constructionism allows disability theorists to challenge familiar, hierarchical categories into which identities are unfairly cast. Garland-Thomson, for example, seeks to "defamiliarize these identity categories ['able-bodiedness' and disabled] by disclosing how the 'physically disabled' are produced by way of legal, medical, political, cultural, and literary narratives that comprise exclusionary discourse."[32] Garland-Thomson thus problematizes the standard identity distinctions between the physically abled and disabled.

In addition, by highlighting the plasticity of identity, cultural constructionism empowers disability studies scholars to rename their own identities by first casting off identities thrust upon them—identities posing as objective and universal. Since language possesses such performative power, disability theorists focus their work on the social, cultural, and political junctures where language—for better or for worse—shapes their reality. This performative power of language has clear precedents. Harlan Lane, for example, notes how

> [a]lcoholism has changed from a moral failure to a disease; child abuse from an economic problem to a criminal one; homosexuality from disease to personal constitution to human rights; disability from tragic flaw to social barriers. Social problems, it seems, are partly what we make of them; they are not just out there lying in the road to be discovered by passers-by.[33]

Disability theorists thus seek a role in identifying and rectifying these social problems by renaming their very nature—by decentering the language of the medical model and deploying a new vocabulary that redefines the experience of disability as well as the obstacles encountered by those with disabilities.

In many cases, deploying a new vocabulary leads to exploding prior constructions of disability. As with minorities, the disabled are often cast as Other, which leads to objectification, depersonalization, and fear-mongering. As Susan Wendell observes, "If you are 'other' to me, I see you primarily as symbolic of something else—usually, but not always, something I reject and fear and that I project onto you."[34] In other cases, deploying a new vocabulary means combating paternalistic and mawkish attitudes toward people with disabilities. Nancy L. Eiesland and Don E. Saliers note how, during the early 1990s, disability activists demonstrated against the Jerry Lewis Muscular Dystrophy Telethon, "whose paternalistic portrayal of people with disabilities and pandering to the fears and pity of able-bodied viewers were repudiated."[35]

While cultural constructionism constitutes the theoretical orientation of disability studies, getting this message of the disability rights movement out serves as the practical goal of the field. It is here that theory gives way to praxis. As Jim Swan writes, "If we ask what's new about the new field of disability studies, there's a clear answer: it is people with disabilities making themselves heard politically, socially, culturally."[36]

GENRE

Being heard in this fashion demands a particular sort of discourse. Specifically, deploying a new vocabulary not only to deconstruct old identities and attitudes but also to forge new ones requires a genre that authenticates and empowers the voice of the speaker by providing an insider's perspective. For this reason, autobiography has become a popular genre in the field, as it has in other branches of cultural studies. James Olney observed in 1980 that "autobiography has become the focalizing literature for various 'studies,' such as American studies, black studies, women's studies, and African studies, because autobiography—the story of a distinctive culture written in individual characters and from within—offers a privileged access to an experience . . . that no other variety of writing can offer."[37]

When readers gain this privileged access, the identity of the autobiographer becomes concrete and familiarized, displacing the caricaturized identities that spring from fear and prejudice. As David T. Mitchell and Sharon L. Snyder explain, "Autobiographical narratives demand that the disabled subject develop a voice that privileges the agency of a bona fide perspective of disability."[38] Such is the voice Nancy Mairs develops in her autobiography, *Waist-High in the World: A Life among the Nondisabled*, which she describes as a "Baedeker for a country to which no one travels willingly: the observations and responses of a single wayfarer who hopes, in sketching her own experiences, to make the terrain seem less alien, less perilous, and far more amusing than the myths and legends about it would suggest."[39] She continues, "There are readers—not a lot of them, perhaps, but even one is enough—who need, for a tangle of reasons, to be told that a life commonly held to be insufferable can be full and funny. I'm living the life. I can tell them."[40]

A CHRISTIAN APPROACH TO DISABILITY STUDIES

How should Christians respond to disability studies? *Why* should they even engage this burgeoning discipline? In Manifesto #41 from the Institute on Disability Culture, Steven E. Brown notes a void in disability discourse: "There are a core of people within the disability rights movement with whom I've engaged in discussion about the need to focus not only on what happens with our minds and bodies, but with our spirits."[41] The spiritual component of human experience and, more importantly, its importance for human flourishing, have received short shrift within the field. The notion that being whole ultimately has less to do with bodily health and more to do with spiritual health requires a Christian perspective for articulation. The Christian perspective should also be mobilized to direct righteous anger toward those who oppress the disabled, whether linguistically, socially, theologically, or architecturally; concomitantly, Christians should join the chorus of voices that call for new constructions of the disabled identity. Christian scholars should thus participate in the work of resisting the cultural forces that in one way or another demean the disabled, who, like their able-bodied brothers and sisters, bear the image of God.

THEOLOGY AND DISABILITY STUDIES

Many Christian scholars have been slow to engage disability studies because of an allegiance to a long-standing theology that places the theodicy squarely at the center of dilemmas concerning illness and impairment. When confronted with the issue of disability, many Christian scholars feel compelled to address that weighty question, "Why does God allow bad things to happen?" Though well intentioned, and though important for a well-conceived Christian theology, the theodicy has often proved to be inadequate and even hurtful. Eiesland recalls the "folk theodicies" directed toward her when she was a child: "'You are special in God's eyes. That's why you were given this disability'; 'Don't worry about your pain and suffering now, in heaven you will be made whole'; and 'Thank God it isn't worse.' I was told that God gave me a disability to develop my character. But at age 6 or 7, I was convinced that I had enough character to last a lifetime."[42] Likewise, in an almost hostile tone, Reynolds Price affirms how he avoided the theodicy questions: "But with all the morbidity of such parlor games, some vital impulse spared my needing to reiterate the world's most frequent and pointless question in the face of disaster—*Why*? *Why me*? I never asked it; the only answer is of course *Why not*?"[43] The hostility directed toward theodicies is also evident in Lewis Smedes' *My God and I: A Spiritual Memoir*, which moves beyond folk theodicies to consider (and reject) more sophisticatedly conceived theodicies. Contemplating the events of September 11, 2001, Smedes writes, "I do not want God to 'make it plain.' If he could show us that there was a good and necessary reason for such a bad thing to have happened, it must not have been a bad thing after all. And I cannot accommodate that thought. In fact, I have given up asking *why* such bad things happen."[44] Alvin Plantinga employs even stronger language in condemning the theodicy: "If God is omnipotent, omniscient, and wholly good, why is there any evil? . . . The Christian theist must concede that she doesn't know—that is, she doesn't know in any detail. . . . And here I must remark that many of the attempts to explain why God permits evil—theodicies, as we might call them—seem to me shallow, tepid, and ultimately frivolous."[45]

Stanley Hauerwas has raised the sort of objections to the theodicy that open up a space for disability studies to assert itself as a valid alternative discourse whereby Christian scholars can engage issues of illness and impairment. Hauerwas de-problematizes the problem of evil,[46] not by claiming to have arrived at any promising, new answers to the age-old question, "Why does God allow bad things to happen?"; rather, he seeks to wrest the fact of suffering from the theoretical assumptions that make the problem of evil a problem in the first place. Hauerwas de-problematizes the problem of evil by questioning the claim that there exists a philosophical problem to begin with. He notes that "the assumptions that there is something called the problem of evil which creates a discourse called 'theodicy' occurred at the same time that modern atheism came into being."[47] According to Hauerwas's account, evil counts as a strike against God's existence only when evil is viewed through an interpretive lens that holds God's existence in skeptical abeyance to begin with. Enlightenment thought—with its posture of tradition-free, autonomous inquiry—creates this conceptual scheme which in turn transforms evil into a problem that undermines God's supposed existence or nature. Claims about God and evil are thus wrenched from the interpretive community (the community of faith) which had traditionally framed those claims, supplying them with contextual meaning. Alasdair MacIntyre points out that only after the seventeenth century did the existence of evil become a problem that challenged the "coherence and intelligibility of Christian belief per se."[48] Prior to this time, truth claims about God and evil achieved coherence within a narrative that held certain presuppositions about those very truth claims. According to an Enlightenment model, on the other hand, as Hauerwas contends, the assumption is that "we are most fully ourselves when we are free of all traditions and communities other than those we have chosen from the position of complete autonomy." "In such a context," Hauerwas concludes, "suffering cannot help but appear absurd, since it always stands as a threat to that autonomy."[49] The issue of God and evil thus hinges upon methodological assumptions, context, and perspective.

Hauerwas's argument holds important implications for a Christian approach to disability studies. First, it frees Christian scholars from the spurious need to defend God's existence whenever one of his creatures becomes disabled; the energy expended in theodicy-making can be used instead to gather the knowledge and mobilize the political mechanisms whereby people with disabilities can live a life free from culturally instilled hostility. By revealing that disability need not be a "problem" from a theological perspective, Hauerwas's argument can point us to the fact that disability *is* a problem from a sociocultural perspective.

Second, Hauerwas's emphasis on perspective provides support for the theoretical stance of disability studies. Hauerwas writes, "No two sufferings are the same: my suffering, for example, occurs in the context of my personal history and thus is peculiarly mine."[50] Thus, divergent perspectives on illness assume divergent phenomenological distances from those very objects of inquiry. An individual with multiple sclerosis, for example, assumes a different distance from suffering than does an individual free from multiple sclerosis. Indeed, there exists an enormous phenomenological distance between encountering illness at a safe cognitive and emotional remove, and confronting illness when it invades the individualized space of personal experience and indelibly marks the human psyche.

This phenomenological distance to illness tends to bifurcate discursive approaches to the issues surrounding illness. On the one hand, the approach of disability studies—the disability narrative, autobiography, memoir, etc.—occupies the personalized space of illness. Such an approach eliminates that phenomenological distance and gives representation to concrete, particularized experiences of suffering. The philosophical/theological discourse of theodicy, on the other hand, often operates from a de-individualized vantage point that, if successful, will render universally binding conclusions—solutions to the problem of evil. In order to do so, such a discourse necessarily maintains that phenomenological distance, combating the problem of evil from an abstract, de-particularized, and, to use Hauerwas's word, autonomous perspective; concrete instances of illness are held at bay while the theodicy-maker squares off against the universal problem of evil. Such universalized discourse can be both reductive to the "problem" that it tackles and unfair to the person it claims to represent. The philosophical/theodicy approach thus mimes the Enlightenment approach against which Hauerwas inveighs.

Eschewing such an Enlightenment approach with its neutral postures, disability studies works from an unapologetic, self-conscious perspective that lends authenticity to its representations of disability. Through autobiographical narratives, disability studies particularizes disability. Consequently, disability studies can avoid the generalizations, stereotypes, and caricatures that result from a universalized discourse (such as the theodicy) that, despite the best of intentions, oppresses through distorted constructions of disability and disability experience. In addition, by embracing perspectivalism, disability studies opens a place at the table for the Christian scholar perspective.

The Bible and Disability Studies

What might the Christian scholar perspective look like? As people of the Book, Christians adhere to a perspective shaped by Holy Scriptures. Unfortunately, many scholars outside the Christian community have argued that such a perspective as well as the Book that forms it ill-serves people with disabilities who search for spiritual fulfillment. Jane S. Deland, for example, claims that the "Biblical record which has shaped the Judeo-Christian and cultural attitudes toward disease and disability also has helped to marginalize and ostracize people with disabilities and disease by seeming to portray an image of a capricious and arbitrary God. God is imaged as one who sends disease or disability as punishment or as a test of faith or endurance; healing comes for an ill-defined divine purpose."[51] Deland, for example, notes how healing stories in the New Testament directly link healing to faith: those with a strong faith are healed; those with a weak faith are not. "Two morals," writes Deland, "can be drawn from such stories: God rewards pro-active people who seek to participate in the healing process; people with disease/disabilities who are not healed are not trying hard enough or do not have enough faith. In the latter, as Denise Hopkins notes, "The victim is victimized twice."[52] What is required for the Christian perspective is a biblical hermeneutic that reanalyzes Scripture from the vantage point of disability theory.

In an issue of *The Disability Rag and Resource* focusing on religion and disability, P. J. Magik catalogs common Judeo-Christian responses to disability: Disability can be a punishment from God, a test of faith, or the sins of the fathers visited upon the children, among others.[53] Such responses are often occasioned by biblical passages that, from a disability perspective, can be problematic. For example, John 5 explains that near the Pool of Bethesda a "great number of disabled people used to lie—the blind, the lame, the paralyzed" (5:3; NIV hereafter). Jesus there heals one who "had been an invalid for thirty-eight years" (5:5). Jesus heals the man, and, when he later finds him at the temple, he proclaims, "'See, you are well again. Stop sinning or something worse may happen to you'" (5:14). Jesus' words might imply that the man originally became disabled because of some sin and that, if that sin is not eliminated, the disability will return and become even worse—disability as punishment. In Matthew 17, Jesus' disciples are unable to heal a demon-possessed boy. After Jesus heals the boy himself, the disciples ask Jesus why they failed: "'Because you have so little faith'" (Matthew 17:20). Similarly, Bartimaeus is healed of his blindness when he evidences persistent faith.[54] After Bartimaeus doggedly pursues him, Jesus exclaims, "'Go, your faith has healed you'"—disability as a test of faith. These and other passages can potentially cause anguish for those for whom disability is a reality.[55] One can draw dangerous conclusions from these verses of Scripture: If a person with a disability is not healed, then that person must be egregiously sinful; or, if health doesn't improve, then that person must lack faith. For people with disabilities, such conclusions can lead to spiritual frustrations and ultimate alienation from the church. Isolated within the public sphere for physical difference, such persons likewise find themselves singled out through spiritual interpretations of that difference—interpretations that generate stigmatization. Disability is read as a physical sign of spiritual defect.

How might disability theory recast these biblical texts? Informed by a disability perspective, one might relocate the focus of these verses from the implications it has on people with disabilities to the person of Jesus Christ. That is, these passages primarily endeavor to reveal the authority and divinity of Jesus; they are not meant to provide normative guidelines for interpreting the spiritual significance of disability. As Eiesland and Saliers argue, many of the Gospel stories are "not primarily about the people healed, but focus instead on the healer, Jesus. In other words, they are Christological stories passed along to describe some reality about who Jesus the Christ was and is."[56] We should read these stories for what they say about Jesus' identity, not for what they say about the disabled. N. T. Wright places Jesus' miracles in their proper context when he observes that Jesus' healings, "at their deepest level of understanding on the part of Jesus and his contemporaries, would be seen as part of his total ministry, specifically, part of that open welcome which went with the inauguration of the kingdom"; Jesus' healings, Wright continues, "take place in the context of what is called 'faith' . . . and raise the question of Jesus' authority and status. . . ."[57] Thus placed within their proper context, the Gospel accounts of Jesus' healings need not be problematic for Christians with disabilities.

By focusing on Jesus' identity, a disability hermeneutic can unveil a biblical image of Jesus that resonates more strongly with disabled Christians. Deland notes how theologians have fleshed out images of God as "Father, Judge, King, and Shepherd."[58] The primary image of Jesus is that of healer—an image that "attest[s] to the power of faith to bring health and wholeness."[59] For people with disabilities, these images of God and Jesus can be, at best, irrelevant, and, at worst, harmful. So what is an alternative image?

Eiesland has written extensively on the image of the "disabled God."[60] Without robbing God of His omnipotence,[61] Eiesland points to images of the post-resurrection Jesus with impaired hands and impaired feet. "Jesus," Eiesland writes, "the resurrected savior, calls for his frightened companions to recognize in the marks of impairment their own connection with God, their own salvation."[62] Jesus' resurrected body still bears the marks of his earthly impairment, marks with which his disabled followers can identify. That power of identification constitutes a moment of validation of the disabled body as well as a moment of spiritual empowerment. Vinay Samuel observes in another context that, by limiting himself on the cross, "God himself limits himself in order to understand our limitations."[63] In addition, the image of the disabled God provides a clear object lesson for the fair treatment of people with disabilities. As disabled God, Jesus encourages us to treat his disabled children with respect. More, the image of the disabled God defuses the secular premium placed on self-sufficiency and independence; instead, it underscores the importance of community and mutual concern. When we look upon our disabled brothers and sisters, we look upon images of the disabled God.

In addition, a disability hermeneutic might point to other stories in Scripture that defuse the possible negative implications of the verses discussed above. In Luke 13, for example, Jesus explains that suffering is not tied to levels of sinfulness. When told about the "Galileans whose blood Pilate had mixed with their sacrifices," Jesus replies, "'Do you think that these Galileans were worse sinners than all the other Galileans because they suffered this way? I tell you, no!'" (Luke 13:2–3). And concerning those "who died when the tower in Siloam fell on them," Jesus replies, "[D]o you think they were more guilty than all the others living in Jerusalem? I tell you, no!'" (Luke 13:4). Jesus thus contravenes the notion that suffering—and by extension, disability—is linked to sin.

In John 9, Jesus makes perhaps his strongest statements about sin and disability; in fact, this chapter of John is a pivotal chapter for people with disabilities. Observing a man born blind, the disciples ask Jesus, "'Rabbi, who sinned, this man or his parents, that he was born blind?'" (John 9:2). Jesus replies, "'Neither this man nor his parents sinned . . . but this happened so that the work of God might be displayed in his life" (9:3). This discussion and the story that ensues provide a rich source for disability theory–inspired analysis. Not only does the story sever the sin/disability link, but, as Eiesland and Saliers note, unlike other healing stories in the Gospels, it provides a well-developed representation of a person with a disability: "He appears not simply as a broken figure in need of compassion and healing but as a person in his own right. We are able to get to know him as a thoughtful, brave, amusing, but above all, ordinary person."[64] In effect, the story of the man born blind in John 9 recapitulates the function of disability studies itself. By particularizing the identity of the blind man, the story precludes the sort of rhetorical moves that marginalize people with disabilities: reductive generalizations about how "different" the disabled are as well as universalizing discourse that invalidates the particularity of the experience of disability. More, as Eiesland and Saliers observe, when the man is healed, people who knew him do not believe that he is the same man who was born blind. By insisting that he is, the man shows that his disability never defined his identity; it was never his "defining characteristic."[65] Like many people with disabilities, the man resists the identity that is externally forced upon him. He is, in fact, more than both his disability and his newfound ability. Insights such as these materialize when disability theory provides a theoretical lens for biblical interpretation.

ENABLING A CHRISTIAN APPROACH TO DISABILITY STUDIES

Having outlined the basic contours of disability studies—from its rejection of the medical model of impairment to its adherence to cultural constructionism—and having explored some reasons for the dilatory Christian response to these issues, this essay calls for such a moment of encouragement and empowerment. As the field continues to grow, the stakes increase for a Christian approach to disability studies, which presents issues and poses questions that should challenge Christian scholars from across the disciplinary spectrum. This paper touches on just some of those issues and questions. For example, Christians can debate the merits of cultural constructionism as the reigning epistemology of disability studies. Certainly God possesses certain knowledge of the disability identity—knowledge that overarches the historically specific permutations of social identities. What implications does this hold for cultural constructionism? The dominant genre of disability studies can also prove to be fruitful for Christian inquiry. Tobin Siebers identifies the autobiographical approach of the field as the "literature of witnessing," an epithet redolent of Christian testimony.[66] How are disability testimony and Christian testimony parallel? How might critical methodologies historically employed to analyze the Christian testimony yield insights into disability testimony?

Opportunities for Christian theologians to engage disability studies likewise abound. How does one, for example, reconcile the theodicy with disability studies? Does the theodicy, as this paper suggests, deflect attention away from the issues that figure prominently in disability discourse? Or can the theodicy and disability studies be harmonized? Also, what difference might a disability-inflected biblical hermeneutic make? Can such a hermeneutic remain faithful to the integrity of the biblical text?

As a prolegomenon, this essay also calls for a distinctly Christian analysis of issues in the field that lie outside the parameters of the essay's scope. After all, the essay can only skim the surface of disability studies; the issues multiply as the field grows. For example, disability studies scholars have analyzed concepts of normalcy. What is a "normal" human being? Are the disabled abnormal? What implications does an affirmative answer to that question have on the lives of people with disabilities? Lennard Davis has argued that the term "normal" was invented 150 years ago with the development of mathematical statistics; with these innovations came the notion of the "average citizen," an exclusionary category that ostracizes the disabled.[67] Certainly Christians can contribute to this conversation about normalcy and, like Davis, can trouble this concept of "normal," though on a different basis. Drawing from her own experience, Nancy Mairs writes, "Perhaps because I have embraced a faith with crucifixion at its heart, I do not consider suffering an aberration or an outrage to be eliminated at any cost, even the cost of my life."[68] This essay calls for the continued formulation of perspectives such as this—a perspective that further paves the way for a Christian approach to disability studies.

NOTES

1. Quoted in Simi Linton, *Claiming Disability: Knowledge and Identity* (New York: New York University Press, 1998), p. 33.

2. Robert F. Murphy, *The Body Silent* (New York: Henry Holt, 1987), p. 117.

3. Ibid.

4. Rosemarie Garland-Thomson, *Extraordinary Bodies: Figuring Physical Disability in American Culture and Literature* (New York: Columbia University Press, 1997), p. 41.

5. In the film, boxer Maggie Fitzgerald (played by Hillary Swank) receives a spinal cord injury during a fight that leaves her severely paralyzed. She ultimately succeeds in convincing her manager, Frankie Dunn (Clint Eastwood), to terminate her life.

6. A CNN/USA Today/Gallup Poll conducted on March 18–20, 2005, found 56 percent of Americans in agreement with the original removal of Terri Schiavo's feeding tube (http://www.cnn.com/interactive/allpolitics/0503/poll.gallup/content .1.html). A CBS news poll conducted on March 21–22, 2005, found 61 percent agreeing with the decision to remove the feeding tube (http://www.cbsnews .com/stories/2005/03/23/opinion/polls/main682675.shtml).

7. Helen R. Betenbaugh, "The Church and Disability: A Trinity of Issues," *Disability Studies Quarterly* 15.3 (Summer 1995): 32–33.

8. This thesis does not imply that I am the first to think Christianly about disability issues. Nancy Eiesland, for example, has done extensive work situating disability within a Christian perspective. (See Eiesland's *The Disabled God* [Nashville: Abingdon, 1994].) What distinguishes this essay is its attempt to introduce a Christian approach to disability studies as an academic discipline—to survey the field and explore areas where Christians can enter the discussion. Eiesland analyzes disability in general through the lens of theology, in effect formulating a theology of disability.

9. Lennard Davis, "Introduction: The Need for Disability Studies," in *The Disability Studies Reader*, ed. Lennard J. Davis, 1 (New York: Routledge, 1997).

10. Linton, *Claiming Disability*, p. 2.

11. Quoted in Stanley Hauerwas, "Salvation and Health: Why Medicine Needs the Church," in *The Hauerwas Reader*, 542 (Durham: Duke University Press, 2001).

12. Helen Deutsch, "Exemplary Aberration: Samuel Johnson and the English Canon," in *Disability Studies: Enabling the Humanities*, ed. Snyder, Brueggemann, and Garland-Thomson, 199 (New York: Modern Language Association, 2002).

13. Ibid.

14. Lennard Davis, "Dr. Johnson, Amelia, and the Discourse of Disability in the Eighteenth Century," in *"Defects": Engendering the Modern Body*, ed. Helen Deutsch and Felicity Nussbaum, 62 (Ann Arbor: University of Michigan Press, 2000).

15. Paul Longmore in *Human Disability and the Service of God: Reassessing Religious Practice*, ed. Nancy Eisland and Don Saliers (Nashville: Abingdon, 1998), p. 1.

16. See G. Thomas Couser, "Signifying Bodies: Life Writing and Disability Studies," in *Disability Studies: Enabling the Humanities*, 112.

17. Davis, "Dr. Johnson, Amelia, and the Discourse of Disability in the Eighteenth Century," p. 62.

18. Linton, *Claiming Disability*, p. 110.

19. Ibid.

20. Ibid., p. 111.

21. Irving Kenneth Zola, *Missing Pieces: A Chronicle of Living with a Disability* (Philadelphia: Temple University Press, 1982), p. 201.

22. Arthur Frank, *The Wounded Storyteller* (Chicago: University of Chicago Press, 1995), p. 6.

23. Paul Redding, "Science, Medicine, and Illness: Rediscovering the Patient as a Person," *Troubled Bodies: Critical Perspectives on Postmodernism, Medical Ethics, and the Body*, ed. Paul A. Komesaroff, 88 (Durham, NC: Duke University Press, 1995).

24. Frank, *The Wounded Storyteller*, p. 6.

25. Linton, *Claiming Disability*, p. 133.

26. Longmore, p. 221.

27. Garland-Thomson, *Extraordinary Bodies*, p. 6.

28. Michel Foucault, *Discipline and Punish: The Birth of the Prison* (New York: Vintage, 1977), p. 25.

29. Of course, not everyone in the field subscribes to cultural constructionism. See Michael Bérubé, afterword in *Disability Studies: Enabling the Humanities*, ed. Snyder, Brueggemann, and Garland-Thomson, 340 (New York: Modern Language Association, 2002).

30. Mark Jeffreys, "The Visible Cripple (Scars and Other Disfiguring Displays Included)," in *Disability Studies: Enabling the Humanities*, p. 32.

31. Couser, "Signifying Bodies," p. 112.

32. Garland-Thomson, *Extraordinary Bodies*, p. 6.

33. Harlan Lane, "Constructions of Deafness," in *The Disability Studies Reader*, p. 154.

34. Susan Wendell, "Toward a Feminist Theory of Disability," in *The Disability Studies Reader*, p. 271.

35. Nancy L. Eiesland, "Barriers and Bridges: Relating the Disability Rights Movement and Religious Organizations," in *Human Disability and the Service of God: Reassessing Religious Practice*, ed. Nancy Eiesland and Don Saliers, 202 (Nashville: Abingdon, 1998).

36. Jim Swan, "Disability, Bodies, Voices," in *Disability Studies: Enabling the Humanities*, p. 283. This quotation raises the question of advocacy within academics. Is political action incompatible with scholarship? Longmore admits that disability studies has "encountered strong opposition. Some critics condemn it for

pushing parochial ideologies and political agendas, for lacking intellectual credibility, and for contributing to the 'balkanization' of learning" (*Why I Burned My Book*, p. 5). Norah Vincent dismisses disability studies for reasons along these lines: "The ostensible goal [the Society for Disability Studies] has been to spread acceptance of the disabled into 'ableist' culture. But like their queer studies/gay rights counterparts—who shifted focus from acceptance of gay culture to a more chauvinistic gay pride—disability mavens are advocating a surreal ideology one might call 'disability pride'" ("Enabling Disabled Scholarship," Salon.com, August 18, 1999). A defense of advocacy within scholarship lies outside the scope of this essay; as a prolegomenon, the essay encourages further analysis of this issue. My analysis in these pages reveals my own position: advocacy (and even the cultivation of pride) for the historically oppressed is a valid direction for scholarship.

37. James Olney, "Autobiography and the Cultural Moment," in *Autobiography: Essays Theoretical and Critical*, ed. Olney, 13 (Princeton, NJ: Princeton University Press, 1980).

38. David T. Mitchell and Sharon L. Snyder, "Introduction: Disability Studies and the Double Bind of Representation," in *The Body and Physical Difference: Discourses of Disability*, ed. Mitchell and Snyder, 2–3 (Ann Arbor: University of Michigan Press, 1997).

39. Nancy Mairs, *Waist-High in the World: A Life among the Nondisabled* (Boston: Beacon, 1996), p. 6.

40. Ibid.

41. Steven E. Brown, Manifesto #41 from the Institute on Disability Culture, available at http://www.dimenet.com/disculture,cgi/getlink.cgi?98r.

42. Eiesland, "Barriers and Bridges," p. 218.

43. Reynolds Price, *A Whole New Life* (New York: Atheneum, 1994), p. 53.

44. Lewis B. Smedes, *My God and I: A Spiritual Memoir* (Grand Rapids, MI: Eerdmans, 2003), p. 125.

45. Alvin Plantinga, "Epistemic Probability and Evil," in *The Evidential Argument from Evil*, ed. Daniel Howard-Snyder, 70 (Bloomington: Indiana University Press, 1996).

46. I use the term "evil" here in its technical, philosophical sense to mean intense, undeserved suffering. This term has perpetuated the (often unspoken) notion that the disabled are spiritually flawed, that evil has afflicted them and become a part of their being. I use the term briefly here because it is historically prevalent in the philosophical issue that I am engaging.

47. Stanley Hauerwas, *Naming the Silences* (Grand Rapids, MI: Eerdmans, 1990), p. 41.

48. Alasdair MacIntyre, quoted in Kenneth Surin, *Theology and the Problem of Evil* (Oxford: Basil Blackwell, 1986), p. 97.

49. Hauerwas, *Naming the Silences*, pp. 53–54.

50. Ibid., p. 3.

51. Jane S. Deland, "Images of God through the Lens of Disability," *Journal of Religion, Disability & Health* 3.2 (Summer 1999): 54.

52. Ibid., p. 57.

53. P. J. Magik, "Disability for the Religious," *Disability Rag & Resource*, November/December 1994, 24–25.

54. Mark 10:52.

55. See Matthew 9:1–8; Mark 2:1–12; Mark 2:15–17; and Mark 7:24–30.

56. Quoted in Colleen C. Grant, "Reinterpreting the Healing Narratives," in *Human Disability and the Service of God: Reassessing Religious Practice*, p. 73.

57. N. T. Wright, *Jesus and the Victory of God* (Minneapolis: Fortress, 1996), pp. 192, 194.

58. Deland, "Images of God through the Lens of Disability," p. 48.

59. Ibid.

60. See Nancy L. Eiesland's *The Disabled God: Toward a Liberatory Theology of Disability* (Nashville: Abingdon, 1994).

61. I adhere to Daniel Howard-Snyder's definition of God's omnipotence: "God's power is limited to what is possible; not even an omnipotent being has the power to do what is absolutely impossible" ("God, Evil, and Suffering," in *Reasons for the Hope Within*, ed. Michael J. Murray, 85 [Grand Rapids: Eerdmans, 1999]).

62. Eiesland, *The Disabled God*, p. 100.

63. Vinay Samuel, "God, Humanity, and Disability," *Transformation* 15 (1998): 15.

64. Eiesland and Saliers, *Human Disability and the Service of God*, p. 79.

65. Ibid.

66. Tobin Siebers, "Tender Organs, Narcissism, and Identity Politics," in *Disability Studies: Enabling the Humanities*, 50.

67. See Lennard Davis, *Enforcing Normalcy: Disability, Deafness, and the Body* (New York: Verso, 1995).

68. Nancy Mairs, "Sex and Death and the Crippled Body: A Meditation," in *Disability Studies: Enabling the Humanities*, p. 169.

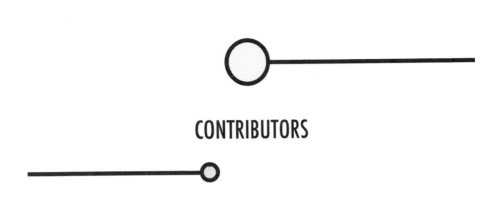

CONTRIBUTORS

Adrienne Asch is Edward and Robin Milstein Professor of Bioethics at the Wurzweiler School of Social Work and professor of epidemiology and population health at the Albert Einstein College of Medicine.

Drew Batavia (d. 2003) was associate professor of public health policy at Florida International University at the time of his death and a former partner at the Miami law firm of McDermott, Will & Emery. He helped write the Americans with Disabilities Act.

Martha Beck is the author of several books, including *Expecting Adam* and *Leaving the Saints*, and a partner at NorthStar, Inc., a life-coaching consulting and seminar company.

Michael Bérubé is Paterno Family Professor in Literature at Pennsylvania State University and the author of *Life as We Know It*.

Diane Coleman is an attorney, the executive director of the Progress Center for Independent Living in Oak Park, Illinois, and a volunteer organizer for American Disabled for Attendant Programs Today (ADAPT).

Barry Corbet (d. 2004) was the editor of *New Mobility* magazine, a publication covering disability culture and lifestyle.

Ruthanne L. Curry is a family nurse practitioner in private practice in Gainesville, Florida. As the mother of two children, one of whom has a physical disability, she and her husband, Dr. R. Whit Curry Jr., continue to advocate for integrating all children with differing abilities into community life.

Hugh Gregory Gallagher (d. 2004) was cofounder of AUTONOMY, INC., the author of the Architectural Barriers Act of 1968, and often called the father of the disability rights movement. In 1995 Gallagher won the Henry B. Betts Award for his lifetime work for the disabled. He was also the author of *FDR's Splendid Deception*.

Terry Galloway is a playwright, an essayist, a poet, and a performer. She is the author of and starred in her acclaimed solo show, "Out All Night and Lost My Shoes."

Carol J. Gill is a psychologist, president of the Chicago Institute of Disability Research, adjunct assistant professor of physical medicine and rehabilitation at Northwestern University Medical School, and research chair of the Health Resource Center for Women with Disabilities at the Rehabilitation Institute of Chicago.

Gerard Goggin has a PhD in literature from the University of Sydney and is an Australian Research Fellow working on an Australian Research Council–funded five-year project on mobile phone culture and regulation.

John Hockenberry is a correspondent for *Dateline NBC* and a former correspondent in broadcast news at National Public Radio and ABC News.

John Hull is honorary professor of practical theology at the Queen's Foundation for Ecumenical Theological Education, Birmingham, England, and emeritus professor of religious education at the University of Birmingham.

Samuel Joeckel is assistant professor of English at Palm Beach Atlantic University.

Harriet McBryde Johnson (d. 2008) was an attorney in Charleston, South Carolina, and a disability rights activist and advocate.

Douglas Lathrop is managing editor of *New Mobility* magazine.

Paul K. Longmore is professor of history and director of the Institute on Disability at San Francisco State University.

Nancy Mairs is an essayist, a poet, a teacher, and author of *Waist-High in the World: A Life Among the Nondisabled* and other autobiographical texts that depict her life with multiple sclerosis.

Arlene Mayerson is directing attorney at Disability Rights Education and Defense Fund and codirector of the Disability Rights Legal Education Clinic.

Robert Molsberry is the senior pastor of the United Church of Christ-Congregational in Grinnell, Iowa, and author of *Blindsided by Grace: Entering the World of Disability.*

Cal Montgomery is a member of the Autistic Network International and speaker and widely published writer on disability-related issues.

Christopher Newell (d. 2008) was associate professor at the School of Medicine, University of Tasmania, Australia.

William J. Peace is an independent scholar, freelance writer, and the author of *Leslie A. White: Evolution and Revolution in Anthropology* and *The Bad Cripple.* His articles on disability appear in such publications as *Ragged Edge* and *Disability Studies Quarterly.*

Oliver Sacks, MD, a clinical professor of neurology for much of his career at the Albert Einstein College of Medicine and the New York University School of Medicine, is now at Columbia University College of Physicians and Surgeons. He is a prolific author, the best known of his books being *Awakenings.*

John Schatzlein is a disability consultant with the Minnesota Department of Health.

Richard K. Scotch is professor of sociology and political economy at the University of Texas at Dallas and the past president of the Society for Disability Studies.

Peter Singer is Ira W. DeCamp Professor of Bioethics at Princeton University and laureate professor at the Centre for Applied Philosophy and Public Ethics, University of Melbourne.

William G. Stothers is deputy director at the Center for an Accessible Society, San Diego.

S. Kay Toombs is emeritus professor of philosophy at Baylor University, author of *The Meaning of Illness*, and editor of *The Handbook of Phenomenology and Medicine* and *Chronic Illness: From Experience to Policy.*

David Wasserman, JD, is a research scholar at the University of Maryland's Institute for Philosophy and Public Policy.

John Williams is a weekly columnist on assistive technology for *Business Week Online.*